D0719246

365 DAYS OUT IN BRITAIN

Produced by AA Publishing

Consultant: Richard Cavendish

Editorial contributors:
Richard Cavendish
Lesley Ellis
Lawrence Garner
Sally Varlow

Mapping produced by the Cartographic Department of
The Autombile Association
©The Automobile Association

This book was produced using QuarkXpress™ and
Microsoft Word™ on Apple Mackintosh™ computers.
Printed and bound by Graficromo SA, Spain
Colour origination by Aylesbury Studios Ltd, Bromley, Kent

The contents of this publication are believed correct at the
time of printing. Nevertheless, the publishers cannot
accept responsibility for errors or ommisions, or for changes
in details given.

© The Autombile Association
©Revised and updated edition 1994
Reprinted 1996

All rights reserved. No part of this publication may be reproduced, stored in a retrieval system or transmitted in any
form or by any means – electronic, mechanical, photocopy-
ing, recording or otherwise _ unless the written permission
of the publisher has been given beforehand.

Published by AA Publishing (a division of
Autimobile Association Developments Limited,
whose registered office is Norfolk House,
Priestly Road, Basingstoke, Hampshire RG24 9NY.
Registered number 1878835).

ISBN 0 7495 09872 (paperback)
ISBN 086145-765-X (hardback)

Contents

About this book

What shall we do today? is a familiar question. *Out and About in Britain* provides the answer, showing that wherever you are, and whatever the time of year, there is always something special to see or do.

This book combines the best of all that Britain has to offer by linking ceremonies, festivals and events to places to visit. So, whether you are interested in airfields or zoos, nature reserves or industrial heritage, Hare Pie Scrambling or Tar-barrel Rolling, it is the perfect guide to an unusual and entertaining day out.

Out and About in Britain is divided into six regional sections, each of which opens with an introduction, a special feature highlighting some aspect of the region, a calendar of events and a location map.

The hundreds of attractions described in the book are grouped into 365 'days', each comprising a selection of places that could be visited during one outing. The 'days' are grouped into seasons – Spring, Summer, Autumn and Winter – although these are intended for guidance only and the places mentioned have much to offer at all times of the year. However, a visit during the season indicated means you may be able to enjoy one of the events featured as well.

The pages are colour coded according to the season as follows.

SPRING
March, April, May

SUMMER
June, July, August

AUTUMN
September, October, November

WINTER
December, January, February

OPENING TIMES

Unless otherwise stated in the text, places of interest are open during the season in which they are listed.

Although detailed opening times are not given in this book, the address and telephone number of the relevant Tourist Information Centre can be found at the top of each numbered 'day'. Some Information Centres specify seasonal opening only, which means they are generally open between April and September only.

Many places mentioned in the book are in the care of the National Trusts and English Heritage.

ENGLISH HERITAGE

EH (AM) CADW Visitors can join English Heritage at any of its staffed properties, and receive benefits such as free admission to all English Heritage properties. Further information is available from English Heritage, 429 Oxford Street, London W1R 2HD.

Ancient Monuments in Scotland (with the exception of Holyrood House) are the responsibility of the Scottish Development Departments, Room 214, 20 Brandon Street, Edinburgh EH3 5RA. Membership of the Friends of Historic Scotland can be purchased from the above address.

Ancient Monuments in Wales are the responsibility of Cadw, Brunel House, Fitzalan Road, Cardiff CF2 1UY. Heritage in Wales Membership, entitling the subscriber admission to all the Welsh sites, can be purchased from the above address. In general, the standard times of opening for all Ancient Monuments, except Scotland, are as follows:

April – September: daily 10 – 6
October – March: daily 10 – 4

Standard times of opening for all Ancient Monuments in Scotland are as follows:

April – September weekdays 9.30 – 6.30 Sundays 2 – 6.30
October – March weekdays 9.30 – 4.30 Sundays 2 – 4.30

All monuments in England and Wales are closed on 1 January and 24 – 26 December. Those in Scotland are closed on 25 and 26 December, also 1 and 2 January.

THE NATIONAL TRUSTS

NT Indicates properties in England and Wales administered by the National Trust for Places of Historic Interest or Natural Beauty, 42 Queen Anne's Gate, London SW1H 9AS.

NTS National Trust for Scotland, 5 Charlotte Square, Edinburgh EH2 4DU.

MAPS

Each section of the book has a location map of the region. The main headings for each day out in the region are shown on the map in red and the red stars locate the customs and events described at the side of the main text.

CUSTOMS AND EVENTS

A month-by-month calendar of customs and events occurring in that region throughout the year can be found at the beginning of each section.

A selection of the most interesting and unusual occasions are described beside the appropriate 'day'.

*E*ngland's south-western counties form one of the country's prime tourist areas, famous for beaches and beauty spots, but there are unexpected pleasures here too. You can burrow underground, for instance: through weird rock formations under the Mendip Hills at Wookey Hole, among the eerie, echoing iron mines of the Forest of Dean, or with a kind of prosaic claustrophobia in the labyrinth of medieval tunnels beneath Exeter's prim post-war shopping precincts. There's another labyrinth up on the ceiling of Somerset among the grassed-over quarry workings of Ham Hill, which could well be the best place for hide-and-seek in all Britain.

Keeping on the surface, for rolling chalk country you could scarcely beat Salisbury Plain, and there are also Gloucestershire's dramatic Cotswold edge, the swoop of Somerset's roller-coaster Quantocks and the great granite humps of Exmoor, Dartmoor and Bodmin Moor. There is spectacular cliff scenery, of course, along the whole length of the north Devon and north Cornwall coasts, where the sea thunders against titanic ramparts of sheer rock, and on the shimmering chalk coast of Dorset as well. And again, there's stranger scenery: the sea of sand dunes at Braunton Burrows, the china clay moonscape outside St Austell.

Enjoyable wildlife ranges from red squirrels on Brownsea Island to swans and their cygnets at Abbotsbury, exotic butterflies at Compton House and peculiar multi-horned sheep like ambulating hat-racks at the Cotswold Farm Park. Stately homes go all the way from medieval Clevedon Court to a 20th-century fortress at Castle Drogo, and in between you can enjoy Tudor Cotehele, Elizabethan Montacute, the ample Victorian kitchens at Lanhydrock, and the Indian eccentricity of Sezincote. Some of Britain's most rewarding gardens are here, too, including Hidcote Manor in Gloucestershire, Compton Acres in Dorset and the semi-tropical paradises of Cornwall.

Traces of famous people are blazed across the counties: the legendary King Arthur at Glastonbury and Tintagel, Drake at Plymouth, Thomas Hardy and T E Lawrence (Lawrence of Arabia) in Dorset, Brunel in Bristol, and at Morwenstow the local vicar, the wonderfully eccentric Robert Hawker, who once dressed up as a mermaid and sat on a rock in the sea off Bude, singing melodiously, to the astonishment of the inhabitants.

Relics of prehistory, too, are in great abundance. Stonehenge and Avebury take pride of place, but there's the whale-backed Cotswold tomb of Belas Knap, the standing stones and stone circles of Dorset, Dartmoor and the Land's End area, the barrows like guardians round the mysterious Mendip village of Priddy (where legend says Jesus lived as a boy), and the towering earthworks of Maiden Castle which the Romans stormed.

Addicts of cities and cathedrals can feast themselves on Bath's noble terraces, the west front of Wells Cathedral, Salisbury's soaring spire and the huge Crécy window at Gloucester, the size of a tennis court. Finally, one oddity not to miss: the gleaming Art Nouveau front of Bristol's Edward Everard Building, by the man who designed the meat-hall at Harrods.

Durdle Door, west of Lulworth Cove. One of the most distinctive rock formations in Dorset, the 'elephant's trunk' is all that remains of a band of limestone almost worn away at this point

The
West Country

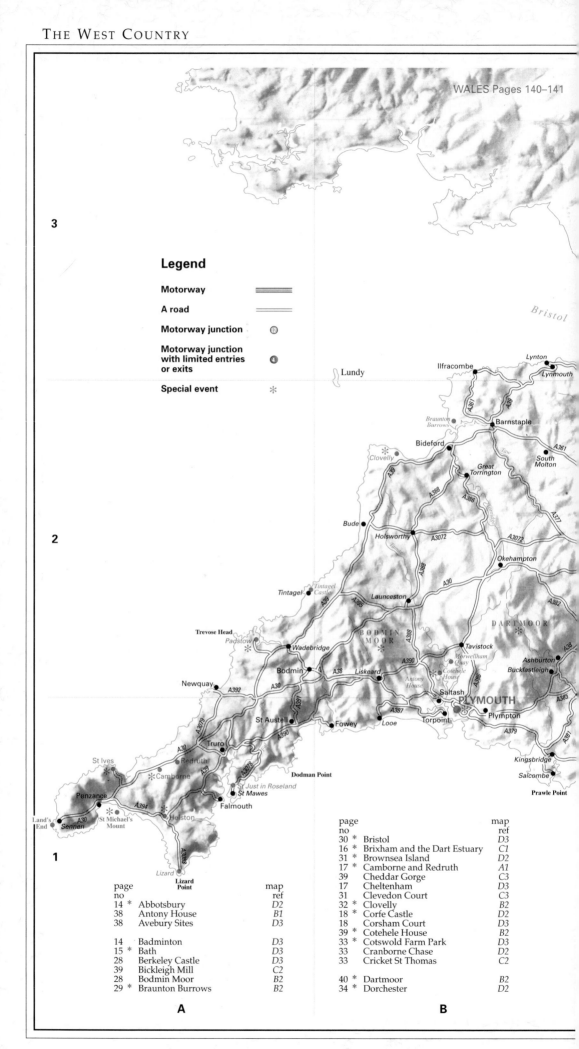

WALES Pages 140–141

3

Legend

Motorway	
A road	
Motorway junction	⑫
Motorway junction with limited entries or exits	④
Special event	✳

Bristol

Lundy

Lynton
Lynmouth
Ilfracombe
Barnstaple
Braunton Burrows
Bideford
A361
South Molton
Great Torrington
Clovelly
A39
A388
A386
A377
Bude
Holsworthy
A3072
A3072
Okehampton
A388
A30
DARTMOOR ✳
Tintagel *Tintagel Castle*
Launceston
A382
A386
A388
BODMIN MOOR
Tavistock
Ashburton
Trevose Head
Padstow
Wadebridge
Morwellham Quay
Buckfastleigh
A390
Liskeard
Cotehele House
A386
Bodmin
A38
Antony House
Saltash
A385
Newquay
A392
A30
PLYMOUTH
A387
A379
St Austell
Fowey
Looe
Torpoint
Plympton
A3075
A390
Truro
Redruth
A39
Kingsbridge
St Ives ✳
✳ Camborne
A30
Dodman Point
Salcombe
St Just in Roseland
St Mawes
A3078
Falmouth
Prawle Point
Penzance
A394
✳ Helston
Land's End
A30
Sennen
✳ St Michael's Mount
A3083
Lizard
Lizard Point

2

1

A   B

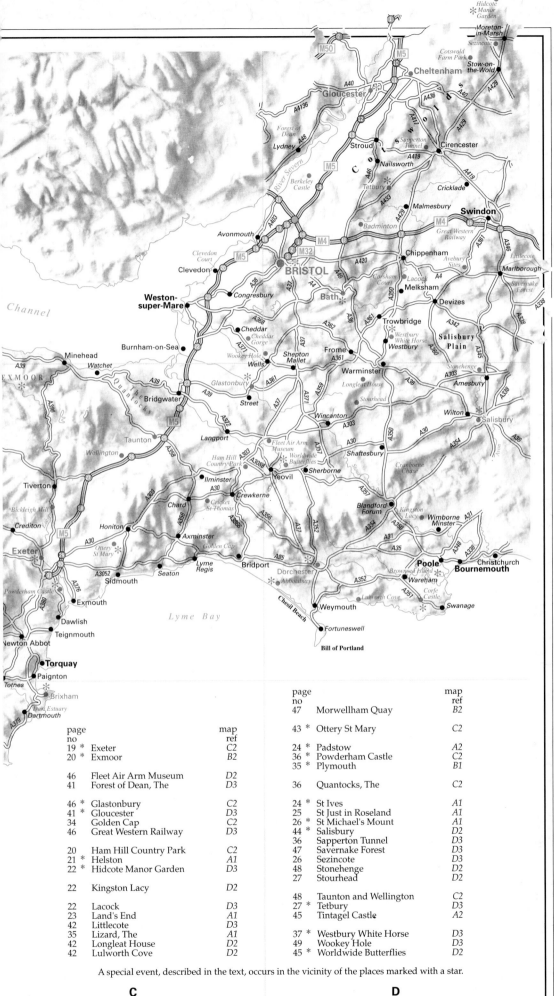

A special event, described in the text, occurs in the vicinity of the places marked with a star.

C   **D**

9

Calendar
of Events

Spring

MARCH

Cornwall Brass Band Association Annual Contest
Truro, Cornwall
(early March)

EASTER

St Endellion Easter Festival of Music
St Endellion Church, Cornwall (Easter)

APRIL

Sudeley Castle Events
Winchcombe, Gloucestershire
(April to October)

Trevithick Day
Camborne, Cornwall
(April – last Saturday)

Badminton Three Day Event
Badminton House, Avon
(late April or early May)

Thornbury Arts Festival
Thornbury, Avon
(late April or early May)

MAY

Minack Theatre Festival
Porthcurno, Cornwall
(throughout the summer – from May)

Hobby Horse Festival
Padstow, Cornwall
(1 May)

May Day Hobby Horse Celebration
Minehead, Somerset
(1 May)

Blessing the Fishing Fleet
Brixham, Devon
(Rogation Sunday)

Furry Dance
Helston, Cornwall
(early May)

Abbotsbury Garland Day
Abbotsbury, Dorset
(mid May)

Cheltenham Festival of Speech, Drama and Dancing
Cheltenham, Gloucestershire
(May – 2nd and 3rd weeks)

Devon County Show
Exeter, Devon
(May – 3rd week)

North Somerset Agricultural Show
Long Ashton, Avon
(May – 4th week)

Rush-bearing Ceremony
St Mary Redcliffe Church, Bristol, Avon
(Whit Sunday)

Cheese-rolling Ceremony
Cooper's Hill, near Gloucester
(Spring Bank Holiday)

Heavy Horse and Steam Engine Rally
Cricket St Thomas Country Park, Somerset
(Spring Bank Holiday)

Scuttlebrook Wake
Chipping Campden, Gloucestershire
(Spring Bank Holiday)

Woolsack Races and Medieval Fair
Tetbury, Gloucestershire
(Spring Bank Holiday)

Newquay Surf Classic
Newquay, Cornwall
(late May)

Bath International Festival of Music and the Arts
Bath, Avon
(late May to early June)

Royal Bath and West Show
Shepton Mallet, Somerset
(late May or early June)

Summer

JUNE

Double-handed Transatlantic Race
Plymouth, Devon
(early June)

Royal Cornwall Show
Wadebridge, Cornwall
(June – 2nd week)

Sidmouth Arts Festival
Sidmouth, Devon
(June – 2nd and 3rd weeks)

St Nectan's Day
Hartland Point, Devon
(Sunday nearest 17 June)

Festival of Antique Lace and Flowers
Maiden Newton, Devon
(June – 3rd week)

Glastonbury Abbey Pilgrimage
Glastonbury, Somerset
(June – 4th week)

International Trawler Race
Brixham, Devon
(June – 4th week)

Wessex Game and Country Fair
Cricket St Thomas Country Park, Somerset
(June – last week)

Bournemouth Flower Festival
Bournemouth, Dorset
(late June)

Exeter Festival
Exeter, Devon
(late June – mid July)

JULY

Annual Historic Vehicles Gathering
Powderham Castle, Devon
(early July)

Tregony Annual Sheepdog Trial
Tregony, Cornwall
(July – 1st week)

Cheltenham International Festival of Music
Cheltenham, Gloucestershire
(July – 1st and 2nd weeks)

Tavistock Carnival Week
Tavistock, Devon
(July – 1st or 2nd week)

Minehead and Exmoor Festival
Minehead, Somerset
(July – 2nd and 3rd weeks)

World of Music and Dance Festival
Clevedon, Avon
(mid-July)

Tolpuddle Martyrs Procession
Tolpuddle, Dorset
(July – 3rd Sunday)

Stroud Show
Stroud, Gloucestershire
(July – 3rd week)

World Wine Fair
Bristol, Avon
(July – 3rd and 4th weeks)

Knill Ceremony
St Ives, Cornwall
(25 July 1996 and every 5th year)

Culdrose Air Day
Royal Naval Air Station, Portland, Cornwall
(July – 4th week)

Exeter Classic Motorcycle Club Annual Dartmoor Run and Show
Exeter, Devon
(July – 4th week)

Bristol Harbour Regatta
Bristol, Avon
(late July)

Poole Fisherman's Regatta
Poole Harbour, Dorset
(late July)

Dawlish Regatta
Dawlish, Devon
(late July to early August)

St Endellion Summer Festival of Music and Drama
St Endellion, Cornwall
(late July to early August)

International Festival of Folk Arts
Sidmouth, Devon
(late July to early August)

Breakers off the north coast of Cornwall provide some of the best surfing in Britain and it is at Newquay that the Surf Classic is held every spring

AUGUST

International Balloon Fiesta
Long Ashton, Avon
(early August)

Sacred Music Festival
Tewkesbury Abbey,
Gloucestershire *(early August)*

Bournemouth Regatta and Carnival
Bournemouth, Dorset
(August – 1st week)

Gloucester Festival
Gloucester
(August – 1st or 2nd week)

Lyme Regis Carnival Week and Regatta
Lyme Regis, Dorset
(August – 1st or 2nd week)

Marhamchurch Revel
Marhamchurch, Cornwall
(August – 2nd week)

Priddy Sheep Fair
Priddy, Somerset
(mid-August)

Bournemouth Clowns Festival
Bournemouth, Dorset
(August 3rd week)

Dawlish Carnival Week
Dawlish, Devon
(August – 3rd week)

International Air Day
RAF St Mawgan,
Cornwall
(August – 3rd week)

Poole Yachting Week
Poole Harbour, Dorset
(August – 3rd week)

Weymouth Carnival
Weymouth, Dorset,
(August – 3rd week)

Fowey Royal Regatta and Carnival Week
Fowey, Cornwall
(August – 3rd week)

Needles International Powerboat Race
Poole, Dorset
(August – 3rd week)

Port of Dartmouth Royal Regatta
Dartmouth, Devon
(August – last week)

Edington Festival of Church Music
Edington Priory, Wiltshire
(August – last week)

Bournemouth Kite Festival
Hengistbury Head,
Dorset
(August Bank Holiday)

Bourton-on-the-Water Game
Bourton-on-the-Water,
Gloucestershire *(August Bank Holiday)*

Plymouth Navy Days
HM Naval Base,
Plymouth, Devon *(August Bank Holiday Weekend, 1995 and every other year)*

Autumn

SEPTEMBER

Great Dorset Steam Festival
Tarrant Hinton, Dorset
(September – 1st week)

International Kite Festival
Long Ashton, Avon
(early September)

Widecombe Fair
Widecombe in the Moor,
Devon *(September – 1st or 2nd week)*

Salisbury Festivities
Salisbury, Wiltshire
(September – 2nd and 3rd weeks)

Barnstaple Old Fair
Barnstaple, Devon
(September – 3rd week)

Frome Cheese Show
Frome, Somerset
(September – 3rd week)

Painswick Clipping Ceremony
Painswick, Gloucester
(September – 3rd week)

Pewsey Carnival and Torchlight Procession
Pewsey, Wiltshire
(September – 3rd week)

OCTOBER

Callington Honey Fair
Callington, Cornwall
(October – 1st week)

River Dart Sponsored Struggle Raft Race
Buckfastleigh to Totnes,
Devon *(October – 1st week)*

Cheltenham Festival of Literature
Cheltenham,
Gloucestershire
(October – 1st and 2nd weeks)

Exeter Carnival Procession
Exeter, Devon
(October – 2nd week)

Tavistock Goose Fair
Tavistock, Devon *(October – 2nd Wednesday)*

Cirencester Mop Fair
Cirencester,
Gloucestershire
(Monday before 11 October and Monday after)

Pack Monday Fair
Sherborne, Dorset
(October – 1st Monday after 10 October)

Taunton Illuminated Carnival and Cider-barrel Rolling Race
Taunton, Somerset
(October – 3rd week)

Punky Night
Hinton St George,
Somerset
(October – last Thursday)

NOVEMBER

Tar-barrel Rolling
Ottery St Mary, Devon
(5 November)

Turning the Devil's Boulder
Shebbear, Devon
(5 November)

Hatherleigh Fire Festival
Hatherleigh, Devon
(1st Wednesday after 5 November)

Punky Night in October

Winter

DECEMBER

Flowering of Glastonbury Thorn
Glastonbury, Somerset
(December or January)

Paper Boys Custom
Marshfield, Avon
(26 December)

JANUARY

Blessing the Plough Ceremony
Exeter Cathedral, Devon
(1st Sunday after 6 January)

Wassailing the Apple Tree
Carhampton, Somerset
(17 January)

SHROVETIDE

Shrovetide Football
Corfe Castle, Dorset
(Shrove Tuesday)

Shrovetide Hurling
St Ives, St Columb Major and St Columb Minor,
Cornwall
(Shrove Tuesday)

KING ARTHUR'S COUNTRY

The West Country is the heartland of the Arthurian legends, the wealth of stories which grew up about a great warrior-king who ruled England long ago from his capital city, many-towered Camelot, where he held court among fair ladies and the heroic knights of the Round Table. The knights rode out in search of brave deeds, notably in the quest of the Holy Grail, the wonder-working cup of the Last Supper. Although the stories are fictitious, the likelihood is that at the core of them lie distant memories of a real man – a powerful war-leader of the Britons against the invading Saxons in the period in the 5th and 6th centuries after the Roman army had withdrawn and left the province of Britain to its own devices.

Background: Glastonbury Tor
Below: Cadbury Camp, believed to be Camelot

An enjoyable tour can be made of Arthurian sites in the South West. One place closely connected in folk tradition with King Arthur and his knights is Cadbury Castle at South Cadbury in Somerset. This is not a castle of the medieval kind, but a hill-fort on a commanding hill. In the 16th century it was identified as Camelot and there was a local belief that Arthur and his knights were sleeping inside the hill, ready to awake and ride out when England had need of them.

Archaeological excavations in the 1960s revealed that in the period after the Roman withdrawal the fortifications at Cadbury were strengthened on a massive scale, unmatched at this time anywhere else in the country. Cadbury was evidently the base of a formidable warlord with ample resources of men and money. Was he the original Arthur? Close by are the little River Cam and the village of Queen's Camel – names which recall Camelot.

A dozen miles away is Glastonbury, which has the strongest links with the traditions of Arthur and the Grail of any place in Britain. The founder of Glastonbury Abbey, according to legend, was Joseph of Arimathea, the rich man who took Jesus's body down from the cross for burial. It was

said that he brought with him to England the cup of the Last Supper, in which he had caught some of the blood welling from Christ's wounded side. Close to the foot of Glastonbury Tor, Joseph thrust his staff into the ground; it miraculously took root and put out buds. It was the ancestor of the celebrated Glastonbury Thorn, which flowers in winter every year, around Old Christmas Day in January. There is one of these trees in the abbey grounds today, and one outside the parish church.

A belief grew up that the Grail was kept secretly at Glastonbury until the Dissolution of the Monasteries, when it was smuggled away into Wales. Alternatively, it is said to lie deep in Chalice Well, near the base of the Tor, whose waters have a reddish tinge.

In 1191 the Glastonbury monks, digging in their cemetery, discovered what they maintained was the grave of King Arthur and his queen, the beautiful Guinevere. The bodies were afterwards reburied in a black marble tomb in the abbey church, in front of the high altar, and the site is marked among the ruins today. This is linked with the tradition that when Arthur was mortally wounded in his last battle he was taken to Avalon, the Isle of Apples, which is identified with Glastonbury.

In Dorset, the Iron Age hill-fort of Badbury Rings, between Wimborne and Blandford, is a candidate for the site of Arthur's greatest victory over the Saxons,

Above: Tintagel Castle – one legend claims the infant Arthur was washed up here by the waves
Below: the Chalice Well cover near Glastonbury Tor – hiding place of the Holy Grail?
Bottom: Dozmary Pool, where Arthur's sword was said to have been returned to the Lady of the Lake

the battle of Mount Badon. Liddington Castle, near Badbury in Wiltshire, is another, or the battle may have been fought somewhere close to Bath.

Arthur's chief counsellor in his youth was Merlin, the master magician, and legend makes Merlin responsible for Stonehenge. The huge stones to build it were allegedly brought from Ireland and erected on Salisbury Plain by Merlin, who fitted them together by magic art.

Moving to Cornwall, it was Merlin, again by magic art, who engineered the conception of Arthur at Tintagel Castle. Later in the legends, Tintagel is the stronghold of King Mark of Cornwall and the place where the lovers Tristan and Iseult lie buried. On the other side of Cornwall, outside Fowey, is the memorial stone of a man called Drustan, who may possibly have been the original Tristan.

Cornwall also claims the site of Arthur's last battle, at Camlann, where he slew the traitor Mordred. This is said to have happened at Slaughter Bridge on the River Camel, outside the town of Camelford (the names again recall Camelot). Dozmary Pool, a desolate lake on Bodmin Moor, is one of the places where Sir Bedivere is said to have thrown Excalibur, Arthur's great sword, into the water when the king lay mortally wounded. In the later stories, however, the last battle is generally set on Salisbury Plain and it is there that Arthur's glorious kingdom is finally and tragically destroyed.

1

ABBOTSBURY
DORSET

On the B3157, at the western end of Chesil Beach, 8 miles south-west of Dorchester. Tourist Information Centres: the King's Statue, The Esplanade, Weymouth (01305) 765221 and St George's Centre, Reforne, Portland (01305) 861333 (limited opening).

Abbotsbury has many attractions, including the famous subtropical gardens, the 14th-century St Catherine's chapel, the parish church and the magnificent thatched Abbey Barn, which dates from about 1400. The mild climate encourages early spring displays of camellias, azaleas, rhododendrons and magnolias in the 20-acre gardens. Later in spring the touching yet fearsome protectiveness of swans with newly hatched cygnets can be seen at Abbotsbury Swannery, behind Chesil Beach. The colony of mute swans, maintained here since the 14th century, numbers 400 at present, and they coexist with ducks. The latter are still trapped for ringing in decoys (a sort of curved netting tube) of 17th-century design.

IN EASY REACH Chesil Beach, the 12-mile long, straight shingle reef containing a lagoon, forms a link between the mainland and the Isle of Portland, a strange, treeless place that has been exploited for centuries for its superb building stone. There is a surprising amount to see on Portland, including the modern lighthouse at the Bill, the local museum (Avice's cottage in Thomas Hardy's book *The Well-Beloved*) with displays of maritime and historical interest, and Portland Castle.

A bridge links Portland with Weymouth, a sprawling town which has absorbed its neighbour Melcombe Regis. It is in the Melcombe area that you will find the huge sandy beach and the Regency terraces that mark it out as a historic watering place. The Lodmoor Country Park has a Sea Life Centre, a butterfly farm and much more, while the RSPB has a reserve there and at Radipole Lake. Enquire about guided walks at the visitor centre in the Swannery car park in Weymouth.

Garland Day

Two Garlands, each about 2ft high and mounted on a pole, are made by the village children of Abbotsbury on Garland Day, 13 May, which is the 'old' May Day. One is made of garden flowers and the other of wild flowers. They are carried round the houses where they are shown and money is given to the children. This is the whittled-- down remnant of what was once a much more elaborate May Day custom, involving garlanding the local fishing boats (see right).

2

BADMINTON
AVON

Off the B4040, 5 miles east of Chipping Sodbury. Tourist Information Centre, The Colonnades, 11-13 Bath Street, Bath (01225) 462831.

The Three Day Event at Badminton in April or early May is the supreme test of skill and toughness for horse and rider, but part of its attraction is undoubtedly the imposing backdrop of Badminton House. Since the house is rarely open, this may be your best chance to examine the magnificent Palladian mansion, a study in severe symmetry. The substantial main house, with twin cupolas, is flanked by L-shaped wings connected to low pavilions, giving a frontage of immense breadth. Badminton is especially noted for the enormous tombs of the Dukes of Beaufort in the church.

IN EASY REACH Six miles to the north-east, off the A433, is the famous Westonbirt Arboretum, with over 18,000 trees and shrubs. Go there in May to avoid the crowds and to see the fine displays of flowering shrubs. Horton Court, a National Trust property north-west of Badminton off the A46, has a notable 12th-century hall (limited opening only). Dyrham Park, also on the A46, 6 miles south-west of Badminton, was built at the turn of the 17th century, and is a most elegant house with an interior that has hardly been altered. It is set in 263 acres of ancient parkland with views over the Severn Valley.

3

BATH
AVON

Tourist Information Centre, The Colonnades, 11-13 Bath Street (01225) 462831.

The Roman Great Bath, which was originally roofed and surrounded by dressing rooms. In the background is the abbey

A concert in Bath's Green Park area – one of the many events at the city's famous festival

●

Bath Festival

The annual Bath Festival, one of the most prestigious in Britain, was directed in its early days by Yehudi Menuhin. It began primarily as a music festival and has always been strong in concerts., ballets and other musical events, but there is also a rich supporting programme of plays, lectures and exhibitions.

●

The Bath Festival of Music and the Arts in May–June each year has international status. It is a highly civilised occasion for a highly civilised city, and you could hardly choose a better time to spend a day in Bath. The season has just begun, and there is room to move – a luxury not always available in high summer.

Perhaps your first visit should be to the Huntingdon Centre in the Paragon, because this beautiful Georgian chapel houses displays explaining Bath's history and the fine scale model will help you to plan your tour. You will certainly want to see the Roman Baths, for there are no comparable remains from this period anywhere else in Britain. Built around a natural hot spring, they were the centre of a Roman resort which flourished here for four centuries. The main feature is the Great Bath itself, but other evidence of Roman life is displayed in the museum.

Close by stands Bath Abbey, one of the last monastic churches to be built. In fact it was still unfinished at the Dissolution of the Monasteries, and was acquired as the parish church. It is an impressive building with an interesting west front, but 19th-century restoration left an interior that is rather featureless apart from some good memorials.

There is some fine architecture wherever you look in Bath, but it is seen at its most spectacular in the Royal Crescent, one of Britain's greatest building achievements, and in the nearby Circus. The interior of No 1 Royal Crescent has been restored as an example of a fine 18th-century house. This is the place for the connoisseur of fine arts, and so is the Holburne Museum and Craft Study Centre in Great Pulteney Street, which houses collections of silver, porcelain, paintings, furniture and glass of all periods, including notable contemporary work.

Bath has an astonishing range of museums, most of them devoted to special interests. One of the most popular is the Museum of Costume in the elegant Assembly Rooms – a remarkably comprehensive collection covering the period from the 16th century to the present day. The Bath Industrial Heritage Centre in Julian Road is something completely different. The cluttered, appallingly dangerous factory of J B Bowler, brass-founder and mineral-water manufacturer, has been reconstructed to show the firm's history. The centre also traces the story of the famous Bath stone. The nature of the displays at the Postal Museum in Broad Street is self-explanatory, but it is worth noting that the first Penny Black stamp was posted at this old post office in 1840.

William Herschel, composer and astronomer, lived in New King Street in the late 18th century, and his house now contains a fascinating collection of his possessions. Another distinguished and slightly later resident was the eccentric writer William Beckford, and you can discover more about his curious career at the Beckford Tower and Museum in Lansdown. (There are fine views from the tower.) The Octagon, a handsome building in Milsom Street has been adapted as the National Centre of Photography, with a museum of historic photographs and equipment, as well as changing exhibitions of other photographs. Finally, don't overlook the American Museum just outside the town, at Claverton Manor. It illustrates vividly domestic life in America between the 17th and the 19th centuries.

4

BRIXHAM AND THE DART ESTUARY
DEVON

Tourist Information Centres: The Old Market House,
The Quay, Brixham (01803) 852861 and 11 Duke Street, Dartmouth (01803) 834224.

The ceremony to bless the fishing fleet at Brixham is a reminder of how many livelihoods once depended on bringing home good catches. They still bring back fish at Brixham, but the prosperity of the town, like that of most of the old harbours of Devon and Cornwall, relies increasingly on a good harvest of holidaymakers.

In this respect Brixham appears, at first, to have fewer advantages than most. The harbour still has the functional look of a working port, and the houses that rise above it are unpicturesque Victorian dwellings. Brixham's domestic past is set out in the museum at the top of Fore Street, with a strong maritime emphasis, and there is a fishing museum and aquarium, on the Quay.

Most of the area's holiday attractions lie to the south-west around the Dart Estuary (see below), but a mile east of Brixham is Berry Head, a country park and nature reserve with fine views over Torbay. There are extensive walks here, taking in an Iron Age settlement and the remains of the defences against Napoleon. A three-mile path to the south passes along unspoilt coast.

Kingswear stands on a steep slope beside the Dart Estuary and has a modern marina and an old castle (not open) that was an essential defence work in the 15th century. Dartmouth Castle, over the water, was its twin in age and purpose – in times of danger a chain would be stretched between the two forts. Dartmouth itself is famous for its naval college, which looms above the steeply rising houses, but the town has other attractions, including the Butterwalk, many fine old houses in the waterfront area, and St Saviour's Church with its celebrated rood screen. The old Customs House and some pleasant 17th-century dwellings can be found at Bayard's Cove.

You can travel on the estuary aboard one of the ferries, or embark on an exceptionally attractive river trip to Totnes, a town rich in historic buildings of many ages, including a notable church and Norman castle. To the east of Totnes is Berry Pomeroy Castle, on the edge of a steep drop. It is reached by way of a pleasant wooded drive, and the 14th-century gatehouse and outer walls rub shoulders with the remains of a large Tudor house, abandoned by the Seymour family in the 17th century. The Dart Valley Railway (limited opening in spring) has steam trains running for seven miles from Paignton to Kingswear stopping at Goodrington sands, a popular beach, and at Churston, before connecting with the ferry crossing at Dartmouth.

Back on the coast and south of Dartmouth, Slapton Ley is Devon's largest freshwater lake. It is separated from the sea by a narrow shingle ridge, and a memorial recalls the days when residents in the area were evacuated so that this strip of shore could be used as a training ground for the Normandy invasion in World War II. Now the lake is part of a nature reserve for marsh birds, dragonflies and rare plants.

●

Blessing the Fleet

Brixham is still a thriving fishing port, one of the few left in the country. The local fishermen work together as a co-operative and the fish market is one of the most active in Britain. The Fisheries Museum and the Marine Aquarium here are consequently close to the life of the town and once a year, on Rogation Sunday (the Sunday before Ascension Day), a special service is held to bless the Brixham fishing fleet and bring it prosperity. Another lively occasion in the town is the trawler race round the harbour in June.

●

Cheerfully colourful houses cluster round Brixham Harbour on Devon's south coast

CAMBORNE AND REDRUTH
CORNWALL

Tourist Information Centre, Municipal Buildings, Truro (01872) 74555.
Information also available from Kerrier District Council Offices,
Dolcoath Avenue, Camborne (01209) 712941.

The Cornish beam engine was possibly the greatest single factor in the prosperity of the county's tin and copper mining industry, and in the 1850s no fewer than 650 of them were being used in Cornwall to pump out water or to power winding gear. Surprisingly, the National Trust owns some of these engines, and you can see two of them at East Pool on the main road between Redruth and Camborne. A third is still in place at the South Crofty Mine at Pool (viewing by appointment only). The Redruth–Camborne area was a great mining centre, and memories of the boom years as well as minerals and ores are preserved at the technical museum at the Camborne School of Mines. A little further afield, north towards St Agnes, is the engine house of Wheal Cotes, a ruined tin mine.

●

Trevithick Day

To honour the town's most famous son, the great engineer Robert Trevithick (above), and commemorate Camborne's role in the Industrial Revolution, Trevithick Day is held every year on the last Saturday in April. The main event is a dance (with many of those taking part dressed in the Cornish colours of black and gold), which proceeds up the main street to the music of the town band. The dance is led by a traction engine and more of them come lumbering along at the rear of the procession. There are also street choirs, street theatre, stalls, exhibitions and a children's dance.

The Gwennap Pit, a mile east of Redruth, is a former mine-working that became famous as an amphitheatre used by John Wesley during one of his frequent visits to this strongly nonconformist area. It has since been grassed over and seats have been cut. To the south-west of Redruth, commanding wide-ranging views, is the granite hill of Carn Brae, topped by a monument of 1836 to one of the local Basset Family, with the remains of a hill-fort and a castle.

●

CHELTENHAM
GLOUCESTERSHIRE

Tourist Information Centre, 77 Promenade (01242) 522878.

The lucky discovery of a medicinal well in the early 18th century and the endorsement by George III and the Duke of Wellington of its beneficial effects transformed Cheltenham from an obscure town into a centre of fashion. The lawns, flowers and trees so characteristic of the town are seen at their best in The Promenade and the neighbouring Imperial Gardens. Perhaps only Bath can match the grand scale of the Regency architecture here, exemplified in the imposing Municipal Offices – a deflating name for such a magnificent terrace – and in the many fine roads and squares nearby. Royal Crescent is the residential showpiece, but the shops in Montpellier Walk, with their curious statuary are equally splendid in their way.

There are some notable individual buildings, too. At the end of Montpellier Walk is the Rotunda, now a bank but originally a pump room, while the fine Queen's Hotel occupies the north side of Imperial Gardens. But perhaps the most elegant single building is the great domed and colonnaded Pittville Pump Room and Museum, standing in its own park to the north of the town.

One of Cheltenham's most valuable assets is the Art Gallery and Museum in Clarence Street, which contains one of the country's foremost collections of arts and crafts, as inspired by William Morris and his followers. The art gallery displays Dutch and British paintings from the 17th century to the present day. The museum is rich in ceramics of many ages from Britain and abroad in addition to fine collections of furniture and glass. In Clarence Road, on the way to Pittville Park, is the birthplace of Gustav Holst – a handsome house, most of which has been reconstructed to show a typical Regency interior from kitchens to nursery. The ground-floor rooms display many of Holst's possessions.

IN EASY REACH Tucked away on side-roads, about 7 miles north-west of Cheltenham, is Deerhurst, where the church is thought to be England's oldest. Also at Deerhurst, and only a stone's throw away, Odda's Chapel dates from 1056, and has been restored after being discovered as part of a farmhouse. You can climb to the top of Cleeve Hill, at 1,082ft the highest point in the Cotswolds, by making for Cheltenham racecourse, to the north-east of the town, while Leckhampton Hill, to the south, has excellent walks that take in the famous rock pinnacle called the Devil's Chimney.

Above left: the grassy amphitheatre at Gwennap Pit. Each year, on Whit Monday, Methodists hold a service here to celebrate Wesley's associations with the area

---

7

CORFE CASTLE
DORSET

On the A351, 6 miles west of Swanage.
Tourist Information Centre, Shore Road, Swanage (01929) 422885.

Shrove Football

On Shrove Tuesday (in February or March) the members of the Ancient Order of Purbeck Marblers and Stone-cutters meet in solemn conclave in Corfe Castle town hall. The Purbeck stone-cutters used to have the right to take their stone from Corfe to Owre Quay on the coast. To keep the right of way open they kicked a football the whole length of the road after their Shrove Tuesday meeting. Today this has degenerated into kicking an old football about in the village street (see right).

The month of March is a good time to come to Corfe. Without summer visitors the grey old village (built almost entirely of Purbeck stone) looks like the working community it used to be, and blends in easily with the castle silhouetted bleakly above it. The castle ruins, on a motte that commanded the only road into the Isle of Purbeck, are remarkably extensive with towers that survived determined attempts to blow them up in 1646 during the Civil War.

IN EASY REACH The Isle of Purbeck is an ideal place for walking and local pamphlets show many opportunities. You will find everywhere the relics of quarrying, both for humble building stone and the famous marble. There are nature reserves (some needing permits) at Hartland Moor, Godlingston Heath and Studland Heath. For shorter walks in unspoilt coastal terrain, and fine views across to the Isle of Wight, go to the Durlston Country Park, south of Swanage.

To the north-west of Corfe Castle is Wareham, a pleasant market town and former port that is still a great sailing centre. A particular attraction is St Martin's, a notable church of Saxon origin, containing a memorial to Lawrence of Arabia, who lived and died nearby.

8

CORSHAM COURT
WILTSHIRE

Off the A4, 3 miles west of Chippenham.
Tourist Information Centre, Neeld Hall, High Street, Chippenham (01249) 657733.

The handsome old town of Corsham with its 17th- and 18th-century Flemish architecture pays tribute to its days as a weaving centre. You can hardly miss the huge entrance gate at Corsham Court, next to the church, whose splendid Georgian state rooms are full of fine 18th-century paintings and furniture. 'Capability' Brown – not usually employed as an architect – was commissioned to enlarge the house in the 1740s, and his work included a splendid triple-cube picture library designed to display an impressive collection of paintings belonging to wealthy cloth merchant Paul Methuen. The Methuens have owned the house for over 200 years and do so to this day. There is a Georgian bath-house in the grounds, as well as a 15th-century gazebo and peacocks strutting about.

IN EASY REACH On the western outskirts of Chippenham, between the A4 and the A420, stands charming Sheldon Manor, sole survivor of a medieval village. The porch of the house dates from 1282, the little separate chapel comes from the 15th century, and inside is a most engaging collection of ornaments, oddments, oak furniture and glass. Keep an eye out for the quilt made of the skins of duck-billed platypuses.

North-west of Sheldon Manor, off the B4039, is Castle Combe, an idyllic picture-postcard village in honey-coloured Cotswold stone with old cottages, a stone-canopied market cross, a church and a little, triple-arched bridge over the brook. The film of *Doctor Doolittle* was made here.

9

EXETER
DEVON

Tourist Information Centre, Civic Centre (01392) 265700.

The Exeter Festival starts towards the end of June and sends this bustling county town into a holiday mood – a good time for a visit before the arrival of the summer crowds. Earlier, in May, the Devon County Show also brings a touch of excitement.

There is a great deal to enjoy, and most people will start at the cathedral, one of the glories of the South-West. The twin towers, unusually placed at the transepts, are Norman, but rebuilding in the Gothic style produced two magnificent results – the elaborately carved west front and the interior roof that forms the longest stretch of Gothic vaulting in the world. Extending over the full length of nave and chancel, it is a marvellous sight, enhanced by the refurbishing which has restored colour to the intricate corbels and bosses. The astronomical clock in the north transept is a famous feature, and so are the misericords on the choir stalls beyond the fine 14th-century chancel screen.

The secluded Cathedral Close has a harmonious mixture of buildings, including the splendid Mol's Coffee Shop. St Martin's Church, close by, is one of several exceptional small churches, like St Mary Arches, where there are some interesting memorials, and St Mary Steps, where the elaborate clock is famous. The Rougemont Gardens are one of the city's showpieces, and another is Southernhay, where elegant Georgian terraces stand round well-kept gardens. Notable individual buildings include the Tucker's Hall, the porticoed Guildhall and the ambitious Royal Albert Museum in Victorian Gothic, which houses some distinguished collections, including Exeter silver.

The importance of the river in Exeter's history is symbolised by the fine Custom House on the Quay and the two restored warehouses that accommodate the Maritime Museum – a glittering collection of nearly 170 working boats. Finally a curiosity – in the arcade in the High Street is the entrance to medieval aqueducts that form a series of unique underground passages. People queue up to go through them: an odd, slightly eerie experience. 'We are now immediately beneath the perfume counter of Boots,' says your guide.

Inset below: Figurehead of The Cygnet, one of the more unusual boats in Exeter's Maritime Museum. It was used to ferry passengers to a larger craft, The Swan, which used to be moored at Starcross on the Exe Estuary

●

Exeter Festival

The Exeter Festival, which lasts for two and a half weeks at the turn of June and July each year, was first held in 1980. The emphasis is principally on music – involving anything from Vivaldi, Bach and Mozart through the great 19th-century composers to present-day and avant-garde compositions, and also covering ballet, opera and choral works. Other events are arranged as well, however, and may include plays, films, poetry readings, puppet shows and children's entertainments. The main picture (below) shows members of the Welsh National Opera Company taking part in a performance in Exeter Cathedral.

●

EXMOOR
SOMERSET AND DEVON

Tourist Information Centres: 17 Friday Street, Minehead (01643) 702624 and Town Hall, Lynton (01598) 52225. National Park Centres at Dulverton, Dunster, County Gate, Lynmouth and Combe Martin.

●

May Day Celebration

*A*t Minehead the peculiar-looking creature called the Sailors Horse (see above) first appears on the streets on the last night of April. He comes out again early on May Day, when he bows solemnly three times to the rising sun and again during the next two days, when he also tours the surrounding district. His attendants, who collect money from locals and visitors, are called Gullivers.

●

Lorna Doone Farm at Malmsmead. A footpath leads south along Badgworthy Water to the legendary Doone Country

*S*pring officially reaches Minehead on May Day, when the Hobby Horse dances through the streets to scare off the Danes. If there are no Danes about the ceremony becomes an excuse for a spring festival, and also a chance for the visitor to sample the pleasures of Exmoor.

The National Park is an area of high, wild moorland, the source of fast-flowing streams. Much of it is grazed by sheep and beef cattle, but there is an abundance of wildlife too – apart from the famous ponies there are red deer, foxes, otters, badgers, buzzards, merlins and ravens. Human habitation is sparse by contrast, but hamlets like Luccombe, Winsford and Selworthy have churches that are well worth visiting. Many people like to explore the settings of *Lorna Doone* at Malmsmead, Badgworthy Water and Oare, in the north of the Moor, and exploration of all kinds is made easier by over 600 miles of public footpaths.

One church not to be missed is at Culbone. It is a tiny building embedded in coastal woodland 4 miles west of Porlock. The medieval village of Dunster, south-east of Minehead, has an unusual octagonal Yarn Market in its village street, which is lined by charming houses and dominated by a massive castle (open to the public) at one end. On the other side of the Moor, nine miles south-east of Lynton, Arlington Court dates from 1822 and has fascinating collections of all kinds built up by a Victorian lady. It also has a large number of horse drawn vehicles, and Shetland ponies and Jacob sheep grazing the parkland.

11

HAM HILL COUNTRY PARK
SOMERSET

*Near the A303, 5 miles west of Yeovil.
Tourist Information Centre, Petter's Way, Yeovil (01935) 71279.*

*T*urning this steep and hummocky hill into a country park has made this interesting area much more accessible. Many people come here simply to enjoy the panoramic views, but the maze-like quarries, the source of the famous Ham building stone, have their own fascination. Inevitably a strongpoint like this became the site of an Iron Age hill-fort, the largest in Europe, the ramparts of which still survive. The obelisk on the top is a war memorial for the village of Stoke-sub-Hamdon below. Other places to visit within the park are High Wood, colourful in the spring with many rhododendrons, and Bateman Barn, the site of a Roman villa excavated in 1907. Most of the buildings in the village are built of Hamstone. Apart from quarrying, the major source of employment was the glove industry, originally there were seven factories but only one remains today.

IN EASY REACH The area around Ham Hill abounds with fine houses in the care of the National Trust. Montacute House is very grand indeed. It stands 4 miles west of Yeovil, an H-shaped Elizabethan mansion noted for its fine furniture, tapestries and heraldic glass. There is a superb formal garden with mixed borders and old roses, and also a landscaped park. Formal gardens are also the attraction at the 17th-century Tintinhull House, (house not open) 5 miles north-west of Yeovil, but in this case they were laid out in the present century. The garden is divided by walls and hedges into themed areas with a kitchen garden. Lytes Cary Manor (limited opening) and Barrington Court, noted for its beautiful Gertrude Jekyll garden, are other National Trust properties further afield. At East Stoke, St Mary's Church, which dates back to Norman times, has a 13th century tower and 15th century interior wall paintings.

12

HELSTON
CORNWALL

On the A394, midway between Falmouth and Penzance.
Tourist Information Centre: Station Road, Penzance (01736) 62207. Information also available from Kerrier District Council Offices, Camborne (01209) 712941.

To learn about the town of Helston and its Furry Dance, a good first port of call is the Folk Museum in Church Street. You will find that Helston was once important as one of the 'Stannary Towns', where the quality of tin was officially assessed before it could be sold. Nowadays the older part of the town is a place of harmonious Georgian and Victorian architecture, although the Angel Hotel is of 16th-century origin. The Market Hall of 1839 is in a distinguished classical style, and so is St Michael's church, rebuilt in the 18th century.

●

Furry Dance

Grey toppers and smart spring bonnets adorn couples both young and old as they dance sweetly through the crowded streets of Helston on Flora Day (see left). They dance to the catchy tune wrongly – to the irritation of the locals – called the 'Floral Dance'. It is actually the 'Furry Dance'. The whole town is hung with greenery, flowers and bunting for this tremendous occasion (usually staged on 8 May), which welcomes in the spring and the promise of summer.

●

IN EASY REACH Across the Lizard peninsula, the Helford Estuary is really a flooded valley with innumerable creeks and inlets where the trees grow down to the shore. Fans of Daphne du Maurier can seek out Frenchman's Creek, and everyone should visit the Cornish Seal Sanctuary and Marine Animal Rescue Centre, near Gweek, where injured seals are nursed back to health. Elsewhere in the district the most ambitious man-made attraction is Flambards Theme Park, at Culdrose to the east of Helston. It features a beautifully detailed Victorian village, a display of historic aircraft and a vivid portrayal of Britain in the Blitz. For the adventurous there is a chance to explore deep underground at the Poldark Mine, 3 miles north of Helston. More traditional pleasures can be found at Glendurgan Garden, near Mawnan Smith, with its water gardens and maze. Trelowarren House (limited opening), 3 miles south of Helston, is mainly early Tudor with 17th-century additions and is noted for its pre-Reformation chapel. Five miles north-west of Helston is the splendid Godolphin House – originally 15th-century, but with a unique colonnaded front added in the 1630s.

HIDCOTE MANOR GARDEN
GLOUCESTERSHIRE

Off the B4632, 4 miles north-east of Chipping Campden.
Tourist Information Centres: Woolstaplers Hall Museum, Chipping Campden (01386)
840101 (seasonal opening only) and Bridgefoot, Stratford-upon-Avon (01789) 293127.

Even the hard-to-please connoisseur will acknowledge the originality of the garden at Hidcote Manor. When Laurence Johnston, an American bought the Manor in 1906 he created tiny 'boxes' bounded by tall hedges that effectively make each plot a new and subtly different experience. The plants are not exotic, but the skilful use of flowering shrubs was unusual at the time, and Johnston did much to popularise them. Not far away, the gardens of Kiftsgate Court are distinguished for roses and rare shrubs.

IN EASY REACH Chipping Campden was one of the Cotswold towns that grew rich on wool, and a visit to the magnificent church confirms the fact with an outstanding range of memorials and effigies. There are many more treasures out in the High Street, which is lined by fine buildings of a variety of ages. Several of these buildings were restored early in the 20th century after the formation of a pioneering preservation society by newcomers associated with the Guild of Handicrafts. There is an intriguing small folk museum, with exhibits including mantraps, sewing machines and jelly moulds, at the Woolstaplers Hall.

Scuttlebrook Wake

Scuttlebrook Wake is the traditional Whitsuntide celebration in the historic market town of Chipping Campden, culminating in the crowning of the May Queen in the market square, and a procession. The evening before, eccentric and boisterous sports and contests of strength

(known as the 'Cotswolds Olympics') are held on Dover's Hill nearby. The hill is named after Robert Dover, who founded the games early in the 1600s. The illustration (above) shows the 'Hay Tossing' contest.

14

KINGSTON LACY
DORSET

On the B3082, 1½ miles north-west of Wimborne Minster.
Tourist Information Centre, 29 High Street, Wimborne Minster (01202) 886116.

Kingston Lacy is one of the National Trust's most splendid properties. It is basically a 17th-century mansion – severely square and self-contained – but in the 18th and 19th centuries distinguished experts made changes to both house and park. What the visitor sees now is a succession of magnificent ground-floor rooms, the marble staircase and the state bedroom. Thanks to a much-travelled 19th-century owner, the furnishings and decorations have a cosmopolitan quality, with fine Italian work very prominent. The pictures are memorable – Lely, Van Dyck, Romney, Rubens and Brueghel are represented together with minor Dutch and Italian masters. There is also a fine landscaped park, with guided walks round the estate buildings.

IN EASY REACH The pleasant market town of Wimborne Minster is built around its famous Minster, an imposing Norman church with fine central and bell towers. Inside are some notable monuments and a very old astronomical clock with a quarterjack – a lifesize soldier who strikes the quarter hours on his bells. Wimborne's history is related in the Priest's House Museum. East of Wimborne off the A31 is Stapehill Abbey, a busy working crafts centre with landscaped gardens, parkland and many attractions under cover. Further east at Hampreston are the Knoll Gardens filled with ponds, waterfalls, rockeries, woodland glens and formal areas.

15

LACOCK
WILTSHIRE

On the A350, between Chippenham and Melksham.
Tourist Information Centres: Neeld Hall, High Street, Chippenham (01249) 657733
and Church Street, Melksham (01225) 707424.

When England's sheep supported the thriving medieval wool trade, Lacock flourished at the heart of wool country. Now one of the best preserved medieval small towns in the country, many of the buildings date from those prosperous times. Strolling through the old streets, you see sturdy stone cottages – some dating back to the 13th century.
The National Trust owns most of Lacock, as well as Lacock Abbey, with its great black walnut trees. The original cloisters, sacristy, chapter house and nuns' parlour have survived, although after the Reformation the nunnery was converted into a grand Tudor mansion with twisted brick chimney-stacks, a courtyard, a clock-tower and half-timbered gables. In the 18th century fashionably Gothic alterations were made, including the Great Hall and gateway. The Fox Talbot family were squires of Lacock Abbey and it was here that William Henry Fox Talbot carried out his pioneering experiments in photography producing the world's first photographic negative in 1835. The 16th-century barn in the village now houses a museum of his work.

IN EASY REACH Bowood House, off the A4, near Calne (5 miles east of Lacock), is probably at its best in spring, when daffodils, narcissi and bluebells carpet 100 acres of stunning grounds created by 'Capability' Brown in the 1760s. Its centrepiece is the long, 40-acre lake, and added later were the cascade, hermit's cave and little Doric temple. Terraced gardens stocked with roses, clipped yews and statuary make a stage on which the house is set. In late spring there are wonderful walks in 40 acres of separate woodland planted with gorgeous and unusual rhododendrons and containing the mausoleum of the Landsowne family, the owners of the house.

Italianate terraces, with statues and clipped yews, at Bowood House

The house itself is long, low and classical, beautifully proportioned and the survivor of what was once a far bigger mansion. Designed by Robert Adam, it houses the laboratory where Joseph Priestley discovered the gas oxygen. The orangery is hung with interesting paintings, ancient Roman statuary is on view in the sculpture gallery, and displays of clothing include Lord Byron's celebrated Albanian fancy dress. Porcelain, Indian curios and silver are also on view. You can take the children outside to rampage in the sizeable adventure playground and pop into the garden centre to buy a shrub or two.

16

LAND'S END
CORNWALL

Tourist Information Centre, Station Road, Penzance (01736) 62207.

There is something compelling about the idea of standing on the most south-westerly point of mainland Britain. Millions have done it, and people who mutter about 'commercialisation' here forget that Land's End was commercialised in Victorian times when Grace Thomas set up her First and Last House and sold refreshments to visitors. In more recent years innovative exhibitions have been set up to trace the geology, wildlife and maritime history of the area. You also get magnificent scenery for your money – the 200-acre site is the setting for wild coastal walks, tumbled granite, the jagged reefs, the Longships and Wolf Rock lighthouses, and perhaps even a view of the Scillies, more than 25 miles away to the west.

The coastal path provides a fine short walk northward to Sennen among endlessly changing cliff scenery. Sennen Cove has a good beach, and there is a famous Iron Age hill-fort on Mayon Cliff nearby. If you continue round the sweep of Whitesand Bay you reach Cape Cornwall, marked by a chimney-stack on its summit. This was a famous mining area, with its centre at St Just, and among the many remains the most famous are at nearby Botallack mine, with its recently-restored engine houses perched just above the sea. The old Count House has been converted into a restaurant and has splendid views.

Equally famous in this area are the prehistoric remains, best discovered on an Ordnance Survey map. Several can be reached from the minor road leading from Madron to Morvah. Close to the prominent ruins of the Ding Dong Mine is the 6th-century inscribed stone known as Mens Scryfa. Lanyon Quoit, a Neolithic chambered tomb with three stones supporting a huge capstone, stands right beside the road. Further west towards Trewellard is the Iron Age fort called Chun Castle, with Chun Quoit nearby.

---------------------------------- 17 ----------------------------------

PADSTOW
CORNWALL

On the A389, west of Wadebridge.
Tourist Information Centre, Shire House, Mount Folly Square, Bodmin (01208) 76616.

●

Hobby Horse

The earliest records of the Padstow hobby horse (see right) go back only to the early years of the 19th century, though the custom is no doubt very much older. The day begins at the crack of midnight on the last night of April, with the singing of a 'morning song' outside the Golden Lion pub. The two 'horses' leap and prance in the streets for most of the day.

●

Once a year on May Day this otherwise quiet port erupts as the Old 'Oss and the Teazer lead an uninhibited festival that has its roots in ancient fertility rites. This spring celebration provides added spice for the visitor to the Camel Estuary, where there is much to see and enjoy.

Padstow itself is a very ancient port – the old name 'Petrockstow' reflects the fact that it was also the site of the first monastery established by Cornwall's best-known saint. The harbour trade declined as sand built up on the Doom Bar, and there has been little scope for development since, so it remains a place of harmonious stone houses with one or two outstanding buildings, such as the 15th-century Merchants' Guild House and Raleigh's Court House, a Tudor tax office on the south quay.

IN EASY REACH Exhilarating cliff walks abound near the Camel Estuary, particularly at Pentire Point, Rumps Point and Trevose Head, seen at their best when the spring flowers are out. The Trevose lighthouse is open to the public. A short distance south along the coast, the Bedruthan Steps are rock stairs set in majestic cliff scenery. Further inland, Little Petherick is a delightful place – its small church has an astonishingly rich interior. There are other churches in the area for the connoisseur: At St Ervan, St Enodoc, St Kew and at Wadebridge (St Breock's). East of Pentire Point lie the unspoilt Port Isaac, Port Gaverne and Port Quin (now in National Trust ownership). The Longcross Victorian Gardens, a mile south-east of Port Quin, are a pleasant place to stroll while enjoying the coastal views.

---------------------------------- 18 ----------------------------------

ST IVES
CORNWALL

Tourist Information Centre, Guildhall (01736) 796297.

Apart from its function as a market town, St Ives was an early centre for artists, and the tradition has continued, so life goes on throughout the year. In addition, it enjoys the late spring and summer boom that comes from having a generous ration of four sandy beaches on each side of the headland known as the Island. The old fishing quarter, where the early artists set themselves up among the locals, is still a delightful place of small cottages, shops, cobbled lanes and alleyways. Barbara Hepworth was one of the artists who worked here, and the museum and sculpture garden named after her contains some of her work. She also sculpted a notable Madonna and Child for St Ia's Church, a fine building which should not be missed. The Tate Gallery presents displays of modern art relating to Cornwall.

IN EASY REACH The Zennor Wayside Museum, on the B3306 west of St Ives, is an extensive privately assembled collection of tools, industrial relics and domestic items covering every aspect of life in the area from 3000BC to the 1930s. Zennor Quoit nearby is believed to be the largest chambered tomb in the country. To the east of St Ives, at Cornucopia, in Lelant, there is a model village and miniature displays on many themes. Paradise Park, a conservation theme park with an otter sanctuary and endangered species of birds and animals, is off the B3302 south of Hayle. The remarkable Iron Age village of Chysauster can be seen off the B3311, south of St Ives. It incorporates the remains of four pairs of houses with circular rooms and gardens, set in the oldest surviving village street in England.

19

ST JUST IN ROSELAND
CORNWALL

On the eastern side of the Fal Estuary, south of Truro on the A3078.
Tourist Information Centres: 28 Killigrew Street, Falmouth (01326) 312300 and
Municipal Buildings, Truro (01872) 74555.

The church of St Just in Roseland stands on a hill overlooking Carrick Roads, Falmouth's famous deep-water anchorage. When you pass through the elaborate lych-gate the church appears to be beneath your feet, so steep is the way down. It lost much of its character after restoration, but contains a notable 16th-century memorial brass. However, most visitors do not come to see the church but the decorative churchyard, a riot of subtropical trees and flowering shrubs. Opinions will differ as to whether it is really the most beautiful churchyard in the world, but there certainly are few, if any, in Britain to surpass it for exotic spring and summer colour.

IN EASY REACH Flushing and St Mawes, on opposite sides of the Fal Estuary, both have waterfront architecture of great charm, and St Mawes has in addition an unusual Tudor castle, built for the defence of the estuary. It comprises a substantial tower and three cannon emplacements in a clover-leaf pattern. Pendennis Point, at Falmouth's eastern extremity, carries a castle built at the same time and is equally functional as a fort designed solely for cannon. Further inland a major attraction is Trelissick Garden, on the B3289, 4 miles south of Truro. The grounds slope down to the river and feature magnificent rhododendrons and hydrangeas as well as specimen trees. A visit to Truro really needs a day to itself, but if time is limited at least try to look at the 19th-century cathedral. J L Pearson designed a building which skilfully incorporated part of an old parish church. It is in the Early English style, with twin west towers, and the clean local stone is decorated with crisp carving.

Knill Ceremony

One of the strangest occasions in Britain is held every fifth year at the monument to John Knill, Mayor of St Ives and benefactor to the town in the 18th century. On 25 July, the day of his death, 10 small girls in white dresses dance for at least 15 minutes and then sing a psalm: this is under the terms of his will. Two elderly widows attend the ceremony to make sure it is correctly performed. The Mayor and the Town Council attend as well. The illustrations (left and above) show the 1986 ceremony.

20

ST MICHAEL'S MOUNT
CORNWALL

Off the coast at Marazion, 3 miles east of Penzance.
Tourist Information Centre, Station Road, Penzance (07136) 62207.

Cornwall is rich in dramatic scenery, but there is no more striking sight in the county than St Michael's Mount, especially on a clear spring day when the details of the granite hill and its castle stand out sharply. At high tide it becomes an island, but when the causeway reappears it is possible to walk to this astonishing place.

A monastery was established on the Mount in 1047, and it remained a religious centre until the early 15th century, when it began to develop as a fortress. After the Civil War it was acquired by the St Aubyn family, who converted the monastery into a private house. The family still lives here, but the house is administered by the National Trust and open to the public.

The castle is no romantic ruin – much restoration and extension has taken place over the centuries – but the new work blends happily with the medieval remains. The great south-east wing is entirely Victorian and a stunning architectural achievement. Inside the castle the Blue Drawing Rooms, created from the former Lady Chapel, are outstanding in the 18th-century Gothic style, and the Chevy Chase Room and armoury are also impressive.

Minack Theatre

The Minack Theatre at Porthcurno stages plays in a rock amphitheatre created in the 1930s by Rowena Cade. The setting on the edge of the cliffs with the sea in the background lends an enchantment to the performances.

IN EASY REACH Penzance, just along the coast, is a modest holiday resort worth visiting for its exotic Egyptian House in Chapel Street. Other attractions include the Penlee Museum of local folk history, a maritime museum and an aquarium. For 'traditional' Cornish harbours you need to go further west to Newlyn and Mousehole. Two other places not to be missed are Trengwainton Gardens, at Madron, 2 miles west of Penzance, with a subtropical flora and splendid native shrubs, and the unique natural auditorium of the Minack Theatre at Porthcurno.

21

SEZINCOTE
GLOUCESTERSHIRE

Off the A44, 3 miles south-west of Moreton-in-Marsh.
Open Thursday and Friday afternoons (house May to July and September only).
Tourist Information Centres: Council Offices, High Street, Moreton-in-Marsh (01608) 650881 (limited opening) and Hollis House, Stow-on-the-Wold (01451) 831082.

The Canal Pool and slim cypresses adorning one of the terraces at Sezincote

The house at Sezincote was built in 1805 for an East India Company grandee and designed to make him feel at home – in fact it is said to have been the inspiration for the Prince Regent's Royal Pavilion at Brighton. The bow-fronted and balconied main house is surrounded by an onion dome, a motif repeated frequently elsewhere. An elegant low wing extends from one side. The garden, landscaped by Humphrey Repton, contains an Indian shrine, a famous Oriental water garden and some fine trees.

IN EASY REACH Snowshill Manor (open May to September), 5 miles to the west, appears more conventional but is equally fascinating. Behind the Tudor façade is an extraordinary jumble of assorted collections more or less as the early 19th-century owner, Charles Wade, left them. Some of them are junk, some are valuable, but all are interesting. You will never see a house like it. The Batsford Arboretum, north-west of Moreton-in-Marsh, is at its best in spring when the daffodils bring a homely touch to this collection of exotic and native trees, which otherwise has a strong Japanese emphasis. The 1,200 or more species within its 50 acres make Batsford a place of subtle beauty.

22

STOURHEAD
WILTSHIRE

Off the B3092, 3 miles north-west of Mere.
Tourist Information Centre, The Square, Mere (01747) 861211.

Bridge, Lake and South Bank at Stourhead, as depicted in about 1770 by C W Bampfylde. Over two centuries the trees have obviously grown larger, but the view is still easily recognisable today

In late spring the rhododendrons bring brilliant, exotic colour to this 2,600-acre estate, once the home of banker Henry Hoare. His son Henry laid out the famous pleasure grounds in 1741 and they probably constitute the most breathtaking 18th-century landscape garden in Europe, with every tree, shrub and hillock choreographed to present splendid views. Lakes, grottoes, statues, surprising little follies, classical temples and dainty bridges make up an elegant fantasy landscape, like an 18th-century painting brought to life.

Be sure to inspect King Alfred's Tower, 150ft high on top of Kingsettle Hill, itself 800ft above sea-level, but worth the climb for the view. The tower, a red brick folly built in 1772, is said to mark the spot where Alfred stood against the Danes in 879. The gardens contain rhododendrons, some of them very rare, which grow alongside tulip trees, beeches and conifers on the wooded lower slopes of the valley of the Stour. The Palladian house itself is elegant, not exceptional perhaps, but still worth seeing. It was built in 1721 by Colin Campbell and contains furniture by the younger Chippendale and fine paintings.

Both the mansion and park are actually part of the village of Stourton, which stands at the park entrance, and all now belong to the National Trust. Stourton consists of St Peter's Church, the medieval Bristol High Cross – brought here in the late 18th century, an inn and an attractive group of stone cottages.

23

TETBURY
GLOUCESTERSHIRE

On the A433, 10 miles south-west of Cirencester.
Tourist Information Centres: The Old Court House, Tetbury (01666) 503552 (seasonal opening only) and Town Hall, Market Lane, Malmesbury (01666) 823748.

The merry-making of Tetbury's Woolsack Races in late May takes place against a background of harmonious buildings, most of them in local stone. The architecture is mainly a mix of medieval, 17th-century and Georgian, and is seen at its best in Long Street. However, as with most old Cotswold wool towns, it pays to investigate side turnings and odd corners. Tetbury takes special pride in its imposing market hall, supported on pillars, and its elaborate church of 1781, which is a very early example of the Gothic revival.

IN EASY REACH When driving in the area around Tetbury, you should not hesitate to be diverted by villages like Sherston or Easton Grey. But try to get to the old market town of Malmesbury (5 miles south-east) which is dominated by the impressive ruins of the 12th-century Norman abbey – its particular glory is the south porch. Follow the self-guided circular Malmesbury Town Trail (leaflet from the Tourist Information Centre), or the marked river walk. Another place not to be missed is Chavenage, 2 miles north of Tetbury signposted off the B4014 (limited opening May to September). It is an Elizabethan manor house whose owner during the Civil War had Parliamentarian sympathies, so Cromwellian relics are a feature of the interior, together with some good furniture and tapestries. In more recent years the house has been the location for the television series *Grace and Favour, Poirot, The House of Elliot* and *The Noel Edmunds House Party*.

Woolsack Races

Tetbury has a long history as a prosperous market town at the heart of what was once an important wool-producing area. This past is remembered today at the Spring Bank Holiday, when relay teams race up and down the steepest streets (between pubs), with woolsacks weighing 50lb (see above). There is also an all-day medieval market.

—————————— **24** ——————————

BERKELEY CASTLE
GLOUCESTERSHIRE

Off the A38, midway between Gloucester and Bristol.
Tourist Information Centre, Subscription Rooms, George Street,
Stroud (01453) 765768

Berkeley has everything you might expect of a castle – rambling architecture, a keep, superb state apartments and a particularly notorious dungeon (Edward II was brutally murdered in it). Branches of the Berkeley family have lived here for 800 years, and since the 14th century they have transformed the castle from a fortress into a richly furnished house. The principal rooms are magnificent in size, design and decoration, with the 60ft Great Hall as the centrepiece, but you can also visit the kitchens and that dungeon. Outside there are fine terraced gardens, an extensive park and a butterfly farm. The neighbouring small town of Berkeley has a museum devoted to the life and work of Edward Jenner, pioneer of vaccination.

IN EASY REACH The Wildfowl Trust, at Slimbridge, 5 miles north-east of Berkeley Castle, needs no introduction. Peter Scott's original modest project has now grown to 800 acres, and much scientific work is carried out. But this is not only a place for specialists – it is geared equally to the family outing, and a late spring or early summer visit, with hundreds of young birds on view, will delight children.

Due east of Slimbridge, on the other side of the M5, is Frocester, where the huge 14th-century tithe barn – 200ft long – is still in use. Seven miles south-west of Stroud, off the B4066, the tiny village of Owlpen boasts a distinguished manor with a record of building from the 15th to the 18th centuries.

—————————— **25** ——————————

BODMIN MOOR
CORNWALL

Tourist Information Centre, Shire House, Mount Folly Square, Bodmin (01208) 76616.

● *Royal Cornwall Show*

To the south of Wadebridge (at the west of Bodmin Moor) is the county showground where the Royal Cornwall Show is held every year in June (see right). This is the premier agricultural show in the county, and one of the major shows in Britain, with championship cattle, horse and sheep classes. There are competitions and displays in every aspect of farming and horticulture, as well as hundreds of trade stands.

●

Bodmin Moor is on a smaller scale than Exmoor or Dartmoor, but it has much the same character as the other south-western 'deserts' and possibly more variety. During a single day's drive you can see the bleak northern moors, dominated by Roughtor and Brown Willy, each over 1,300ft, the lower hill 'ranges' to the east, the lonely farms with their walled pastures, prehistoric remains, ancient churches, old and new industrial sites, and modern holiday enterprises.

Information about walking opportunities is readily available, and the main road system brings into easy reach some very desirable targets like Brown Willy, the Moor's highest point, or Dozmary Pool, the mysterious lake close to Bolventor that is supposedly the last resting place of the sword Excalibur. The Golitha Falls are a well-established beauty spot near St Neot, and you should certainly not miss Altarnun, where St Nonna's is one of Cornwall's finest churches. The prehistoric remains are most thickly concentrated in the south-east corner of the Moor, and at the other extreme the park at Colliford Lake is a recreational area with lakeside walks and a rare breeds centre.

● *Fowey Regatta and Carnival*

In August a watery festivity arrives with a splash in a harbour deep in Daphne du Maurier country. This is the Royal Regatta and Carnival in Fowey, a port once famous for its piratical seamen, the Fowey Gallants, who in medieval times raided and looted the coasts of France.

●

IN EASY REACH Two miles south-east of Bodmin is the magnificent Lanhydrock House (National Trust), basically 17th-century, but largely rebuilt after a fire in 1881. The outstanding features here are the original gallery, with its vast plasterwork ceiling, and the network of domestic quarters. Four miles north-west of Bodmin, off the A389, Pencarrow House in its fine 19th-century grounds is home to an excellent collection of paintings.

Bodmin itself, if not the liveliest spot in the west, has a fine church and the regimental museum of the Duke of Cornwall's Light Infantry. Further south the National Trust has acquired much of the land surrounding the Fowey Estuary, and a notable coastal walk starts at Pont Pill.

The Hurlers, a prehistoric stone circle near Minions on the east side of Bodmin Moor. A local legend said that the stones were men who had been petrified as a punishment for hurling a ball on the Sabbath

26

BRAUNTON BURROWS
DEVON

On the A361, 6 miles north-west of Barnstaple.
Tourist Information Centre, The Library, Tuley Street, Barnstaple (01271) 388583.

Covering a total area of about 2,000 acres at the northern end of the Taw and Torridge Estuary, Braunton Burrows may well be the largest expanse of sand dunes in England. The 17th-century naturalist John Ray, was the first to catalogue the wildlife here, and although the northern edge has been marred by a beach-side car park and golf course, over 1,500 acres remain unspoilt as a National Nature Reserve (open to the public), still harbouring rare birds and plants. Where the dunes meet the sea are plants like sea stock, sea holly and sea bindweed. Further inland you come to sea sponge and wild thyme, and further in still there are marsh orchids and water germander, yellow rattle and red campion. There are masses of snails and insects to look for here, too.

IN EASY REACH Braunton itself has an interesting church and a rare example of strip farming in its Great Field. Immediately to the west of the Burrows are the famous 3-mile-long Saunton Sands, while the nearby village of Croyde has an unexpected and fascinating Gem, Rock and Shell Museum.

For dramatic cliff scenery and outstanding views, go north-west from Croyde to Baggy Point, a 400ft headland with excellent walks. Marwood Hill Gardens, inland from Croyde and Braunton, will provide a change from the salt air – its 5 acres of gardens have a lake and a remarkable display of flowering shrubs. While here call in at the church, which has many other attractions including a magnificent rood screen.

27

BRISTOL
AVON

Tourist Information Centre, St Nicholas Church, St Nicholas Way (0117) 9260767.

●

Rush-bearing Ceremony

The Lord Mayor and Corporation of Bristol in full civic splendour attend the rush-bearing service and process through the church of St

Mary Redcliffe on Whit Sunday every year. The floor of the nave is strewn with rushes and the pews are garlanded with numerous bouquets of flowers.

●

The dramatic 700ft span of the Clifton Suspension Bridge high above the Avon Gorge

First and foremost, Bristol is an ancient port and, although large ships no longer tie up here, the Floating Harbour has been put to imaginative use. In high summer there is often a festival atmosphere here, with water craft of all kinds from sailing dinghies to powerboats. The best way to explore the harbour is by ferry boat – take a complete tour or stop off at different points to visit various places – while further east there is a variety of land-based attractions. A short walk from the city centre will bring you to the Industrial Museum (much more fun than it sounds) and while you are here it is worth walking round to the redeveloped Bathurst Basin. The Industrial Museum acknowledges Bristol's debt to Isambard Kingdom Brunel, and a little further west is one of his pioneering achievements – the SS *Great Britain*, the first ocean-going propeller-driven ship, now forming the centrepiece of the Maritime Heritage Centre. One of the city's most exciting museums is the Exploratory Hands-on Science Centre where visitors are encouraged to handle the exhibits.

Bristol's old city centre and commercial district is best toured with the help of the 'heritage walk' pamphlet. It will guide you to some memorable sights, such as St Mary Redcliffe, one of England's greatest parish churches, and to the fine buildings in King Street, which include a spectacular timber-framed pub called the Llandoger Trow. Other places on the walk are the Dickensian Christmas Steps, the Edward Everard Building, and St Nicholas Church. By branching off to the Broadmead shopping centre, you can see the well-preserved New Room, the earliest Wesleyan Chapel in Britain.

Another face of Bristol is seen on a plateau above the old centre. (You can reach it by way of Denmark Street, where Harvey's have established an excellent wine museum). The cathedral stands commandingly on College Green, and is a much underrated building with many treasures. From here the shopping centre off Park Street takes you into fine Georgian streets and on to Brandon Hill, where the Cabot Tower provides the best viewpoint in the city. Also here is one of the first urban nature reserves in Britain. Beyond the Tower the City Museum and Art Gallery mingles with the university buildings. There are outstanding displays of ceramics and glass here, but also plenty for children to enjoy.

Finally there is Clifton, the elegant suburb to the west, and the best way to reach it is to drive along the Avon Gorge. This way you will get the 'classic' view of Brunel's Clifton Suspension Bridge, a delicate engineering miracle spanning the Gorge, 250ft up. There are contrasting attractions in Clifton. One is the pleasure of strolling round splendid early Regency terraces like Cornwallis Crescent and Royal York Crescent. Another is visiting the brilliant modern interior of the Roman Catholic Cathedral. A third is the Zoo, well worth a visit for its extensive gardens, varied collections of mammals, birds, reptiles and fish and its adventure playground.

If you cross the Suspension Bridge (an experience in itself) you will reach two of the open spaces on the outskirts of the city. The Avon Gorge Nature Reserve and Leigh Woods both have enjoyable walks in former parkland.

28

BROWNSEA ISLAND

DORSET

In Poole Harbour. Reached by ferry from Poole Quay or Sandbanks.
Tourist Information Centre, The Quay, Poole (01202) 673322.

Brownsea Island first achieved a niche in history when Lord Baden-Powell organised a boys' camp there, thus launching the Boy Scout movement. A subsequent owner closed it completely to the outside world and did nothing to stop nature running wild, so when the National Trust acquired it and opened it up in 1961 it was already a nature reserve of sorts. Now the 500 acres are managed as a haven for an enormous variety of wildlife.

The 19th-century mansion and 250 acres of scientific reserve are closed off, but otherwise you can wander freely, enjoying the views of the mainland. A leaflet tells you what to look out for, but red squirrels, herons and deer are among the many attractions.

IN EASY REACH A 500-yard channel forms the entrance to Poole Harbour, one of the world's largest anchorages. Its centre of activity is the Quay. The most-visited building along here is the Poole Pottery Factory and showrooms, where you can learn about the complete process and buy the products. Opposite the Quay, in the High Street, are the Waterfront and Scalpen's Court Museum buildings.

To the west of the town and overlooking the harbour is Upton Country Park, where a 19th-century house (partly open) is surrounded by 55 acres of traditional parkland of great variety. On the other side of the town, between Canford Cliffs and Parkstone, is Compton Acres – an astonishing spread of exotic gardens featuring bronze and marble statuary.

Clowns Festival

The annual Clowns Festival at Bournemouth, just along the coast from Poole, is a very recent and extremely successful attraction. In August clowns come from all over Britain, and some from other countries of Europe, to perform in public gardens, parade on the streets and dart into shops (see above).

29

CLEVEDON COURT

AVON

Off the B3130, 1½ miles east of Clevedon.
Tourist Information Centre, Beach Lawns, Weston-super-Mare (01934) 626838.

Clevedon Court's south façade shows the unusual rectangular windows, some with ornate tracery – just one of the attractions of this old manor house

This is a marvellous survival – a 14th-century manor house with a tower and chapel of even earlier date. The house has not entirely escaped alteration. An early 18th-century owner gave the Great Hall an upper storey, and the terraced gardens date from the same period, but it remains an outstanding showpiece, now in the care of the National Trust. The former owners, the Elton family, had literary leanings, and the novelist Thackeray was a visitor. Perhaps the most famous association, however, is with Arthur Hallam, close friend of the poet Tennyson, who was buried in Clevedon churchyard, a fact recorded in Tennyson's *In Memoriam*. The house has an unusual collection of the glass for which nearby Nailsea was famous.

IN EASY REACH The town of Clevedon is one of those nice old resorts that restore your faith in the seaside. There are no garish attractions – just a small beach, a Victorian pier, a landscaped esplanade, quiet streets and pleasant shops. To the north of the town, at Walton-in-Gordano, is The Manor House with its 4-acre garden, specialising in shrubs and trees. To the east is the splendid hill-fort of Cadbury Camp. There is good cliff walking to the north of Weston-super-Mare, where Worlebury Hill rises to command magnificent views across the Bristol Channel. At its western end is a hill-fort noted for its storage pits. There is information about this and much else concerning the area at Woodspring Museum in Weston.

The picturesque village and harbour of Clovelly first became popular with holidaymakers in the mid-19th century. Many of the cottages bear the initials of Christine Hamlyn, the local landowner in the early 20th century who was responsible for much of the restoration of the village.

CLOVELLY
DEVON

Off the A39, 12 miles west of Bideford.
Tourist Information Centre, The Quay, Bideford (01237) 477676.

Clovelly must be everyone's idea of a romantic Devon harbour. Idyllically set in a gap in the cliffs, it has preserved its lovely old houses although it no longer has the thriving herring trade that once created bustle in its 16th-century harbour. The most scenic approach is by way of Hobby Drive, a private road about ½ mile beyond Bucks Cross on the A39. For a small charge it is possible to drive through lodge gates on to a spectacular coast road.

The best-known feature of the village is its cobbled main street, dropping so steeply between the immaculate cottages that steps are necessary. This excludes traffic, although there is a Land Rover service from the car park for those with walking difficulties. Do not miss the church with its old pews and fine memorials to past lords of the manor. A nearby path leads away to Gallantry Bower, a cliff where you will get unsurpassed views of Lundy Island.

IN EASY REACH Seven miles west of Clovelly, Hartland Point has exciting cliff scenery, part of a savage stretch of jagged coastline. The elaborate lighthouse is open to the public. Further on south is Morwenstow, whose Victorian vicar was the colourful Robert Hawker. He organised many sea rescues, and the churchyard contains a ship's figurehead as a memorial to a drowned crew. A walk from the village green to Vicarage Cliff will bring you to his favourite view.

Finally, between Bideford and Barnstaple, is Tapeley Park, overlooking the Taw and Torridge Estuary. There are guided tours of the elegant house, which dates from the reign of William and Mary, and is the Devonshire home of the Christie family, of Glyndebourne. The gardens are mainly the work of Lady Rosamond Christie who helped plan the beautiful Italian Garden.

●

St Nectan's Day

On the Sunday nearest 17 June (St Nectan's Day) a special mass is celebrated beside the saint's holy well at Hartland Point and local children walk in procession carrying foxgloves. After being decapitated by robbers, St Nectan, a 6th-century Welsh hermit, was said to have picked up his head and carried it to his well. Where blood dropped to the ground, foxgloves are said to have grown.

●

31

COTSWOLD FARM PARK
GLOUCESTERSHIRE

*Near Guiting Power, 10 miles east of Cheltenham. Tourist Information Centre,
Municipal Offices, The Promenade, Cheltenham (01242) 522878.*

It is some years now since Joe Henson decided to devote part of Bemborough Farm to the preservation of rare breeds of livestock. Now his Cotswold Farm Park is a premier tourist attraction, and it still outclasses its many imitators in its setting and its range of stock. The farm is on the broad uplands nearly 1,000ft high, and there is a great sense of space – you walk along wide paths between generous enclosures containing history-book animals like the spectacular Highland cattle, the striped 'Iron Age' pigs and the famous Cotswold sheep. Children will be particularly drawn to the pets' corner and the farm trail.

IN EASY REACH To the north-west, just outside Winchcombe, is Sudeley Castle. It is basically of 15th-century date and had close associations with Tudor royalty before being ruined after the Civil War. Victorian restoration began in the 1830s. It is set in fine formal gardens and parkland, where the church has an elaborate Victorian memorial to Katherine Parr. One of the most exciting prehistoric sites in England is nearby, at Belas Knap, off the A46, 2 miles south of Winchcombe. A superb viewpoint, this Neolithic barrow is 200ft long, with three chambers into which you can crawl.

Sudeley Castle Events

Many special events are held throughout the season in the castle grounds, including craft shows, a horse show, a gardens weekend and a classic car roadshow. One of the most popular events on the programme is the Gloucestershire Game Fair.

32

CRANBORNE CHASE
DORSET

*Between the A350 and the A354.
Tourist Information, Bell Street, Shaftesbury (01747) 853514.*

Cranborne Chase is a broad expanse of chalk upland, once a royal hunting forest with its own intimidating laws. (King John's hunting lodge can be seen at Tollard Royal). It is still heavily wooded in places, with old trees and newer plantations, and remains comparatively deserted, with narrow lanes connecting small settlements that must once have been clearings in the forest. There are good walks here, but you need to get information first to avoid trespassing.

The Chase has its share of prehistoric earthworks, but the most remarkable survival in the area is Ackling Dyke, part of a Roman road from Dorchester to Salisbury. It can be seen as a substantial causeway to the south-east of the village of Sixpenny Handley. Garden lovers should not miss Cranborne Manor, north-west of Cranborne. Originally laid out in the 17th century by John Tradescant, the grounds have been replanned since and now feature a knot garden, a herb garden, flowering cherries, roses and much more. At Shaftesbury very little remains of the town's rich past, but it is worth visiting for the views its plateau-edge situation affords, and for the picture-postcard street called Gold Hill.

33

CRICKET ST THOMAS
SOMERSET

*On the A30 between Chard and Crewkerne.
Tourist Information Centre, Guildhall, Fore Street, Chard (01460) 67463.*

Fans of the actress Penelope Keith will already know Cricket St Thomas – it was the setting for the television comedy series *To the Manor Born*. In real life, the 1,000-acre estate here provides space for a wide variety of animals and birds, including elephants, camels and sealions in wildlife enclosures designed to blend in with the surroundings as far as possible. The Shire horses at the National Heavy Horse Centre and the working railway are other popular attractions.

IN EASY REACH 'A garden for all seasons' is the claim of Clapton Court, on the B3165, 3 miles south of Crewkerne. In its 10 acres there is certainly immense variety, with terraces, lawns, woodland, water features and a rose garden. Another fine garden can be seen at Forde Abbey, a mile east of Chard. Here the distinctive feature is the bog garden, containing unusual Asiatic plants, and the whole 30 acres are splendidly landscaped around a unique crenellated house that was once a Cistercian abbey. Further east, Parnham House is off the A3066, 1 mile south of Beaminster in Dorset, and is famous as the home of John Makepeace's furniture workshops and School for Craftsmen in Wood. The house is basically 16th-century, with later additions including work by John Nash. Visitors can see the main rooms and workshops and walk in the 14-acre garden.

• 34 •

DORCHESTER
DORSET

Tourist Information Centre, 1 Acland Road (01305) 267992.

The town of Dorchester lost most of its medieval buildings through a succession of fires, and its character now is agreeably Georgian and Victorian, but it is worth seeking out older survivals like the Old Tea House and Judge Jeffreys' Lodging in High West Street. The Walks are Dorchester's unique feature – tree-lined lanes following the Roman walls. A copy of the detailed town trail will guide you round these and other places of interest. Near Dorchester's southern boundary is Maumbury Rings, an amphitheatre which the Romans adapted from a Neolithic temple site. The public gallows were set up here in the 18th century. Enthusiasts for militaria should make for the Military Museum at the Keep in Bridport Road, and children will love the blend of prehistory and hi-tech at the Dinosaur Museum in Icen Way. Also don't miss the excellent Dorset County Museum in High West Street

IN EASY REACH Two miles south-west of the town is spectacular Maiden Castle – a 45-acre, flat-topped earthwork with fearsome ramparts. It is usually called an Iron Age hill-fort, but research has shown at least three main stages of development, from a small village of about 2000BC, through a period of Iron Age occupation until its capture by the Romans in about AD43, and finally as the site of a pagan temple in the 4th century.

Thomas Hardy was born and wrote several novels at Higher Brockhampton, 2 miles north-east of Dorchester, off the A35. His cottage can be visited only by appointment, but the gardens are public. Beside this same stretch of road is Athelhampton, a 15th-century house with some of the best formal gardens you are likely to see – very highly recommended. A little further away (10 miles north-east of Dorchester) is Milton Abbas, an 18th-century 'new' village, erected when the local landowner demolished the old one in order to extend his park.

• 35 •

GOLDEN CAP
DORSET

National Trust coastal estate to the east of Lyme Regis. Tourist Information Centre, Guildhall Cottage, Church Street, Lyme Regis (01297) 442138.

Miles of unspoilt coastline, with beaches, dramatic cliffs, panoramic views, rolling downland, woods, old-fashioned meadows – this is the National Trust's Golden Cap Estate. Dominating the estate is Golden Cap itself, at over 600ft the highest cliff on the south coast. Recommended walks up to the Cap are from the car park at Langdon Hill Wood or from the Anchor Inn at Seatown, and a whole network of paths start at the Trust's information centre at Stonebarrow Hill. Go to the car park at Charmouth to get useful information from the Heritage Coast Centre, including tips on how to find some of the fossils on the beaches.

IN EASY REACH Paths from Golden Cap lead to Lyme Regis, an unspoilt seaside resort which so impressed Jane Austen that she used it as a setting in *Persuasion*, including the famous curving breakwater known as the Cobb. Among other attractions here are the seafront thatched cottages, the Philpot Museum and the Umbrella Cottage, but the main pleasure is simply strolling round this charming old town.

Tolpuddle Martyrs

*E*veryone has heard of the Tolpuddle Martyrs, pioneer trade unionists, but not so many know their story. If you pause for a while in Tolpuddle, along the A35 from Dorchester, you will leave much better

informed, because their memory is kept proudly alive, especially in July, when commemorative processions bring the village to life. In the churchyard is Eric Gill's memorial to James Hammett, the only Martyr to die here. At the centre of the village a seat stands by a tree under which the six are reputed to have met, and the pub name also commemorates them. A memorial arch leads to the Methodist chapel, but the most striking memorial is the pleasant row of six cottages erected by the TUC in 1934 for retired farm workers. There is a small museum here too.

Above right: golden cliffs and beaches at Eype Mouth, at the eastern end of the National Trust Estate

---

36

THE LIZARD
CORNWALL

Tourist Information Centres: 28 Killigrew Street, Falmouth (01326) 312300 and Station Road, Penzance (01736) 62207.

Kynance Cove, just to the west of Lizard Point, shows the typical jagged cliffs and stacks carved out of the multicoloured serpentine rock of the peninsula

In high summer the Lizard peninsula is crowded, but the Cornish heather is out, and its pink and lilac flowers are almost unique to this area of heathland, cliffs and coves, reputed to be the warmest part of England. Apart from the lighthouse there is not much worth lingering for at Lizard Point, unless you need a granite ashtray, but on no account miss the very attractive village of Landewednack just to the north.

Back on the east coast, Cadgwith is a tiny picture-book harbour, while Coverack is a larger fishing village with a safe beach and good cliff walking. The old tower and spire of the church at St Keverne, a little further north still, was designed as a warning to ships approaching the notorious Manacle rocks to the east of the village.

Moving inland, you cross the Goonhilly Downs, a nature reserve whose name has become familiar because of the satellite tracking station and its immense equipment. You will probably pass it on the way to Mullion, another village with an outstanding church (look for the pew carvings). Mullion Cove, with its small harbour, and Kynance Cove to the south are delightful places, although in the high season you will probably enjoy them either very early or very late in the day.

37

PLYMOUTH
DEVON

Tourist Information Centre, Island House, The Barbican (01752) 264849.

The combination of war damage and later redevelopment has left Plymouth with modern office blocks and shopping precincts, but the old nucleus of the city, huddled to the west of Sutton Harbour, has been lovingly preserved (and sometimes reconstructed) in the district known as the Barbican. The Black Friars Distillery in Southside Street (home of the famous Plymouth Gin) has been much altered, but dates back to the 15th century. Prysten House, behind St Andrew's Church, is of the same age, and its rough stone and little courtyard give it great character. The church, itself gutted by bombs, deserves a visit to see its John Piper windows and splendid new floor of Delabole slate. Paradoxically, Plymouth's oldest street is New Street, and it contains the Elizabethan House, authentically restored. The town's showpiece, however, is the 16th-century Merchant's House in St Andrew's Street, with a façade almost entirely made up of windows. It now houses a museum of social and commercial history. The Pilgrim Fathers did not actually start their journey here, but Plymouth has claimed them as its own and they have a memorial on the shores of Sutton Harbour.

Plymouth's best-known feature is probably the Hoe, a beautifully landscaped area facing the Sound. It is dominated by Charles II's Citadel – a huge and astonishing ramparted fortress – but equally impressive is John Smeaton's handsome Eddystone Lighthouse, re-erected here in 1882 and providing one of the best viewpoints in the city. While you are at the Hoe, don't miss the small aquarium near the Citadel.

If you despair of seeing all this, plus Plymouth's other attractions, in a day, there are open-top buses or boat cruises available. The Phoenix Wharf is the embarking point for cruises up the Tamar River or for regular trips around the naval dockyard.

●

Navy Days

Plymouth means the navy, and traditional Navy Days are held here every other year in August (see above). Apart from giving you the rare chance of going on board, the navy stages air displays and events on the river as part of its thank-you to one of its oldest homes.

●

38

POWDERHAM CASTLE
DEVON

Off the A379, 8 miles south of Exeter.
Tourist Information Centre, Civic Centre, Exeter (01392) 265700.

The Earl of Devon's family has occupied Powderham Castle for nearly 600 years, although most of the present building is the result of reconstruction during the last two centuries. The castle overlooks the Exe Estuary from the western side, in fine natural parkland complete with a herd of deer and a heronry. The house has very elaborate rooms, including a splendid banqueting hall, a music room by Wyatt and a chapel converted from a medieval barn. The rich variety of furniture, china and paintings complements the ornate decoration.

Historic Vehicles

Numerous special events are staged at Powderham Castle during the season, including horse shows and craft fairs. Perhaps the best-known one is the annual historic vehicles gathering in early July at which horse-drawn transport vies with antiquated, puffing, steam-driven conveyances.

IN EASY REACH The Exe Estuary is full of seabirds and sailing craft – a pleasant setting for the villages that surround it. Kenn is a very pretty place with thatch and colourwash and a church with an elaborate chancel screen. The church is also the best feature of nearby Kenton. At the head of the estuary, Turf is situated at the end of the Exeter Canal, first cut in 1567, while close by, but on the other side of the river, is the ancient port of Topsham, a sailing centre with a delightful waterfront and a wealth of attractive buildings. While you are on this side of the estuary, you might like to visit the Woodbury area. The common provides good walking country with fine views over both the Exe and Otter Valleys. In addition there is Woodbury Castle, an easily accessible Iron Age hill-fort, and the common also has several Bronze Age barrows.

About 4 miles south of Powderham, a long sandy spit extends far across the mouth of the estuary. This is Dawlish Warren, once a lonely place, but now built-up at the shore end as a beach resort. Further out on the spit is a nature reserve, and organised walks are programmed in the summer.

39

THE QUANTOCKS
SOMERSET

Tourist Information Centre, 50 High Street, Bridgwater (01278) 427652
(seasonal opening).

The Quantock Hills, rising to 1,250ft and once bleak moorland, are now well-wooded, with deep combes, and you can learn about their natural history by calling at the visitor centre at Fyne Court, Broomfield. The centre also provides literature about hill walks. Along the roads at the foot of the hills are a string of pleasant villages, whose churches are almost always worth exploring – good examples are Stogursey (a fine Norman survival), Spaxton, Goathurst and Combe Florey. Several of them have the carved bench ends characteristic of the area. At Enmore, Barford Park is an elegant Queen Anne house with particularly fine woodland and water gardens.

IN EASY REACH Samuel Taylor Coleridge lived at Nether Stowey, at the north of the Quantock Hills between 1796 and 1803. During this time he wrote *The Ancient Mariner* and *Christabel*, but equally important for English poetry was the fact that William and Dorothy Wordsworth came to live 3 miles away at Alfoxton Park in 1797. Their discussions resulted in the publication of the *Lyrical Ballads*, a book which gave poetry a new direction. The parlour of the cottage (administered by the National Trust) has been preserved as a memorial to the poet.

To the west of the hills, Combe Sydenham Hall, on the B3188, is undergoing long-term restoration. At present only the Court Room is open to visitors, but the country park has well-planned waymarked walks. Near Washford, at the northern end of the B3188, are the remains of 13th-century Cleeve Abbey which forms part of an interesting complex of buildings.

40

SAPPERTON TUNNEL
GLOUCESTERSHIRE

Off the A419, 3½ miles west of Cirencester.
The tunnel is near Tunnel House Inn, on the Coates to Tarlton road.
Tourist Information Centre, Corn Hall, Market Place, Cirencester (01285) 654180.

The Thames-Severn Canal, from Stroud to Lechlade, was a dubious commercial enterprise and certainly no engineering miracle. The ambitious 2½ mile Sapperton Tunnel was always subject to collapse, but its grandiose west portal survived, and you can see it by walking the towpath from a point near the old canal pub called the Tunnel House Inn. In fact you can walk enjoyably about 8 miles along the towpath from here to Stroud through the 'Golden Valley', cut by the Frome and once heavily industrialised. On the way you will see encouraging signs of canal restoration.

IN EASY REACH The lovely small town of Cirencester nearby, was an important Roman city, and its history during this period is vividly revealed at the Corinium Museum in the town centre. More evident today is its status as a major medieval wool town – a stroll through its streets reveals a wealth of handsome buildings of the 17th century and earlier, and its cathedral-like parish church is a symbol of a wealthy community. Look for the three-storey south porch, the medieval pulpit and the memorials in the Trinity Chapel and Lady Chapel.

The hilly village of Chedworth, 8 miles north of Cirencester, is famous for its Roman Villa, where you can see finely preserved mosaics and baths, together with a museum of artefacts. A pleasant walk to the site begins just outside Chedworth on the Yanworth road. Also in this area is Denfurlong Farm, where visitors can see the workings of a modern dairy farm. Bibury, 8 miles north-east of Cirencester, is widely held to be the most beautiful Cotswold village. Its showpiece is Arlington Row – a line of 14th-century weavers' cottages. Arlington Mill nearby is a museum devoted to rural bygones and crafts.

41

WESTBURY WHITE HORSE
WILTSHIRE

Off the B3098, between Westbury and Bratton.
Tourist Information Centre, Edward Street, Westbury (01373) 827158.

Just outside Westbury, on the edge of Salisbury Plain, a huge, awkward-looking horse has been carved into the steep chalk slope of Bratton Down. The best place to see it is from the B3098, about 1½ miles east of the town. A stylish animal in its way, it is not the creature it once was – the original Saxon horse was 'new modelled' in 1778, and altered from 'cart breed' to 'blood breed' by a presumptuous Mr Gee. At the top of the hill is Bratton Castle, a large prehistoric earthwork with a longbarrow. There is a superb view from the summit.

Church Festival

A week in August every year is devoted to church music, performed as part of the services in the church in Edington, near Westbury. Four services are held every day during the week, beginning with matins in the morning and ending with compline by candlelight at night. The festival was founded in 1956 and is now firmly established and of an extremely high standard.

IN EASY REACH In Westbury itself there are handsome Georgian houses around the market square, an interesting Perpendicular church and Chalcot House, a small Palladian mansion with a Boer War collection. East of Westbury along the line of the Downs lies Edington Priory, a huge 14th-century church, dwarfing its tiny village, which in August every year plays host to an annual festival of church music.

The tiny village of Dilton, just outside Westbury, has a fascinating church, which escaped the attentions of Victorian restorers and remains as it was in the 18th century. A little further away, to the north-west at Rode, the Bird Gardens have a collection ranging from flamingos to vultures. At Farleigh Castle, north again at Farleigh Hungerford, you can see the tower in which a 16th-century Hungerford imprisoned his wife for 4 years.

The White Horse at Westbury. The people standing on its eye give some idea of its size

--------- 42 ---------

ANTONY HOUSE
CORNWALL

Off the A374, 2 miles north-west of Torpoint.
Tourist Information Centre, Island House, The Barbican, Plymouth (01752) 264849.

Across the Tamar from Plymouth stands Antony House, an 18th-century mansion with fine furniture, books and china, surrounded by wooded gardens and lawns which roll down to the river. The estate belonged to the Carew family from the late 15th century until 1961, when it was passed to the National Trust, but the family still live there. Built of silvery-grey Pentewan stone with colonnaded wings of red brick, the architect of the house is unknown, but its style resembles that of James Gibb who designed Oxford's Radcliffe Camera.

IN EASY REACH Nearby is Mount Edgcumbe Country Park where there are hundreds of acres of coastal parkland with exceptional views, and further west along the coast is the charming Murrayton Monkey Sanctuary (limited opening in autumn). Here a colony of Amazonian woolly monkeys live as near naturally as possible in spacious, wooded enclosures. A little further westwards still is Looe – onetime pilchard-fishing community and now a popular holiday resort from which fishing and boating trips operate. The Town Museum is situated in the old Guildhall.

--------- 43 ---------

AVEBURY SITES
WILTSHIRE

On the A361.
Tourist Information Centres: Great Barn, Avebury (016723) 425 (seasonal opening only) and Neeld Hall, High Street, Chippenham (01249) 657733.

Ancient standing stones at Avebury. Their natural outlines – tall and straight or diamond shaped – may have been chosen to symbolise male and female forms

This little village lies at the heart of a remarkable complex of prehistoric remains. Avebury Circle itself is the biggest megalithic ceremonial monument in Europe, large enough to contain half a dozen cathedrals. It consists of a circular bank, getting on for a mile round and over 20ft high originally, surrounding a ditch 30ft deep. Within this are three circles of stones. The outer one is the largest in Britain, originally composed of about 100 giant standing stones, weighing in at 40 tons or more each. An avenue of stones leads south-east to another site, known as The Sanctuary. Seen early in the morning or at dusk, especially on a misty day, many claim that Avebury has a more powerful atmosphere than Stonehenge.

Avebury dates back to about 2600BC. North-west of it, on Windmill Hill, stands an even older monument, a Neolithic earthwork going back to about 3700BC. Silbury Hill to the south remains a mystery: man-made and 130ft high, it is the largest artificial prehistoric mound in Europe. It may have taken up to 200 years to build, but no one knows its purpose. We do know that West Kennet Long Barrow, a little further south still and built in about 3500BC, was a burial place. Pottery, tools and weapons unearthed at the Avebury sites can be seen in the Alexander Keiller Museum, behind Avebury church.

Off the A4 east of Avebury, at Lockeridge Dene and Piggle Dene, the National Trust owns land on which can be seen the 'grey wethers' or sarsen stones of the kind used to build the Avebury and Stonehenge circles. On the northern edge of the Marlborough Downs, off the B4005, is the impressive hill-fort of Barbury Castle, with a monument to the writer Richard Jefferies, who loved this spot.

44

BICKLEIGH MILL
DEVON

On the A396, 3 miles south of Tiverton.
Tourist Information Centre, Phoenix Lane, Tiverton (01884) 255827.

For years tourists have flocked to Bickleigh Bridge to gaze at the idyllic view of riverside gardens and thatched cottages. Nowadays a good many of them move on to gaze in equal fascination at the huge waterwheel and cumbersome mechanics of the old mill, restored to working order after years of neglect. The ground floor here is given over to craft products in every kind of material, while upstairs you can find an impressive range of woollen goods and some up-market garments in a variety of natural fibres. Associated with the mill is a re-creation of a Victorian farm, with shire horses, rare livestock and displays of traditional farming skills. Mechanisation is not ignored – a Motor Centre has farm machinery and historic cars on show.

IN EASY REACH Nearby is Bickleigh Castle (limited opening in autumn), where the attractions include a *Mary Rose* exhibition and a display of escape and espionage equipment. The 18th-century Killerton House lies further south and features family possessions, but its main glory is the 15-acre garden with magnificent trees and a Victorian 'Norman' chapel. Knightshayes Court, 2 miles north of Tiverton, is a Victorian mansion with an imposing interior containing fine furniture, china and paintings. Much of the astonishing interior work is by William Burges and J D Crace.

45

CHEDDAR GORGE
SOMERSET

On the B3135, 8 miles north-west of Wells.
Tourist Information Centres: The Gorge, Cheddar (01934) 744071 (seasonal opening only) and Town Hall, Market Place, Wells (01749) 672552.

Autumn, when the leaves are turning and the crowds have gone, sees Cheddar Gorge at its best. The steep limestone cliffs with the road winding through far below never fail to impress. Gough's and Cox's Caves allow spectacular trips underground, and there are many well-signposted family walks.

IN EASY REACH Near Churchill, 6 miles north of Cheddar, is the fine hill-fort called Dolebury Camp, while at Priddy, 4 miles to the south-east, there are many Bronze Age barrows and the mysterious earth rings known as the Priddy Circles. The village has an interesting church and is a popular caving centre. Just to the east of Churchill, Burrington Combe is a dramatic wooded valley, superb in autumn, and the same can be said for Ebbor Gorge – an unspoilt ravine with a nature reserve to the south of Priddy. The museum at Axbridge interprets the life, ancient and modern, of the Mendips.

46

COTEHELE HOUSE
CORNWALL

Off the A390, 5 miles south-west of Tavistock.
Tourist Information Centres: Town Hall, Tavistock (01822) 612938 (seasonal opening only) and Island House, The Barbican, Plymouth (01752) 264849.

In the early 16th century the Edgcumbe family built themselves a fine manor house overlooking the River Tamar. When they moved in the late 17th century they left the house more or less intact and continued to maintain it. As a result Cotehele House is a remarkable Tudor survival, now in the care of the National Trust. Perhaps the most impressive interior feature is the lofty Great Hall, with splendid roof timbers and walls bearing a collection of weapons and armour, but all the rooms contain objects of beauty, including furniture of the 17th and 18th centuries.

The grounds are of equal interest, formed on several levels with pools, terraces and fine trees that are seen to advantage in autumn. The buildings include a medieval dovecot and barn. A short distance away is Cotehele Quay, where a branch of the National Maritime Museum has been established with a Tamar barge as its centrepiece.

IN EASY REACH Buckland Abbey, a few miles to the east, also has superb gardens as well as a medieval tithe barn. Originally a religious institution, as its name suggests, it was converted to a house in the 1570s by Sir Richard Grenville. A decade or so later it was sold to Sir Francis Drake. It now houses a naval museum with 'Drake's Drum' among its exhibits.

●

Honey Fair

The quiet town of Callington, to the west of Cotehele, once had a prosperous wool industry, but today is known for its annual honey fair, held in the first week of October. Revived a few years ago, the event does involve beekeeping exhibitions and honey on display in the town hall, but is mainly an opportunity for a fun-fair and stalls selling knick-knacks on the streets.

●

●

Goose Fair

The traditional Goose Fair, or Goosey Fair, on the second Wednesday in October has been a fixture in the town of Tavistock, 5 miles north-east of Cotehele, since as long ago as 1105. All through medieval times geese were the principal commodity on sale, but nowadays the streets are packed with stalls selling a million and one things. Roundabouts, fairground rides and amusements, and a procession in the evening complete a cheerful day.

●

DARTMOOR
DEVON

Tourist Information Centre, Civic Centre, Exeter (01392) 265700. Also (seasonal opening only), 3 West Street, Okehampton (01837) 53020. National Park Centre, Haytor Road, Bovey Tracey (01626) 832047.

Combestone Tor, on a minor road south of Dartmeet, shows the rocky, windswept scenery typical of Dartmoor

•

Widecombe Fair

The fame of the fair held in September at Widecombe in the Moor rests on the song about 'old Uncle Tom Cobbleigh and all'. (Incidentally, all the characters named in the song were real people.) It is not a particularly old fair, going back only to 1850. Ponies and sheep from Dartmoor are sold at the fair.

•

Raft Race

In October, to raise money for charity, the local Round Table organises a lively

raft race over 6 miles of the River Dart, from Buckfastleigh down to Totnes. It attracts 400 or more rafts as entrants.

•

A great granite plateau formed by volcanic action, the Moor is a place of stony soil, bogs, frequent mists and rain, and vast expanses of green broken by rocky tors. It is rich in minerals, and has been exploited in the past for tin, copper, iron, arsenic, and fluor. Somehow prehistoric peoples flourished here, and their relics include Bronze Age 'Beaker burials' at Fernworthy and Lakehead Hill, as well as stone circles and settlement sites (there is a particularly fine example at Grimspound). Wildlife includes foxes, otters and badgers, while new conifer plantations provide a habitat for the merlin, chiffchaff and redpoll. And, of course, there are the famous ponies.

Widecombe, famous for its fair, is a good example of an isolated Moor settlement. Tin mining paid for the splendid church of St Pancras, a prominent landmark with its disproportionately high tower. Among the cluster of buildings nearby, the 16th-century Church House is outstanding. A few miles to the east, Haytor, one of the best-known rock outcrops, can be seen. (Just to the north of it look out for the granite rails of an old 7-mile tramway that carried stone down into the Teign Valley.)

Many fast-flowing rivers rise on Dartmoor, and 4 miles south of Moretonhampstead, on the B3344, the Becky Falls cascade dramatically after rain. There are many paths and nature trails here. Even more spectacular is the Lydford Gorge on the western side of the Moor. Lydford can be found off the A386, 8 miles north of Tavistock, and the old mining village is of interest in itself, but the great attraction is its ravine, where the River Lyd descends for 2 miles between walls up to 60ft high, swirling over pot-holes like the eerie Devil's Cauldron.

Man's struggle to civilise the wilderness is symbolised by St Michael's Church near North Brentor, a few miles south of Lydford off the A386. Despite its lonely, exposed position, this tiny building attracts large congregations in the summer. The church is a reminder that the local stone has always been a fine building material. Two other outstanding examples of its use can be seen back on the other side of the Moor at Buckfast Abbey, on the A38 about 20 miles south-west of Exeter, and at Castle Drogo, off the A382 north-west of Moretonhampstead. They are both modern buildings; the abbey was built by French monks between 1906 and 1932 (it is famous now for its wine and honey) while Castle Drogo is an immense private house of the same period by Sir Edwin Lutyens. It stands on a 900ft bluff overlooking the Teign Valley.

After visiting the splendour of Castle Drogo it is something of an antidote to look in at the old Nonconformist village of Sticklepath, a few miles to the north-west on the A30. The Museum of Water Power at the Finch Foundry recalls the hard work and ingenuity needed to make a living here, while the Quaker graveyard evokes the humility of the former inhabitants.

48

THE FOREST OF DEAN
GLOUCESTERSHIRE

Tourist Information Centre, 27 Market Place, Coleford (01594) 836307.

The Forest of Dean has a unique history. The Romans exploited it for iron, it became a royal hunting forest after the Norman Conquest, it was progressively reclaimed for industry, and now it is a favourite recreational area. Its towns like Cinderford and Coleford, are unglamorous, but the wide expanses of heathland, planted with broadleaved and coniferous trees, make marvellous walking country, and the Forestry Commission has mapped several trails. The local tourist board produces pamphlets with suggestions for drives as well as walks.

Intensive coal mining and iron processing have left pits, spoil heaps and other traces throughout the Forest, and this activity is vividly explained at the Dean Heritage Centre in Soudley, by means of displays and reconstructions. At the Clearwell Caves, near Coleford, you can go down into some very ancient iron mines which form an exciting cavern system. The Dean Forest Railway at the Norchard Centre, north of Lydney, is a reminder of the part played by local railways. Engines and rolling-stock are on display in the yard and there are train rides available on certain days.

Little Dean Hall, 1½ miles from Cinderford, off the A4151, claims to be England's oldest house, and certainly investigations have revealed building work over a remarkable time span. The grounds offer a stunning view over the Severn and also contain the largest known Roman temple in rural Britain which was unearthed here in 1984. A little further east, off the A48, is Westbury Court, with its unique late 17th-century water gardens.

49

GLOUCESTER
GLOUCESTERSHIRE

Tourist Information Centre, St Michael's Tower, The Cross (01452) 421188.

Gloucester Cathedral, described by Celia Fiennes who visited it in 1698 as 'large, lofty and very neate', is still an impressive sight today

Most people know that Gloucester has a cathedral, but few realise that it also boasts a fine Victorian dockland area.

The cathedral is a treasure-house of human skills – almost superhuman in the case of the immense nave pillars. The stone-carver's art is present everywhere, but nothing matches the effigy and intricate canopy of the tomb of Edward II, murdered at Berkeley Castle. There is supreme craftsmanship, too, in the vast east window, commemorating knights who fought in the Hundred Years War, while the work of modern artists has enriched the Chapel of St John the Baptist.

The docks are a different kind of architectural treat. Seen at their best from the North Quay, massive but strangely elegant 19th-century warehouses stand around a series of basins that formed the terminus of the big Gloucester-Sharpness Canal. They are now being developed for various leisure and commercial purposes, including the award-winning National Waterways Museum – where there are boats to visit and demonstrations to watch, Robert Opie's Packaging Collection – a nostalgic museum of packages and advertisements covering the last 100 years. The House of the Tailor of Gloucester, in College Court is devoted to the life of Beatrix Potter.

IN EASY REACH Painswick is a handsome small town south of Gloucester, best known for a churchyard with 99 yew trees and some remarkable tombs. The charming Rococo Garden here is being restored to its unusual early-18th-century character. The Benedictine Prinknash Abbey, at nearby Cranham, is noted for its pottery and bird park. Also in the area there is excellent waymarked walking on Cooper's Hill, the scene of ancient Whit Monday cheese-rolling festivities.

Clipping Ceremony

In the clipping ritual at Painswick in September each year hundreds of children from the neighbourhood go in procession round the church and then link hands to form a circle round the building and so 'clip' or embrace it. There is dancing, a hymn and a special service in the church, and each child is given a bun and a silver coin. The ceremony was revived in 1897, but how much further it goes back is unknown.

50

LITTLECOTE
WILTSHIRE

Off the B4192, near Hungerford.
Tourist Information Centre, District Museum, The Wharf,
Newbury, Berkshire (01635) 30267.

Littlecote House is an impressive Tudor manor house built between 1490 and 1520, with splendid panelling and beautiful plaster ceilings inside. The Great Hall houses a unique collection of Civil War armoury and contains an extraordinary shovelboard table, which stretches 30ft, and can seat up to 40 people for dinner.

Outside in the grounds you can meet the animals in the working farmyard – home to both domestic and rare breeds. Wander through the formal Tudor-style rose gardens, the medieval gardens and past the knot gardens, then visit the craft village and on to the car museum. Stop for a taste of medieval rivalry at the jousting tournaments (daily May to September) and don't leave until you have inspected the excavations at the ancient Roman site which includes the superb Orpheus mosaic, first discovered in the 18th century. All staff at Littlecote are dressed in medieval costume to add to the atmosphere of an enjoyable day out.

IN EASY REACH Hungerford, 2 miles to the south-east of Littlecote, has an impressive, wide main street. Henry VIII gave the old Bear Inn to two of his wives in succession and William III made himself comfortable there in 1688. The Kennet and Avon Canal runs through here on its way from Reading to Bath. On the River Kennet, further west along the B4192, is the pleasant village of Ramsbury, which a thousand years ago was the centre of the bishopric of Wiltshire. In the large church are fragments of Anglo-Saxon crosses with patterns carved on them.

51

LONGLEAT HOUSE
WILTSHIRE

On the A362, west of Warminster.
Tourist Information Centres: Central Car Park, Warminster (01985) 218548/846154
and The Square, Mere (01747) 861211.

Close encounters with lions – one of the attractions of a visit to Longleat

One of the grandest country houses in England, Longleat is a great spreading Elizabethan pile, built in Italian Renaissance style and surrounded by one of 'Capability' Brown's better-than-nature-could-do landscapes. The view from Heaven's Gate is particularly spectacular and the place is famous for its safari park, opened in 1966, the late Marquess of Bath's pioneering venture based on African big-game parks.

Inside, the house is gorgeous with decoration, gilded and painted Italian ceilings, inlaid marquetry work and sumptuous marble. The rooms are full of treasures, including paintings, early-16th-century tapestries, furnishings and artefacts which reflect the tastes and interests of the Thynne family throughout the centuries. Outside, you can drive through lolling prides of lions, wandering giraffes, prowling cheetahs and chittering monkeys. Take a boat trip to see the hippos and sea-lions, then you can get lost in the world's largest maze, visit the re-created Victorian kitchens to catch a glimpse of life 'below stairs', flutter through the butterfly gardens and browse among a multitude of exhibitions and other attractions. And for anyone with children in tow, the railway and the pets' corner should not be missed.

IN EASY REACH Just across the A362 from Longleat is Cley Hill, a striking-looking hill about 800ft high, with the earthworks of an Iron Age hill-fort on top. It is in the care of the National Trust and has an odd reputation as a magnet for flying saucers, which have been reported in the vicinity. Warminster, 4 miles to the east, has a long main street with some attractive Georgian houses and fine old inns. The church is mainly a product of a 19th-century restoration by Sir Arthur Blomfield.

52

LULWORTH COVE
DORSET

Reached by the B3071.
Tourist Information Centre, Town Hall, East Street, Wareham (01929) 552740.

Late autumn is the time to visit Lulworth Cove. The summer crowds have gone, and if a strong sea is running you can appreciate the calm of this perfect natural harbour, protected by tall cliffs which allow the narrowest of entrances.

The cliff scenery is the best reason for coming here – erosion by the sea has produced some spectacular results, like Stair Hole next to the Cove or the great arch of Durdle Door – and the way to appreciate it is by using the Dorset Coast Path, especially the stretch westwards to Ringstead Bay. (The path in the other direction may be closed during the week for military purposes – telephone Bindon Abbey 462721 to check.)

IN EASY REACH The strange story of Lawrence of Arabia is recalled at Clouds Hill, off the B3390, a mile north of Bovington Camp and 7 miles north from Lulworth. This is the cottage which he rented when he enlisted in the Tank Corps as 'Private Shaw'. After his discharge from the RAF in 1935 he returned here, but was killed in an accident shortly afterwards. The spartan rooms that he occupied are as he left them. There are Hardy associations in the locality too. Bindon Abbey, near Wool, is the ruin where Tess of the D'Urbervilles lay down in a stone coffin during her miserable honeymoon. The real Turbervilles are commemorated at Bere Regis church to the north, but a more compelling attraction here is the 15th-century roof.

53

OTTERY ST MARY
DEVON

On the B3174, 6 miles south-west of Honiton.
Tourist Information Centres: Old Town Hall, The Flexton, Ottery St Mary (01404)
813964 (seasonal opening only) and Civic Centre, Exeter (01392) 265700.

This town is best known as the birthplace of the poet Coleridge, whose father was vicar of what is undoubtedly the grandest parish church in Devon. Modelled on Exeter Cathedral, it has the same twin towers unusually placed at the transepts and some magnificent interior features, including the fan-vaulted 'Dorset Aisle' dating from 1520. Seek out the clock in the south transept (reputed to be 600 years old) and the three 16th-century memorial brasses. Set around the church are some solid and handsome Georgian houses, and the pleasant streets with their small shops recall a more leisured age.

IN EASY REACH A mile or two south-west of Ottery St Mary, Fernwood offers a 2-acre woodland garden with a rich array of conifers and flowering shrubs. Children may prefer the Farway Countryside Park, 6 miles to the east, with its farm animals, adventure playground, pets' corner and pony rides. Both are only open till the end of September.

Down on the coast, Sidmouth remains a soothing, old-fashioned resort, with a wide esplanade lined with early Victorian houses and an astonishing number of attractive Georgian buildings and terraces. Bicton Park lies just outside Budleigh Salterton, further west along the coast, and its fine gardens are not too grand to provide adventure for children.

●

Tar-barrel Rolling

Events occur throughout the day in Ottery on 5 November, but the climax comes at night. A carnival procession, a bonfire and the burning of Guy Fawkes in effigy is followed by the carrying of fiercely blazing tar-barrels perilously through the packed crowds (see above). The bearers carry the barrels on their shoulders and wear old clothes and thick protective gloves.

●

54

SALISBURY
WILTSHIRE

Tourist Information Centre, Fish Row
(01722) 334956.

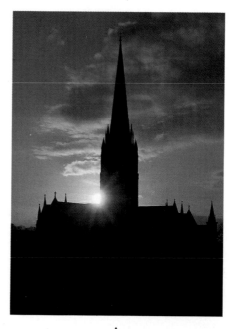

The graceful spire of Salisbury Cathedral (right) added in 1334, outlined against a sunset

The Salisbury Giant is a relic of the days when the guilds used to march in procession on great civic occasions, with the merchant tailors proudly parading the giant, who was called St Christopher. Accompanying him would be his sword-bearer, his mace-bearer, Morris dancers and a hobby horse called Hob-Nob (or Hooden or Old Snap), who also appeared on May Day. Nowadays the giant and Hob-Nob stand side by side in the Salisbury and South Wiltshire Museum (see above). A replica of the giant is still sometimes carried in procession today, and Hob-Nob himself is allowed out on very special occasions.

Among lush water-meadows by the River Avon, Bishop Poore laid the foundation stone of his new cathedral in 1220. Today, 700 years after its consecration, Salisbury Cathedral still stands among the meadows and is little changed. The only major addition is the lovely 14th-century spire, teetering on foundations which are only 4ft deep.

Inside, the cathedral is uncluttered. The historic 14th-century clock mechanism in the nave is in working order and is probably the oldest of its kind in Europe. You can walk through the cloisters with their huge cinquefoil openings and look at the octagonal chapter house. Then walk out into the beautiful leafy close, lined with some 80 grand houses. Grandest of the lot is Mompesson House, built in 1701 and now a National Trust property, worth seeing for its sumptuous plasterwork and elegant staircase. The late-14th-century King's House is home to the Salisbury and South Wiltshire Museum, with finds from Stonehenge as well as the Salisbury Giant, a costume, lace and embroidery gallery and local history collections. The Wardrobe houses the Museum of the Duke of Edinburgh's Royal Regiment (formerly the Wiltshires and Berkshires), bursting with regalia, uniforms, weapons, medals and other regimental paraphernalia.

The city streets are rich in historic buildings, which seem to pop up in the oddest places. Even the Odeon Cinema, behind its modern façade, boasts a 15th-century foyer, which was once the home of a wealthy merchant named John Halle, whose coat of arms still adorns the chimney-piece. The city also has a remarkable assemblage of ancient inns, such as the old George, where Pepys once slept, and the King's Arms, where Royalists plotted the escape of Charles II after the Battle of Worcester. Also don't miss seeing some of Salisbury's almshouses: the pretty College of Matrons, Edward Frowd's 18th-century buildings or the little almshouse of Trinity.

IN EASY REACH Five miles to the west of the city, on the A30, is the carpet-making town of Wilton. At the Royal Carpet Factory you can see modern manufacturing methods and, by contrast, a working exhibition of traditional working skills. And for something really unusual, how about the Burnbake Gallery of Arts and Crafts from HM Prisons? However, the jewel in Wilton's crown is gracious Wilton House, the 17th-century home of the Earls of Pembroke, famous for its beautifully proportioned Double Cube and Single Cube room, and for an art collection with paintings by Rembrandt and Van Dyck. Adults, as well as children, will probably enjoy the doll's house and an exhibition of more than 7,000 model soldiers.

On a windy hill just north of Salisbury, off the A345, is one of England's most dramatic ancient monuments – the towering earthworks of Old Sarum. Over 1,900 years old, it was originally an Iron Age fort, later a Saxon settlement and later still a Norman fortress, town and site of the first cathedral, whose outline can still be seen. Although long deserted, Old Sarum went on returning two Members of Parliament, at one time including the Elder Pitt, until rotten boroughs were abolished in 1832.

55

TINTAGEL CASTLE
CORNWALL

On the B3263, north-west of Camelford. Tourist Information Centres: North Cornwall Museum, Camelford (01840) 212954 (seasonal opening only) and Shire House, Mount Folly Square, Bodmin (01208) 76616.

There is not much left of Tintagel Castle – the great attractions here are the Arthurian legend and the spectacular site. Although there are traces of a Celtic settlement, there is in fact no reason to think that King Arthur, whoever he was, had any connections with Tintagel.

But this becomes irrelevant when you see the site. The castle, which was built and adapted from the 12th to the 14th centuries, stood on dramatic rocks high above the sea, divided between the mainland and a headland that is now almost an island. Simply walking the narrow causeway between the two is an experience in itself, and lovers of cliff scenery will find the whole expedition exhilarating. While in the village don't miss the Old Post Office. It is a rare example of an ordinary 15th-century house based on a hall that extended the full height of the building.

IN EASY REACH In nearby Camelford the North Cornwall Museum and Gallery (closed after September) is dedicated to recalling life in north Cornwall over the last 100 years. The emphasis is on traditional work, but home life is made vivid by a reconstruction of a moorland cottage at the turn of the century. One of the most impressive sights in the area is the Delabole Slate Quarry, on the B3314 west of Camelford. Slate has been extracted here since the 15th century, and now it is reckoned to be the largest man-made hole in England. There is a Slate Museum nearby. One of the outlets for the Delabole slate was to build Boscastle Harbour, 4 miles north-west of Tintagel. It sits uncomfortably in a cleft of the rocks, and the harbour seems impossibly tortuous – ships had to be carefully towed in. A breakwater first built in 1584 shields a tiny beach, while the functional village divides itself between the top and bottom of the cliffs.

56

WORLDWIDE BUTTERFLIES
DORSET

At Compton House, on the A30 midway between Yeovil and Sherborne. Tourist Information Centres: Petters Way, Yeovil (01935) 71279 and 3 Tilton Court, Digby Road, Sherborne (01935) 815341.

In the colder days of autumn it is nice to know that there is somewhere warm to go for a day out, and this is certainly true of Compton House where 25 years of expertise have gone into building up Worldwide Butterflies. Visitors today can see an unrivalled collection of species in reconstructions of their natural habitats. The expert or aspiring enthusiast can visit the comprehensive specialist library, but most visitors will be content simply to revel in the colours of the butterflies and their backgrounds. The very active breeding and hatching areas are on view, and if you want to start your own collection you can buy eggs, caterpillars and books for guidance.

The other attraction here is the Lullingstone Silk Farm, where the complete process of silk manufacture is explained by a combination of film and actual exhibits. All this comes with the bonus of Compton House itself, and its delightful gardens.

IN EASY REACH Just along the road, the mellow town of Sherborne is always a pleasure to wander in. The centrepiece of the town is the abbey, which has a history of building, and adaptation over 1,200 years, and there is a splendid mansion built by Sir Walter Raleigh and called Sherborne Castle (open to the public till late September). Don't confuse this with the fragmentary Old Castle. Sherborne Museum, in the Abbey Gate House, Church Lane, has exhibits including a model of the Norman Castle and local geological material. Four miles east of the town, Purse Caundle Manor boasts a celebrated 14th-century Great Hall, while Sandford Orcas Manor, 4 miles north of Sherborne, is an immaculately preserved example of a small Tudor manor house. Both close at the end of September. Finally, 10 miles south of Sherborne is the Cerne Abbas Giant cut into the hillside. He is thought to date from pre-Saxon times and is rather rude.

Pack Monday Fair

Sherborne's annual Pack Monday Fair in October was once the principal horse-trading event in the region. Today it consists of a fun-fair, with stalls in the streets. The fair is by ancient custom heralded at midnight the night before by several hundred people, traditionally known as Teddy Roe's Band, who walk through the town blowing bugles and whistles, banging cans together, shouting and making a terrible noise. It is said that this odd custom commemorates the noisy celebrations when the building of Sherborne Abbey was finally completed in 1490.

One of Britain's rarest and most beautiful butterflies, the swallowtail, which can be seen at Compton House

57

FLEET AIR ARM MUSEUM
SOMERSET

At the Royal Naval Air Station, Yeovilton, 6 miles north of Yeovil.
Tourist Information Centre, Petters House, Petters Way, Yeovil (01935) 71279.

Here is one solution to the problem of finding a day out in the depths of winter – this museum is open every day except for Christmas itself. The role of the navy's aircraft was very much in the news during the Falklands War, so it is no surprise to find that this campaign is strongly featured in a display which includes captured Argentinian aircraft. But older battles are not forgotten, and there are special exhibitions paying tribute to the legendary Fairey Swordfish and telling the story of the Wrens, as well as a feature on the Japanese kamikaze pilots. In an array of over 50 aircraft, the major exhibit is *Concorde 002*. The permanent displays include a vast collection of models, photographs, uniforms and equipment used in naval aviation.

IN EASY REACH Ilchester, 2 miles away to the west, is on a Roman road, the Fosse Way, and there are Roman bricks in the walls of the church. At Yeovil, to the south, the impressive church is built of Ham stone. The Wyndham Museum here, in Hendford Manor Hall, covers local history and has special collections of costume and firearms. Two miles further south is the village of East Coker, where T S Eliot lies buried in the churchyard.

Glastonbury Thorn

Around the New Year the Glastonbury Thorn comes into flower, as it has supposedly done ever since Joseph of Arimathea arrived here with the Holy Grail. In sight of the Isle of Avalon (Glastonbury Tor) he stuck his staff in the ground, whereupon it flowered as a hawthorn. This attractive legend is an example of Glastonbury's powerful associations with both early Christianity and King Arthur, who is said to have been buried in the abbey where the site of his tomb is marked.

58

GLASTONBURY
SOMERSET

Tourist Information Centre, The Tribunal, 9 High Street (01458) 832954.

Modern Glastonbury is a busy market town, with an L-shaped main street forming two sides of the grounds containing the hauntingly atmospheric abbey ruins. You can see a specimen of the famous Thorn in the churchyard of St John's, which has a fine tower and a splendid interior. Few medieval buildings remain, but the George and Pilgrim Hotel and the Tribunal (a 15th-century Grade I listed building now housing a local museum) are notable exceptions, and another impressive survival is the great Abbey Barn, which now forms part of the excellent Somerset Rural Life Museum. Not far away you can drink from Chalice Well, a spring that probably served a Neolithic settlement. (According to one legend, the Holy Grail lies buried in it.)

Glastonbury Tor has always been a place of pilgrimage, and it was once surmounted by the church of St Michael. The tower is still there, and you can climb to it by a path that starts in Dod Lane.

Cutting the thorn tree in the grounds of St John's Church, Glastonbury. Each Christmas a sprig of the thorn is sent to the reigning monarch

IN EASY REACH To the south and west of Glastonbury are the Somerset Moors and Levels, the strange area of reclaimed land that forms Somerset's heartland. It was down here, to the north of Westonzoyland, that the Monmouth Rebellion was crushed by James II's army at Sedgemoor in 1685. Some of the rebels were imprisoned in Westonzoyland church, which is well worth a visit. To the south, Burrow Mump provides good views over the Levels, and across the Isle of Athelney, associated with King Alfred's campaign against the Danes.

59

GREAT WESTERN RAILWAY
WILTSHIRE

On Faringdon Road, Swindon.
Tourist Information Centre, 37 Regent Street, Swindon (01793) 530328.

What better home for this museum than Swindon, a railway town which grew up around the massive GWR workshops in the 19th century. In the museum you can marvel at Victorian engineering glories and the ranks of historic locomotives with glowing liveries and brass, displays of nameplates, models, posters and tickets. Don't miss the re-created foreman's house in the original 'model' village built for its workers by the company in Bath stone. The little museum is furnished as a typical Victorian working-class home.

IN EASY REACH Three miles west of Swindon, off the A3102, lies Lydiard Country Park. Explore the 1½ mile nature trail and keep an eye open for resident wildlife. Lydiard Mansion, once the seat of the St John family, dates from medieval times originally but was largely rebuilt in the 1740s: it is worth seeing for its elegant Georgian decoration. Next door is the little 14th-century parish church of Lydiard Tregoze – no village, just St Mary's church – full of fine and unusual memorials to the St John family. At Coate, in south-east Swindon off the B4006, is the Richard Jefferies Museum, with reconstructions of this celebrated writer and naturalist's study and cheese room, and with books and manuscripts.

60

MORWELLHAM QUAY
DEVON

Off the A390, 4 miles south-west of Tavistock.
Tourist Information Centres: Town Hall, Tavistock (01822) 612938 (seasonal opening only) and Island House, The Barbican, Plymouth (01752) 264849.

An important official at the copper mine was the 'Assayer', who tested the purity of the ore. A reconstruction of his office is just one of the fascinating exhibits at Morwellham

Since the 12th century Morwellham had been important as the nearest river port to Tavistock, and in 1817 a canal was built to link the port with the town. The discovery in the early 1840s of a rich vein of copper 5 miles away turned Morwellham into a thriving centre. Copper from the Devon Great Consols Mine, in its day the largest copper mine in Europe, was shipped downriver, together with arsenic and manganese. After 50 years of activity the mines closed and Morwellham was abandoned.

In 1970 work was started on restoring the quays and their industrial remains, and the whole area is now an open-air museum. Relics have been preserved in place, workshops have been reconstructed, and it is now possible to ride into the copper mine on a tramway. In addition the canal basin and the entrance to the 2-mile tunnel under Morwelldown have been preserved. An interpretation centre tells the story of Morwellham, and excellent leaflets guide you round the widespread exhibits. The museum is open all the year round, but a winter visit seems to evoke something of the old atmosphere of this former industrial site.

IN EASY REACH Another attraction in the area which is open throughout the year is the Paperweight Centre at Yelverton, off the A386, 5 miles east of Morwellham. This has a glittering display of paperweights of all sizes and designs.

61

SAVERNAKE FOREST
WILTSHIRE

Off the A346, outside Marlborough.
Tourist Information Centres: The Car Park, George Lane, Marlborough (01672) 513989 and The Wharf, Newbury, Berkshire (01635) 30267.

Maybe 1,000 years old, this ancient forest is now an area of gentle woods and glades, a sanctuary for Wiltshire wildlife and a place for quiet walks and picnicking. Aisles of straight-boled trees, planted over 200 years ago by 'Capability' Brown, lead past spreading age-old oaks. Forty years ago charcoal burning returned briefly to the area when Savernake became a site for the manufacture of gasmasks during World War II.

IN EASY REACH On the north-west skirt of the forest lies Marlborough, its impressively wide old High Street lined by pretty tile-hung and colonnaded buildings. From here you can drive or walk up onto the Marlborough Downs, strolling along the windswept tops dotted with the peculiar boulders known as sarsen stones and enjoying the panoramic views. South of the A4, between Marlborough and Hungerford, is the Bedwyn Stone Museum at Great Bedwyn. This open-air museum explains the ancient secrets of the stonemason, and the neighbouring church has a fine sequence of carvings.

—————————— **62** ——————————

STONEHENGE
WILTSHIRE

On the A360, west of Amesbury.
Tourist Information Centre, Redworth House, Flower Lane, Amesbury (01980) 622833.

●

Very little is known about Stonehenge (see above right) the most famous of all prehistoric megalithic monuments. From time to time the public imagination is caught by theories of sun-worship rites and primitive astronomical computers, but it is likely that these have as little factual base as the neo-druidical Midsummer's Night Eve ceremonies which were once enacted here.

●

Almost insignificant at first sight, seen against the backdrop of Salisbury Plain, Stonehenge (managed by English Heritage) becomes massively astonishing as you move close. Thirty mighty upright stones support giant lintels in a circle 108ft across. Within that is another circle of 16 stones, within that a horseshoe of 10 more, within that again another horseshoe of 19 more. At the heart of them all lies the great 'altar stone'.

Built in successive stages between about 5,000 and 3,000 years ago, this is one of the world's most famous ancient monuments and a remarkable tribute to the engineering and logistical skills of Britain in the Bronze Age. Archaeologists are still uncertain why some of the stones, weighing 4 tons or so each, were brought here from the faraway Preseli Mountains in Wales and why the gigantic sarsen stones, weighing in at anything from 25 to 50 tons apiece, were dragged here from 20 miles away, to be erected by human muscle power. However, like other stone circles, Stonehenge seems to be laid out in a sophisticated geometrical and astrological pattern, but the theory that it was used as a temple or an astronomical observatory is not based on fact.

IN EASY REACH The National Trust owns many acres of the farmland around Stonehenge, and the area is studded with the barrows of the aristocracy of the time, who were buried close to the sacred centre, as distinguished men of later generations were buried in Westminster Abbey. The Trust's land includes an important concentration of barrows at Normanton Down, ½ mile to the south of Stonehenge.

Many of the finds from Stonehenge, Avebury and other Wiltshire sites, including weapons, jewellery, gold and amber ornaments, and other objects, are impressively displayed in the award-winning Devizes Museum. The town is on the A360, 15 miles or so north of Stonehenge.

—————————— **63** ——————————

TAUNTON AND WELLINGTON
SOMERSET

Tourist Information Centres: The Library, Corporation Street, Taunton (01823) 274785
and The Museum, Fore Street, Wellington (01823) 664747 (seasonal opening only).

In the Great Hall of Taunton Castle, Judge Jeffreys vengefully sent hundreds of victims to execution or transportation after the failure of the Monmouth Rebellion, and his restless ghost is said to stalk the precincts. Today the building is home to the Somerset County and Military Museum. Three miles north, off the A361, are the gardens of Hestercombe House, a superb example of cooperation between Sir Edwin Lutyens and Gertrude Jekyll. Whilst east on the A361 lie the mysterious Somerset Levels, home to the ancient craft of willow-growing and basket making. Heading west on the A38 towards Wellington, a diversion can be made to the Sheppy Cider Works at Bradford on Tone which is open to visitors to enjoy both the product and the cider museum.

When Arthur Wellesley became Duke he chose Wellington as his peerage title, and the town considered it fitting to erect a substantial memorial on the Blackdown Hills. Designed by Thomas Lee, this obelisk, vaguely Egyptian in character, tapers elegantly towards a pointed top, and is today a prominent feature of the landscape. A doorway in the base gives access to interior stairs and views towards the Quantocks and Exmoor. There are several good walks and picnic places nearby on National Trust land; and there is a car park about ½ mile west of the monument.

Often gaudy, these richly carved and decorated fairground animals bring back nostalgic memories for many visitors to Wookey

---
64
WOOKEY HOLE
SOMERSET

Off the B3139, 3 miles north-west of Wells.
Tourist Information Centre, Town Hall, Market Place, Wells (01749) 672552.

No one has yet discovered where the River Axe comes from, but it emerges at Wookey Hole, and over the years the mysterious limestone caverns here have been a magnet for explorers. Nowadays visitors can walk comfortably through skilfully-lit underground chambers, and it is a memorable experience to see these eerie lakes, waterfalls, stalagmites and stalactites. In these fantastic surroundings it is easy to understand the belief that the caverns housed the 'witch of Wookey'.

In addition to going underground you can visit the long-established paper mill, see a re-creation of a traditional fairground by night, use up pennies in a pier arcade or experience an intriguing waxwork display. A museum tells the story of exploration in the caves.

IN EASY REACH Wells is England's smallest city. The old town centre clusters round the cathedral, which you reach by passing from a gracious market square through a medieval gateway. The building is full of riches, including an intricate west front, an octagonal Lady Chapel, good memorials, a finely roofed Chapter House and a 14th-century clock. The moated Bishop's Palace (closed in winter) is a magnificent survival, and you should on no account miss the nearby medieval street called Vicar's Close. The city also boasts a parish church – St Cuthbert's – which comes close to rivalling the cathedral.

You can discover some of the history of this remarkable city at the museum on Cathedral Green, and for a bird's eye view climb to the Tor Hill Wood park just east of the cathedral. To the south-east of Wells, at Pilton, there is a notable church, with a 15th-century roof, and a magnificent stone tithe barn which belonged to Glastonbury Abbey. The village's manor house has a productive vineyard open to the public.

J Hassell's drawing of the Witch of Wookey in Wells Museum shows some embellishment, but it does not take much imagination to see the Witch and other figures in the caverns at Wookey

The south-east of England has always been the most prosperous region of the whole country, and consequently the one most impressively equipped with fine buildings and historic treasures. London dominates the whole area, inevitably, but outside London, too, there are exceptional and varied rewards for today's visitor.

Windsor Castle, the largest inhabited castle in the world, is a kind of architectural pageant of the history of the monarchy. In sheer splendour it is outdone by Blenheim Palace, one of the heavy loads which Sir John Vanbrugh laid on the groaning earth; it covers 4 acres and contains some 200 rooms. On a smaller scale, one of the Rothschild houses in Buckinghamshire, Waddesdon Manor, is so packed with gorgeous and precious objects that it is physically exhausting. And there's still the Prince Regent's wondrous pleasure-dome, the Brighton Pavilion, to enjoy, and the glittering Robert Adam interiors at Syon House and Osterley Park.

Where there's wealth, there are gardens, and the south-east's range of them stretches from official Kew and Wisley to the 30,000 rose bushes in the Gardens of the Rose at St Albans and the 'old' roses at Mottisfont Abbey, and on to what is perhaps the most romantically beautiful garden in all England, at Scotney Castle in Kent. Where there's wealth, there are also things beautiful and rare, or simply very odd: like the world's largest collection of fleas at Tring, the Père David deer at Woburn Abbey, the working duck decoy at Boarstall, and the ancient aircraft in the Shuttleworth Collection which totter triumphantly about the sky on flying days, apparently held together by faith and sticky tape.

As a magnet for talent and ambition, London and the south-east are associated with famous people almost innumerable: from Henry VIII and his wives at Hampton Court to Queen Elizabeth I at Hatfield House, and Queen Victoria and the Prince Consort at Osborne House on the Isle of Wight. London and Rochester have the closest links with Charles Dickens of any places in Britain. Milton wrote Paradise Lost in his cottage at Chalfont St Giles, Bunyan delivered himself of Pilgrim's Progress while in Bedford Gaol, Jane Austen created Emma and Mansfield Park at Chawton, and George Bernard Shaw fired off salvoes of wit from Ayot St Lawrence. Sir Winston Churchill was born at Blenheim and lived at Chartwell.

The area is equally well stocked with handsome cities and prosperous towns, from Winchester, Canterbury and Oxford to Brighton, Lewes and Tunbridge Wells. But there is some of England's most enjoyable countryside here as well, a wealth of downland and woodland, from the New Forest and the Hampshire trout streams, eastwards along the South Downs to Beachy Head and the white cliffs of Dover. To the north lie the Weald and the North Downs, and just across the Thames Estuary are the creeks and marshes of the Essex coast, teeming with bird life. And then, swinging westwards across the hornbeams of Epping Forest, the map-hovering eye comes to the glorious Chiltern beechwoods and sweet Thames running softly down to London again, to the bustle of the capital and the sea.

Brighton – acknowledged 'Queen' of the south coast resorts since receiving the Prince Regent's patronage. Today it is as popular as ever, with traditional seaside attractions and year-round entertainment

South & South East England

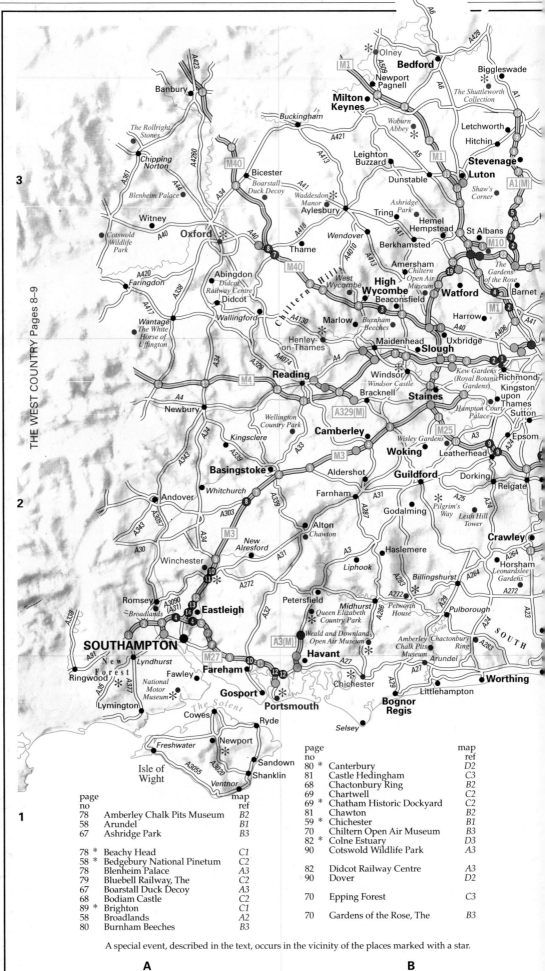

3

Banbury

A423

A6

M1   Olney   ✳
A509   **Bedford**   ✳ Biggleswade

The Rollright
Stones
Buckingham   Newport
Pagnell   *The Shuttleworth
Collection*
**Milton
Keynes**   A1

Chipping
Norton   A421   A5   Letchworth
Hitchin
Leighton
Buzzard   **Stevenage**
Woburn
Abbey ✳   M1   **Luton**
Witney   Bicester   A41   Dunstable   *Shaw's
Corner*
Blenheim Palace   Boarstall
Duck Decoy   Waddesdon
Manor ✳   St Albans   A1(M)
Cotswold
Wildlife
Park   Aylesbury   Tring   Hemel
Hempstead   M10   *The Gardens
of the Rose*
A40   **Oxford** ✳   Thame   Wendover   Berkhamsted   Amersham   M1   Barnet
Faringdon   M40   West
Wycombe   *Chiltern
Open Air
Museum*   **Watford**
Abingdon   Marlow   **High
Wycombe**   Beaconsfield   Harrow   A41
Didcot
Railway Centre   Burnham
Beeches   M1
Wantage   Didcot   Henley-
on-Thames   A4   Maidenhead   Uxbridge   A406
*The White
Horse of
Uffington*   Wallingford   **Slough**
A4   Windsor   *Kew Gardens
(Royal Botanic
Gardens)*   Richmond
Reading   *Windsor Castle*   Kingston
upon
Thames
Newbury   Bracknell   **Staines**   *Hampton Court
Palace*   Sutton
Wellington
Country Park   A329(M)   M25   A3   Epsom
Camberley   *Wisley Gardens*   Leatherhead
Kingsclere   **Woking**   Dorking
A303   **Basingstoke**   Aldershot   M3   **Guildford**   Reigate
Andover   Whitchurch   Farnham   A31   Godalming   *Pilgrim's
Way*   *Leith Hill
Tower*
2   New
Alresford   Alton   A3   Haslemere   **Crawley**
Chawton   Liphook   Billingshurst   A264   *Leonardslee
Gardens*
Winchester   A272   Petersfield   *Petworth
House*   Pulborough
Romsey   *Broadlands*   **Eastleigh**   Midhurst   *Queen Elizabeth
Country Park*   *Amberley
Chalk Pits
Museum*   *Chanctonbury
Ring*
SOUTHAMPTON   *Weald and Downland
Open Air Museum*   Arundel
New   Lyndhurst   M27   **Havant**   **Worthing**
Forest   Fawley   **Fareham**   Chichester   Littlehampton
Ringwood   *National
Motor
Museum*   **Gosport**   ✳   **Bognor
Regis**
Lymington   **Portsmouth**
Cowes   Ryde   Selsey
Freshwater   Newport   Sandown
*Isle of
Wight*   Shanklin
Ventnor

1

A special event, described in the text, occurs in the vicinity of the places marked with a star.

A   **B**

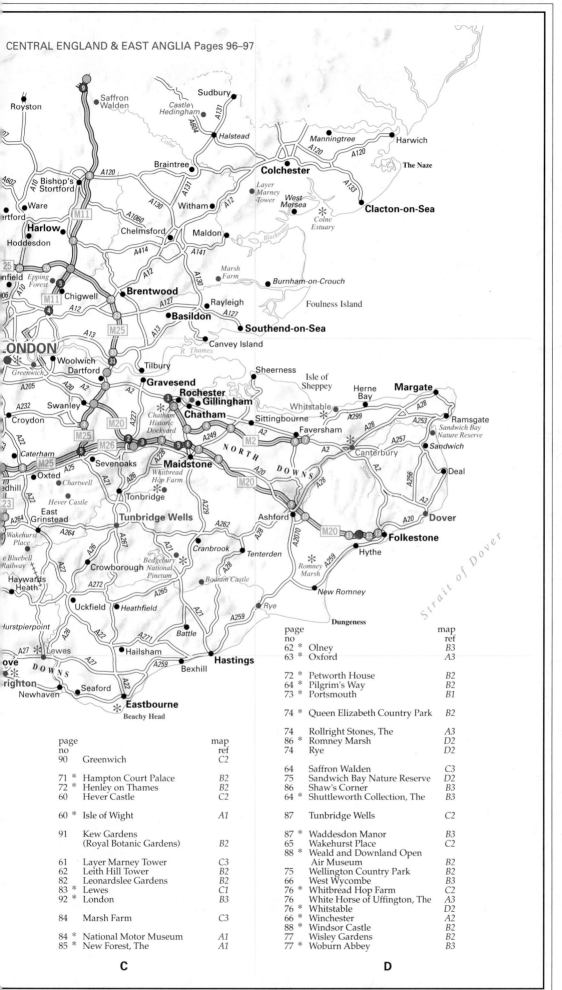

CENTRAL ENGLAND & EAST ANGLIA Pages 96–97

Royston

Saffron
Walden

Sudbury

*Castle
Hedingham*

A131

A604

Halstead

Colne

Manningtree

Harwich

The Naze

Braintree

A120

A120

Bishop's
Stortford

A602

A10

A120

A131

Colchester

Layer
Marney
Tower

West
Mersea

A12

Clacton-on-Sea

Ware

A130

Witham

A12

M11

A1060

Chelmsford

Maldon

*Colne
Estuary*

Harlow

A414

A141

Hoddesdon

Blackwater

A12

A25

*Epping
Forest*

A130

*Marsh
Farm*

Burnham-on-Crouch

M11

Chigwell

A10

Brentwood

A12

Rayleigh

Foulness Island

A13

M25

Basildon

A127

A127

Southend-on-Sea

LONDON

R Thames

Canvey Island

Woolwich

Tilbury

Sheerness

Isle of
Sheppey

Herne
Bay

Margate

Greenwich

Dartford

A205

A20

A2

Gravesend

Rochester

Whitstable

A299

Ramsgate

A232

Swanley

Gillingham

A28

A253

*Sandwich Bay
Nature Reserve*

Croydon

Chatham

*Chatham
Historic
Dockyard*

Sittingbourne

Faversham

A257

Sandwich

Caterham

A2

M20

A249

M2

Canterbury

Deal

M25

M26

A228

A2

A256

A25

A2

Sevenoaks

NORTH

DOWNS

A2

Oxted

Maidstone

*Whitbread
Hop Farm*

A20

A28

Dover

Chartwell

A21

A26

Tonbridge

M20

A20

Folkestone

Hever Castle

East
Grinstead

A264

A229

Ashford

M20

Hythe

*Wakehurst
Place*

A264

A267

A262

A28

A2070

*Bluebell
Railway*

A22

A26

Cranbrook

Tenterden

*Romney
Marsh*

A259

Crowborough

*Bedgebury
National
Pinetum*

A21

A28

Bodiam Castle

New Romney

Haywards
Heath

A272

Uckfield

A265

Heathfield

A21

Rye

Dungeness

Hurstpierpoint

A22

A271

Battle

A259

DOWNS

Lewes

A27

Hailsham

Hastings

Brighton

A27

Seaford

A22

Bexhill

Newhaven

Eastbourne

Beachy Head

C

D

Calendar of Events

Spring

MARCH

Ideal Homes Exhibition
London
(early March to early April)

Tichbourne Dole
Tichbourne, Hampshire
(25 March)

Oxford versus Cambridge Boat Race
Putney to Mortlake,
London
(late March or early April)

EASTER

Easter Food and Craft Day
Wellington Country
Park, Stratfield Saye,
Hampshire *(Easter)*

Hampstead Heath Fair
London *(Easter)*

British Marbles Championship
Tinsley Green, W Sussex
(Good Friday)

Long Rope Skipping
Alfriston, E Sussex
(Good Friday)

Biddenden Dole
Biddenden, Kent
(Easter Monday)

Easter Parade
Battersea Park, London
(Easter Monday)

Harness Horse Parade
Regent's Park, London
(Easter Monday)

APRIL

Boat Jumble
Beaulieu, Hampshire
(April – 2nd week)

Hocktide Festival
Hungerford, Berkshire
(April – 2nd week)

East Hertfordshire Festival
Stevenage, Hertfordshire
(mid-April)

MAY

Chichester Festival Theatre Season
Chichester, W Sussex
(May to September)

Garland Ceremony
Charlton-on-Otmoor,
Oxfordshire
(1 May)

May Day Celebrations
Elstow, Bedfordshire
(1 May)

May Morning Ceremony
Magdalen College,
Oxford *(1 May)*

Folk Festival
Winchester, Hampshire
(early May)

Crab Fair
Ventnor, IOW
(May Bank Holiday)

May Celebrations
Ickwell, Bedfordshire
(May Bank Holiday)

Festival of the Arts
Brighton, E Sussex
(May – 1st to 3rd weeks)

Battle Arts Festival
Battle, E Sussex
(May – 2nd or 3rd week)

Royal Windsor Horse Show
Windsor, Berkshire
(May – 2nd or 3rd week)

Chelmsford Cathedral Festival
Chelmsford, Essex
(mid-May)

D-Day Military Vehicle Rally
Portsmouth, Hampshire
(Spring Bank Holiday)

Morris Dancing
Bampton, Oxfordshire
(Spring Bank Holiday)

Surrey County Show
Guildford, Surrey
(Spring Bank Holiday)

Bedford River Festival
Bedford
(late May)

Blessing the Sea
Hastings, E Sussex
(late May)

Hertfordshire Show
St Albans, Hertfordshire
(late May)

Arundel Corpus Christi Carpet
Arundel, W Sussex
*(Corpus Christi – Thursday
after Trinity Sunday)*

Chelsea Flower Show
London
(late May to early June)

Dickens Festival
Rochester, Kent
(late May or early June)

Summer

JUNE

Whitbread Hop Farm Events
Beltring, Kent
*(various dates - June to
August)*

Trooping the Colour
Horse Guards Parade,
London
(June – 2nd Saturday)

International Folklore Festival
Folkestone, Kent
(June – 3rd or 4th week)

Stour Music Festival
Boughton Aluph, Kent
(June – 2nd half)

Game and Country Fair
Penshurst, Kent
(late June)

Round the Island Yacht Race
Cowes, IOW
(late June)

Royal Ascot
Ascot, Berkshire
(late June)

Wimbledon Lawn Tennis Championships
London
(late June to early July)

JULY

Henley Royal Regatta
Henley on Thames,
Oxfordshire
(July – 1st week)

International Organ Festival
St Albans, Hertfordshire
(July – 1st week)

British Rose Festival
Hampton Court Palace,
Surrey
(July – 1st or 2nd week)

City of London Festival
London
(July – 1st three weeks)

Hampshire Country Fair
Queen Elizabeth Country
Park, near Petersfield,
Hampshire
(July – 2nd week)

Wellington Country Fair and Sheep Dog Trials
Stratfield Saye,
Hampshire
(July – 2nd week)

Black Cherry Fair
Chertsey, Surrey
(July – 2nd Saturday)

Kent County Show
Maidstone, Kent
(mid-July)

Royal Tournament
London
(mid-July)

Royal Isle of Wight Agricultural County Show
Cowes, IOW
(July – 3rd week)

Cowes Regatta, Isle of Wight

The Lord Mayor setting off from the Law Courts during London's most famous show

Glorious Goodwood
Goodwood Racecourse,
W Sussex
(July – last week)

**Blessing the Waters
(Oyster Ceremony)**
Whitstable, Kent
(25 July)

Ebernoe Horn Fair
Ebernoe, W Sussex
(25 July)

**Brighton Antiques
Fair**
Brighton, E Sussex
(late July)

AUGUST

**Deal Summer Music
Festival**
Deal, Kent
(August – 1st half)

Broadstairs Folk Week
Broadstairs, Kent
(August – 2nd week)

Cowes Week
Cowes, IOW
(August – 1st week)

**Margate Carnival
Week**
Margate, Kent
(August – 2nd week)

East Cowes Carnival
East Cowes, IOW
(mid-August)

**Hampshire County
Show**
Royal Victoria Country
Park, Netley Abbey,
Hampshire
(mid-August)

Venetian Fête
Hythe, Kent
*(20 August – alternate
years)*

**Greater London Horse
Show**
Clapham Common,
London
(August Bank Holiday)

Navy Days
Portsmouth, Hampshire
*(August Bank Holiday,
biennial next in 1994)*

**Whitbread Beltring
Fayre**
Whitbread Hop Farm,
Beltring, Kent
(August Bank Holiday)

**Island Steam
Extravaganza**
IOW Steam Railway,
Havenstreet, IOW
(late August)

Arundel Festival
Arundel, W Sussex
*(late August to early
September)*

Guildford Show
Guildford, Surrey
*(late August to early
September)*

Autumn

SEPTEMBER

Shetland Pony Show
Wellington Country Park,
Stratfield Saye,
Hampshire, *(September)*

**Oyster Proclamation
and Feast**
Colchester, Essex
(September and October)

Buckinghamshire Show
Aylesbury,
Buckinghamshire
(September – 1st week)

**English Wine Festival
and Regional Food
Fair**
Alfriston, E Sussex
(September – 1st week)

Hop Hoodening
Canterbury, Kent
(September – 1st Saturday)

St Giles's Fair
Oxford
(September – 1st full week)

Rye Festival
Rye, Kent
*(September – 1st and 2nd
week)*

Auto Jumble
Beaulieu, Hampshire
(September – 2nd week)

**International Air
Show**
Farnborough,
Hampshire
(September – 2nd week)

**Horse of the Year
Show**
Wembley, London
(mid-September)

**International Boat
Show**
Southampton,
Hampshire
(mid-September)

Newbury Show
Newbury, Berkshire
(mid-September)

**World Carriage Driving
Championships**
Windsor, Berkshire
(mid-September)

OCTOBER

Canterbury Festival
Canterbury, Kent
(October)

**Trafalgar Day
Ceremonies**
Portsmouth, Hampshire
(21 October)

Titchfield Carnival
Titchfield, Hampshire
(October – last Monday)

Bonfire Procession
Littlehampton,
W Sussex
(late October)

**Steam Threshing and
Autumn Ploughing**
Weald and Downland
Open Air Museum,
Singleton, W Sussex
(late October)

NOVEMBER

Guy Fawkes Night
Battle, E Sussex
*(November – Saturday
nearest to 5th November)*

Guy Fawkes Night
Lewes, E Sussex *(5
November)*

Torchlight Procession
East Hoathly, E Sussex
(early November)

**Traditional Bonfire
Celebrations**
Edenbridge, Kent
(early November)

**London to Brighton
Veteran Car Run**
(November – 1st Sunday)

Firing the Poppers
Fenny Stratford,
Buckinghamshire
(11 November)

Lord Mayor's Show
London
(November – 2nd Saturday)

Winter

DECEMBER

Royal Smithfield Show
London
(early December)

**Bampton Mummers'
Play**
Bampton, Oxfordshire
(24 December)

Hoodening
Folkestone, Kent
(26 December)

Mummers' Play
Crookham, Hampshire
(26 December)

JANUARY

**International Boat
Show**
London
(January)

Epiphany Procession
Chichester Cathedral,
W Sussex
*(1st Sunday after 6
January)*

**Dicing for the Maids'
Money**
Guildford, Surrey
(January – last Thursday)

FEBRUARY

Boat Jumble
Historic Dockyard,
Chatham, Kent
(late February)

Sussex Beer Festival
Hove, E Sussex
(late February)

SHROVETIDE

Pancake Day Race
Olney, Buckinghamshire
(Shrove Tuesday)

LINES OF DEFENCE

In May 1940, when nothing seemed to stand between Hitler and England but a few miles of sea, Pevensey Castle on the Sussex coast was hastily put into some sort of order against invasion. Pillboxes for machine guns were cunningly disguised as part of the castle walls, and are still not easily spotted today. The castle had been refortified before in its long history: against Napoleon, and against the Spanish Armada. It was at Pevensey that William the Conqueror made his landfall in 1066 and the fortress was already there: built by Roman engineers 800 years earlier still against the Saxons, the ancestors of the modern English.

All along the southern and south-eastern coast today's visitor sees formidable defence works of the past. The very first human (or humanoid) visitors to Britain walked here, on dry land all the way, 300,000 or so years ago. There was no English Channel then, but long afterwards the sea-level rose until the Channel was formed, about 10,000 years ago. Since then the Channel has played two contradictory roles: as a barrier against invasion, but also as the bridge across which people, ideas and influences have come to Britain from abroad.

As the nearest part of Britain to the Continent, the south and south-east coasts have been the areas most open to both foreign influence and foreign attack. When the stammering Emperor Claudius's legions invaded Britain in AD43 they made their base at Richborough on the Kent coast, where they eventually constructed a fortress whose towering walls are still impressive.

Two hundred years later, Saxon pirates in swift longships were preying on ships in the Channel and plundering the coast. To deal with this, around AD270, the Romans built a chain of fortresses along the coast from

the Solent to The Wash: at Portchester in what is now Hampshire, at Pevensey in Sussex, at Lympne, Dover, Richborough and Reculver in Kent, and at Bradwell and Walton across the Thames Estuary in Essex, with Burgh Castle and Brancaster continuing the line on the East Anglian coast. So huge were these strongholds that later generations thought they had been built by giants, not by men.

At Portchester you can still see the complete circuit of the Roman walls, studded with bastions where the catapult artillery was mounted. Here, as elsewhere, the Normans took over the Roman defences. The empty central area of Portchester Castle, tamely marked out now with football pitches, once rang to the clangour of knights, men-at-arms and archers gathered by Edward III for the invasion of France which led to the battle of Crécy. A generation later, Henry V assembled his

Above: an artist's impression of Anderida, the fort built by the Romans at Pevensey
Left: Richborough Castle – a superb example of the Romans' Shore defence system against the Saxons
Right: Bodiham Castle, now safe in the hands of the National Trust
Below: Pevensey Castle, built by the Normans on the Roman fort
Bottom: Portchester Castle – one of the best-preserved of the Roman fortifications

army here for the campaign which culminated at Agincourt.

The threats of piracy and raiding had not gone away meantime. Places like Rye and Winchelsea in East Sussex were repeatedly looted by marauders from across the Channel. Romantically beautiful Bodiam Castle was built in the 1380s against a threatened French invasion. The Cinque Ports (originally Sandwich, Dover, Hythe, Romney and Hastings) with their 'limbs' or assistants, provided ships and seamen for the king's navy in time of need, and their local museums vividly reflect their history and traditions.

The Tudors built new coastal fortresses. Southsea Castle in Hampshire, for instance, Deal Castle and Walmer Castle on the Kentish shore and Upnor Castle on the Medway near Rochester were all constructed in Henry VIII's time, employing the latest techniques of defensive warfare. In the 18th century the focus turns more to smugglers and their doings in areas like Romney Marsh, but late in the century the threat of Napoleon's flotilla of invasion barges inspired the building of the Royal Military Canal at Hythe, the fortified gun platforms called Martello towers along the coast and other shore strongpoints. Examples can be explored today at Eastbourne in Sussex, Dymchurch and Dover in Kent and Harwich in Essex.

Far more formidable are the defences thrown up against the possibility of French invasion in the 1860s. At Portsmouth, for example, the fortified islets in the Solent date from this time, as do the fortresses like Fort Brockhurst and Fort Widley which guarded the naval dockyard against assault from the landward side. They are impressive today for their sheer massiveness, their labyrinthine tunnels and passages burrowed through cliffs, and the characteristically Victorian efficiency of their gun emplacements and magazines. Similar forts are open to the public on the Isle of Wight – Fort Victoria and the Needles Old Battery – and at Chatham in Kent and East Tilbury in Essex. And at Dover Castle and Fort Amherst in Chatham you can see how the fortresses of an earlier day returned to service against the air attacks of World War II.

Below: Shoeburyness Battery, established in 1858 as a practice ground

65

ARUNDEL
WEST SUSSEX
Tourist Information Centre, 61 High Street (01903) 882268.

In the 1870s the 15th Duke of Norfolk, the leading Roman Catholic layman in England, resolved to rebuild his ancestral fortress at Arundel in medieval grandeur and on a supercolossal scale. Opinions about the result range from 'magnificent' to 'preposterous'. The oldest part of the castle today is the impressive Norman keep. Inside, enjoy the chapel – a striking expression of the 19th-century Roman Catholic revival – the gargantuan barons' hall, the hushed 10,000-volume library, the family portraits, and the giant stuffed owls. The family tombs are in the church of St Nicholas.

Arundel's Roman Catholic cathedral, also built by the 15th Duke, has an annual Corpus Christi carpet of flowers. The 'carpet' lasts two days and is then ceremonially trodden on – an Italian custom that so impressed the Duke he decided to start it here in Sussex. Near the castle entrance is a Heritage Museum of local history, and bordering the estate (on Mill Road) is the Wildfowl and Wetlands Trust sanctuary, with its viewing gallery, landscaped grounds and hides where you can watch the swans, ducks and geese.

IN EASY REACH A little further afield to the west are the beautiful ruined church of medieval Boxgrove Priory at Boxgrove; Denmans in Fontwell, a 20th-century walled garden planted for all-year-round interest; and the National Trust village of Slindon, with 17th-century cottages, a shingle beach marooned 5 miles inland by the receding sea, and a stretch of Roman road.

66

BEDGEBURY NATIONAL PINETUM
KENT

Off the B2079, south of Goudhurst.
Tourist Information Centre, The Old Fish Market, The Pantiles,
Tunbridge Wells (01892) 515675.

This is the Forestry Commission's star collection of conifers, the largest in Europe, with magnificent Californian redwoods, and a superb assemblage of spring-flowering rhododendrons and azaleas. The pinetum was established in 1925 and some of the trees planted in its early days are already more than 100ft tall. There are yews and junipers here as well as exotic conifers – more than 200 species altogether. Marked trails (details from the visitor centre) guide you through the 150 acres, past two lakes and streams. Picnics are allowed, and very enjoyable.

IN EASY REACH For one of the dreamiest spring sights in Kent, head north-west to romantic Scotney Castle Garden (off the A21, 1 mile south-east of Lamberhurst). It lies at the foot of a deep, wooded valley that suddenly opens out to reveal a ruined tower standing in a moat, with masses of daffodils and azaleas. More daffodils drift under the fruit trees at the Owl House, a 16th-century smuggler's (owler's) haunt a mile or so the other side of Lamberhurst. Later come azaleas, and roses dripping off their trellises. Also in the area are Bewl Water, the largest stretch of inland water in the South-East, with water sports, picnic spots and walks, and Lamberhurst Vineyard, open for tasting, buying and guided tours.

South-west of Goudhurst is Finchcocks Living Museum of Music set in a fine Georgian baroque manor. Finchcocks is filled with historic keyboard instruments, whose music follows you through the house, especially during the September concert festival. Further east on the A262 is Vita Sackville-West's delectable garden at Sissinghurst Castle. 'Sleeping Beauty's garden', she called it when she first saw it, 'crying out for rescue'. It is exquisitely English, and operates a ticketed system to avoid crowding.

67

BROADLANDS
HAMPSHIRE

On the outskirts of Romsey, on the A31.
Tourist Information Centres: Bus Station Car Park, Broadwater Road,
Romsey (01794) 512987 and the Guildhall, The Broadway, Winchester (01962) 840500.

It was Lord Mountbatten of Burma who first opened Broadlands to the public, and the stables today house an exhibition and audio-visual show which cover his highly eventful career: the Royal Navy, supreme command in South East Asia, the Viceroyalty of India. In the previous century Broadlands was the home of another exceptionally distinguished figure,

Biddenden Dole

Far back in the 12th century, Siamese twins named Elisa and Mary Chulkhurst were born in the village of Biddenden (on the A262, east of Goudhurst). They were joined at the hips and shoulders, and when one of them died at the age of 34, the other soon succumbed. They are said to have left land to provide a yearly gift of

bread and cheese for the poor of the parish. Bread and cheese and tea are still handed out to widows and pensioners on Easter Monday each year, and everyone present at the distribution of the Biddenden Dole is given a special biscuit with a picture of the twin sisters on it.

the John Bullish foreign minster and prime minster, Lord Palmerston. Beautifully situated on the River Test, the house was rebuilt and the grounds landscaped a century earlier still by John Holland and 'Capability' Brown, and the rooms contain notable furniture, family portraits and Wedgwood china.

IN EASY REACH Lord Mountbatten's grave is in the south transept of Romsey Abbey, one of the two or three finest Norman buildings in the country. The abbey also contains two ancient roods, or figures of Christ crucified, from the earlier Saxon church. In Romsey market-place, nearby, is a statue of Lord Palmerston.

On a minor road, 4 miles west of Romsey, is another remarkable church, at East Wellow, with wall paintings of the 13th century, including a St Christopher. In the churchyard is the grave of Florence Nightingale, who lived close by at Embley Park. In the other direction, north-east of Romsey, is the Hillier Arboretum at Ampfield. At its peak of attractiveness in the spring, it rejoices in one of the largest tree and plant collections in Europe, with 3,000 species of trees and 10,000 species and varieties of woodland plants.

Tucked away off the B3084, north of Romsey, is a special treat. Bowered in romantic seclusion among gigantic trees on the bank of the Test, Mottisfont Abbey is an unforgettable blend of medieval priory and 16th-century mansion. In the walled gardens is the National Trust's sweetly scented assemblage of old fashioned roses.

68

CHICHESTER
WEST SUSSEX

Tourist Information Centre, 29a South Street (01243) 775888.

The Romans built Chichester and their street pattern remains – a regular criss-cross of narrow roads meeting at the city centre, where the splendid octagonal stone Market Cross, built in 1501 by Bishop Story, still gives shelter from the odd shower.

Nowadays Chichester is probably best known for its Festival Theatre and arts events. The modern concrete theatre, built in 1961, contrasts sharply with the tall, slim spire that tops the Norman cathedral. But the cathedral has its modern side too: vivid paintings, tapestries, sculptures and stained glass, by Graham Sutherland, John Piper and Marc Chagall. Outside are quiet, flint-walled precincts, where Keats wandered while preparing his poem on *The Eve of St Agnes*, and streets of handsome Queen Anne and Georgian houses, such as Pallant House, carefully restored and containing Walter Hussey's mostly modern art collection. Don't miss the 18th-century corn store, now a local museum, in Little London, one of the prettiest old streets, or the enchanting Mechanical Music and Doll Collection at Church Road, Portfield.

IN EASY REACH Chichester Harbour, with its 50 miles of shoreline and 3,000 acres of water, tidal flats and saltmarsh, is a haven for yachts and, in winter, for vast flocks of waterfowl.

On the A27, west from the city, is Fishbourne Palace; remains of the largest Roman residence yet found in Britain. It is incongruously surrounded by a housing estate, but don't let that deter you. The many mosaics, including the 'boy on a dolphin' are beautiful, the underground heating fascinating and there is a reconstructed Roman garden.

Further west on the A27 is Bosham, a huddle of harbourside cottages that look ready to float at high tide, yet the village was important enough to appear in the Bayeaux Tapestry. The Saxon church is claimed as the burial place of King Canute's daughter, and the muddy creek as the place where Canute ordered the sea to go back.

Festival Theatre

The Chichester Festival Theatre season begins in May and runs for 5 months with a challenging and enjoyable drama programme. For the rest of the year the theatre plays host to concerts, jazz and pop music, ballet, opera and a Christmas show. The theatre was specially built to incorporate a 'thrust stage' – with the audience on three sides of it – on the model of the Festival Theatre at Stratford, Ontario, which Tyrone Guthrie's productions had made famous. The Chichester Festival Theatre opened in 1962, with Laurence Olivier as the first director. The illustration (left) shows Joanna Lumley and June Whitfield in a production of An Ideal Husband during the 1987 Festival.

---------------------------------- **69** ----------------------------------

HEVER CASTLE
KENT

*Off the B2026, east of Edenbridge. Tourist Information Centre, The Old Fish Market,
The Pantiles, Tunbridge Wells (01892) 515675.*

If Henry VIII didn't court Anne Boleyn here, he should have done. Once the family home of the Boleyns, it is almost a stage set for a royal romance, especially in spring when thousands of daffodils carpet Anne Boleyn's orchard, right up to the banks of this moated Tudor mansion. Dating partly from the 13th century, it stands compact and four-square round a courtyard with a drawbridge across the moat, leading to a maze and a delightful walled Italian Garden, created this century and dotted with classical statues. Thousands more daffodils edge the lake and white narcissi smother the Spring Garden, beside the Rhododendron Walk.

Behind the house is a mock-Tudor village, added this century, like the Italian Garden, when wealthy American William Waldorf Astor bought and restored the house and filled it with fine furniture and armour. Enjoy, too, the lovely old church at the entrance to the castle, and the inn.

IN EASY REACH A mile or two east of Hever is Chiddingstone Castle: late-18th-century Gothic, it now houses Japanese lacquer and swords, and relics of the royal house of Stuart. Chiddingstone village main street is an enchanting little row of well-preserved timber-framed shops and houses in the care of the National Trust and filmed in *A Room with a View*. A footpath leads to the original chiding stone, where scolds and shrewish wives were publicly chided.

Penshurst Place, on the B2176, south of Chiddingstone Causeway, is one of England's greatest medieval manors, with a huge baronial hall dating from 1340 and a series of state rooms. It was the birthplace of Elizabethan courtier-poet Sir Philip Sidney, but the house seems gaunt and impressive rather than poetic. Not so the walled gardens and park, nor the village with its ancient gateway to the church, full of Sidney memorials.

---------------------------------- **70** ----------------------------------

ISLE OF WIGHT

*Reached by ferries from Southampton, Portsmouth and Lymington. Main Tourist
Information Centres: 67 High Street, Shanklin (01983) 862942 and The Esplanade,
Sandown (01983) 403886. Others in Ventnor, Yarmouth, Ryde, Cowes and Newport.*

Island Events

Traditional carnivals are still very much part of the Island's summer scene. Each town hosts a Carnival week of events, with an early evening Carnival procession and a final illuminated procession. Regattas are held annually in Ryde, Sandown, Shanklin, Bembridge and Seaview. The Cowes Festival, held in the days following Cowes Week combines the annual Carnival events with other attractions such as Dragon Boat Racing, fireworks and the Folk Festival, culminating in the annual Power Boat Race on August Bank Holiday weekend. The larger villages host a variety of unique annual events such as the Niton Mackerel Fayre, the Bembridge Festival and Chale's two-day horticultural show. The Island's agricultural show at the County Ground, Northwood, in July provides a day of livestock competitions and horse events. The Garlic Festival at Newchurch in August and the Steam Extravaganza at the Steam Railway Centre for four days at August Bank Holiday are both great attractions.

Queen Victoria and Prince Albert bought themselves a holiday home on the Isle of Wight in the 1840s, so that they and their children could enjoy bathing and the sea air, and it was this which gave the impetus to the island's development as a popular holiday destination. Known for its seaside resorts, it also possesses many attractive inland villages and churches, and a thousand miles of footpaths, including a 65-mile coast path.

Queen Victoria spent much of her long widowhood at Osborne House (open Easter to October), her home outside Cowes, which her son Edward VII, presented to the nation. The royal apartments and state rooms remain much as they were on the old queen's death in 1901, an Aladdin's cave of Victorian treasures, ornaments and bric-a-brac. In the grounds can be seen the discreet royal bathing machine and the Swiss Cottage, in which the little princes and princesses played.

High on a hill to the west of Newport stands imposing Carisbrooke Castle, where Charles I was held prisoner for almost a year. His night-cap can be seen in the museum and there is also the only surviving donkey wheel in Britain: the donkeys still draw water up from a 160ft well.

From Carisbrooke the Tennyson Trail runs for 15 miles to the western extremity of the island at Alum Bay. The trail passes through Brighstone Forest and emerges on to Brighstone Down, proceeding across East Afton Down to Freshwater Bay and Tennyson Down where the air, the great poet said, was worth sixpence a pint. The Tennyson Monument commands wonderful views of the island's most celebrated landscape feature – the jagged chalk cliffs called The Needles, with a lighthouse at the seaward end. The Needles Old Battery, a fort of 1861, has been restored. Alum Bay itself is known for its multi-coloured sandstone cliffs.

Near Chale, close to the southern point of the coastline, is the island's top children's attraction – Blackgang Chine Theme Park (a chine is a deep ravine), with fantasy worlds including a Wild West town, models of dinosaurs, a whale's skeleton and a smugglers' cave, a working saw mill and an exhibition on lifeboats.

To the north-east, Godshill is the island's showpiece village, and crowded in summer. In the church is the unique lily cross, a wall painting of Christ crucified on a flowering lily. Also here are a toy museum, a model village, and a natural history centre with displays of butterflies, shells and stones.

Strung along the sandy south-east shore are the resorts of Ventnor, Shanklin and Sandown. Ventnor climbs up a steep cliff from the sea in a series of terraces

*Above: Queen Victoria
and Osborne House, as
depicted in the Osborn-
Smith Wax Museum at
Brading*

*Left: The Needles, at the
western extremity of the
Isle of Wight, are
composed of chalk rock.
The chalk, which forms
the 'backbone' of the
island, was laid down
over 60 million years ago*

of Victorian and Edwardian flavour. The botanic garden here has a splendid collection of rare and subtropical plants, and there is a fascinating museum of smuggling history.

Inland, Brading has a fine medieval church with effigies of the Oglander family, plus the Lilliput museum of antique dolls and toys, the Wax Museum and the remains of a Roman villa. The many other enjoyable attractions on the island include the Isle of Wight Steam Railway, based at Havenstreet, the Shipwreck Centre at Bembridge and the Robin Hill Country Park at Downend.

71
LAYER MARNEY TOWER
ESSEX

*Off the B1022, north-east of Tiptree. Tourist Information Centre,
1 Queen Street, Colchester (01206) 712920.*

This is the tallest Tudor gatehouse in England, and an impressive sight, with two great turrets each eight storeys high, studded with rows of windows and topped with ornate Italianate cresting – notice the splendid little dolphins. Climb to the top of the gatehouse for magnificent views of the surrounding countryside and looking south, of the Blackwater Estuary.

Sir Henry Marney built the tower in 1520 as the gateway for a great house. Unfortunately he died before the house was completed. Alongside is the church, which he remodelled and which contains his tomb along with his son's and that of one of his ancestors. Before you leave, inspect the beautiful carving and original St Christopher wall painting, then tour the formal garden with its clipped yew trees and rose beds.

IN EASY REACH Where Mr Crittall set up his metal window factory in the 1920s, at Silver End, 7 miles to the west, he also built homes for his workers in an interesting 'model' village. The houses are a mixture of neo-Georgian and 'international modern' style. To the north, at Coggeshall, off the A120, is Paycocke's House, a splendidly ornamented merchant's house built by Thomas Paycocke in about 1500 with beautiful overhanging carved beams and a richly decorated interior. It is now in the care of the National Trust.

72

LEITH HILL TOWER
SURREY

On the summit of Leith Hill, approached from the A29 and the B2126.
Tourist Information Centre, The Undercroft, 72 High Street, Guildford (01483) 444007.

Much of the Leith Hill woodland, renowned for dazzling displays of spring bluebells and rhododendrons, is now in the care of the National Trust along with the tower itself, which stands on the highest point in south-east England, at 965ft. The tower, which is 64ft high, was built in 1766 by Richard Hull, the owner of Leith Hill Place (not open), to the south-west. He had himself buried under the tower, standing up and, according to the local story, quite possibly upside-down. You can climb to the top of the tower for spectacular views over the Weald.

IN EASY REACH Just to the north of the hill are the charming red-brick cottages and wood-fringed lake at Friday Street. The village pub, the Stephen Langton Inn, recalls a church dignitary who played a leading role in the signing of the Magna Carta. Further north, on the A25, is Abinger Hammer, known for its 19th-century clock, jutting out into the road from the Clock House. The hour bell is struck by a figure called Jack the Smith.

Further north still at Great Bookham, Polesden Lacey, another National Trust property, is a charming Edwardian house, formerly owned by a noted society hostess between the wars, Mrs Ronnie Greville. Besides photographs of the great and famous who came to stay, there is her art collection to admire. Nearer Dorking, Box Hill is a very popular walking spot, with fine views.

73

OLNEY
BUCKINGHAMSHIRE

On the A5. Tourist Information Centre, 10 St Paul's Square, Bedford (01234) 215226.

Pancake Race

On Shrove Tuesday every year in Olney since 1445 (or so it is said) the pancake race has been run between the market place and the church. Each pancake must be tossed and caught in the frying pan at least three times on the way. The winner receives a prayer book, and a kiss from the verger.

This small town on the Great Ouse is famous for its annual pancake race. The church of St Peter and St Paul, at one end of the pancake racecourse, has a stone spire, a rare sight in Buckinghamshire, rising to a majestic 185ft. In the market place, at the other end of the course, the Cowper and Newton Museum preserves the memory of Olney's most famous inhabitant, the poet William Cowper, who lived here from 1767 to 1786. The museum, which is in his house, also has displays on lace-making, which was once the main Olney industry.

John Newton, the curate of Olney, was a close friend of Cowper's and together they wrote many well-loved hymns: *Glorious things of thee are spoken, How sweet the name of Jesus sounds, God moves in a mysterious way,* etc. Newton's body was brought back to Olney long after his death and buried in the churchyard.

IN EASY REACH The area to the south and west of Olney has many country houses worth visiting. Chicheley Hall, outside Newport Pagnell, is a handsome red-brick mansion with a collection relating to Admiral Lord Beatty, the World War I hero. Further west, just north of Buckingham, the breathtakingly splendid house and grounds at Stowe (now a school, but open to the public during the Easter and summer holidays) were created for the Duke of Buckingham. Florence Nightingale often stayed at beautiful Claydon House, off the A413, where mementoes of the 'Lady with the Lamp' will be found.

OXFORD
OXFORDSHIRE

Tourist Information Centre, St Aldates (01865) 726871.

You will have to get up early if you want to enjoy one of Oxford's most attractive old customs, the May Morning ceremony at Magdalen College. When May has been welcomed in, there is a chance to inspect the 15th-century college itself, wealthiest and perhaps most beautiful in Oxford, with glorious grounds, spring flowers, a famous river walk, deer park and cloister. Across the High Street from the college is the University Botanic Garden, founded in 1621 as a physic garden. The oldest of its kind in England, its grounds and greenhouses are full of fascinating specimens.

A stroll down the High Street leads on to many other colleges of the university: Queen's College, founded 1340, with its elegant 17th-century buildings – St Edmund's Hall, founded 1278 – 15th-century All Souls – University College, possible the oldest of all, where Shelley studied and was expelled (see his monument in the Front Quad) – 13th-century Merton with its medieval library – and magnificent 16th-century Christ Church, which has Oxford Cathedral as its chapel. The cathedral's William Morris/Burne-Jones windows are well worth seeing, as is the picture gallery and Tom Tower above the main college gate. Built by Wren in 1681, it houses Great Tom, a gigantic 6¼ ton bell which is rung every night at 9.05pm to signal college gate closing time. To the north of High Street, Exeter College has a unique 17th-century dining hall, and 15th-century Lincoln College is known for its John Wesley rooms, restored with fine panelling and old oak furniture. In Radcliffe Square, nearby, stands the imposing 18th-century Radcliffe Camera, 145ft high, domed and circular. It is now part of the Bodleian Library, the main part of which is across the square. Opened in 1602, the Bodleian houses over five million books.

North of the Bodleian, along Parks Road, you will find two of Oxford's marvellous museums: the University Museum (natural history collections including life-size dinosaur models and dodo relics in an unusual Victorian-Gothic building) and the Pitt-Rivers Museum with its displays of archaeology, anthropology and musical instruments. Other museums worth a visit include the Museum of the History of Science, with early scientific instruments, photographic, medical and electrical equipment; the Museum of Modern Art; the Museum of Oxford which traces the history of the city and the university; and most famous of all, the Ashmolean Museum with its magnificent collections of archaeology, fine art, prints and ceramics.

Make sure to see some of the city's beautiful old churches. Oxford is known for its sumptuous stained glass, both in the city churches and the college chapels. St Mary's has been the University Church since the 14th century: there are fine views from its tower top, and an interesting video on Oxford's history. St Peter's, in the east, has 15th-century glass and a late Norman chancel, while St Michael's has 13th-century glass, the oldest in Oxford, and an 11th-century tower. Carfax, at the centre of the old city, is a 14th-century tower where four streets meet and is all that remains of St Martin's Church, demolished in 1896. The old clock-jacks can be seen on the tower. Finally, before you leave the city, find time to take a quiet walk along the banks of the Isis (as the Thames is called here), to watch the punts gliding by and enjoy the peaceful green of the riverside meadows.

●

May Day Morning

People gather very early on the morning of May Day on Magdalen Bridge in Oxford. At 6am, from high above on top of the tower of Magdalen College, the strains of a hymn in Latin float sweetly down, sung by the college choir. The hymn is followed by a madrigal, and then morris dancers dance in Radcliffe Square and Broad Street (see above). How this custom started is not known, but it was going strong by about 1650, when the choir sang at 4am. Later, musical instruments played and the whole concert went on for two hours, to be drastically reduced one very wet May Morning late in the 18th century.

●

Surrey Show

Stoke Park on the north-eastern edge of Guildford is the local council's principal open space and recreation area, and the venue for the Surrey County Agricultural Society Show every year on Spring Bank Holiday Monday. This is the biggest one-day event of its kind in the county, with the usual cattle judging, agricultural machinery displays, craft stalls and trade stands. The two-day Guildford Show, around the turn of August and September, is also held in Stoke Park.

An odd ceremony called Dicing for the Maids' Money is conducted in the guildhall at Guildford on the last Thursday in January. Under the rules of a 17th-century charity, two maidservants throw dice in the presence of the Mayor to determine which of them gets the larger and which the smaller of two sums of money.

75

PILGRIMS' WAY
SURREY

South of Guildford.
Tourist Information Centre, The Undercroft, 72 High Street, Guildford (01483) 444007.

The Pilgrims' Way is an ancient track along which pilgrims once travelled from Winchester across southern England to the shrine of St Thomas Becket at Canterbury. A section of it outside Guildford, now part of the waymarked North Downs Way, provides a pleasant walk up the wooded hill called Chantries, with good views from the top, and on to the solitary church of St Martha, above Chilworth. The Way crosses the A25 at Newlands Corner where there is a large car park. Further east, the National Trust nature reserve of Hackhurst Down is renowned for its junipers.

IN EASY REACH Guildford, the busy county town of Surrey, has an attractive riverside area along the Wey. The modern Yvonne Arnaud Theatre is situated here. The guildhall in High Street is distinguished by its substantial and handsome clock, of 1683. Guildford Museum covers local history, with an excellent needlework collection and material on Lewis Carroll, the author of *Alice in Wonderland*, who often stayed with his sisters in Guildford. Rising above the town on Stag Hill is the modern cathedral, designed by Sir Edward Maufe in the 1930s and completed in 1961.

At Compton, a couple of miles west of Guildford, are two 'musts'. The first is the Watts Gallery crammed with works by the Victorian painter and sculptor George Frederick Watts. Nearby is the weirdly symbolic, Byzantine-style mortuary chapel designed by his adoring widow. The second is Losely House, built in the 1560s, and known for its panelling, ceilings and unique chalk chimney-piece, and also for its farm tours and farm produce.

To the north of Guildford, Clandon Park at West Clandon was built in the 1730s by a Venetian architect, Giacomo Leoni. Inside are the old kitchens, the museum of the Queen's Royal Surrey Regiment and the Gubbay collection of porcelain, furniture and needlework. Nearby, at West Horsley, is Hatchlands, another imposing 18th-century house, with interiors by Robert Adam.

76

SAFFRON WALDEN
ESSEX

Tourist Information Centre, 1 Market Place, Market Square (01799) 510444.

Fields of crocuses covered this area in medieval times and yielded precious saffron, a yellow spice so valuable it made the little town wealthy. Today its legacy is visible in the pretty, prosperous old houses elegant with Essex pargetting (decorative plasterwork). The parish church of St Mary, second largest in the county, has a fine 19th-century spire 200ft high. Notice the funny, grotesque figures along the north wall and, inside, the delicate carvings and memorial brasses. The museum has displays of local history, archaeology, geology, wildlife, costume and toys. Don't miss the Saxon sword or the immensely rare feathered cloak once worn by Hawaiian kings and made from the feathers of birds long extinct.

IN EASY REACH Audley End House lies west of Saffron Walden off the B1383, and is an early-17th-century mansion. It was originally of gigantic size, but Vanbrugh remodelled and demolished half of it in 1721. Worth special notice are the marvellous Jacobean Great Hall, the Robert Adam interiors, the quaint Gothic-style chapel, and the attractive grounds. While in the area go and meet the residents of Mole Hall Wildlife Park at Widdington, south of Saffron Walden off the B1383. Here there is also a butterfly pavilion and pretty gardens to be enjoyed.

77

THE SHUTTLEWORTH COLLECTION
BEDFORDSHIRE

At Old Warden Aerodrome, west of Biggleswade, on a minor road off the A1.
Tourist Information Centre, 10 St Paul's Square, Bedford (01234) 215226.

Nowhere else in the world can you watch, actually flying, a machine identical to the one in which Louis Bleriot made the historic first crossing of the English Channel by air in 1909. All the other veteran aircraft in this collection, upwards of 30 of them are still airworthy too – perilously frail and kite-like as some of them look. They can be seen cavorting about in the air at frequent flying days and pageants.

Richard Ormonde Shuttleworth, a pilot and racing driver, started the collection in the 1930s. He was killed flying in 1940. His 1898 Panhard Levasseur car and the 1909 Bleriot are still on display, together with other aircraft including a Spitfire and early cars, cycles and fire-engines.

IN EASY REACH Close to the aerodrome is the Swiss Garden, laid out by the lakeside early in the 19th century. A few miles to the north-west, Bedford is known for its links with John Bunyan, author of *Pilgrim's Progress*. A statue of him, 9ft tall, stands outside St Peter's Church, and scenes from his much-loved book are carved on the doors of the Bunyan Meeting House in Mill Street. Next door, the Bunyan Museum preserves his iron violin and other curiosities, as well as editions of *Pilgrim's Progress* in practically every language in the world. While in Bedford, don't miss the Cecil Higgins Art Gallery and Museum in Castle Close, a 'must' for its superbly displayed ceramics, glass and lace.

Bunyan grew up at Elstow, just south of Bedford, where the imposing church of St Helen and St Mary, with its unusual detached bell-tower, has memories of him: so, too, does the old market house called the Moot Hall. The pretty village of Ickwell, near Biggleswade, is noted for its May Day celebrations. East of Bedford at Willington, the National Trust administers the 16th-century stone dovecot and stable buildings. Further east at Sandy, is the RSPB nature reserve with woodland walks, a wildlife garden and observation hides.

●

May Day Dancing

A red-and-white striped maypole is a permanent fixture on the village green at Ickwell, a few miles north-east of Old Warden, whose May time celebrations go back at least to the 16th century. Some dancing around the maypole goes on during the early hours of May Morning itself, but the main event occurs on the Bank Holiday Monday, when the May Queen is crowned. Dancers, grown-ups as well as children, circle and weave intricate patterns with ribbons around the maypole, and mummers play the fool and collect money from the crowds. The village of Elstow, nearer Bedford, also celebrates the coming of May in style, with the choosing of a May Queen, and in Bedford itself in May there is a spectacular river festival on the Ouse with road and river parades in alternate years.

●

A DH88 Comet, part of the Shuttleworth Collection at Old Warden

────── 78 ──────

WAKEHURST PLACE
WEST SUSSEX

*Near Ardingly on the B2028 north of Haywards Heath.
Tourist Information Centres: 187 High Street, Lewes (01273) 483448
and 9 The Causeway, Horsham (01403) 211661.*

Wakehurst is run as an outpost of the Royal Botanic Gardens at Kew, an important collection of exotic trees and shrubs planted in the mature gardens of an Elizabethan mansion. Woodland and lakes linked by a pretty watercourse make this a beautiful place to walk. It is especially colourful in early spring with daffodils and later the dazzling rhododendrons and azaleas. Within the house, home of the Culpeper family, close relatives of herbalist Nicholas Culpeper, are natural history displays and tea-rooms.

IN EASY REACH Not far away are the ancient heaths and woodlands of Ashdown Forest where you can follow the Forest Way Footpath, from East Grinstead to Groombridge, or the Weald Way, from Tonbridge to Uckfield, passing some of 'Winnie the Pooh's' haunts around Hartfield. Borde Hill Garden, 1½ miles north of Haywards Heath has rhododendrons, azaleas, magnolias and camelias, also woodland walks and two lakes. South of East Grinstead is Standen, a large, late-Victorian family house, minutely preserved and furnished, as it was originally, with William Morris fabrics and wallpapers. It was designed by Philip Webb, an architect whose output was not large, as he insisted on overseeing all parts of his buildings. Not far away, at West Hoathly, is the Priest House. Dating from the 15th century, this is now a small folk museum with an emphasis on samplers and needlework.

79

WEST WYCOMBE
BUCKINGHAMSHIRE

On the A40. Tourist Information Centre,
6 Cornmarket, High Wycombe (01494) 421892.

The National Trust protects most of this village on the old London-Oxford road, and many of the houses date from the 15th to the 18th centuries. West Wycombe Park, reposing in its grounds with a lake and classical temples, is the great house of the Dashwoods. It was rebuilt about 1765 for the notorious and wildly unconventional Sir Francis Dashwood, the leading figure in the 18th-century Hellfire Club. The club met in the caves in the hill which dominates the village, and they are now open to the public.

IN EASY REACH The village of Bradenham, set among its beautiful beechwoods on either side of the A4010, to the north, and Hughenden Manor, a mile or so north of High Wycombe, are also National Trust properties. Benjamin Disraeli lived at Hughenden Manor from 1848 until his death in 1881 and remodelled it in a mock-Tudor style. In High Wycombe itself is the Wycombe Local History and Chair Museum on Castle Hill, which explains everything there is to know about the Windsor chair and the now vanished 'bodgers', or turners, who used to make chairs in the Chiltern woods. Further east, near Beaconsfield, is Bekonscot Model Village (off the B474), laid out in a rock garden and one of the best of its kind.

80

WINCHESTER
HAMPSHIRE

Tourist Information Centre, The Guildhall, The Broadway (01962) 840500.

The Round Table in Winchester's Great Hall is thought to originate from the early 14th century. Near by is a large statue of Queen Victoria – by Sir Arthur Gilbert

•

Folk Festival and Tichborne Dole

For two days in early May the annual Folk Festival in Winchester brings street dancing and entertainments, folk singing and a ceilidh to the city. Events alter from one year to another, but the liveliness and good humour remain the same.
A few miles away to the east of Winchester, at Tichborne, 25 March every year sees the payment of the Tichborne Dole, which has been distributed to the needy since the 13th century, in bread or money. Nowadays the dole is given in flour to each parishoner. The custom was started by a dying Lady Tichborne who persuaded her skinflint husband to set aside, in order to grow corn for the poor, as much land as she could painfully crawl round before a burning torch went out.

•

At the Hospital of St Cross, among the water-meadows of the Itchen, visitors can still receive the traditional 'wayfarer's dole' of bread and beer, issued to passing travellers ever since the almshouse was founded in 1136. The elderly gentlemen who have found safe haven here wear black or claret caps and gowns, and worship in the hospital's cross-shaped church, completed in 1225.

Winchester was once the capital of England and legend has it as one of the contenders for Camelot, the capital of King Arthur. In the Great Hall, which is all that remains of the Norman castle, the Round Table is hanging on the wall. Or at least a circular table, 18ft across, hangs there, with the names of Arthur's knights written round the edge in Gothic script. The city was certainly the capital of the great Wessex king, Alfred, who is commemorated in a statue in The Broadway.

One of Britain's most prosperous towns, a visit to Winchester is richly rewarding. The cathedral, from the outside is long and low, and going in at the west end, you find yourself admiring the full length of the longest medieval Gothic building in the world (556ft).

Outside The Close, in College Street, is the house in which Jane Austen died, and further along the street is Winchester College, founded in 1382 by the Bishop William of Wykham, and one of the country's leading boys' schools. Inside is a war cloister which contains memorials to Wykamists who died in World War I and all battles since then.

The city's museums should not be missed. The City Museum, in The Square, has a fascinating collection of local bygones. In the Peninsula Barracks is the Royal Hussars (Prince of Wales Own) Regimental Museum. One of the best military museums in Britain, it illustrates the history of the Regiment now known as the King's Royal Hussars. The Westgate Museum in the High Street is a small museum of arms, armour and historical objects

IN EASY REACH Just outside Winchester to the south, Marwell Zoological Park specialises in breeding species threatened by extinction, and the rare animals here include snow leopards, Asian lions and scimitar-horned oryx. To the south-west of Winchester are the colourful Hillier Gardens and Arboretum. To the east, the Mid-Hants Railway runs steam trains along the 'Watercress Line' between Alresford and Alton.

81

ASHRIDGE PARK
HERTFORDSHIRE

Either side of the B4506, north of Berkhamsted.
Tourist Information Centre, The Library, Kings Road, Berkhamsted (01442) 877638.

The huge house built in 1808 by James Wyatt for the Duke of Bridgewater is open occasionally and the gardens, laid out by Humphry Repton, are open at weekends. More accessible is the National Trust's Ashridge Estate: 4,000 acres of delightful and varied countryside, embracing downs, heaths and beechwoods, stretching across the Buckinghamshire border to Ivinghoe Beacon, the viewpoint where the Ridgeway long-distance footpath begins, or ends. The Bridgewater Monument, erected in 1832 to honour the 3rd Earl of Bridgewater, the father of the canal age, is a column 108ft tall and also the starting point for a 1½ mile nature trail.

IN EASY REACH The world's largest collection of fleas can be examined at the Zoological Museum in Tring. However, there is no need for caution as they are all safely dead, as are the vast mammals, birds, insects and fishes from all over the world which were first gathered here by Lionel Walter Rothschild in the 1890s and which are now in the care of the British Museum.

To see some living creatures, go to the Tring Reservoirs nature reserve, between Tring and Marsworth. The reservoirs were dug by navvies in the 19th century to supply water to the Grand Union Canal. Now they are home to legions of birds, dragonflies, assorted water beetles and seven kinds of leeches.

Across in Bedfordshire, off the B4540 south of Dunstable, Whipsnade Zoo, set in 60 acres of beautiful parkland, led the way in keeping larger animals in sizeable enclosures instead of cramped cages. Whipsnade is home to almost 2,500 animals and its conservation and breeding programmes for endangered species are known and respected worldwide. Additional attractions are the children's farm, railway and roadtrain.

82

BOARSTALL DUCK DECOY
BUCKINGHAMSHIRE

Near Brill, on a minor road off the B4011.
Tourist Information Centre, County Hall, Walton Street, Aylesbury (01296) 382308.

Now you see it, now you don't. The principle has been used to catch ducks at Boarstall for close to 300 years. One of the few working duck decoys in the country, it is now in the care of the National Trust. A dog vanishing and reappearing from behind a succession of straw screens arouses the insatiable curiosity of the ducks, which are lured deeper into a channel of water covered by netting stretched over hoops, gradually getting progressively smaller. The trapped ducks are not eaten any more, though, merely ringed. Demonstrations of the process can be seen on spring and summer weekends. The 13-acre site also has a nature trail through the woods, and an exhibition hall with natural history displays.

A male mallard duck emerges from a dive. Teal, as well as mallard, use the pool at Boarstall as a daytime retreat, and occasionally other wildfowl such as wigeon, shovelers or tufted duck may be seen

IN EASY REACH This is an area of particularly attractive countryside and endearing backwater villages, to explore by car or on foot. Brill Post Mill has stood on the hill above its exceptionally pretty village since the 17th century. To the west, the Otmoor area has a curiously wild and mysterious atmosphere for a district in the heart of England. The church is garlanded on May Day at Charlton on Otmoor. Between Boarstall and Stanton St John to its south-west lies Bernwood Forest, one of the best places in Britain for butterflies, and nearby are the Waterperry Gardens and Horticulture Centre. Here an 80-acre estate surrounds Waterperry House (not open), where there are fine herbaceous borders, a rock garden, a riverside walk, lawns and trees. Herbaceous, alpine, shrub and fruit nurseries and glasshouses provide all-year-round plants and produce for sale at the garden shop.

--------------------------------- 83 ---------------------------------

BODIAM CASTLE
EAST SUSSEX

At Robertsbridge, off the A229, south of Hawkhurst.
Tourist Information Centre, 88 High Street, Battle (01424) 773721.

Bodiam is everyone's idea of a romantic, picture-book castle – high, solid walls and battlemented towers, silently reflected in a moat of lilies. Though it was never attacked by the French, against whom it was built in 1386, it was gutted in the Civil War and left an uninhabited shell ever since. An audio-visual show about life in a medieval castle helps fill some of the gaps in your imagination and a few floors have been replaced.

Before fighting the Battle of Hastings, William the Conqueror vowed that if he was the victor he would build an abbey by way of thanking God. St Martin's Abbey at Battle was the result. It is said that the high altar was placed on the spot where King Harold fell

IN EASY REACH Across the River Rother lies Great Dixter – domestic architecture seen at its best. It consists of a large 15th-century timber-framed house, made larger by Sir Edwin Lutyens, who also designed the garden, with a flower meadow and orchard, ideal for daydreaming on a summers afternoon.

Go south via Sedlescombe's pretty village green and church to Battle Abbey built by William to commemorate his victory over Harold at the Battle of Hastings. Visit the excavated foundations of the abbey, and the exhibition in the Great Gatehouse. Buckleys Yesterday World, also on Abbey Green, offers 'a day in a bygone age' with many authentic Victorian and Edwardian shop and room settings.

About 7 miles north-west of Battle, at Burwash, is Rudyard Kipling's principal home in Sussex, Bateman's. Built for an ironmaster in 1634, it has many of the author's possessions, notably his 1928 Rolls Royce, and a working watermill that grinds flour for sale – and for scones in the tea-shop.

--------------------------------- 84 ---------------------------------

CHANCTONBURY RING
WEST SUSSEX

At Washington, off the A283 between Storrington and Steyning, north of Worthing.
Tourist Information Centre, Chapel Road, Worthing (01903) 210022.

Of all the many viewpoints and beauty spots that crown the South Downs, Chanctonbury Ring is probably the most famous. This is not so much for the views, though on a fine summer morning you can see for miles and miles across the patchwork Weald, but rather for the clump of beech trees planted here, in 1760, 815ft up beside a prehistoric hill-fort. Savagely battered by the winds of October 1987, they are still unmistakable, outlined against the sky.

IN EASY REACH Cissbury Ring, due south but still high on the Downs above Findon is another, much larger, hill-fort with ramparts and remains of Stone Age flint mines, re-used in Roman times. Reach it from Findon on the A24, north of Worthing.

At the foot of the Downs is Bramber, once a key Norman stronghold. The castle at Bramber was dismantled after the Civil War, leaving only a gateway and easily traceable sections of the wall. On a ridge of the South Downs, its location offers wonderful views. If rushed, ignore these ruins and spend extra time at St Mary's, the best late-15th-century half-timbered house in the county: close-beamed, with excellent panelling and rare painted wall-leather.

85

CHARTWELL
KENT

Off the B2026, south of Westerham.
Tourist Information Centre, Buckhurst Lane, Sevenoaks (01732) 450305.

Chartwell's fascination lies not only in the house, but also in its owner, Sir Winston Churchill, who bought it in 1924. Many of the rooms have been left as they were in his lifetime, filled with his paintings, books, documents, medals and uniforms. The honours he received, his much-prized Nobel award, and photographs with other world leaders, only serve to underline the comparative modesty of the place and his great love for it: for the studio where he painted in the garden, the terraced grounds and the famous black swans on the lake. Crowded it may be, but it's worth queuing for.

IN EASY REACH Westerham village green, to the north, has two statues: one is naturally Sir Winston, the other is the sword-waving figure of General James Wolfe, victor at Quebec in 1759. His boyhood home, Quebec House, a small, red-brick, gabled house, has several rooms on show and exhibits in the stable block. More Wolfe mementoes are nearby at Squerryes Court, another pleasing 17th-century house.

To the south-east, off the B2042, are good viewpoints on the North Downs including Toy's Hill and Ide Hill, noted for its bluebells. Here the National Trust has open ground and a 4-acre garden, Emmetts. On the A225 on the south-eastern outskirts of Sevenoaks, is Knole, a glorious great Tudor mansion – one of the largest in England – set in a wide-rolling deer park. It is said to have a room for every day of the year and a staircase for every week. The contents are stunning.

86

CHATHAM HISTORIC DOCKYARD
KENT

Tourist Information Centre, Eastgate Cottage, High Street, Rochester (01634) 843666.

What Chatham lacks in conventional charm, the Historic Dockyard more than makes up with huge quantities of history. This 80-acre Georgian and Victorian dockyard, in a bend of the River Medway before it joins the mouth of the Thames and the open sea, is packed with scheduled ancient monuments. In its towering and cavernous old shipbuilding sheds – 'covered slips' – the lines were laid for countless famous vessels. Around them stand warehouses, timber stores, period houses and the dockyard church – just inside the ornate gateway (possibly designed by Vanbrugh). Visit the working ropery and flag loft, and the visitor centre, with

displays and ship models. Finally, before you leave Chatham, look at Fort Amherst, off Dock Road, an underground Napoleonic fort built to protect the Royal Naval Dockyard from landward attack. Not all of it is on show, but there is a working gun battery and various other displays.

IN EASY REACH It was work at the dockyard that brought Charles Dickens's father here, and the family lived at Ordnance Terrace (see the plaque). But it was neighbouring Rochester that really inspired Dickens. The Norman castle keep – climb it for the views of the meandering Medway – and the cathedral, Restoration House, the Royal Victoria and Bull Hotel, the Corn Exchange, the Guildhall (now an entertaining museum) and the Six Poor Travellers almshouse all appear in various forms in *Pickwick Papers*, *Great Expectations*, *Edwin Drood* and other books. The full story is told at the Dickens Centre at Eastgate House, full of tableaux and pictures, all delightfully presented.

Dickens Festival

At the turn of May and June, liveliness and nostalgic charm bring the streets of Rochester to life in the annual Dickens Festival (see left), celebrating the novelist's lifelong love affair with the city. (He wanted to be buried there, outside the west door of the cathedral, but Westminster Abbey claimed him.) There are appropriate readings and plays, the local citizens dress up in Victorian costume and all the well-loved characters, headed by a beaming Mr Pickwick, grace the occasion and lead the jollifications. One of the local pooches even takes the part of Bill Sikes's dog.

87

CHILTERN OPEN AIR MUSEUM
BUCKINGHAMSHIRE

At Newland Park, near Chalfont St Peter. Off the A413.
Tourist Information Centre, 6 Cornmarket, High Wycombe (01494) 421892.

Five centuries of life in the Chilterns are reflected in this collection of farmhouses and other local buildings, including a toll-house, a Victorian loo, a cart shed and several granaries. One of the most interesting buildings is the cruck-framed barn originally built at Arborfield, near Reading, in about 1500. As far as possible the original building methods and materials are employed in all the reconstructions. There is also an Iron Age house reconstructed from archaeological evidence, from which a nature trail explores some of the 45 acres of local woods and chalk grassland.

IN EASY REACH Bertram Mills, the circus entrepreneur, is buried in St Giles's churchyard at Chalfont St Giles, a few miles north. John Milton lived here at a cottage in Dean Way in the 1660s, escaping from the Great Plague in London. It was here that he wrote *Paradise Lost* and there is a first edition of it in Milton's Cottage, off the B4442, which preserves other relics of the poet, with portraits and busts, and objects of local interest.

A couple of miles to the west is the quiet village of Jordans, where William Penn, the Quaker leader and founder of the American state of Pennsylvania, lies buried with his two wives and many lesser Penns in the graveyard of the Friends' Meeting House. Nearby is the Mayflower Barn, believed to be built partly of timbers which came from the ship on which the Pilgrim Fathers sailed to the New World.

Close to Amersham, off the A404, is Chenies Manor House, delightfully homely in Tudor red-brick, with amazing chimneys and a pretty garden. In the church you can press your nose against the glass like a Dickensian urchin to peer in at the grandiose Russell family monuments in the Bedford Chapel.

88

EPPING FOREST
ESSEX

Off junction 26 of the M25.
Tourist Information Centre, The Castle, Hertford (01992) 584322.

Epping Forest may be a surprising find – nearly 6,000 acres of lovely old woodland right on London's suburban doorstep. Once a royal hunting forest, the area is now owned by the City of London and open to everyone. Wander through it and admire the wildlife – listen for nightingales. Afterwards, you might like to make for High Beach, on a beech-topped ridge to the west, where Alfred, Lord Tennyson lived before he became famous. Here you can also admire the views and visit the Conservation Centre.

Don't miss seeing the Queen Elizabeth Hunting Lodge, off the A110 at Chingford. A timber-framed hunting lodge built, in fact, for Elizabeth I's father Henry VIII, it now houses the Epping Forest Museum, with displays of history and natural history – including over 1,400 different species of beetles.

IN EASY REACH Take junction 6 off the M11 (or 27 off the M25), or drive through winding lanes and little villages to arrive at Greensted near Chipping Ongar. There you can admire the little church with its 9th-century nave made of great split oak trunks, its pretty Tudor dormer windows and its delightful weatherboarded Saxon spire. Alternatively, or in addition, take junction 7 off the M11 for Parndon Wood Nature Reserve on the southern edge of Harlow. Here, in the 52-acre woodland, you can enjoy a stroll along a nature trail or lie in wait for wildlife in a hide.

89

THE GARDENS OF THE ROSE
HERTFORDSHIRE

At Chiswellgreen, on the south-west outskirts of St Albans.
Tourist Information Centre, Town Hall, Market Place, St Albans (01727) 864511.

Home of the Royal National Rose Society, the 12 acres of gardens surrounding the Society's headquarters contain what is possibly the finest collection of roses in the world, more than 1,600 varieties blooming on 30,000 bushes. In addition to the permanent displays of roses with their companion plants there are also trial grounds where visitors can see the very latest varieties and developments in rose growing. The gardens stay open into October, but are at their peak around the turn of June and July. The British Rose Festival, a spectacular display of roses, is held at Hampton Court.

The British Rose Festival

The British Rose Festival, a spectacular event held at Hampton Court in July each year, is organised by the Royal National Rose Society. At the Festival there are magnificent displays of roses on an exiting new theme each year; the latest new rose introductions and competitions for rose exhibitors and floral artists. The Society was founded in 1876 and became 'royal' in 1965. It organises shows and competitions, and awards gold medals and certificates of merit for outstanding new roses. The Society's progress would have delighted its first president, S Reynolds Hole, a clergyman who was a passionate enthusiast and propagandist for roses. He was Dean of Rochester, where he introduced over 130 varieties of rose to the deanery gardens.

IN EASY REACH St Albans is known for its Roman remains and its cathedral. Verulamium was a major Roman town, on the bank of the River Ver. To be seen today are part of the city wall, the foundations of houses and a temple, and the semicircular theatre, which held an audience of 1,600. Mosaics, jewellery, glass, coins and other objects reflecting life in Roman Britain are on show in the Verulamium Museum.

There are good views from the 77ft clock-tower in the marketplace, from which the curfew bell used to be rung, and the Fleur de Lys and the Fighting Cocks are two of the oldest inns in England. The Museum of St Albans houses a collection of craft tools and reconstructed workshops, and in the Organ Museum (Sundays only) are mechanical musical instruments. On the outskirts of the city, a mile to the west, Gorhambury House was built by Sir Robert Taylor in the 1780s. Part of the older house survives. It was Sir Francis Bacon's country house.

At Hatfield, to the east of St Albans, is one of the stateliest showplaces in England. Hatfield House was built early in the 17th century for Robert Cecil, principal minister of Elizabeth I and James I. It belongs to his direct descendent, the Marquess of Salisbury. Inside the domed and pinnacled palace are impressive state rooms, a giant Great Hall with a notable Jacobean screen, a splendid staircase and long gallery, a Georgian kitchen, and paintings, furniture, armour and tapestries assembled by generations of Cecils. It also houses the National Collection of Model Soldiers. The ample grounds of Hatfield House, with their mulberry trees, contain the one surviving wing of the old royal palace of Hatfield, in Tudor red brick.

90

HAMPTON COURT PALACE
SURREY

On the A308. Tourist Information Centre, Town Hall, Old Town Hall, Richmond 0181-940 9125.

Cardinal Wolsey planned and built it, Henry VII took it away from him in 1530, and it is certainly a house fit for a king. Wolsey's palace had 500 rooms, of which close to 300 were for guests and the rest for his staff. Henry made it bigger still. The stately gatehouse opens onto Tudor courts in magnificent red brick. Further in are the state apartments set round the Fountain Court, built by Sir Christopher Wren in the 1690s and a delight to the spirit. Things not to miss include the astronomical clock, made for Henry VIII in 1540, the Great Hall and the chapel royal, with the corridor outside haunted by Catherine Howard, copious carvings by Grinling Gibbons, the Tudor tennis court (still played on), the sumptuous gardens and the notorious maze.

Neatly trimmed bushes, statuary and colourful flowers can be seen in the Sunken Garden at Hampton Court

●

Black Cherry Fair

The Black Cherry Fair at Chertsey is held in July on St Anne's Hill, where a 14th-century abbot had built a chapel. Little is left of the chapel but the low hill commands good views. The fair, on the second Saturday in July, involves parades in costume, craft stalls, a procession of floats through the town and the solemn crowning of the Black Cherry Princess. The original black cherries probably grew and ripened at this time of year on the abbey's fruit trees.

IN EASY REACH On the Thames to the west of Hampton Court, the old market town of Chertsey grew up around its Benedictine abbey. It was to this abbey that Henry VI, in the 15th century, granted the proceeds of the Black Cherry Fair, still celebrated in July each year. The town museum in Windsor Street has a good local history collection, including a Viking sword, and holds various exhibitions throughout the year. About 2 miles north on the A320, Thorpe Park provides fun for all the family. Attractions include Space Station Zero, a ghost ride and a farm.

To the south of Hampton Court, on the A307 at Esher, is Claremont Landscape Garden, the earliest English landscape garden to have survived, laid out by Vanbrugh and extended by Kent. It now covers about 50 acres and its main attractions include a lake with an island pavilion, a grotto and a turf amphitheatre.

●

91

HENLEY ON THAMES
OXFORDSHIRE

Tourist Information Centre, Town Hall, Market Place (01491) 578034.

Regatta Week

Regatta is an Italian word for a race between Venetian gondolas, but no gondolas compete in what is now the most prestigious regatta in the world. It has been held regularly on the Thames at Henley since 1839. The course of 1 mile 550 yards corresponds to no distance raced in any other rowing event, and to allow stands for spectators to be set up close to the finish, the races have to be rowed against the flow of the river.

Arrive at Henley in the first week of July and you will find the town bulging with boat crews and visitors for the Royal Regatta, one of Britain's most famous boating events. But even at other times of year you can admire the river and the handsome bridge, built in 1786. The town itself is home to more than 300 buildings of architectural interest, including old coaching inns, St Mary's Church with its 16th-century chequerboard tower, and Fawley Court and Museum designed by Sir Christopher Wren with its displays of Polish royal documents, sabres and military equipment.

IN EASY REACH Follow the Thames south 3 miles to Wargrave (on the A321), a prettily sited riverside village over the Berkshire border, or go north-west of Henley, off the A423, to Greys Court, an interesting Jacobean house with medieval ruins, lovely gardens, a maze and a Tudor wheelhouse and donkey wheel. To the north of Greys Court, in a dip of the Chilterns off the B480, is Stonor Park, a medieval and 18th-century house, historic 'secret' Catholic stronghold and home of the Stonor family for 800 years. There are fine paintings and tapestries inside, and enjoyable gardens and a deer park with marvellous hilly views.

92

PETWORTH HOUSE
WEST SUSSEX

On the A285 and A272, north-east of Chichester. Tourist Information Centre, 29a South Street, Chichester (01243) 775888.

Horn Fair

One of the world's strangest cricket matches is played on St James's Day (25 July) at the Horn Fair in Ebernoe, near Petworth. The Ebernoe Cricket Club challenges one of the other local sides to a match, during which a sheep is roasted whole on the edge of the village green. At the end of the game, the batsman who has scored most runs for the winning side is presented with the head and horns of the sheep as a trophy. The custom was revived in 1864.

Whichever way you approach Petworth, you'll come through tiny Wealden villages and hamlets, seemingly untouched by modern times, until you spy Petworth House perched on a sandstone hill. The house has a proud air, like its builder, Charles, 6th Duke of Somerset, who married the estate's young Percy family heiress in 1682. The long west front is magnificent. The rest looks plain and severe, especially the side that backs onto the town, and it is not improved by the prison-like wall that encircles the house and its huge deer park – a 'Capability' Brown classic complete with serpentine-shaped lake. But Petworth's great glory is as an art gallery rather than a stately home. It has masses of early landscapes by Turner, who stayed and painted here; portraits by Van Dyck and Romney, who also came often to paint; Greek and Roman antiquities; and superb wood carvings, much by Grinling Gibbons himself, that appear to grow out of the walls and festoon the rooms.

IN EASY REACH Petworth itself is scarcely more than a large village, of charming old houses – dozens turned into antiques shops – cobbled alleyways, and narrow streets that perform endless sharp bends round the central marketplace and the high wall of Petworth House.

Westwards from the town the A272 runs beside the deer park to Cowdray Park, best known for polo but originally the grounds to Cowdray House, now an imposing palace ruin that is said to result from a curse placed on Sir Anthony Browne and his family by a monk, about 1540. Some say the curse was a protest against Sir Anthony's excessive property grabbing after the Dissolution of the Monasteries.

After Cowdray comes Midhurst, another delightful old town. Its tile-hung, timber and Georgian houses include the splendid Spread Eagle Inn. Curfew is still rung at 8pm in memory of the travellers who would have wandered outside the town all night but for the sound of the bell.

93

PORTSMOUTH
HAMPSHIRE

Tourist Information Centre, The Hard (01705) 826722.

Although much of historic Portsmouth was lost to the ferocious bombing of World War II, it still remains the world centre for maritime heritage and, together with Southsea just along the front, it brims over with interesting things to see. Its history is bound up with that of the navy and two of its great occasions are the Navy Days (held in August in alternate years), when the ships and their crews play host to the public, and the Trafalgar Day ceremonies, which honour Nelson's final victory. HMS *Victory*, Nelson's flagship at Trafalgar and the greatest of the wooden walls which kept

•

Navy Days and Military Vehicle Rally

The Navy Days, a biennial event (alternates with Plymouth) usually held at the end of August in the Royal Dockyard in Portsmouth, give the public an opportunity to see the Royal Navy at close quarters. Besides visiting a wide selection of warships and exhibits, you can enjoy flying displays by jet planes or watch parachutists and marching bands. Portsmouth's Navy Days were the first to be instituted in 1927. Over the Spring Bank Holiday weekend in May another exciting event in Portsmouth is the Military Vehicle Rally, during which hundreds of tanks, armoured cars and fighting vehicles parade in the city, with bands, helicopter stunts and aerobatics displays.

•

This carving of Nelson, which came from HMS Trafalgar, *can now be seen on the dock near HMS* Victory

Napoleon at bay, is the star of Portsmouth's many attractions. Close by is another veteran warship, or what is left of her – the hulk of the *Mary Rose*, of 700 tons, which sank in the Solent when sallying out to repel a French invasion force in 1545. In the accompanying exhibition, you can see many of the multitude of objects, from pocket sundials to a chamber-pot, which went down with the ship and her crew. Not far away, a third warship can be inspected. This is HMS *Warrior*, the world's first iron-hulled, armoured battleship, launched in 1860 and now restored. Close to all three ships is the excellent Royal Naval Museum.

There are boat trips to see the harbour, which is the reason for Portsmouth's existence. The world's first dry dock was built here in 1495, and an efficient self-guiding trail leads you on an enjoyable walk through the Portsmouth Point area to see the 15th-century and later defences, and the houses and pubs, in the oldest part of the town. In Old Commercial Road the house in which Charles Dickens was born is now a small museum to his memory.

The D-Day Museum, Clarence Esplanade, contains the giant Overlord tapestry, telling the story of the D-Day invasion, but is more worthwhile for its re-creation of life in wartime Britain.

IN EASY REACH Across the narrow entrance to Portsmouth Harbour is Gosport, where the Royal Navy Submarine Museum tells the story of underwater warfare, with submarines from their earliest days to the last survivor of World War II, HMS *Alliance*. Portchester Castle, commanding the north shore of the harbour, was one of the Saxon Shore forts constructed by the Romans to guard the south coast against raiders. Exceptionally well preserved, it was afterwards taken over by the Normans and it was here that Edward III and Henry V assembled their armies to invade France.

—————————— 94 ——————————

QUEEN ELIZABETH COUNTRY PARK
HAMPSHIRE

Off the A3, 2 miles south of Petersfield.
Tourist Information Centre, County Library, 27 The Square, Petersfield (01730) 268829

●

Country Fair and Sheepdog Trials

If you want to buy a shepherd's crook, head for the Queen Elizabeth Country Park, where the Hampshire Country Fair and Sheepdog Trials are held in July each year on the lower slopes of Butser Hill (also popular with grass skiers). This is very much a farming occasion, with classes for sheep, pigs and ducks, young farmers' events in the arena and local pony clubs competing. There are innumerable craft displays and craft stalls, and an interesting self-sufficiency section, which shows you how to keep bees and other livestock and how to re-use paper and other waste. Meanwhile, county teams take part in the sheepdog trials, which go on all through the day.

●

Queen Elizabeth Country Park, situated at the western terminus of the South Downs, was opened by the Forestry Commission and the County Council in Jubilee Year (1977), hence its name. It comprises 540 acres of open chalk downland on Butser Hill (which rises to 888ft) and 860 acres of beech and coniferous forest. Numerous footpaths criss-cross the area, some of which have marked trails and there is a Park Information Centre, to make sure you get the most out of your visit.

IN EASY REACH Butser Ancient Farm 3 miles south off the A3 sets out to reconstruct an Iron Age Farm dating to approximately 300BC and includes a reconstruction of a prehistoric round-house, fields growing early varieties of cereals, kilns, a herb garden and, of course, livestock.

In the opposite direction from the Queen Elizabeth Country Park is the spiritual home of cricket, Broadhalfpenny Down, a couple of miles north-east of the village of Hambledon. Here was the pitch on which the Hambledon Club took on and sometimes defeated the rest of England in the 1770s and 1780s, and where the rules of the game were first authoritatively formulated. A granite monument marks this hallowed site, overlooked by the old Bat and Ball Inn.

High on the Downs to the east on the B2146, over the border into Sussex, is late 17th-century Uppark a National Trust property, now being restored after a fire in 1989. It is hoped that the house will reopen in 1995. Meanwhile the garden, landscaped by Repton, and its magnificent views can still be enjoyed.

—————————— 95 ——————————

THE ROLLRIGHT STONES
OXFORDSHIRE

A few miles north of Chipping Norton, off the A34.
Tourist Information Centre, Banbury Museum, 8 Horsefair, Banbury (02195) 259855.

You will find this late-Neolithic stone circle just off the main road from Oxford to Stratford. Alongside it are the Whispering Knights, a cluster of stones that once formed a Neolithic longbarrow. Across the road on a little hill stands the solitary King Stone. It's an eerie spot, rich in folklore. According to one legend this is where an invading Danish king met with Mother Shipton, the local witch. She promptly turned him to stone along with his army (the stone circle) and his whispering retinue (the Knights).

IN EASY REACH North-east of the Rollright Stones, through pretty country lanes, is the village of Alkerton (off the A422). Stop off to see the lovely garden at Brook Cottage. Also off the A422 is Upton House at Edge Hill. It dates back to the late 17th century and contains fine tapestries, pictures and furniture. Banbury is also worth visiting for currant-studded Banbury cakes and the famous cross – rebuilt in 1858, the original having been destroyed by Puritans in 1602. The 18th-century church is worth seeing, and so is Banbury Museum with its local history displays.

Take the B4035 south-west from Banbury and you'll come to Broughton Castle, a moated medieval fortress, turned into a country house in the 16th century. It is known for its plasterwork and chimney-pieces. At Bloxham, also south-west of Banbury, is a landmark visible for miles around, the 198ft church spire. The church also boasts stained glass by William Morris and Burne-Jones.

—————————— 96 ——————————

RYE
EAST SUSSEX

Tourist Information Centre, The Heritage Centre, Strand Quay (01797) 226696.

The sight of Rye rising on a hill above the marshes is one of the joys of Sussex. Though the sea has long since receded, Rye is still at heart a medieval seafaring town, one of the two Ancient Towns linked to the Cinque Ports. Visit the Rye Heritage Centre on the Strand Quay and learn how the French sacked the town and the smugglers gathered in the Mermaid Inn. Then enjoy strolling the steep, cobbled streets, past the old grammar school, the town hall over the marketplace, and hundreds of black-and-white houses and inns. The churchyard of St Mary's at the top of the hill provides a peaceful respite and here the gilded Quarter Boys can be seen striking the quarter hours – but not the hour – on the church clock. Lamb House home of American novelist Henry James and later E F Benson, author of the Mapp and Lucia books based on Rye, is a charming 18th-century building with a delightful garden. From the 13th-century Rye Castle (used for 300 years as the town prison and now housing a museum of Cinque Port material and local history) there are views across the marshes to Rye Harbour and nature reserve.

IN EASY REACH On the road south-east towards Dungeness are Camber Sands – long stretches of dunes backed by holiday centres and caravan sites – and on the other side of the Rother Estuary towards Hastings you pass Camber's ruined Tudor castle and then Winchelsea, Rye's partner as an Ancient Town. Quieter and smaller than Rye, but just as delightful, it too was sacked, leaving the great church of St Thomas in ruins.

97

SANDWICH BAY NATURE RESERVE
KENT

Off the A256 from Sandwich to Ramsgate. Tourist Information Centres: The Guildhall, Cattle Market, Sandwich (01304) 613565 (seasonal opening) and The Argyle Centre, Queen Street, Ramsgate (01834) 591086.

Over 1,000 acres of lonely sand dunes and shingle, freshwater marshes and saltings on either side of the River Stour meandering down to the sea make up this official Site of Special Scientific Interest. This mixture of habitats supports a rich variety of wildlife, and the lime-rich soil formed from sand and shells accounts for the abundance of wild flowers. Many, such as sea holly, are of very restricted distribution in Britain. The Kent coast is well known for its migrant birds and butterflies, and many species pass through the reserve in large numbers every spring and autumn. Access to most of the reserve is unrestricted all year round but visitors are requested to observe the notices. The nearest car park to the area south of the Stour is 1½ miles away, via a toll-road leaving Sandwich to the east.

IN EASY REACH Close by, on the edge of Pegwell Bay's wide sandy flats, is Ebbsfleet, where Saxon leaders Hengist and Horsa landed in AD449 (a replica longship, the Hugin – *Raven* – records the fact). They were followed by St Augustine in AD597 (who merits a stone marker). At Richborough, a little way south, the Romans had earlier built their main invasion port, guarded by a colossal castle whose hulk-like ruins still manage to impress.

Sandwich itself is a little gem – and like many, overlooked. The web of narrow streets and overhanging houses dates back to Sandwich's heyday as a Cinque Port, the seventh largest town in England. When the river silted up and the sea receded it was left, quietly inland, with a huge Norman church, a guildhall and streets of 16th-century Dutch houses with crow-stepped gables, built for the Flemish weavers who settled here.

98

WELLINGTON COUNTRY PARK
HAMPSHIRE

*At Stratfield Saye, east of the A33, near Riseley.
Tourist Information Centre, Town Hall, Blagrave Street, Reading (01734) 566226.*

The lake, which is the central attraction of the Wellington Country Park, is surrounded by woods, with nature trails and picnic areas. This is a good area for birdwatching, and you can keep an eye and ear open for treecreepers, nuthatches and green and spotted woodpeckers. Close by is the National Dairy Museum which explains how dairying became an organised national industry. There is also a charcoal burner's hut, which casts light on an old industry, and a collection of small domestic animals. In addition, leisure activities such as fishing and windsurfing can be pursued here.

IN EASY REACH The country park stands on land donated by the Duke of Wellington whose country house, Stratfield Saye, is on the opposite side of the A33. It is full of mementoes and memories of his ancestor, 'the great duke' or simply 'the duke', to whom the house was given by a grateful nation after Waterloo. It is still redolent of his commanding presence and the common sense which he elevated to the level of genius. Beneath a tree in the grounds is the grave of Copenhagen, his favourite charger, and in the stable block is the huge funeral car on which the great man's coffin was hauled in procession to St Paul's in London.

Closer to Basingstoke, off the A30, near Sherborne St John, is the Vyne, a graceful 16th-century house with a stately 17th-century portico, a lake and fine grounds. Now in the care of the National Trust, it is widely regarded as the most attractive house in Hampshire.

Wellington Country Park is also home to the National Dairy Museum

— 99 —

WHITBREAD HOP FARM
KENT

At Beltring, on the A228 between Tunbridge Wells and Wateringbury.
Tourist Information Centre, The Gatehouse, Old Palace Gardens, Mill Street,
Maidstone (01622) 673581.

Kent has many a conical-roofed oast house, traditionally used for drying hops, but nowhere so many as here at Beltring. Whitbread brewery has preserved whole 'terraces' of the tall Victorian kilns as part of a working hop farm, and added a museum of rural crafts and 'hopping' through the ages. Outside are Whitbread's famous shire horses – on holiday, in retirement, or newly born and training. For miles around are hop gardens, where in autumn the hop vines hang from high poles and wires, waiting to be cut down, their flowers stripped and dried in the oast houses, ready to flavour beer.

IN EASY REACH Take the B2016, northwards through Mereworth (catch sight of the amazing Palladian-style 'castle' here, and its companion church) to Wrotham Heath, on the A25/A20, and pause again at St George's Church, before turning west to Ightham Mote: an unbelievably unspoilt, early medieval manor house, deep-moated, and undisturbed by time.

South of Maidstone, off the A229, Boughton Monchelsea Place is an Elizabethan mansion in a large park; while north of Maidstone are Allington Castle, home of Tudor poet Sir Thomas Wyatt, and Aylesford Priory, restored, with a working pottery. Both are on the River Medway.

— 100 —

THE WHITE HORSE OF UFFINGTON
OXFORDSHIRE

Near Kingston Lisle, on the B4507 west of Wantage. Tourist Information Centre, The
Pump House, 5 Market Place, Faringdon (01367) 242191.

On a windy walk along the top of the Berkshire Downs, you can follow the ancient Ridgeway Path west past Wantage and find White Horse Hill with its wonderful prehistoric figure carved in the chalky hillside. Once thought to have been drawn in celebration of King Alfred's victory over the Danes in 871, the 375ft-long white horse, an extremely peculiar-looking creature, is now thought to be 2,000 years or so old. On top of the hill is the prehistoric earthwork of Uffington Castle, with a fine view. About 8 acres in extent, it is entered by a single gateway, protected by an extension of the perimeter banks.

IN EASY REACH West of White Horse Hill, and also on the Ridgeway Path is Wayland's Smithy, a prehistoric burial place built about 2000BC. It has a strange old superstition: leave your tethered horse and coin at the place, it is said, and when you return the horse will be newly shod, the coin mysteriously disappeared.

Kingston Lisle Park, on the B4507, is a handsome 17th-century house with a remarkable flying staircase and superb gardens, while Ashdown House, a National Trust property near Ashbury to the south, is an impressive 17th-century hunting lodge. It contains Craven family portraits. Another National Trust property worth seeing is Great Coxwell Barn (2 miles south-west of Faringdon), a massive stone tithe barn built by Cistercian monks in the 13th century. The barn, which is 152ft long and 48ft high, is all original, except for the doorways at either end which were 18th-century additions.

— 101 —

WHITSTABLE
KENT

Tourist Information Centre, Horsebridge, Whitstable (01227) 275482.

There is a tradition in Kent that Julius Caesar was drawn to Britain by the Whitstable oysters. Certainly they have attracted countless other visitors over the centuries, and the town's annual July oyster festival is a lively affair of oyster landings and tastings, and a 'blessing of the waters' service: a reminder that this is still fundamentally a fishing port, with small streets and fishermen's cottages, boatyards and tackle shops.

Whitstable is now also a seaside resort with a shingle beach, and a yachting centre. It is possible to take an unusual walk at low tide out along a finger of shingle called 'the Street', which protrudes for a mile or so into the sea. The story of the oysters, which the Romans consumed in prodigious quantities, is told in the local history museum in the High Street.

Game and Country Fair

One of Kent's major annual events comes round in September when 20,000 visitors or more flock to the Whitbread Game and Country Fair at the Whitbread Hop Farm. It involves craft stalls and a range of changing events, which may include military bands, a tug-of-war and other country sports, an assault course, and the world championship pitchfork contest – throwing a bale of hay over a bar set at gradually increasing heights. Other regular summer events at the Hop Farm include a military vehicle rally, the heavy horse show with a vintage tractor and engine rally, and a hot air balloon festival.

Oyster Ceremony

On St James's Day (25 July) the oyster-rich waters at Whitstable are formally blessed in a ceremony held at high tide at the edge of the water on Reeves Beach. The occasion is organised by the Association of Men of Kent and Kentish Men (the former living to the south of the River Medway and the latter to the north). St Peter's Church in Whitstable supplies the clergy and the choir for the service, while fishing boats and other vessels bob about offshore. The custom goes back to the early 19th century at least.

IN EASY REACH About 7 miles south-west stands Faversham, an industrious, underrated little town, once a 'limb' of the Cinque Ports. The Fleur-de-Lis Heritage Centre here provides a first-rate introduction to the area and will direct you to the 18th-century gunpowder mills at Chart, the Maison Dieu at Ospringe and the Dolphin Yard museum of sailing barges at nearby Sittingbourne.

Where the sea meets the mouth of the River Swale, the south Swale Nature Reserve is noted for overwintering wildfowl. There's mostly beach and foreshore here on either side of the sea-wall and along the Saxon Shore Way Footpath. Across the water, on the Isle of Sheppey, is the Elmley Marshes RSPB reserve, off the A249, turning immediately right once you have crossed Kingsferry Bridge. This is one of many excellent places around the Isle of Sheppey for birdwatching – or watching the constant parade of ships in the Thames Estuary.

102

WISLEY GARDENS
SURREY

Off the A3, about 8 miles north-east of Guildford.
Tourist Information Centre, The Undercroft, 72 High Street, Guildford (01483) 444007.

Hours of satisfaction are guaranteed at Wisley for those with green fingers, and for those without, for that matter. The Royal Horticultural Society moved its headquarters to Wisley in 1904 and now has 150 acres of gardens here, with examples of every type of planting. There are gardens for roses, herbs and heathers, a lake, trees and shrubs, impressive rock gardens, plots for vegetables and fruit, woods, glasshouses and a special area to encourage disabled people to take up gardening. In addition, there is a restaurant, a gift shop and, naturally, a plant centre. As well as all this, the Society runs an advisory service here, covering all aspects of gardening.

IN EASY REACH Off the A3 at Cobham, is Painshill Park, a marvellous 'mood' landscape garden, constructed in the 18th century, by the Hon Charles Hamilton, to induce a succession of appropriate emotions in the visitor strolling from one area to another. Many new shrub beds have been planted with appropriate plant material giving an insight into 18th-century plantings. Open Sunday only mid-April to mid-October with free optional guided tours lasting nearly 2 hours, it is a thoroughly enjoyable visit. Also near Cobham (off the A245) is Stoke D'Abernon, where the grey flint church contains the oldest brass in England. The figure shown is Sir John D'Abernon, Sheriff of Surrey, who died in 1277.

103

WOBURN ABBEY
BEDFORDSHIRE

Off the A5, east of Bletchley.
Tourist Information Centre, Vernon Place, Dunstable (01582) 608441.

Grandest of the grand houses of Bedfordshire, Woburn Abbey has been the country seat of the Russells, Dukes of Bedford, since 1550. The Palladian mansion was built by Henry Flitcroft in the 1740s for the 4th Duke, and inside is a remarkable art collection, with works by Rembrandt, Claude, Poussin, Van Dyck, Tintoretto, Gainsborough, Reynolds, Velázquez, Cuyp, Teniers, Murillo and Canaletto. Also on view is fine furniture, silver, gold plate and porcelain, including the Sèvres dinner service given to the family by Louis XIV.

Outside, the 3,000-acre park was landscaped by Humphrey Repton and is home to nine species of deer, including the very rare Pere David variety, as well as many other rare animals and birds. The wild animal kingdom is Britain's biggest drive-through safari park. An antiques centre with 40 shops is supported by a pottery and garden centre, picnic areas and gift shops.

IN EASY REACH To the west, on the Buckinghamshire border, is Stockgrove Country Park, with its ancient oak woods. To the north-east is the shell of 17th century Houghton House, often identified as the 'House Beautiful' of *Pilgrim's Progress*. Also in the charge of English Heritage is Wrest Park at Silsoe, worth visiting for its noble formal gardens, with a canal, fountains and elegant statuary. The tombs of the de Greys of Wrest Park can be seen in the Flitton de Grey Mausoleum, west of Silsoe. At Wing in Buckinghamshire, Ascott was one of several Rothschild houses in the county, and is now a National Trust property.

Events at Woburn and Firing the Poppers

Woburn Abbey and Deer Park play host to a wide variety of activities, especially during the summer months. Dates vary from year to year and the events may range from art exhibitions within the abbey, to historic vehicle shows or sheepdog trials in the grounds. The curious custom of Firing the Poppers occurs at the village of Fenny Stratford, not far from Woburn, on St Martin's Day every year, in November. The poppers (see below) are little miniature cannons, weighing about 6lbs. The verger of St Martin's Church primes them with gunpowder and they are fired by the vicar, the verger, the churchwardens and invited guests at intervals during the afternoon.

•

— 104 —

AMBERLEY CHALK PITS MUSEUM
WEST SUSSEX

On the B2139, between Amberley and Houghton, north of Arundel.
Tourist Information Centre, 61 High Street, Arundel (01903) 882268.

The woods and water-meadows of the Arun Valley may seem a curious, even inappropriate setting for a regional industrial heritage centre. But the early-19th-century limeworks and chalk quarry – a huge white gash in the hillside some discreet distance from the thatch-and-timber prettiness of the village – have become an important open-air museum. There are tools and equipment from iron-founding, brick-making and other traditional South-East industries, plus a vintage wireless collection, demonstrations by blacksmith, printer, boatbuilder and potter, an audio-visual introduction to the pits, and nature and geology trails round the 36-acre site. Special events include a September steam weekend, when traction engines and trains are steamed up at night so that photographers can shoot the sparks.

IN EASY REACH To the north-west, on the other side of the valley, is Bignor Roman Villa, off the A29. It is often missed by visitors, but it has some of the loveliest mosaics, one 80ft long, uncovered anywhere outside Italy. Between Pulborough and Storrington, off the A283, is Parham House (only open till early October). It is much like other Elizabethan mansions, but has exceptionally fine needlework, a 4-acre walled garden and a church in the park, with Gothic box-pews

Wine Festival

The English Wine Centre at Drusillas Corner, Alfriston, which incidentally boasts a historic corkscrew collection, as well as the zoo park and the vineyard, stages the English Wine Festival and Regional Food Fair in September each year to introduce visitors to the pleasures of home-grown vintages by allowing them to sample a variety of English wines and ciders. Wine cultivation almost died out in England after the Middle Ages and was kept alive only by a few obstinate eccentrics until the years after World War I, when there was a new interest. Business is now booming and there are more than 70 English vineyards open to the public.

•

— 105 —

BEACHY HEAD
EAST SUSSEX

Off the B2103, west of Eastbourne.
Tourist Information Centre, Cornfield Road, Eastbourne (01323) 411400.

Here the white chalk hills of the South Downs meet the sea in a sheer drop – 575ft, to the rocks, waves and lighthouse. There is little to divert from the grandeur of the cliffs, except a new Countryside Centre next to the pub, or a nature trail and the start – or end – of the South Downs Way Footpath. The Heritage Coast sweeps all the way to Seaford, past Birling Gap, whose rocky beach was notorious for smugglers. For dramatic views of the Seven Sisters cliffs and Cuckmere Valley, explore the Seven Sisters Country Park with its excellent interpretation centre and the Living World at Exceat, a living exhibition of small creatures. Neighbouring Friston Forest is an experiment to create a broadleaved forest only a mile from the sea; here there are enjoyable walks along good paths and trails.

IN EASY REACH Eastbourne sits sedately in the shelter of Beachy Head and is rated one of the sunniest resorts in Britain. It has plenty of parks, a few museums, an art gallery, and several theatres. East along the A259 is Pevensey, where William the Conqueror first landed and the Normans built a castle, now ruined, within the Romans' massive fort, one of their chain of Saxon shore forts. Polegate, where the A22 meets the A27 north of Eastbourne, has little of note, except a tall, red-brick tower mill, built in 1817 and still intact, with a milling museum.

A little further afield, west along the A27 is Wilmington. Here there are remains of a Benedictine priory, a small farming museum and the 'giant' Long Man of Wilmington, cut out of the turf on the Downs. Next, still going west along the A27 is Drusillas Zoo Park – with small animals that appeal to small visitors, and a vineyard where autumn beer, cider and English wine festivals are held. Nearby in Alfriston, is the National Trust's first building, a modest, thatched, medieval Clergy House, and one of the oldest inns in England, The Star.

— 106 —

BLENHEIM PALACE
OXFORDSHIRE

At Woodstock, on the A34, 8 miles north of Oxford.
Tourist Information Centres: Hensington Road, Woodstock (01993) 811038 (seasonal opening only) and St Aldates, Oxford (01865) 726871.

The largest and grandest house you'll find anywhere in England, Blenheim Palace was given to John Churchill by Queen Anne and a 'grateful nation' after his great victory over the French at Blenheim in 1704. Of staggering splendour and built on a massive scale, it took Sir John Vanbrugh 17 years to complete and is his greatest classical masterpiece. The gigantic pillared north front, the roof bristling with sculptures, the fabulous state rooms rich with gold decoration, pictures and tapestries, the Great Hall

Blenheim Palace – the only non-royal residence in the country to be so named – is currently the home of the 11th Duke of Marlborough

with its huge Corinthian columns, the enormous library are all breathtaking. You can see the room where Winston Churchill was born, with its relics and exhibition, and admire the fine furniture and family portraits.

Outside are 2,000 acres of gorgeous gardens and grounds, landscaped by 'Capability' Brown between 1764 and 1774. It was he who created the famous Blenheim lake with its grand cascade, built the temple to Diana and Gothicised buildings on or near the estate. The deer park is dotted with magnificent oaks and cedars, and you can tour the arboretum and inspect the 134ft column erected in the grounds in memory of the 1st Duke of Marlborough and his battles – the trees around it are laid out as a plan of the Battle of Blenheim. Rosamond's Well is named in memory of Fair Rosamond Clifford who is said to have lived here in a secluded bower built for her by Henry II, her secret lover. A puff along the miniature steam railway line and a motor-launch ride about the lake will get you back in time for a visit to the butterfly house and the plant centres. Before leaving you may like to let the children loose in the park's adventure playground, where there are plenty of amusements.

IN EASY REACH Just outside the palace gate lies Woodstock. Elegant with Georgian architecture, the town also boasts much older buildings. In the churchyard at Bladon, not far away, are the Churchill family graves, including the last resting place of Sir Winston Churchill. If you have time and want to see more examples of grand living, Ditchley Park at Enstone, to the north-west, is another magnificent 18th-century house designed for the Lee family by James Gibbs, with interiors by William Kent (limited opening). Even more impressive work by Kent can be found at Rousham House, Steeple Aston (off the A423), where he created the gorgeous landscape garden, featuring cascades, classical temples and statues, in the woods rising up above the River Cherwell.

107

THE BLUEBELL RAILWAY
EAST SUSSEX

Sheffield Park Station is on the A275 between Newick and Forest Row. Horsted Keynes Station is off the B2028 north of Haywards Heath. Tourist Information Centre, 187 High Street, Lewes (01273) 483448.

The Bluebell, as its name suggests, has the best of both worlds: a wonderfully scenic route – 5 miles of woodland glades and pastures – and the largest collection of old locos and carriages in the region. Start at the southern end, Sheffield Park Station, where you will find a picnic site as well as the museum and many engines and carriages dating back to 1865; chug past Freshfield Halt to Horsted Keynes Station, hop off for more exhibitions and a buffet bar; and then return to Sheffield Park. At weekends there is a restaurant train, and special events include Santa Specials in December. If you think you've been here before, you were probably watching a Sherlock Holmes film, or maybe *Mahler*, to name but two.

IN EASY REACH On the other side of the A275 is Sheffield Park Garden, one of 'Capability' Brown's and another of the Sussex forest-ridge gardens famed for flaming autumn trees – here reflected in five large lakes – and rhododendrons and azaleas in spring. Now a National Trust property, it was laid out between 1769 and 1794 for the 1st Earl of Sheffield. Inside the garden is the entrance to Wings Haven Bird Sanctuary, a bird hospital for macaws, parrots, and many other types of birds.

108

BURNHAM BEECHES
BUCKINGHAMSHIRE

Off the A355, 3 miles north of Slough. Tourist Information Centre, The Library, St Ives Road, Maidenhead, Berkshire (01628) 781110.

Gorgeous in their autumn livery of reds, russets and browns the pollarded beeches of this famous beauty spot did duty for Sherwood Forest in the classic Errol Flynn film of *Robin Hood*. Footpaths wind through the woods, which shelter deer, owls and newts, among other residents. Some of the trees are 450 years old and more, and have probably been pollarded since the early 16th century. The resulting crop of timber would have been used for firewood and poles in neighbouring manors or in London.

IN EASY REACH Cliveden Reach is a particularly beautiful stretch of the Thames at Cliveden, north-east of Maidenhead, where the Astors' house is now a hotel, though the formal gardens are open to the public. There are a variety of features to be seen in the gardens, including fine lawns with box hedges, topiary, a rose garden and Oriental-style water gardens with spring and autumn-flowering shrubs. At Stoke Poges, on the B416 to the south of Burnham Beeches, is the churchyard which inspired the poet Gray to compose his celebrated *Elegy*. He lies buried just outside the church, and in a field close by is a suitably mournful 18th-century monument to him. Langley Country Park, to the south-east, with a deer park and gardens, commands fine views of Windsor Castle.

109

CANTERBURY
KENT

Tourist Information Centre, 34 St Margaret's Street (01227) 766567.

Hop Hoodening Day, in September, once the annual celebration of the hop harvest is now more a morris dance festival when the cathedral grounds are filled with colour and music – rather as one imagines the arrival of Chaucer's pilgrims. A celebration of the arts – the Canterbury Festival – takes place in October. At the Canterbury Tales medieval adventure you are invited to step back in time and join the Wife of Bath and the rest of Chaucer's characters. It's great fun, but don't miss the real thing: the soaring cathedral and the site of Thomas Becket's martyrdom which drew

Detail from one of 12 windows in Canterbury Cathedral's Trinity Chapel. Each window depicts a miracle worked by the intervention of St Thomas

them here; the radiant blue and red stained glass windows, the finest 13th-century stained glass in England, showing bible stories and St Thomas's many miracles; and the tomb of the Black Prince, who sleeps beneath reproductions of his coat of armour, helmet and shield.

There are dozens of churches and religious houses up alleyways and back streets, best explored on foot. These include St Martin's Church, the oldest in England still in use; the Poor Priests' Hospital, restored and now the Heritage Museum; and the Greyfriars, set astride the River Stour, which flows gently through the Franciscan gardens. If you've time, there are also the new Roman Museum, with underground remains and a hypocaust; the 14th-century West Gate, with arms and armour in a former prison; and the Royal Museum, with local history, art gallery and Buffs' regimental museum.

IN EASY REACH For many pilgrims following the route along the North Downs, the pretty village of Chilham (off the A252) was the last overnight rest before Canterbury. Enjoy the village square and the grounds of Chilham Castle, an imposing 17th-century manor with a Norman keep, with a heronry claimed as the biggest and oldest in England, and a Raptor Centre where birds of prey can be seen, with flying displays some afternoons.

110

CASTLE HEDINGHAM
ESSEX

Off the A604, north of Halstead.
Tourist Information Centres: Town Hall, Market Hill, Sudbury (01787) 881320 and Market Square, Saffron Walden (01799) 510444.

Beautifully preserved, Castle Hedingham is one of Europe's best surviving examples of Norman architecture, with the massive walls of the keep looming hugely above the flat, grassy surround. The garrison chamber, the banqueting hall with its minstrels' gallery and the elegant Tudor bridge should all be seen. If the weather is suitable, a picnic in the inner bailey could then precede a tour of pretty Castle Hedingham village. The little railway station is now a museum, with displays of locomotives and rolling stock. If you're there on one of the special steaming days, jump aboard for a nostalgic, picturesque ride along the Colne Valley Line.

IN EASY REACH Thaxted, 10 miles or so west of Castle Hedingham, is a little town with timbered houses, a 15th-century guildhall on wooden posts, a beautiful 14th- to-15th century church with a tall spire, and a handsome windmill dating from 1805. Nearby Finchingfield on the B1053 is an attractive village arranged around a green and duckpond, with a 15th-century guildhall and museum of antiquities, and lovely Tudor Spains Hall, with its gardens (limited opening only). At Great Saling, off the A120 north-west of Braintree, is Saling Hall with its splendid 12-acre garden, and a park with specimen trees, a water garden and a walled garden dating back to 1698.

111

CHAWTON
HAMPSHIRE

Off the A31, near Alton.
Guildhall, The Broadway, Winchester (01962) 840500.

A sextet of the most admired novels in the English language were either written or revised in Chawton. Jane Austen's House, a substantial red-brick building on the old main road between London and Winchester, was where the authoress spent the last eight years of her life, from 1809 until 1817, when she died in Winchester. The brilliance of the novels makes a most striking contrast with the quiet domestic scene and the poky little parlour where Miss Austen wrote – ready to hide her work instantly if anyone else came in. What the visitor sees today are books and family portraits, letters and jewellery, china, Miss Austen's sewing box and quilt, the cup-and-ball game she played with her nephews and nieces, and other humble bygones. Outside is the old wash-house, with the donkey cart on which she took the air in the local lanes, and the pretty garden (stalked now by singularly large and handsome cats), where visitors are welcome to picnic.

IN EASY REACH South-east of Chawton, on the B3006, is Selborne, one of the most famous villages in England. In 1789 *The Natural History and Antiquities of Selborne* was published by Gilbert White, with the fruits of years of patient observation of the wildlife and plants of the area. His house, The Wakes, is today the Gilbert White Museum, and also displays material connected with Francis Oates, the 19th-century explorer, and his nephew, Captain Lawrence Oates, who died heroically on Captain Scott's expedition to the South Pole. There are delightful walks from Selborne, for example to Selborne Hangar (National Trust), the beechwood above the village.

●

Hoodening

Hoodening is an old hobby horse custom, still kept up here and there in Kent. The hooden horse was a man disguised as an animal and equipped with a horse's skull or a horse's head made of wood with real, snapping teeth, a ribbon-decked mane and a horse-hair tail.
Accompanied by a Mollie, or man-woman figure with a besom and by morris dancers, hand-bell ringers or carol singers, he would prance about, bucking and snapping his jaws, and visit farms and houses to bring good luck and prosperity in the coming year.
Hoodening used to be a Christmas custom, but in Canterbury the Hop Hoodening now takes place on the first Saturday in September, when the morris men and country dancers perform outside the cathedral in the presence of the Hop Queen. They later visit Wickhambreaux before returning to Canterbury.

●

112

COLNE ESTUARY
ESSEX

South of Colchester.
Tourist Information Centre, 1 Queen Street, Colchester (01206) 712920.

•

*Oyster Proclamation
and Feast*

*Oysters have been
cultivated in the Colne
Estuary since Roman
times, and perhaps
earlier still, and the
rights to the Colne
Fishery have belonged
since the 12th century to
Colchester Corporation.
In September each year
the Mayor and
Councillors of
Colchester, in full
regalia, sail by fishing
boat to the oyster beds,
where a proclamation is
read out, affirming
Colchester's rights. A
loyal toast is drunk in
gin and the assembled
company eat gingerbread
after which the Mayor
lowers the first oyster
dredge of the new season
and eats the first oyster
brought up (whatever its
condition). Later, in
October, the mayor and
guests tuck in to an
elaborate oyster feast.*

•

The small island of Mersea sits at the mouth of the River Colne. Its west side is a busy yachting centre, its east side quiet countryside fringed by saltmarshes, mudflats and shingle. This is an important site for wildlife, which find rich pickings here. Arm yourself with binoculars and take a gentle walk to watch the wonderful variety of wildfowl and waders in the Nature Conservancy Council Reserve. Then make for Cudmore Grove Country Park to enjoy 35 acres of grassy open space with picnic spots and access to a pleasant stretch of beach. Back along the B1025, 4 miles inland is Fingringhoe Wick, a Norfolk Naturalists' Trust reserve on the west bank of the Colne Estuary. A marvellous place for birdwatching, it has an interpretation centre and marked nature trails. Just south of Fingringhoe is Abberton Reservoir, sanctuary for thousands of overwintering birds. Another absolute must for bird enthusiasts, this site boasts possibly the largest reservoir population of wildfowl in Britain. There is no direct access, but views from the road are excellent.

IN EASY REACH Ancient Colchester stands to the north on the River Colne. It was once a Roman garrison town where Boudicca swept down and slaughtered the occupying forces. See the old Roman walls and gate. Colchester Castle is a great squat Norman stronghold, now a museum with fascinating archaeological finds. Other museums to visit are the Hollytrees, an elegant Georgian townhouse; Tymperleys Clock Museum, the Museum of Natural History; Holy Trinity Church, with its displays of folk history and crafts; and the Minories Art Gallery, a Georgian house with exhibitions of contemporary arts and crafts. Elaborately gabled Bourne Mill, off the B1025 in the south of the town, is a 16th-century fishing lodge converted to a mill, now restored to working order.

113

DIDCOT RAILWAY CENTRE
OXFORDSHIRE

On the A4130, off the A34, south of Oxford.
Tourist Information Centre, 8 Market Place, Abingdon (01235) 522711.

The Great Western Railway transformed Didcot in the 1840s, when Brunel built his famous line to the west and the village became a stopping point for the great trains thundering to Bristol, South Wales and the Midlands. Today the town's Railway Centre celebrates that golden age of the mighty GWR, with its magnificent working museum of locomotives, coaches and other rolling stock. The huge collection covers 100 years of steam railway, from the boom days of the 1850s to nationalisation in the 1950s. Many weekends have special 'working' days when you can enjoy the sight, sound and soot of engines in steam, and even take a ride on a restored train.

IN EASY REACH Abingdon, north of Didcot off the A34, is an old market town and once county town of Berkshire. The 17th-century County Hall, built by Wren's master mason, is the scene of Abingdon's peculiar bun-throwing ceremony – to mark coronations and other royal occasions, town councillors stand on the roof and toss buns to the assembled townsfolk. Inside the hall is Abingdon Museum of local history and geology.

*Both young and old can
enjoy the nostalgia of old
steam trains and
carriages at Didcot*

South-east of Abingdon, off the A415, is the Pendon Museum in Long Wittenham. Nostalgic scenes of rural England in the 1930s are miniaturised here with tiny thatched cottages and minutely accurate model trains. Clifton Hampden, on the A415 from Abingdon, is a beautiful timber-framed village on the Thames. John Masefield lived here and Jerome K Jerome knew it well.

114

LEONARDSLEE GARDEN
WEST SUSSEX

*At Lower Beeding, which is at the junction of the A279 and A281, south-east of
Horsham. Tourist Information Centre, 9 Causeway, Horsham (01403) 211661.*

It is debatable whether autumn leaves or spring-flowering shrubs are the best thing about Leonardslee valley gardens. Both blaze with unbelievable warmth. Much of the woodland is natural – mature oak, beech and silver birch from the ancient forest of St Leonard that borders the garden. Other trees include huge specimen cedars, pines and maples, planted on the sides of the ravine and reflected in a series of little lakes. If you come first for autumn colour, come again in spring for the acres of camellias, azaleas, magnolias and rhododendrons, many raised here at

Leonardslee, that smother the valley with dense bright flowers and dark green leaves. Leonardslee is also home to deer and wallabies.

IN EASY REACH The Leonardslee lakes are really hammer-ponds, dug over 300 years ago and remnants of the huge iron industry that make the Weald the 'Black Country' of Tudor times. So much of the primaeval forest that covered the South-East, known to the Saxons as Anderida, was felled to fuel iron-smelting that Queen Elizabeth was petitioned by her shipbuilders to curb it. What is left of the forest includes St Leonard's, between the A264 and the A23 south-west of Crawley; Worth, around the B2036, east of Crawley; and Tilgate, which has a forest park, on the southern edge of Crawley.

Near Handcross, to the north-east of Leonardslee, is another gorgeous forest-ridge garden, Nymans, off the B2114. Lavishly planted with rare trees and shrubs, this one is of pure romance: roses tumbling over a ruin, white pigeons on a gazebo roof, huge waxy magnolias, and a heather garden. Nearby is High Beeches with twenty acres of landscaped woodland and water gardens. Borde Hill Garden, north of Haywards Heath and further east still, has much the same mixture as Nymans, but the formal gardens lead on to wilder woods and glades.

Glyndebourne House (below) is the romantic setting for the world-famous opera festival, now held in a fine new concert hall in the grounds

— 115 —

LEWES
EAST SUSSEX

Tourist Information Centre, 187 High Street (01273) 483448.

Except on 5 November, when it goes berserk, Lewes is a peaceful old place, whose Georgian houses line steep streets. It's a good place for browsing in the numerous antique shops and bookshops. Until the county was split in two in 1974, it was the county town of Sussex.

The ruins of the Norman castle occupy a dominating position on high ground with commanding views. Close by is the 16th-century half-timbered Barbican House, now an archaeological museum. Another place not to miss is Anne of Cleve's House (she did not actually live here, though she did own it). Built early in the 16th century and retaining much of its Tudor atmosphere, it has been turned into a good museum of Sussex folk life – arts and crafts, farming and industry – with a particularly impressive section on the old Sussex iron industry and some fine pieces of decorated ironwork. Bull House, in the High Street, was once the home of Tom Paine, the 18th-century radical agitator, and as a boy John Evelyn, the 17th-century diarist, lived in Southover Grange.

IN EASY REACH At Rodmell, to the south of Lewes on the banks of the River Ouse, is Monk's House, where writers Leonard and Virginia Woolf lived. Here the South Downs Way long-distance footpath crosses the river. Follow it eastwards for Firle Place, home of the Gage family for 500 years, and further east for Charleston Farmhouse where Virginia's sister Vanessa kept house with Clive Bell and artist Duncan Grant, visited by most of the Bloomsbury Group of writers and painters.

At Glynde, off the A27 east of Lewes, are both Glynde Place, a charming Elizabethan manor house, and its better-known neighbour, Glyndebourne, where John Christie opened the 'opera-house in the country' in 1934.

•

Bonfire Night

Lewes literally explodes on Bonfire Night (always 5 November, bar Sundays) with elaborate fancy-dress parades, lighted flares, bands, fireworks and mammoth bonfires.

•

— 116 —

MARSH FARM
ESSEX

At South Woodham Ferrers, off the A130, 5 miles north-east of Wickford. Tourist Information Centre, High Street Precinct, Southend-on-Sea (01702) 215120.

On flat Essex farmland along a finger of the Crouch estuary stands Marsh Farm Country Park. Here you can wander through 320 acres of parkland run as a modern working livestock farm. Waymarked farm trails allow you to admire herds of cattle and flocks of sheep, and you can also inspect the commercial piggery. The nature reserve yields glimpses of Essex wildlife, or there is a breezy walk along the sea wall to watch waters busy with seabirds and dinghies. Make for the visitor centre to view displays, and if it is wet eat lunch in the indoor picnic area.

IN EASY REACH Five miles south is Rayleigh Windmill on the A1015. Perched on an 11th-century castle mound (nothing remains of the castle), the mill is now a local history museum (limited opening only). Southend-on-Sea, to the south-east, is a traditional seaside town with a 7-mile seafront, award-winning gardens, illuminations, adventure rides, quaint old cottages and modern museums and the only planetarium in the south east outside London. The town's major attraction is the world's longest pleasure pier which has its own museum.

— 117 —

NATIONAL MOTOR MUSEUM
HAMPSHIRE

At Beaulieu, on the B3056, on the southern fringes of the New Forest. Tourist Information Centre at the museum (01590) 612345.

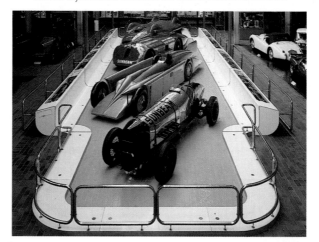

Record-breaking cars in the National Motor Museum. The 350 horsepower Sunbeam (front) broke the land-speed record in 1925 at 150mph, but by 1964 Donald Campbell had to drive at 403mph in Bluebird Proteus *to break the same record*

In the early days of driving, before and after World War I, motoring was very much the preserve of the rich and aristocratic. Sleek, glamourous and powerful, the cars matched their owners, and cavalcades of these luxury conveyances of a vanished age can be seen at certain times of year promenading in the grounds of Lord Montagu's historic estate at Beaulieu (pronounced Bewley). The National Motor Museum, the biggest and best of its kind, has a collection of 250 vehicles, and there is a special 'Wheels' exhibit, depicting the history of motoring – and its possible future – through which visitors are carried in moving 'pods'. Also to be relished in one of the country's most satisfying tourist spots (and, what's more, it stays open all year) are Beaulieu Abbey and an exhibition on monastic life, Lord Montagu's stately home – Palace House – and its gardens, veteran car and bus rides, a model railway and a monorail.

IN EASY REACH Down the beautiful Beaulieu River (boat trips are available) is Bucklers Hard. The Maritime museum tells the story of what was formerly a major shipbuilding centre, for a hundred years after 1745, and scenes from 18th-century life have been re-created in the cottages. On the opposite side of the river, Exbury Gardens are noted for their unrivalled rhododendrons and azaleas. Further east, the Lepe Country Park commands fine views of the busy Solent shipping and across to the Isle of Wight.

Lymington (south-west from Beaulieu on the B3054) was an important port, then a thriving salt town and, in the late 18th century, a bathing resort. It has an attractive High Street, and a church of interest. To the south, sticking out on a promontory and reached across a shingle beach, is Hurst Castle, built in 1544 to defend the Solent approaches.

●

Auto Jumble

Of the numerous events held during the tourist season at the National Motor Museum at Beaulieu, one of the most pleasing is the annual Auto Jumble in September, when hundreds of items to do with motoring go on sale, including some cars and motorbikes. There is a similar Boat Jumble for boating impedimenta in April, with small boats for sale.

●

118

THE NEW FOREST
HAMPSHIRE

Tourist Information Centre,
Main Car Park, Lyndhurst (01703) 282269.

'New' is a relative term and the New Forest was created as a hunting preserve for William the Conqueror 900 years ago: though the idea that villages were destroyed to make it is untrue. Today the forest is a National Nature Reserve of some 90,000 acres, a varied landscape of woods and glades, heaths, moors and bogs, with villages dotted about here and there. The forest is populated with deer and ponies and masses of birds (Dartford warbler, hen harrier, etc). On the insect front, there's a type of cicada which lives nowhere else in Britain. The oak is the traditional forest tree, with regiments of beeches and birches to keep it company, and conifers, which have been planted here since the 18th century. The monarch of the forest's trees is the Knightwood Oak, close to the Bolderwood Ornamental Drive.

Nearby (a mile or so north-east along the A35) is the Holidays Hill Reptiliary, where you can see a sample of the forest's reptiles, frogs and snakes, and the Rhinefield Ornamental Drive. To the north-west are the Bolderwood Walks, laid out by the Forestry Commission, and a deer sanctuary.

Lyndhurst, the 'capital' of the New Forest is dominated by its Victorian Gothic church, with fine Pre-Raphaelite stained glass, and the grave of Alice Liddell (the original Alice in Wonderland). Minstead, off the A31 to the north, is a delightful village, whose church boasts a Georgian interior. To the north-west, and well signposted off the A31, is the Rufus Stone, which marks the spot where William Rufus was shot and killed by an arrow – accidentally or not.

Two other enticing attractions in the area are the New Forest Butterfly Farm, near Ashurst, for exotic butterflies and moths; and the highly enjoyable Paultons Park at Ower, with its acres of gardens and aviaries, where a village-life centre brings the past back to life and craftsmen ply their trades. There's also a gypsy museum, working waterwheel, farm shop, gift shop and plenty of rides and attractions for children.

New Forest Round-Ups

The ancestors of the ponies which wander picturesquely in the New Forest today, living on grass and gorse, used to work on the local small-holdings. They were used for rounding up cattle, pulling carts and traps, and carrying the children to school. The Society for the Improvement of New Forest Ponies, founded in 1891, held annual pony races and imported Welsh stallions to ginger up the breed, but since 1938 no foreign blood has been allowed to intrude on the New Forest strain.

In late summer and autumn, the round-ups or 'drifts' are held, when the local commoners ride over an area of the forest and drive as many ponies as they can into a pound. The ponies are then wormed and those of them which are to be sold or kept on the small-holdings for the winter are loaded into lorries. Pony sales (see below) are held several times a year. It is no kindness to feed the ponies by the way, as this only helps to draw them to the roads, where they are liable to be injured or killed in accidents – and they can bite and kick!

--- **119** ---

ROMNEY MARSH
KENT

Isolated St Thomas Becket Church at Fairford, about 8 miles west of New Romney

Between Rye and Hythe either side of the A259. Tourist Information Centres: 2 Littlestone Road, New Romney (01679) 64044 (seasonal opening) and Harbour Street, Folkestone (01303) 258594.

Events around Romney Marsh

At Rye, to the south-west of the Marsh, a week-long festival is held each September. The emphasis is on classical music, performed by professionals, but folk music and jazz, plays and special events for children also take place. On the other side of the Marsh, every alternate August, a half mile stretch of the Royal Military Canal at Hythe is the stage for one of Britain's most enchanting events, the Venetian Fête. Thousands of spectators come to enjoy the parade of decorated boats, some with humorous tableaux or with scenes from the history of Kent. The floating procession is led by the Mayors of the Cinque Ports in full regalia. As twilight draws on, the boats go east again, all illuminated, to create a fairyland scene.

Where the Wealden hills level down to the sea, lies the lonely expanse of Romney Marsh, dotted with sheep and isolated villages, reclaimed from the sea by drains and ditches first dug in Roman times. It is a remote and a secretive place, stretching from the Royal Military Canal, built against Napoleon's threatened invasion, to the desolate shingle wastes of Dungeness. Strictly speaking there are three marshes – Romney, Denge and Walland – but they merge into one land of legends and smugglers' tales.

To explore the shingly seashore, catch a train on the miniature Romney, Hythe and Dymchurch Railway, running 14 miles from Hythe via New Romney (where there is a large indoor exhibition) to Dungeness. You will pass mile upon mile of shingle, two lighthouses (one new, one old), a nature reserve and bird observatory, and a giant nuclear power station.

The marsh churches – Snargate, Burmarsh, Lydd, Brookland (see the curiously detached, tiered wooden belfry and the font), New Romney, and many more – are the glory of the Marsh. Find time too, for the Martello towers, built like the canal as defence against Napoleon. The one at Dymchurch is well preserved and has a rooftop mounting for a heavy gun.

IN EASY REACH High on the former cliff, looking over the Marsh, is Lympne, known for the castle where Archbishop Thomas Becket once lived, and John Aspinall's Port Lympne Wild Animal Park and Mansion. The house is a 20th-century classic, and the wildlife park has rhinos, elephants and some of Aspinall's famous lions and tigers.

--- **120** ---

SHAW'S CORNER
HERTFORDSHIRE

At Ayot St Lawrence, off junction 6 of the A1(M). Tourist Information Centre, The Campus, Welwyn Garden City (01707) 332880.

A conventional middle-class home for a man who prided himself on outraging bourgeois opinion, Shaw's Corner was George Bernard Shaw's home for the last half of his long, life, his 'final earthplace' as he called it. He bought it in 1906, when he was 50, and died there in 1950 at 94. The rooms on the ground floor remain as they were in his lifetime and the visitor can see the portrait of the great man by Augustus John and his bust by Rodin, his hats, his spectacles and his pen, and the desk from which he fired off salvoes crackling with liveliness and wit. In the garden is the scruffy little shed where he liked to work in the summer. It was in the dining room that he died, and his ashes were scattered in the garden.

IN EASY REACH To the north-east stands Knebworth House, the ancestral home of the Lyttons, rebuilt in fantastically gargoyled Victorian-Gothic in 1843 by Sir Edward Bulwer-Lytton, the novelist who wrote *The Last Days of Pompeii*. The British Raj exhibition is related to Lord Lytton, the novelist's son, who was Viceroy of India. The interior of the house and the gardens were partly redesigned by Sir Edwin Lutyens who was Lord Lytton's son-in-law.

Near Whitwell, to the west is the 1730s formal garden at St Paul's Walden Bury, where the Queen Mother grew up. It was restored by Sir David Bowes-Lyon, her younger brother. Luton Hoo in Bedfordshire, outside Luton, was rebuilt in the 1900s by Mewes and Davis, the architects of London's Ritz Hotel, for Sir Julius Wernher, the diamond magnate. With a park by 'Capability' Brown, it is specially distinguished for its art collection, its astonishing Fabergé jewellery and its mementoes of the Russian Tsars.

121

TUNBRIDGE WELLS
KENT

Tourist Information Centre, The Old Fish Market, The Pantiles
(01892) 515675.

The prettiest part of the town lies round the old High Street and The Pantiles, the famous colonnaded street bordering the iron-impregnated spring which Lord North discovered here in 1606. The fashionable world soon flocked to sample the healthful waters, camping on the common until hotels and boarding-houses were built. The town continued to flourish as a spa until late in the 19th century. You can still sample the spring water, though may not like the taste, and some of the pan-baked tiles that paved round the spring in the 18th century can be seen in the museums. For a taste of the social life in Georgian times visit A Day at the Wells. Pause at the church of King Charles the Martyr, and then head up the hill to the Museum and Art Gallery in the civic centre, which is noted for its collection of Tunbridge Ware inlaid woodwork. The huge sandstone outcrop known as the High Rocks, to the west of the town centre, has weathered into curious shapes and grottoes. There are many good walks here and at Groombridge, to the south-west where the Sussex Border Path, the Wealdway and the Forest Way all meet.

19th-century Tunbridge Ware showing how The Pantiles looked at that time

IN EASY REACH Take the A26 north for Tonbridge, to see the ruined castle on its mound and take a narrowboat trip on the river from Castle Walk. At Matfield, north-east of Tunbridge Wells, the gardens of Crittenden House are noted for autumn colour, and nearby Brenchley is an attractive village with Tudor houses. The 13th-century sandstone church, restored in the mid-19th century, has a beautifully carved rood-screen.

122

WADDESDON MANOR
BUCKINGHAMSHIRE

At Waddesdon, on the A41.
Tourist Information Centre, County Hall, Walton Street, Aylesbury (01296) 382308.

The house was built by Ferdinand de Rothschild in the 1870s and 1880s, in extravagant imitation of a Renaissance French château, to house his collection of furniture, porcelain and paintings. As well as English 18th-century portraits, there are all sorts of small things to look out for: old buttons and lace, birdcages, family photos and mementoes. There's also a sizeable aviary in the grounds and two wonderful fountains.

Recently reopened to the public after 3 years of restoration, this National Trust property has introduced a ticketing system to avoid crowding. You need more than one visit to take in the treasures on view in this great Rothschild pile outside Aylesbury. The clocks alone strike wonder to the heart, and the luxuriant array of paintings, panelling, furniture, carpets and china has visitors literally gasping.

IN EASY REACH A little to the west, off the A41, Wotton House (open till September only) was built in 1704 and refurbished inside by Sir John Soane in 1820. The grounds are by 'Capability' Brown. To the south, of the A418 at Lower Winchendon is Nether Winchendon House, dating from Tudor times and altered in the 18th century. (It is only open by appointment in the autumn). The attractive village of Long Crendon nearby boasts a 14th-century court-house. South-east of Aylesbury, near Wendover, is Coombe Hill which provides a fine viewpoint on the edge of the Chilterns.

●

Buckinghamshire Show

At Weedon Park, near Aylesbury, lovers of the traditional agricultural county show can revel in the delights of the annual Buckinghamshire Show (held in September), with its competitive classes for horses, cattle and sheep. There are also horticultural and domestic competitions for such rival items as cakes and biscuits, home-grown vegetables and home-made wine. Trade stands and craft stalls are further attractions of this show, which has been going since the 1830s.

●

123

WEALD AND DOWNLAND OPEN AIR MUSEUM

WEST SUSSEX

At Singleton, on the A286, north of Chichester.
Tourist Information Centre, 29a South Street, Chichester (01243) 775888.

Steam Threshing and Autumn Ploughing

*A*utumn, after the harvest is safely gathered in, is the time for threshing the corn and ploughing the fields, ready for next year's crop. Visitors to the Open Air Museum's special Steam Threshing and Autumn Ploughing event in October watch the ancient steam threshing machines gobbling and racketing at their work. They mechanised one of the most exhausting, monotonous and grim tasks in the agricultural labourer's calendar, hated by almost everyone in the land, but the labourers fiercely opposed their introduction because the machines took away their work. The ploughing is tackled by teams of horses and by vintage tractors.

*B*uilding by building – over 35 to date, including a toll cottage and treadwheel – the museum is rescuing old houses and workplaces due to be demolished and rebuilding them here as an open-air museum of regional architecture, spread like a village over 40 acres of Downland fields and woods. On a warm day you can feel the coolness in a 15th-century farmhouse or picnic near a charcoal burner's camp, but on most typical autumn days, the heat in the working smithy might be preferable. Other attractions include the village school, and a working mill where flour is ground.

IN EASY REACH The neighbouring estate, also on the A286, includes West Dean Gardens, the grounds of a crafts college that was formerly the home of eccentric, millionaire art collector Edward James. See if you can spot the glass-fibre trees – just one of his 'surrealist jokes'.

Over the next hillside, reached from the A286 or the A285, is Goodwood Racecourse, scene of 'Glorious Goodwood', the July race meeting-cum-social event. Beside the racecourse is The Trundle, a 700ft hill topped with Iron Age earthworks and a Neolithic camp. Southwards lies Goodwood Country Park and the rolling landscaped grounds surrounding Goodwood House (limited opening in autumn). Said to be one of James Wyatt's 'dull designs', it was built in flint for the Duke of Richmond about 1790. He planned an octagon but only completed three sides. The contents, however, are superb and include numerous Old Masters, fine furniture, porcelain and tapestries.

Kingley Vale Nature Reserve and ancient yew forest, planted – legend has it – by Druids, lies some 6 miles west of Goodwood, off the B2141. It is Europe's largest yew forest and is now a National Nature Reserve.

124

WINDSOR CASTLE

BERKSHIRE

Tourist Information Centre, Thames Street, Windsor (01753) 852010.

Events in Windsor

*C*arriage driving is a young but swiftly growing sport, whose yearly round of competitions and tests culminates in the World Carriage Driving Championships, held in September in Windsor Great Park. The three-day event involves a dressage competition, a 16-mile marathon through the park beset by obstacles and hazards, and finally precision driving tests – manoeuvring horses and carriages through cones. Over at the other side of the year, the Royal Windsor Horse Show has been held under royal patronage in May since 1943. Besides the standard jumping competitions, there is a musical ride by the Household Cavalry and more music from the massed bands of the Brigade of Guards.

*T*he enormous fortress which dominates Windsor and the country round it is the largest inhabited castle in the world. It has been one of the principal residences of the sovereigns of England since the days of William the Conqueror, who built it, and almost every king and queen since his time has taken a hand in rebuilding. The general effect the castle makes today is owed mainly to Sir Jeffry Wyattville, who altered it for George IV.

In 1993 a fire at the Castle destroyed a number of both private and state rooms – St George's Hall, the Grand Reception Room and the Private Chapel all suffered damage. Visitors can view the extensive restoration work which will take some years to complete. It is essential not to miss St George's Chapel. Dating from the 15th and 16th centuries, it boasts some of the finest fan vaulting in the world, the helms and banners of knights and the tombs of Henry VII and Charles I. Then there are the state apartments, with their paintings, carvings, armour and porcelain, and Queen Mary's doll's house.

IN EASY REACH Windsor Great Park is a delight, with its gardens and woods, deer and waterfowl, the 3-mile Long Walk created by Charles II, the beautiful 150-acre lake called Virginia Water, fashioned in the 18th century, and Savill Garden with its 20 lovely acres of flowers. The Crown Jewels of the World exhibition, displaying replicas of many royal and imperial jewels, can be found in Peascod Street, and the Combermere Barracks in St Leonard's Road is home to the Household Cavalry museum.

125

BRIGHTON
EAST SUSSEX

Tourist Information Centre, 10 Bartholomew Square (01273) 323755.

If ever one man's spirit pervades a town it must surely be King George IV, chuckling over Brighton. It had already earned its fame when George, then the Prince Regent, bought a 'farmhouse' in The Steine in 1784. But it was the roly-poly prince who really gave Brighton the racy style and fashion that made it so popular, and he would doubtless have approved when, in 1981, Brighton became the first seaside resort with an official nude bathing beach.

Sea-bathing had been declared good for the health in 1750 by a local doctor, Richard Russell, and gradually the little, seaswept village of Brighthelmstone was transformed into a bustling resort. The fishermen's modest cottages are now the boutiques and antiques shops of the Lanes. The Prince Regent had his 'farmhouse' turned into the sumptuous, Oriental-style Royal Pavilion – quite possibly the most bizarre sight in Europe from outside dazzling with gold-plate and chandeliers, inside. The prince's indoor riding school and stables are now the Dome concert hall and beside it, with its entrance in Church Street, is Brighton Museum and Art Gallery, famous for its outstanding collection of Art Nouveau and Art Deco, and costume gallery. Just round the corner is the lovely old Theatre Royal.

Along the seafronts of Brighton and adjoining Hove, are some beautiful Regency squares and terraces, a reminder of past elegance, and the ravaged West Pier. From the other pier, the Palace Pier, and the Sea Life Centre (home to everything from worms to octopus, from sharks to stingrays and hundreds of fish), the Victorian, electric Volks Railway runs (in summer) to Black Rock. Beyond Black Rock is the marina, well worth a visit to see the massive harbour arms sheltering hundreds of yachts and cruisers.

For quieter, more serious moments try Preston Park and Manor – a glimpse of life in an Edwardian gentlemen's house; Booth Museum of Natural History – hundreds of birds and animal skeletons; Hove's Italianate museum of art; and the Engineerium steam museum in a Victorian pumping station.

IN EASY REACH Close behind Brighton are the South Downs, with Jack and Jill, two windmills, standing sentinel on top at Clayton. Join the South Downs Way Footpath here and walk eastwards to Ditchling Beacon with marvellous views all the way, out to sea and inland; below is pretty Ditchling village, noted as an arts and crafts centre, with a 13th-century church, small museum, tea-shops and a vineyard open for visits and tastings. Or turn west for more viewpoints at Newtimber Hill and Devil's Dyck – a dramatic cleft in the Downs, dug, so local legend says, by the Devil to let the sea in and flood Sussex's over-many churches.

Four miles along the seafront (east on the A259) is Rottingdean village, reputedly a smugglers' hideout. Don't miss stained glass in St Margaret's Church by Burne-Jones, or the Rudyard Kipling memorabilia in the Grange: artist and novelist both lived for a time in the High Street.

Events in Brighton

There's always plenty to do in Brighton, even in the heart of winter, and always something going on. One of the best-known regular events, certain of press coverage every year is the London to Brighton Veteran Car Run (see below) early in November, under the auspices of the Royal Automobile Club. A 'veteran' car is one made before 1904. The run starts in Hyde Park in London and the finishing line, all those panting and wheezing miles later, is on Madeira Drive on Brighton's seafront. The run commemorates the motorist's 'emancipation day', 14 November 1896, when the Locomotive Act was repealed. This was the law which restricted the speed of the first motor cars to 4mph and required each one to be preceded by a man 60yds ahead carrying a warning red flag. Other regular Brighton events include an excellent arts festival in May, the Brighton Carnival in July and crafts fairs throughout the year.

---------- **126** ----------

COTSWOLD WILDLIFE PARK
OXFORDSHIRE

Off the A361, south of Burford.
Tourist Information Centre, The Brewery, Sheep Street, Burford (01993) 823558.

Set amongst 200 acres of landscaped gardens and parkland surrounding a Gothic-style manor house, the Cotswold Wildlife Park is home to a large and varied collection of animals, birds, reptiles, fish and invertebrates from all over the world. Rhinos, zebras and ostriches can be seen roaming in large paddocks surrounded by unobtrusive moats, whilst leopards and tigers inhabit the grassed enclosures. The sheltered old walled garden houses many tropical birds such as hornbills and penguins (fed at 11am and 4pm daily except Friday) and here mammals such as monkeys and otters can also be seen at play. Fascinating tropical plants – giant banana palms, sugar canes and exotic passion flowers – flourish in the tropical house alongside colourful birds. Youngsters will appreciate the large adventure playground, the animal brass rubbing centre situated in the house, and the children's farmyard. Other attractions include a reptile house, aquarium, insect house and fruit bat exhibit.

IN EASY REACH Burford is a golden Cotswold medieval wool town off the A40, worth visiting for its steep old high street, stone-built houses with mullioned windows, pretty stone bridge and massive old church. North-east of Burford, off the A361, lies Swinbrook. Its church is lined with tiers of monuments to a wealthy local family, the Fettiplaces. Their effigies lie on their sides, neatly stacked on shelves. Swinbrook was also home to the Mitford family, and Nancy Mitford was buried here. At Minster Lovell, further east, the romantic ruins of the great house of the Lovells stand by the banks of the Windrush, haunted by ghosts and tragic legends.

---------- **127** ----------

DOVER
KENT

Tourist Information Centre, Townwall Street (01304) 205108.

Dover Castle, at the eastern end of the town, overlooking the port, is easily the most important coastal defence-work in the country and one of Europe's most strategic strongholds. The sheer size of its massive keep and curtain walls is breathtaking. The site, fortified from the Iron Age onwards by Romans, Saxons, Normans, and later builders, has a rich and complex past. Inside are trophies, cannons, armouries and Hellfire Corner – underground tunnels used in both world wars. Outside is a Roman lighthouse and Saxon church. The White Cliffs Experience in Market Square, uses stunning high-tech effects to tell the turbulent history of the area. Also to be seen is the Old Town Gaol in Dover Town Hall

IN EASY REACH Walks over the cliffs lead to touching memorials – to the Dover Patrol and to Bleriot (the first man to fly the Channel, in 1909) – and the Pines Garden, 6 acres of trees and specimen shrubs overlooking St Margaret's Bay. Further north along the coast are Walmer and Deal Castles. Walmer, built in Tudor rose shape by Henry VIII, is the Lord Warden of the Cinque Ports' official residence, with relics of past wardens, including the Duke of Wellington's (leather) boots. Deal Castle is similar but bigger, and the town has an early-19th-century time-ball tower containing a 'semaphore to satellites' exhibition.

---------- **128** ----------

GREENWICH
LONDON

Tourist Information Centre, 46 Greenwich Church Street, Greenwich 0181-858 6376.

To see Greenwich at its best, as it was meant to be seen when Queen's House was built for James I's Queen Anne, and King's House for Charles II, you need to approach from the Thames. Regular river boats (covered and heated in winter) from central London may be less romantic than royal barges, but the view is the same: the full sweep of the river bank and the magnificent 17th-century buildings. Inigo Jones, Wren, Vanbrugh and Hawksmoor all took a hand in making them some of the best in Europe.

King's House is now part of the Royal Naval College, visit the galleried chapel, where carol concerts are held and the ornate Painted Hall, where Lord Nelson's body lay in state in 1805. Queen's House is furnished as it would have been in the 17th century when Henrietta Maria, widow of Charles I, lived there. The National Maritime Museum has an impressive collection of boats, barges, models and uniforms, a fitting tribute to Nelson, Drake, Cook and others.

Greenwich as seen from the Old Royal Observatory

The old tea-clipper *Cutty Sark* can be seen in dry dock by the pier, masts towering over the town along with the little ketch, *Gipsy Moth IV*, that Sir Francis Chichester sailed solo round the world.

Up the hill, in Greenwich Park, are the Old Royal Observatory (museum of navigation and astronomical instruments) with the Meridian Line quaintly slicing through it, and the Ranger's House – an 18th-century villa housing 17th-century portraits and the Dolmetsch family's early musical instruments.

IN EASY REACH With time to wander, walk on over Blackheath (for panoramic views) or down into Deptford. Here St Nicholas's Church has the grave of the celebrated playwright Christopher Marlowe, mysteriously murdered in a tavern brawl in 1593, some said to silence him as a spy.

129

KEW GARDENS (ROYAL BOTANIC GARDENS)
SURREY

Close to Kew Bridge. Tourist Information Centre, Old Town Hall, Whittaker Avenue, Richmond 0181-940 9125.

Kew Gardens remain a tonic to the eye and heart at all times of year, even in winter. At the centre of the 300-acre site, facing the pond, rises the noble Palm House of the 1840s, designed by Decimus Burton and made of iron and glass, a kind of miniature Crystal Palace. Burton also designed the Temperate House, as well as the main gates on Kew Green. Bluebells and rhododendrons, roses and water lilies, lilacs and magnolias, a rock garden and an aquatic garden, magnificent trees. – Kew has them all. An additional attraction is the carefully landscaped Princess of Wales Conservatory with its complex computerised systems to control heat, light and humidity, enabling a variety of plant habitats to be viewed within one building. Kew Palace (closed in winter) and the 18th-century church of St Anne on Kew Green are also worth a visit, as are the 19th-century pumping engines in the Kew Bridge Engines Museum.

The Rose Garden and Palm House at Kew. Decimus Burton built the magnificent glasshouse in 1844 to house palms from all over the world

IN EASY REACH At Isleworth, a little way up the Thames, Syon House (closed in winter) looks austere outside and is astoundingly magnificent within. Here is perhaps the finest set of Robert Adam rooms in existence, vibrant with colour, elegance and charm. Also here are a notable garden centre, conservatory, butterfly house, and grounds stretching down to the river. There's another Robert Adam blockbuster at Osterley Park, north of the A4, with a colossal portico and a lovely old stable block. Ham House, outside Richmond, is an outstanding Stuart house which contains much of its original 17th-century furniture.

LONDON

Tourist Information Centres: Victoria Station Forecourt, SW1, Selfridges, Oxford Street, W1 and Liverpool Street Underground Station, EC2. All telephone 0171-730 3488.

London never has a shortage of events and occasions at any stage of the year. In March the Ideal Home Exhibition tells you how you ought to live. Easter brings out cheerful crowds to enjoy the traditional fair on Hampstead Heath, the Easter Parade in Battersea Park and – kingpin of the Easter attractions – the Harness Horse Parade in Regent's Park, where tiny Shetland ponies and gigantic Clydesdales alike show off their finery.
Somewhere around the turn of March and April the Oxford and Cambridge Boat Race oars away from the stakeboats above Putney Bridge. In May or early June, blooms and blossoms in multitudes are covetously admired by crowds at the Chelsea Flower Show. June sees stately royal ceremony when the colour is trooped on Horse Guards parade, and around the end of the month the tennis championships make a spectacle of themselves at Wimbledon.
In July the Royal Tournament at Earl's Court brings thrills, spills and a feast of naval and military nostalgia. The Horse of the Year Show in September is one of the key occasions in the showjumper's calendar, and in November the City prides itself on the colourful floats and marching bands of the Lord Mayor's Show. Finally in December, at the Royal Smithfield Show, the bellowing of champion bulls bring London's year to an oddly countrified close.

The daffodils lifting their yellow trumpets in Hyde Park in the spring, the jingle of silver-glinting cavalry along The Mall in summer, the dome of St Paul's soaring majestically against a cloudy autumn sky, a string of shabby barges butting through choppy winter water on the Thames. Britain's capital city contains so many sights, experiences, ceremonials and pleasures that to talk of making 'an outing' to London makes little sense. All that this brief treatment of the city can do is pick out some of the highlights and a sprinkling of the less well known, but sometimes equally rewarding attractions.

If you hardly know London at all, a good way to give it a preliminary once-over and get yourself roughly orientated is to take one of the London Transport sightseeing bus tours, which take a couple of hours to tour the principal buildings and points of interest. There are also guided walks, and delightful boat trips of varying lengths on the Thames, starting from Westminster Pier and including a circular 1-hour cruise.

London's most popular draws include the changing of the guard at Buckingham Palace, the Tower of London and Westminster Abbey. The guard is changed at 11.30am in the forecourt of Buckingham Palace by regiments of the Brigade of Guards. The façade of the palace which the public sees was built in 1847, though the building behind it goes back to 1703. In the middle of the road in front of the palace, the gilded figure of Victory surmounts the elaborate memorial to Queen Victoria, completed in 1911.

The Tower, grimly battlemented and moated, is indelibly associated with torture, terror and death. At the heart of it is the White Tower, built for William the Conqueror. The stronghold is especially famous today for its collection of armour and weapons, and even more for the fabulous crown jewels.

Westminster Abbey is where the sovereigns are crowned. Built in the 11th century by Edward the Confessor and enlarged and restored ever since, it contains the most stunning array of tombs and monuments in Britain: from those of Henry VII, Queen Elizabeth and Mary, Queen of Scots, to those of Tennyson and Dickens, Handel, Hardy and Kipling.

Across the road from the abbey, the Houses of Parliament were rebuilt in the 1840s after a disastrous fire. Much older is Westminster Hall, which goes back to the 11th century. Big Ben is, strictly speaking, the name of the giant 3½-ton bell which strikes the hours in the 316ft clock-tower at the northern end of the building. The minute hands on the four faces of the clock are each the height of a double-decker bus.

For a breath of fresh air after this solemnity, you can stroll in St James's Park, which is behind the government buildings along Whitehall. Ducks and pelicans swim and squabble in the lake, while the fountains play. Charles II liked to stride along here, with his dogs around him, smiling at passing citizens as they doffed their hats to him.

A life-like waxwork of Charles II can be found in Madame Tussaud's, up near the top of Baker Street (shades of Sherlock Holmes!). The great waxworks collection came to England from France in 1802. It was long celebrated for its Chamber of Horrors, but addicts of the gruesome now sing the praises of the London Dungeon, in Tooley Street, south of the river, where scenes of torture and agonising death are vividly re-created.

Returning to the light of day, there's a bird sanctuary in Hyde Park, where more than 90 species have been recorded. They are undisturbed by the band concerts in the summer. In Trafalgar Square, besides Nelson's Column, there's another bird sanctuary, for enormous numbers of pigeons!

Here too are the National Gallery and the National Portrait Gallery, two of London's numerous and fascinating wet-day retreats. Others are the British Museum, the Tate Gallery, the Wallace Collection in Manchester Square, and the museums complex in South Kensington, including the Victoria and Albert Museum, the Natural History Museum and the Science Museum.

Far right: pomp and ceremony are the order of the day when the Lord Mayor rides through the City in the state coach. It was built in 1757 at a cost of £1,965

Some of the lesser museums are excellent value. In Albert Street, NW1 the little Jewish Museum is crammed with ritual objects, scrolls, lamps, bells and ram's horns. If you're interested in stamps find out all about the Penny Black at the National Postal Museum, King Edward Street. Up the City road is the chapel built for John Wesley in the 1770s and the house he lived in, full of mementoes, while in Gough Square, tucked away behind Fleet Street, is Dr Johnson's House, where the Great Cham lived in the 1750s and where he completed his famous dictionary. In the Barbican complex is the Museum of London, hideous outside, but fascinating inside, with a dramatic diorama depicting the Great Fire.

The City is also of interest for the Wren churches, for some striking modern buildings and above all for St Paul's, masterpiece of Sir Christopher Wren: 'if you seek his monument, look around you'.

And still so many enjoyable things to do and see have been left out – the Nash terraces in Regent's Park, the river views from high up on Tower Bridge, Apsley House where the great Duke of Wellington lived, luxury shopping in Old and New Bond Streets, the spruced-up Covent Garden area with its shops and cafés, the concert halls and galleries on the South Bank – London takes more than a day or two to enjoy, it requires a lifetime!.

The central belt of England stretches from the remote hills along the Welsh Marches to the teeming streets and cheerful pubs of Birmingham and the Black Country – once Britain's industrial heartland – and across the hunting country in Leicestershire and what used to be Rutland to the flat horizons of the Lincolnshire Fens, the Broads in East Anglia and the sea-eroded coastline of Suffolk.

On the way there is certainly no shortage of scenery to delight the eye. In the west are the Shropshire hills and the 'coloured counties' that inspired A E Housman, and the Malvern Hills which Elgar loved. Eastwards lie the heaths and war cemeteries of Cannock Chase, the high country of the Peak District National Park, the dramatic gorge of Dovedale, the remnants of Sherwood Forest and the Charnwood Forest in Leicestershire, and then the rolling Lincolnshire Wolds, the sandy heaths of the Breckland in Norfolk and the bird-haunted dunes and mudflats of the Area of Outstanding Natural Beauty along the North Norfolk coast.

There are great houses, too, in abundance. Warwick Castle, rearing up in grim majesty above the Avon, is one of the most formidable strongholds in all England, and not far away is another tremendous fortress, Kenilworth. Moving from the Middle Ages on to modern times, there could hardly be a stronger contrast than between the medieval simplicity of Stokesay Castle, a rich wool merchant's house in Shropshire, and the pinnacled extravagance of Somerleyton Hall, a wealthy Victorian railway magnate's mansion in Suffolk. In between the two, in date, are some of England's most desirable residences: Burghley House and Blickling Hall from the 16th century; Belton House from the 17th; Holkham Hall from the 18th; Ickworth and Belvoir Castle from the 19th. There are also the unsurpassable splendours of the stately homes of Derbyshire – Chatsworth, Hardwick, Haddon, Melbourne, and Kedleston, where a landscape apparently created by God on a good day was actually designed by Robert Adam.

The theory of gravity struck Newton forcibly at Woolsthorpe Manor in Lincolnshire. Memories of other great figures linger on: Constable in the Stour Valley, Tennyson in Lincolnshire, Dr Johnson at Lichfield, Byron at Newstead Abbey and Benjamin Britten at Aldeburgh.

For gruesome or engaging curiosities, try the reproachful plastercasts of executed murderers' heads at Norwich Castle, tram rides at Crich, or the mighty Wurlitzer cinema organ in the Thursford Collection. You can find out about pork pies at Melton Mowbray and mustard in Norwich. Alternatively, you can watch otters at Earsham or birds at Minsmere, or inspect peculiar things made of shells at Glandford.

There is also a batch of England's noblest cathedrals to savour – Lincoln, Norwich, Ely, Worcester and Southwell. There are handsome old towns to explore: from Ludlow and Bridgnorth to Newark, Buxton, Boston, King's Lynn and Lavenham. The Iron Bridge, now the centre of a complex of fascinating museums, is the country's single most significant monument of the Industrial Revolution. Here, and in the Black Country Museum in Dudley and in the Potteries, you can plunge deep into Britain's industrial past. So no shortage or sameness of pleasures awaits the hopeful visitor.

The Shropshire Union Canal, near Gnosall in Staffordshire. Actually an amalgam of several waterways designed to link the Midlands to the Mersey, its meandering course is now ideal for holiday cruising

Central England & East Anglia

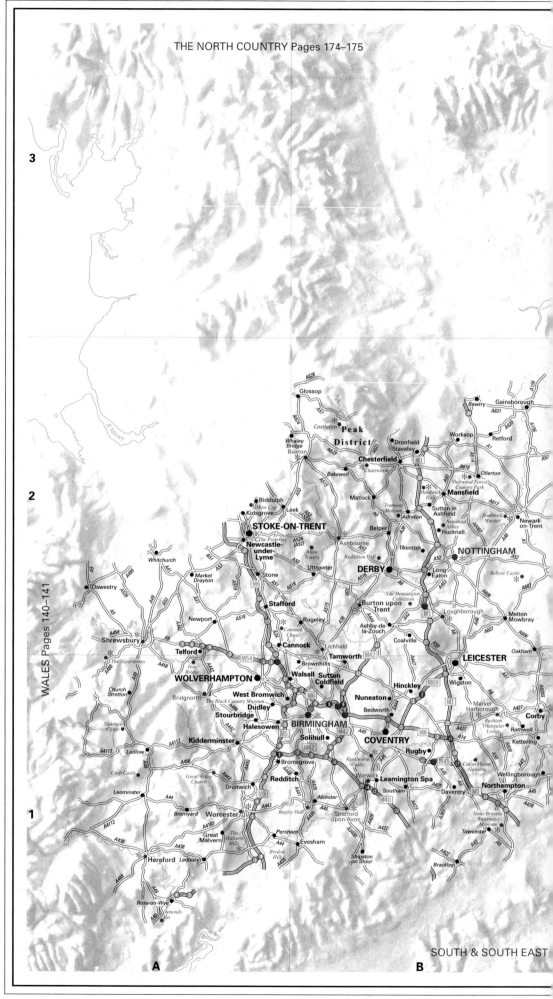

THE NORTH COUNTRY Pages 174–175

3

R. Mersey

2

WALES Pages 140–141

A5

Glossop

Castleton

Peak
District

Whaley
Bridge
Buxton

Bakewell

Dronfield
Staveley

Chesterfield

Chatsworth

Matlock

Bawtry

Gainsborough

Worksop

Retford

Ollerton

Sherwood Forest
Country Park

Hardwick
Hall

Mansfield

Sutton in
Ashfield

Biddulph

Mow Cop

Kidsgrove

Leek

Alfreton

Belper

Southwell
Minster

Newark-
on-Trent

Whitchurch

STOKE-ON-TRENT

The Potteries

Newcastle-
under-
Lyme

Stone

Market
Drayton

Oswestry

A5

Shrewsbury

The Stiperstones

Telford

Iron
Bridge

Church
Stretton

Bridgnorth

Stokesay
Castle

A4113

Ludlow

Croft Castle

Leominster

Bromyard

A4112

Hereford

Ledbury

Ross-on-Wye

Symonds
Yat

Newport

Stafford

Cannock
Chase

Cannock

Rugeley

Lichfield

Brownhills

Walsall

Sutton
Coldfield

WOLVERHAMPTON

West Bromwich

The Black Country Museum

Dudley

Stourbridge

Halesowen

Kidderminster

BIRMINGHAM

Solihull

Bromsgrove

Redditch

Droitwich

Worcester

Pershore

Great
Malvern

The
Malvern
Hills

Bredon
Hill

Evesham

Ragley Hall

Great Witley
Church

Alcester

Stratford
upon Avon

Shipston
on Stour

Alton
Towers

Kedleston Hall

Uttoxeter

Ashbourne

DERBY

Burton upon
Trent

Ashby-de-
la-Zouch

The Donnington
Collection

Tamworth

Nuneaton

Bedworth

COVENTRY

Kenilworth
Castle

Warwick

Leamington Spa

Southam

Ilkeston

Long
Eaton

NOTTINGHAM

Hucknall

Newstead
Abbey

Belvoir Castle

Loughborough

Coalville

LEICESTER

Hinckley

Wigston

Melton
Mowbray

Oakham

Market
Harborough

Rushton
Triangular
Lodge

Rothwell

Kettering

Corby

Wellingborough

Northampton

Daventry

Rugby

Coton Manor
Gardens

Stoke Bruerne
Waterways
Museum

Towcester

Brackley

Tramway
Museum

Hinckley

SOUTH & SOUTH EAST

A

B

1

A special event, described in the text, occurs in the vicinity of the places marked with a star.

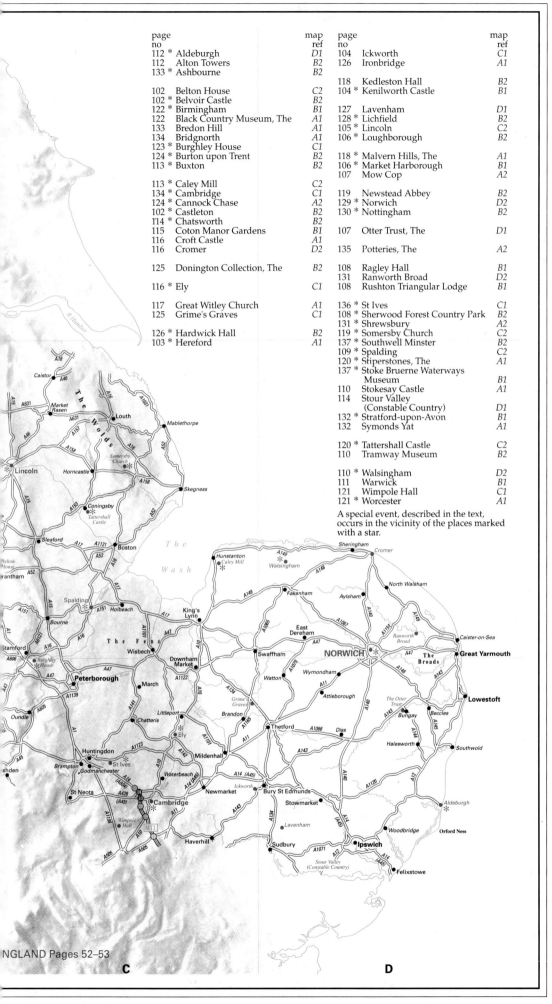

NGLAND Pages 52–53

C

D

Calendar of Events

Spring

EASTER

Pax Cake Custom
Villages near Hereford
(Palm Sunday)

Hare Pie Scramble and Bottle Kicking
Hallaton, Leicestershire
(Easter Monday)

APRIL

Shakespeare's Birthday
Stratford-upon-Avon, Warwickshire
(23 April)

MAY

Festival of the Arts
Lincoln
(May)

Charnwood Arts Festival
Loughborough, Leicestershire
(early May)

Flower Parade
Spalding, Lincolnshire
(early May)

National Classic Motor Show
Birmingham, W Midlands
(early May)

Annual Pilgrimage
Walsingham, Norfolk
(May Day Bank Holiday)

Well Dressing
Tissington, Derbyshire
(Ascension Day)

Leicestershire County Show
Leicestershire
(May – 1st week)

Nottinghamshire County Show
Newark-on-Trent, Nottinghamshire
(May – 1st week)

Sandwell Historic Vehicles Show
Sandwell, W Midlands
(May – 1st or 2nd week)

Bury St Edmunds Festival
Bury St Edmunds, Suffolk
(May – 2nd to 4th weeks)

Aerobatics UK Championship
RAF Cosford, Shropshire
(mid-May)

Derbyshire County Show
Derby
(mid–May)

Leek May Fair
Leek, Staffordshire
(mid-May)

River Severn Raft Race
Arley to Stourport, Hereford & Worcester
(mid-May)

Shropshire and West Midlands Agricultural Show
Shrewsbury, Shropshire
(mid-May)

Malvern Festival
Great Malvern, Hereford & Worcester
(May – 2nd half)

Cyclists' Memorial Service
Meriden, W Midlands
(Sunday nearest 21 May)

Maypole Dancing
Wellow, Nottinghamshire
(Spring Bank Holiday)

Arbor Tree Day
Aston on Clun, Shropshire
(29 May)

Garland Day
Castleton, Derbyshire
(on or near 29 May)

Finishing the garland for Castleton's ancient spring ceremony

Oak-apple Day
Lord Leycester Hospital, Warwick
(29 May)

Belvoir Castle Events
Belvoir Castle, Leicestershire
(late May to August)

Great Witley Festival
Great Witley, Hereford & Worcester
(late May)

Rutland Agricultural Show
Burley on the Hill, Oakham, Leicestershire
(late May)

Staffordshire County Show
Stafford
(late May)

Felixstowe Drama Festival
Felixstowe, Suffolk
(late May to early June)

Summer

JUNE

Festival of Busking
Droitwich, Hereford & Worcester
(early June)

Mayor's Parade
Lincoln
(June – 1st week)

Suffolk Show
Ipswich, Suffolk
(June – 1st week)

Wolverhampton Show
Wolverhampton, W Midlands
(June – 1st week)

Trinity Fair
Southwold, Suffolk
(June – 2nd week)

Festival of Music and the Arts
Aldeburgh, Suffolk
(June – 2nd to 4th weeks)

Three Counties Agricultural Show
Great Malvern, Hereford & Worcester
(mid-June)

Lincolnshire Show
Lincoln
(late June)

Royal Norfolk Show
Norwich, Norfolk
(late June)

Tideswell Wakes Week and Well Dressing
Tideswell, Derbyshire
(late June)

Worcester Carnival Week
Worcester
(late June to early July)

JULY

Lichfield Festival
Lichfield, Staffordshire
(early July)

Royal International Agricultural Show
Stoneleigh, Warwickshire
(early July)

Malvern Victorian Week
Great Malvern, Hereford & Worcester
(July – 2nd or 3rd week)

Ely Folk Weekend
Ely, Cambridgeshire
(mid-July)

Oundle International Festival
Oundle, Northamptonshire
(mid-July)

Shrewsbury International Music Festival
Shrewsbury, Shropshire
(mid-July)

Spilsby Show
Spilsby, Lincolnshire
(mid-July)

Buxton Festival
Buxton, Derbyshire
(mid-July to August)

Cambridge Festival
Cambridge
(July – 2nd half)

East of England Show
Peterborough,
Cambridgeshire
(July – 3rd week)

King's Lynn Festival
King's Lynn, Norfolk
(July – last week)

**Sandringham Annual
Flower Show**
Sandringham, Norfolk
(July – last week)

Charlecote Park Festival
Charlecote Park,
Warwickshire
(late July)

**Ross-on-Wye Annual
Steam Traction Engine
Rally**
Ross-on-Wye, Hereford &
Worcester
(late July)

Stratford Festival
Stratford-upon-Avon,
Warwickshire
(late July)

**Beccles Carnival and
Regatta Week**
Beccles, Suffolk
(late July to early August)

**Church Stretton and
South Shropshire Arts
Festival**
Church Stretton,
Shropshire
(late July to early August)

AUGUST
Three Choirs Festival
Worcester
*(August – 1996 and every
3rd year)*

**Duxford Military
Show**
Duxford Airfield,
Cambridgeshire
(early August)

**Tennyson Memorial
Service**
Somersby or Bag
Enderby, Lincolnshire
*(alternate years, August –
1st Sunday)*

**Robin
Hood Festival**
Edwinstowe,
Nottinghamshire
(August – 1st week)

**Woodmen of
Arden Archery
Contest**
Meriden, W Midlands
(August – 1st week)

**Hot Air Balloon
Festival**
Northampton,
Northamptonshire
(August – 2nd week)

**Aldeburgh Olde
Marine Regatta and
Carnival**
Aldeburgh, Suffolk
(mid-August)

**Skegness Carnival
Week**
Skegness, Lincolnshire
(mid-August)

Alford Festival
Alford, Lincolnshire
*(August Bank Holiday
weekend)*

**Plague Sunday
Service**
Eyam, Derbyshire
(August – last Sunday)

**Leicester International
Air Show**
Leicester
(late August)

Autumn

SEPTEMBER
**Walsall
Illuminations**
Walsall Arboretum,
W Midlands
*(September to early
October)*

**Burghley Horse
Trials**
Burghley House, near
Stamford,
Cambridgeshire
(early September)

**Stourport Land
and River Carnival**
Stourport, Hereford &
Worcester
(September – 1st week)

*Steam events are a regular
feature at Chatsworth
House in Derbyshire*

**Abbots Bromley Horn
Dance**
Abbots Bromley,
Staffordshire
*(Monday after 1st Sunday
following 4 September)*

**Annual East Anglia
Antiques Fair**
Bury St Edmunds,
Suffolk
(September – 2nd week)

Burton Beer Festival
Burton upon Trent,
Staffordshire
(mid-September)

**Dr Johnson's Birthday
Celebration**
Lichfield, Staffordshire
(on or near 18 September)

OCTOBER
Goose Fair
Nottingham
(early October)

**Horse and Tractor
Ploughing
Championships of the
British Isles**
Shrewsbury, Shropshire
(October – 1st Saturday)

**World Conker Knock-
out Championships**
Ashton,
Northamptonshire
(October – 2nd Saturday)

Canterbury Arts Festival
Canterbury, Kent
(mid– October)

Festival of the Arts
Mansfield,
Nottinghamshire
(mid-October)

**Stratford Mop Fair and
Runaway Mop Fair**
Stratford-upon-Avon,
Warwickshire
(mid-October)

**National Festival of
Crafts**
Birmingham,
W Midlands
(October – 2nd half)

**Norfolk and Norwich
Festival**
Norwich, Norfolk
(October – 1st half)

NOVEMBER
**Annual Heaviest
Sugarbeet Competition**
Farmland Museum,
Haddenham,
Cambridgeshire
(early November)

Wroth Silver
Stretton on Dunsmore,
Warwickshire
(11 November)

East Coast Jazz Festival
Norwich, Norfolk
(mid-November)

Winter

DECEMBER
Annual Antiques Fair
Newmarket, Suffolk
(December – 1st week)

**Annual Victorian Street
Fayre**
Bungay, Suffolk
(December – 2nd week)

Broughton Tin Can Band
Broughton,
Northamptonshire
*(1st Sunday after 12
December)*

**Festival of Carols and
Lessons**
King's College Chapel,
Cambridge
(24 December)

JANUARY
Straw Bear Festival
Whittlesey,
Cambridgeshire
*(Friday and Saturday before
Plough Monday)*

FEBRUARY
Cradle Rocking
Blidworth,
Nottinghamshire
*(Sunday nearest
2 February)*

SHROVETIDE
Shrovetide Football
Ashbourne, Derbyshire
*(Shrove Tuesday and Ash
Wednesday)*

ON THE WATERWAYS

One enjoyable way of touring in the Midlands and East Anglia is to concentrate on inland waterways, in which the area is particularly rich. This does not necessarily mean taking to a boat, as there is much of interest to explore by car and on foot.

Until the coming of modern roads in the 18th century and the railways in the 19th, goods, people, news and gossip could move faster and with less effort by water than by land routes. Boats plied busily up and down rivers like the Severn and the Wye, and towns like Hereford and Lincoln thrived as inland ports, with busy wharfs and jostling waterside taverns. As far back as Roman times, a canal was cut westwards from Lincoln so that shipping coming up to the town from the North Sea on the River Witham could go on to the Trent, and so inland.

Now called the Fossdyke Navigation, the canal still connects the Witham and the Trent, and you can take a boat along it and pause for a little something at the White Swan at Torksey Lock.

The great period of canals, however, had to wait until the 18th century. In 1761 Derbyshire wheelwright named James Brindley constructed a canal in Lancashire. It cut the cost of coal in Manchester in half and inaugurated the Canal Age.

The canals were artificial rivers which extended the old river routes and linked them in a cross-country network. The heart of the network lay in the Midlands, and Birmingham, close to the geographical centre of England, has more miles of waterway than

Venice. In fact, the area bounded by Wolverhampton, Cannock, Walsall, Birmingham and Stourbridge contains more than 100 miles of canals. They offer fascinating voyages of exploration and towpath strolls into a forgotten world of engineering and architecture – of locks and tunnels, cuttings and bridges, warehouses and wharfs. The canal system hinged on Birmingham in the same way that the motorway network does today, and one canal actually runs beneath Spaghetti Junction.

The canals were a titanic achievement. You can see Brindley's handiwork at Stourport in Worcestershire, where his Staffordshire and Worcestershire Canal meets the Severn. Brindley made his way by guess and by genius. He had no written calculations, plans or drawings.

His even greater successor, Thomas Telford (also a master road-builder, wittily nicknamed 'the Colossus of Roads'), drove the main line of the Shropshire Union Canal across country on

The photograph below was taken in about 1910 at Buckby, near Weedon

giant embankments and through deep cuttings, with an Olympian disregard of contour lines which still arouses awe today. The cutting at Galton, in Sandwell, for example, is 70ft deep and is crossed by a 150ft bridge, the longest canal bridge in the world in its day.

For a really weird experience, take the trip into the narrow, dank Dudley Tunnel at the Black Country Museum in Dudley: on which you can try your hand, or rather your feet, in the art of 'legging' the boat through by walking along the side walls. Intriguing insights into the lives of the working boatmen and their

Top: entering the Dudley Tunnel from the Black Country Museum

Left: roses, castles and geometric designs traditionally adorn canal boats and ware

Right: a horse-drawn narrowboat rudder, typically decorated with plaited ropes. The main part is called the ram's head

Bottom: at Foxton, the Grand Union Canal negotiates the hill via 10 locks arranged in two staircases

families – and their horses – can be gained at the Waterways Museum at Stoke Bruerne, on the Grand Union Canal in Northamptonshire. There is also a good tunnel here, too – the Blisworth Tunnel – which is 3,056 yards long.

A special aspect of waterways life is canal art. Narrowboats were painted in bright colours with roses, daisies, castles, marigolds and other traditional designs. Every surface inside the boat was decorated too, and so were objects aboard – watering-cans, teapots and mop handles, for instance. It must have been like living inside a kaleidoscope.

To the east of the Midlands canal system lies another network of waterways – the Norfolk and Suffolk Broads, one of England's most popular holiday areas since Edwardian times. The Broads are man-made. They are pits dug over centuries by people cutting peat for fuel, which have

filled up with water and now, with the rivers and cuts that connect them, provide 125 miles of navigable routes. Besides boating and sailing, the Broads area is noted for churches, wildlife and windmills. It is very flat, and one of its delightful experiences is to watch a sailing boat glide swiftly across what at a distance appears to be dry land.

Also very flat, but less crowded by visitors, is the Fen country. The Great Ouse runs from Bedford by way of St Ives and Ely to The Wash at King's Lynn. The River Nene will carry you from Northampton to Peterborough and into the Middle Level complex of waterways around March in Cambridgeshire, while the Witham connects Boston and Lincoln. Here again there is a marvellous blend of history, scenery and wildlife to encounter at the gentle, unhurried pace of a narrowboat or a towpath walk.

131

BELTON HOUSE
LINCOLNSHIRE

Off the A607, 3 miles north of Grantham.
Tourist Information Centre, The Guildhall Centre, St Peter's Hill,
Grantham (01476) 66444.

Serene, civilised and classically symmetrical, Belton House is a masterpiece, built in the 1680s and altered a hundred years later by James Wyatt. Secure in its 1,000-acre park – and safe in the hands of the National Trust – it was home to the Brownlow family and their successors, the Custs, whose likenesses inside make up one of the most enjoyable family portrait galleries in the country. Among a wealth of other attractive items in this delectable house are the wood-carvings of birds and fish, flowers and fruit, wheat and grapes, which spill down the walls or frame pictures. The little church in the grounds is so full of family monuments, you can scarcely see the walls.

IN EASY REACH To the north-east, 11 miles from Grantham, is Sleaford. The church of St Denis here has a splendid west front and ravishing window tracery, and there are fine almshouses and an enormous maltings complex of 1905. A few miles further east on the A17 is Heckington, where there is an eight-sail windmill (open weekends only) and a craft-heritage centre. In the other direction, off the A1 near Colsterworth, 7 miles from Grantham, is the National Trust property Woolsthorpe Manor, the 17th-century farmhouse in which Sir Isaac Newton was born and where, according to tradition, the apple struck him fruitfully on the head.

132

BELVOIR CASTLE
LEICESTERSHIRE

At Belvoir, between the A52 and the A607, 7 miles west of Grantham.
Tourist Information Centre, The Carnegie Museum, Thorpe End,
Melton Mowbray (01664) 480992.

Although Belvoir has been the seat of the Manners family, Dukes of Rutland, for centuries, the turrets, battlements, towers and pinnacles of the present strange-looking house are pure 19th-century mock-medieval, but still impressive on their high ridge overlooking Belvoir Vale. (The name is pronounced Beaver, incidentally.) The sumptuous Elizabeth Saloon, the 150ft Regent's Gallery and the picture gallery hung with Old Masters are exceptionally fine, and the museum of the 17th/21st Lancers the 'death or glory boys', is of interest. Sculptures adorn the beautiful terraced gardens.

IN EASY REACH North of the castle, on the A52, is the village of Bottesford. The church has a chancel that had to be redesigned in the 17th century to provide space for the splendid Manners family monuments of the Tudor and Stuart eras. They are a remarkable sight.

Melton Mowbray, to the south of Belvoir, on the A607, is famous for pork pies and Stilton cheese, which feature prominently in the Melton Carnegie Museum, Thorpe End, along with other local history displays. On Tuesdays the town's street and cattle markets are a lively experience. Just north, off the Scalford Road, is a 140-acre country park with walks, play areas and nature reserves.

Events at Belvoir

The year's programme of events at Belvoir Castle generally begins on the Spring Bank Holiday when a re-enactment group carrys out a siege of the castle from their 17th-century encampment, using early firearms and cannon. On some Sundays, as the season progresses, there are colourful jousting tournaments. The jousting is preceded by tilting at the quintain – which was the knightly way of practicing for combat – and then 'knights' in armour ride at each other with lances, intent on knocking the opponent off his horse.

133

CASTLETON
DERBYSHIRE

On the A625. Tourist Information Centre,
Old Market Hall, Bridge Street, Bakewell (01629) 813227.
Also The Moors Centre, Danby (01287) 660654, see below.

Most visitors to Castleton are bound for the well-publicised caverns. The Blue John Caverns and Mines were originally exploited for the stone (a type of fluorspar) which gives them their name and which has been used decoratively for centuries. You can walk through the many interlinked chambers here, or go underground by boat at the Speedwell Cavern to reach an 'immeasurable vault' and a 'bottomless' pit. The Peak Cavern has the most awe-inspiring entrance, sufficient at one time to accommodate rope-workers' cottages, while Treak Cliff Cavern displays a variety of well-lit natural wonders, including spectacular stalagmites and stalactites.

While you are at Castleton, don't miss the ruins of Peveril Castle and the views from its crags, or the magnificent panorama spread out below the hill-fort on Mam Tor at over 1,600ft. For drama at a lower level, try Winnats Pass, a limestone gorge close to the Speedwell Cavern.

A half-mile underground canal leads to Speedwell Cavern, near Castleton

●

Garland Day

*O*n or near Oak-apple Day, 29 May, a curious figure called the Garland King rides through the streets of Castleton at the head of a procession. His head and the upper part of his body are completely hidden by the 'garland' – a heavy wooden construction shaped like a beehive and covered with a profusion of flowers and greenery (see left). On top of the garland is a small separate posy of flowers which is called the 'queen'. Behind the king rides his woman (formerly a man dressed in woman's clothes), accompanied by a band, and children dressed in white. After stopping to dance at various points on the route, the procession comes to the church and the garland is hauled up to the top of the church's tower and fixed to a pinnacle. The 'queen' posy is placed on the town war memorial.

●

IN EASY REACH Danby a mile or so east is the ideal centre for exploring the contrasting scenery of the Peak District, and the Moors Centre, Danby Lodge, Danby Lane will provide you with all the background information you might want. The northern area offers the more dramatic scenery, being basically a gritstone plateau, with few roads but many fast-flowing streams, which fill the Derwent and Ladybower Reservoirs. To the south, the White Peak gets its name from the light limestone, which is most noticeable in the many miles of drystone walls. The softer stone has worn away to form hidden valleys like Monsal Dale and Lathkill Dale.

134

HEREFORD
HEREFORD AND WORCESTER

Tourist Information Centre, Town Hall, St Owens Street (01432) 268430.

A forbidding ring road encircles Hereford like a moat, but once you have broken through you will find a pleasant old city centre dominated by the mellow cathedral, in which the massive Norman pillars of the nave contrast with delicate later work at the east end. The lady chapel and chantry chapel are outstanding, but the chief glories of the cathedral are its priceless, chained library of nearly 1,500 volumes, and the *Mappa Mundi*, the medieval map of the world, in the north choir aisle.

In the central pedestrian precinct of the city is the Old House, a Jacobean building now housing a museum. In addition to the City Museum, Hereford boasts several specialist exhibitions, among them the display of costume and fine art at the Churchill Gardens Museum and Brian Hatton Art Gallery in Venn's Lane, and the fascinating Museum of Cider in Pomona Place, which should not be missed. There are also enjoyable walks beside the River Wye which flows under the ancient Wye Bridge, past the cathedral grounds and castle ruins.

IN EASY REACH Four miles west of the city, at Swainshill on the A438, are the Weir gardens, fine riverside cliff gardens opened to the public by the National Trust and offering splendid views of the River Wye and the Black Mountains. The gardens are at their most spectacular in early spring when there are lovely displays of naturalised bulbs set in woodland and grassland walks.

●

Pax Cake Custom

*O*n Palm Sunday (the Sunday before Good Friday) at four villages to the south of Hereford – Sellack, Kings Caple, Hentland and Hoarwithy – small biscuits bearing the image of a lamb are handed by the vicar to the worshippers as they come out of church, with the words, 'peace and good neighbourhood'. The biscuits are called pax cakes (from the Latin for 'peace', pax). The custom goes back to the 16th century or perhaps earlier still, and originally cakes and ale were handed out during morning service and eaten and drunk in church, to promote neighbourliness and good feeling at Easter time.

●

135

ICKWORTH
SUFFOLK

On the A143, 3 miles south-west of Bury St Edmunds.
Tourist Information Centres:
6 Angel Hill, Bury St Edmunds (01284) 764667 and
Ancient House Museum, 21 White Hart Street, Thetford (01842) 752599.

Ickworth's rotunda. Its central skylight illuminates a magnificent statue 100ft below – the centrepiece of a fine art collection

Ickworth is a very peculiar house, but extremely grand, which is now administered by the National Trust. It was built by the eccentric Earl of Bristol, between 1794 and 1830, and centres on a colossal rotunda with two curved corridors leading off to flanking wings. The house is filled with treasures amassed by the family – fine furniture and porcelain, one of England's most splendid silver collections, sculptures, and paintings by Gainsborough, Titian and Velasquez. Outside are formal Italian gardens and a 'Capability' Brown park with waymarked woodland walks and a deer enclosure.

IN EASY REACH Bury St Edmunds is a pleasant old market town off the A45. It is full of history and interesting old buildings: the splendid Theatre Royal, one of the few surviving Georgian playhouses in the country, complete with original pit, boxes and gallery; 12th-century Moyse's Hall, once probably a merchant's house, now a museum of local history; and the town hall, designed by Robert Adam. Don't miss the impressive remains of the once great Bury St Edmunds abbey, founded in 945, the beautiful 15th-century church of St Mary, with its marvellous hammerbeam roof, or the cathedral church of St James's. Come in mid to late May for the town's festival with music, films, etc. North-west, off the A1101, the West Stow Country Park and Anglo-Saxon Village holds Saxon craft markets in April and August.

Events around Coventry

On the Green of Meriden, north-west of Kenilworth and west of Coventry, there is a memorial to cyclists killed in the two World Wars. On the Sunday nearest to 21 May each year, a special service is held and wreaths are laid at the foot of the memorial. In the 1930s the ceremony was attended by cyclists in their thousands, today in hundreds. Meriden is also the place where the Woodmen of Arden meet during the summer for archery contests with 6ft yew bows.
Over on the other side of Coventry, near Stretton on Dunsmore, Wroth Silver is paid in coins by representatives of 25 parishes to the Duke of Buccleuch's agent before sunrise at Knightlow Cross on St Martin's Day, 11 November. Why this money is paid, no one any longer knows.

136

KENILWORTH CASTLE
WARWICKSHIRE

Tourist Information Centre, The Library, 11 Smalley Place (01926) 52595.

The great castle at Kenilworth made famous by Sir Walter Scott, deserves a leisurely tour, and a spring visit is recommended to avoid the crowds of the high season. You approach the red sandstone walls across a causeway that bridges the former defensive lake. The sprawling remains reflect several centuries and several distinguished owners, and the result is a complex mixture of early architecture – the enormous keep and curtain wall date from the Norman period, John of Gaunt was responsible for the Great Hall and private apartments in the inner court, while Robert Dudley, Earl of Leicester, modernised the keep and built a fine new gatehouse, later converted into a residence.

IN EASY REACH At Coventry, to the north-east, Basil Spence's cathedral still excites controversy after more than 25 years, but as a centre of Christian activity and a repository of late-1950s art it should not be missed. Other attractions in the city include the Herbert Art Gallery and Museum, the Toy Museum, and a vivid Museum of British Road Transport. At Baginton, to the south of the city, off the A45, a Roman fort has been reconstructed, complete with interpretation centre.

Two fine houses in the area offer contrasting attractions. Baddesley Clinton, off the A4141, 6 miles west of Kenilworth, is a delightful moated manor house, mainly 15th-century, with a notable banqueting hall. At Stoneleigh Abbey, off the B4115, 4 miles east of Kenilworth, restoration following a fire has led to the immaculate refurbishing of the splendid state rooms in a Georgian mansion containing much earlier work. The children will enjoy the amusements in the grounds. Stoneleigh is also well known as the site of the Royal Agricultural Society of England's showground, venue for the 'Royal Show' each July.

137

LINCOLN
LINCOLNSHIRE

Tourist Information Centre, 9 Castle Hill (01522) 529828.

One of the largest churches in England, built mainly between the 11th and 14th centuries, Lincoln Cathedral stands majestically on its hilltop, its three towers dominating the city and the views for miles around. Inside, among many treasures, are two famous windows, the Dean's Eye and the Bishop's Eye, packed with medieval stained glass, 14th-century choir stalls and the soaring angel choir.

Close to the cathedral are scattered remains of the Roman legionary fortress, which stood where Ermine Street climbed the hill in a series of broad steps. The Newport Arch, the Roman north gate, is still used by traffic today, 17 centuries after it was built, though Ermine Street itself is 7 or 8ft below the level of the modern road. Down at the foot of the hill there are trails and river cruises from Brayford Pool.

Back on the hill, Lincoln Castle commands sweeping views of the city. It was built by the Normans and withstood several sieges in its time. Strong 19th-century connections include a unique Victorian prison chapel and a grim little convict's graveyard The Castle is now the home of Lincoln's copy of the *Magna Carta* and an exhibition interprets and displays this important document. Not far away is the excellent Museum of Lincolnshire Life in Burton Road, which has an enormous and varied collection of country bygones. Here you can find out about fen skating, the Lincolnshire Curly Coated Pig, and the Royal Lincolnshire Regiment.

Something else not to be missed is the Usher Art Gallery, Lindum Road, founded by a local jeweller. The star attraction is his fabulous collection of watches, golden and bejewelled, glittering against black velvet, but there are also paintings by local artist Peter de Wint. Other things to see in the city include the bicycles in the National Cycle Museum, and the medieval houses on the appropriately named Steep Hill.

Events in Lincoln

The annual Festival of the Arts at Lincoln occupies the whole month of May and the events are held in the cathedral, the Usher Art Gallery and elsewhere in the city. The festival favours popular music – rock, jazz and folk music – but there are also classical music concerts, as well as modern dance, mime, poetry, film and theatre, and the visual arts. In the following month the city plays host to the Mayor's Parade and the Lincolnshire Show.

Lincoln Cathedral, said to represent the gateway of heaven

Charnwood Arts Festival

The old forest of Charnwood has lent its name to the Charnwood Arts Festival in Loughborough in May. Street theatre and a grand procession are features of the festival, which involves amateur groups and performers as well as professionals, and which likes to cover any aspect of the arts.

138

LOUGHBOROUGH
LEICESTERSHIRE

Tourist Information Centre, John Storer House, Wards End (01509) 230131.

A great deal of mystique seems to surround the ancient business of bell-making. Taylor's of Loughborough are world-famous in the craft, and a visit to their museum and factory in Freehold Street is a unique experience. Don't expect to find gnarled old men secretly practising their trade in dimly lit workshops – modern technology has changed all that – but the museum certainly provides an insight into the mysteries of moulding, casting and tuning bells from the 13th century onwards. It is the only museum of bells and bell-founding in Britain.

The town's handsome 15th-century parish church is naturally noted for its bell-ringing feats, and bells feature again in Loughborough's unusual war memorial, a tall campanile with a 47-bell carillon on which regular recitals are given during the summer months. At the central station the Great Central Railway provides steam rides over an 8 mile route that includes the Swithland Reservoir viaduct.

IN EASY REACH Further afield, to the south-west of Loughborough, Charnwood Forest is an exposed area of rocky outcrops, reaching a high point at Beacon Hill, near Woodhouse Eaves. The centre for walkers and naturalists is Bradgate Park, near Newtown Linford, with over 800 acres of former deer park open to visitors. At Coalville, on the B585, is the major science and industry museum, Snibston Discovery Park, set on the 100-acre site of a former colliery. The most famous feature of Whatton Gardens, 5 miles north-west of Loughborough, off the A6, is the lovely Chinese Garden, set in grounds that also include a splendid arboretum.

Hare Pie Scramble and Bottle Kicking

The Hare Pie Scramble and Bottle Kicking at Hallaton on Easter Monday does not involve pies or bottles, The scramble is nowadays only a token scuffle for pieces of a beef pie. The bottle kicking is the main event and the 'bottles' are actually small wooden, iron-looped barrels filled with ale. They are used as balls in a rugby-like, largely ruleless football match between Hallaton and the neighbouring village of Medbourne, whose team can include anyone not from Hallaton. There is no limit on the numbers involved on either side when the game is played. The ale in the bottles is eventually drunk.

139

MARKET HARBOROUGH
LEICESTERSHIRE

Tourist Information Centres: The Library, Adam and Eve Street, Market Harborough (01858) 462649 and The Library, Catmos Street, Oakham (01572) 724329.

This old market town has an 18th-century town hall, a parish church which dates from the 13th to 15th centuries with a particularly fine tower, and the Harborough Museum, in Adam and Eve Street, which illustrates local history including the town's role as a medieval planned town, hunting centre and social focus for the area. Many other old buildings have survived, perhaps the most famous being the 17th-century grammar school, a timber-framed house that stands on pillars above the street.

IN EASY REACH Canal enthusiasts will want to visit nearby Foxton Locks (to the north-west, off the A6), where a chain of 10 locks climbs a formidably steep hill on the Grand Union Canal. To the north-east, off the B664, is the attractive village of Hallaton, with its stone cottages surrounding a small green and an odd buttercross. On Easter Monday the village hosts the 'Hare Pie Scramble and Bottle Kicking' ceremony.

Further north still is Oakham, county town of the late, lamented Rutland. The Norman banqueting hall in the castle houses a collection of horseshoes of many centuries, and the excellent Rutland County Museum has displays of local agricultural and domestic history. To the east of the town is vast Rutland Water, a centre for water sports where a water industry museum is housed in the former Normanton church – an elegant building perched on a promontory.

140
MOW COP
STAFFORDSHIRE

On a minor road, 2½ miles west of Biddulph.
Tourist Information Centres: Town Hall, High Street, Congleton,
Cheshire (01260) 271095 and 1 Market Place, Leek (01538) 381000.

Crowned by its ruined 'eyecatcher', the rocky hill of Mow Cop (pronounced to rhyme with cow) is now a National Trust property

At 1,100ft, Mow Cop is a superb viewpoint on the border of Staffordshire and Cheshire – a gritstone crag, commanding a panorama of the Cheshire Plain, and the Pennines. On its summit stands what appears to be a fragment of a castle, but this quaint 'ruin' was built here in 1754 by a local landowner to make the view from his house more picturesque.

Mow Cop has strong Nonconformist associations. In the early 19th century prayer meetings held here resulted in the emergence of the austere sect of Primitive Methodists. It is also the starting point of the Staffordshire Way, a long-distance footpath which runs for over 90 miles to Kinver Edge, near Kidderminster.

IN EASY REACH The Greenway Bank Country Park lies 1 mile south of Biddulph on the A527. Once part of a Victorian landscaped estate, it covers over 100 acres, with lakeside and woodland walks and a fine show of azaleas and rhododendrons in the spring. To the east, 3½ miles north-east of Leek on the A523, is Rudyard Lake, after which Rudyard Kipling was named. This reservoir was constructed in the late 18th century to supply the Caldon Canal. There is a picnic place and pleasant walking here. In Leek itself is another link with canals, the Brindley Mill and Museum in Mill Street (open weekend afternoons only in spring), which was designed by the great canal-builder James Brindley in 1752. It was used as a corn mill until the late 1940s, and after a period of dereliction has now been restored to a museum devoted to the life of Brindley and the craft of milling.

141
THE OTTER TRUST
SUFFOLK

At Earsham, 1¾ miles north-west of Bungay, off the A143.
Tourist Information Centres: The Quay, Fen Lane, Beccles (01502) 713196 (seasonal opening only) and The Town Hall, Hall Quay, Great Yarmouth (01493) 846345.

You will find the world's largest concentration of otters at the Otter Trust centre which covers 23 acres of pretty countryside in the Waveney Valley. Any time between April and October, you can seen otters playing by the river bank and admire the latest batch of offspring to come from the Trust's important conservation and breeding programme, a project to release British otters back into the wild in a bid to save them from extinction. After otter antics, take a stroll around the centre's three busy waterfowl lakes and along the pleasant woodland walk.

IN EASY REACH There are a number of other attractions in the area, towards the coast and the ports of Lowestoft and Great Yarmouth. Some have limited opening in spring, so check times carefully to avoid a wasted journey. The East Anglia Transport Museum is at Carlton Colville, 3 miles south-west of Lowestoft on the B1384. It is worth a visit to enjoy the brass, livery and nostalgia of old trams, trolley buses, battery-powered vehicles, old commercial vehicles and narrow-gauge steam trains. Five miles north-west of Lowestoft, off the B1074, is Somerleyton Hall (limited opening), an extravagant mansion built in Anglo-Italian style for a Victorian railway tycoon, Sir Samuel Peto. The state rooms are sumptuous with carvings, paintings and furniture; the 12-acre gardens have specimen trees, rhododendrons, statuary and elegant glasshouses. Find your way through the famous maze, if you can, before taking a ride on the miniature railway.

At Fritton Lake Country World, 5 miles south-west of Great Yarmouth on the A143, explore the woodlands and grassy spaces surrounding a 3-mile-long lake – one of the prettiest in East Anglia. There is boating and fishing in season, a putting green, children's assault course, picnic areas, gardens, birds of prey and a wildfowl reserve to visit. Sections of the massive walls of Burgh Castle, 3 miles west of Great Yarmouth, loom impressively above Breydon Water. Built in about AD286, the castle was one of the 'forts of the Saxon shore', a chain of 11 fortresses built along the east and south coasts from The Wash to the Solent by the Romans to protect the coast from Saxon pirates and raiders.

142
RAGLEY HALL
WARWICKSHIRE

On the A435, south-west of Alcester. Not open until April.
Tourist Information Centres: 1 Bridgefoot, Stratford-upon-Avon (01789) 293127 and
Civic Square, Alcester Street, Redditch, Worcestershire (01527) 60806.

Ragley Hall is one of the most popular stately homes in the Midlands. Owned by the Marquess of Hertford and designed in the late 17th century, it is imposing Palladian in style, with a magnificent portico hinting at the superb entrance hall inside, one of the finest in England. The state rooms contain outstanding furniture and porcelain, and house an important art collection, the most recent major addition being a spectacular mural by Graham Rust. Children are well catered for in 'Capability' Brown's park, which now features an adventure playground, a maze and woodland walks.

IN EASY REACH Alcester and Henley-in-Arden, further north-east on the A3400, are two of the handsomest towns in the Midlands. Look out for the restored Malt Mill Lane at Alcester and the Norman church at Beaudesert in Henley. On the A435, 2 miles north of Alcester, is Coughton Court, a place steeped in the dramatic history of the Throckmorton family, who were 'recusant' Roman Catholics.

143
RUSHTON TRIANGULAR LODGE
NORTHAMPTONSHIRE

In the park of Rushton Hall, off the A6003, 4 miles north-west of Kettering.
Tourist Information Centre, Coach House, Sheep Street, Kettering (01536) 410266.

This is a fascinating piece of pious eccentricity. Sir Thomas Tresham, the owner of Rushton Hall, had the folly built in the 1590s to symbolise the Holy Trinity, and everything about it is related to the number three or its multiples – it has three sides and three storeys and is 27ft high. Each side has three windows and three gables, and the theme is continued in the triangular decoration, and the three-sided chimney. The lodge is now cared for by English Heritage.

IN EASY REACH About 10 miles to the north-east of Kettering, off the A6116, Lyveden New Bield, a National Trust property, is another of Sir Thomas's constructions – an elegant roofless shell of cruciform shape, designed to symbolise the Passion and decorated accordingly. An older survival can be seen nearby at Geddington on the A43, 4 miles north-east of Kettering – a well-preserved Eleanor Cross, one of 12 erected by Edward I to commemorate his dead queen. Deene Park, also off the A43, but 7 miles north-east of Corby, is the home of the Brudenell family, whose most famous member, Lord Cardigan, led the charge of the Light Brigade. The house (limited opening only) is of Tudor origin, but has been added to over several centuries. Just to the west of Deene Park is the shell of one of the most gracious Elizabethan buildings. Kirby Hall is built round a courtyard entered by way of a very beautiful porch. Further west again, Rockingham Castle stands above the Welland Valley, commanding fine views. Behind the Norman walls is an Elizabethan house that has been much adapted and extended. It contains a notable collection of paintings, and there are walks through the wild garden.

144
SHERWOOD FOREST COUNTRY PARK
NOTTINGHAMSHIRE

Visitor Centre (with Tourist Information Centre (01623) 823202)
on the B6034, north of Edwinstowe, 2 miles west of Ollerton.
Tourist Information Centres: Sherwood Heath, Ollerton roundabout (01623) 824545
and also at Newark-on-Trent, Nottingham, Retford and Worksop.

All too little is left of the old royal hunting forest of Sherwood, which covered a 20-mile swathe of country in the area between Nottingham and Worksop; providing a base for Robin Hood and his merry men, and sheltering them from their enemy, the Sheriff of Nottingham. There is a special exhibition about the legendary outlaw at the Edwinstowe Visitor Centre. Marked walks lead among towering ancient oaks and grassy or bracken-covered glades. The most notable tree here is the Major Oak, which has a girth of 30ft and may be all of 500 years old. There are deer here too, many birds and some interesting beetles.

Maypole Dancing

The Nottinghamshire village of Wellow, near Ollerton, is one of the comparatively few places in England with a permanent maypole: in this case made of stainless steel and, strangely, paid for by a grant from the European Economic Community. The May Queen of Wellow is elected every year by the people of village, and the maypole dancing occurs on the Spring Bank Holiday.

IN EASY REACH There is another wildlife sanctuary, and a craft centre, in Rufford Country Park, on the A614, a few miles south of Ollerton. On a minor road, 4 miles east of Ollerton, is Laxton, which is famous for having preserved its medieval open field system of agriculture. Further north, on the fringes of Sherwood Forest, is Clumber Park, lying to the west of the A614. Here the 18th-century landscape gardening achievements of the Dukes of Newcastle are preserved by the National Trust. An enchanting lake, a classical bridge and garden temples, and a splendid Victorian-Gothic church by G F Bodley are amongst the attractions.

Retford, on the A620, is the main market town of north Nottinghamshire. Local history and bygones can be explored here at the Bassetlaw Museum, Grove Street. Five miles to the south, on the B6387 at Lound Hall, is the National Mining Museum, where the exhibits include locomotives, coal-face machinery and miners' equipment.

—— **145** ——

SPALDING
LINCOLNSHIRE

Tourist Information Centres: Ayscoughfee Hall, Churchgate, Spalding (01775) 725468 and 45 Bridge Street, Peterborough, Cambridgeshire (01733) 317336.

Half a million sightseers pour into Spalding for the Flower Parade each May. The town is the centre of the great bulb-growing area in the reclaimed Lincolnshire fenland. In the spring, daffodils and narcissi, hyacinths and tulips, ablaze in their glory, create a magic carpet of shimmering colour at Springfields Gardens, on the north-east outskirts of Spalding on the A151. This 25-acre garden was opened in 1966 as a display centre during the bulb season.

Spalding itself is an old river port on the Welland, which runs through the heart of the town, crossed by seven bridges – the High Bridge of 1838 at their head – with delightful riverside strolls. There are fine old inns, such as the thatched White Horse and the Red Lion, and the church of St Mary and St Nicolas has a 160ft spire. Close by is Ayscoughfee Hall which dates back to the 1430s. It is now a local history museum.

IN EASY REACH To the south of Spalding on the A1073, deep in the fens, once stood the great Benedictine abbey of Crowland. The abbey church with its towering west front is today the parish church. In the village is a peculiar three-way bridge, built in the 14th century at the confluence of two streams, but now left high and dry. Eight miles further south, on the A47, is Peterborough, in Cambridgeshire, a rapidly expanding city with a handsome cathedral and some impressive 17th- and 18th-century buildings. Local history and archaeology are covered in the museum in Priestgate, and rare wall paintings can be seen in the 13th- to 14th-century house, Longthorpe Tower, on the outskirts of the city. Also just outside the city, at Alwalton, is the showground where the East of England Show is held each July. Off the A17, east of Spalding, is the 15-acre Butterfly and Falconry Park.

Flower Parade

The annual Flower Parade at Spalding early in May bills itself as 'the greatest free show in the country'. Spalding is England's bulb capital and the 15 or so giant floats (see above) which go in procession through the town streets, accompanied by bands and entertainers, are decorated with three million tulip heads. Organised by Springfields Gardens, the parade began in 1958 and has been going strong ever since. The floats are all designed and built by the same team and volunteers pin tulip heads into place at the rate of a thousand per square yard.

146

STOKESAY CASTLE
SHROPSHIRE

At Craven Arms, 8 miles north-west of Ludlow, off the A49.
Tourist Information Centres: Castle Street, Ludlow (01584) 875053, 6 School Lane,
Leominster (01568) 616460 (seasonal opening) and the Square, Shrewsbury (01743)
350761.

This is a delightful place – a small fortified manor of the late-13th-century, now in the care of English Heritage. You go in through a separate Jacobean gatehouse covered with lively carvings, and enter a finely timbered Great Hall, with an ancient staircase leading to a tiny retiring room. By climbing an outside staircase you reach the south tower and a solar, with 17th-century panelling. Quiet and empty now, it has an authentic medieval atmosphere.

IN EASY REACH The attractions of Ludlow are famous – a huge and dramatically sited castle, one of the most spectacular parish churches in England, the astounding carved façade of the Feathers Hotel and a generous mixture of the best in medieval and Georgian architecture. There is pleasure of a different kind at Clun (on the A488, 8 miles west of Craven Arms), an old grey town with the remains of a castle set on gigantic earthworks and an unexpectedly rich interior to its fortress-like church. Don't miss the small museum of local history. Aston on Clun, back towards Craven Arms, is famous for its Arbor Tree, a poplar tree decorated with flags every 29 May.

147

TRAMWAY MUSEUM
DERBYSHIRE

At Crich on the B5035, 6 miles south-east of Matlock.
Tourist Information Centre, The Pavilion, Matlock Bath (01629) 55082.

Here is something completely different for all the family – the National Tramway Museum, a huge exhibition hall with impressive static displays, train stands and memorabilia. There cannot be many people who can actually remember living with the unique rattle and grind of trams, yet this museum still evokes instant nostalgia. There are over 50 British and foreign tramcars, many of them in working order and providing rides along a generous length of rail, part of which takes in an area imaginatively converted into a turn-of-the-century urban landscape. Static exhibitions include a display about local lead-mining, and other attractions such as a video theatre, children's playground and shops.

IN EASY REACH On the southern outskirts of Matlock Bath is Cromford, a 'company town' created by the industrialist Richard Arkwright in the 1770s, and a fascinating survival. The original water-powered mill can be visited, and a section of the Cromford Canal has been restored nearby. Matlock Bath is a Victorian spa with its own period charm (and an atmospheric mining museum in the Pavilion), but in recent years it has come to be known for the spectacular cable-car system that carries visitors to the top of the Heights of Abraham. To the south-east of Matlock is the Riber Castle Wildlife Park, set around a Victorian folly and housing a varied collection of birds and animals.

148

WALSINGHAM
NORFOLK

On the B1105, 5 miles south of Wells-next-the-Sea.
Tourist Information Centres: Shirehall Museum, Walsingham (01328) 820510 (seasonal
opening only) and The Green, Hunstanton (01485) 532610.

Visit Walsingham in May to witness the great annual pilgrimage which takes pilgrims to the Anglican church with its image of Our Lady of Walsingham and the 14th-century Slipper Chapel (Roman Catholic). The 12th-century Augustinian priory built round the original shrine is now in ruins, as is the Franciscan friary of the following century, with its cloisters, chapter house and guest hall. The Shirehall Museum has an almost complete 18th-century courtroom including prisoners' lock-up, and an interesting display on the history of the pilgrimage.

IN EASY REACH Holkham Hall, 2 miles west of Wells-next-the-Sea, off the A149, is a great, white-bricked, 18th-century Palladian mansion built by William Kent for the farming innovator 'Coke of Norfolk', afterwards Earl of Leicester. Unfortunately, opening is limited until the summer months, but if you are able to go inside you will see a superb art collection, with

---

Annual Pilgrimage

In the year 1061 the Lady Richeldis, wife of the lord of Little Walsingham, dreamed that the Virgin Mary appeared to her and asked her to build a replica of the house in Nazareth where the Angel Gabriel told Mary that she would be the mother of Christ. A small wooden hut was duly built and over the centuries pilgrims from everywhere in Europe flocked to see the 'holy house' of Walsingham. They included every king of England from Richard I to Henry VIII, which did not prevent the latter from destroying the shrine and having the image of Our Lady burned. Many pilgrims used to stop at the Slipper Chapel in nearby Houghton St Giles, leave their shoes there, and walk the last mile or so to Walsingham barefoot. This chapel is now the principal Roman Catholic shrine. The pilgrimage has been revived in recent times and in the 1930s the Reverend Hope Patten, the Walsingham parson, had a copy of the holy house constructed – though in brick instead of wood, and enclosed in a brick church specially built for it. A new image of Our Lady was made and installed in the shrine, and the annual pilgrimage in May now attracts thousands of participants.

fine furniture and a fascinating display of Victorian and Edwardian agricultural and domestic bygones.

The world's greatest assemblage of steam traction, road, ploughing and barn engines is claimed by the Thursford Collection, off the A148, 6 miles north-east of Fakenham. It includes nine different kinds of mechanical organ, but the star item is the mighty Wurlitzer cinema organ, which you can still hear in concert now and again.

Northwards lies the beautiful North Norfolk coast, a haven for birdlife. A string of important nature reserves stretches for 20 miles. Holme Dunes, to the west towards Hunstanton, has spotted redshank and green sandpipers, hides overlooking wader pools and a nature trail. A boat from Brancaster Staithe will take you to the saltmarshes and sand dunes of Scolt Head Island to see the famous ternery. At Holkham there are mudflats, marshes and dunes with wildfowl and Brent geese. Blakeney Point, reached by ferry, is home to seals and Britain's largest Sandwich tern colony. Finally, travelling eastwards, marsh harriers can be seen at Cley Marshes. While in the Blakeney/Cley area also try to visit the pretty village of Glandford on the B1156. It has a Shell Museum with a beautiful display of shells from all over the world.

—————————— **149** ——————————

WARWICK
WARWICKSHIRE

Tourist Information Centre, Court House, Jury Street (01926) 492212.

This view of Warwick Castle from Castle Bridge is one of the best in the town. The two towers, Caesar's (left) and Guy's, were the work of Thomas Beauchamp and his son

When the Madame Tussaud's organisation took over Warwick Castle, they succeeded in turning it into a genuine family attraction without sacrificing the splendour. From the outside it is a formidable 14th-century stronghold on a commanding site above the River Avon, but within the walls it becomes a magnificent mansion with a series of grand state rooms, luxuriously decorated and furnished and accommodating an important art collection. Skilful waxworks convey the atmosphere of a Victorian royal weekend. There is much to explore here, including the dungeons, and the children will like the grounds.

As a result of a fire in 1694, Warwick town centre is pleasantly 18th-century in character, but fine medieval architecture can be seen in Mill Street and in the attractive cluster of half-timbered buildings that make up the Lord Leycester Hospital, a home for ex-servicemen since the 16th century. St Mary's Church was largely rebuilt after the fire, but fortunately its noblest feature, the Beauchamp Chapel, survived. Richard Beauchamp, a hero of the Hundred Years War, is commemorated by an exquisite gilded bronze effigy that puts to shame the vulgar memorial to the Earl of Leicester nearby.

The handsome Jacobean St John's House at Coten End contains two interesting museums. The ground floor illustrates domestic and social history, while the first floor is devoted to the history of the Royal Warwickshire Regiment, including memorabilia of Field Marshal Montgomery. The Warwickshire Museum in the Market Place covers the history of the county. For something very different go to Oken's House in Castle Street to see the delightful exhibition of nursery bygones, in particular, dolls.

—— **150** ——

ALDEBURGH
SUFFOLK

Tourist Information Centre, The Cinema, High Street (01728) 453637.

Festival of Music and
the Arts

The annual Festival of
Music and the Arts at
Aldeburgh in June is one
of the most prestigious in
the international
calendar. Held every year
since 1948, in its early
days it was dominated
by the personality and
the music of Benjamin
Britten, who founded the
festival with Peter Pears.
Many of Britten's operas
and other compositions
were first performed at
Aldeburgh. The
Aldeburgh Foundation,
which organises the
festival, also runs the
Britten-Pears School for
Advanced Musical
Studies, whose students
play an important part
in the festival.

June is the high point of the year for this quiet little seaside resort, when the famous music and arts festival opens for a season of opera, recitals, concerts and exhibitions. First dreamed up by the composer Benjamin Britten when he came to live in Aldeburgh in 1947, the festival is now a great international occasion with its own concert buildings – the restored and converted maltings which prettily overlook the River Alde in nearby Snape. In fact, you can hear concerts at the Maltings throughout the summer, not just at festival time, and there is also a craft centre to visit, an art gallery and a music library.

Walk into Aldeburgh and along the sloping, shingly beach and you can watch the fishing boats and buy freshly caught fish on the shore. The old Moot Hall, once the town hall and at the centre of Aldeburgh, is now right on the edge of the encroaching sea. Alde House was the home of Elizabeth Garrett Anderson, Britain's first woman medical doctor, and Aldeburgh church has Benjamin Britten's grave (he died in 1976) and a monument to George Crabbe, local poet and author of *The Borough,* the source for Britten's opera *Peter Grimes.*

IN EASY REACH Thorpeness, north of Aldeburgh on the B1353, is an extraordinary little seaside settlement developed in the 1900s as a pioneer self-catering holiday village and sporting a wonderful variety of architectural styles, including such creations as 'the house in the clouds'. Thorpeness Windmill is a handsome working mill, which houses displays on the Suffolk Heritage Coast conservation project.

Further north, off the B1122, is Minsmere RSPB nature reserve, 1,500 acres of marsh, reeds, heath and sandy land ending in low cliffs by the sea. This is home to more than 100 different species of breeding birds, including bitterns and avocets. You may even see the occasional spoonbill. There are good public hides along the shore. The marshes and shingle spit of Orford Ness south of Aldeburgh are also rich in birdlife, though access is not easy. At Orford itself, on the B1084, with its seashore walks and its strange-looking castle built by Henry II with an 18-sided polygonal keep, look out for the local delicacy, smoked herrings known as Orford Butleys.

—— **151** ——

ALTON TOWERS
STAFFORDSHIRE

Off the B5032, 4 miles east of Cheadle.
Tourist Information Centre, Market Place, Ashbourne, Derbyshire (01335) 43666.

*The Corkscrew was the
first 'white knuckle' ride
to be installed at Alton
Towers when part of the
estate was turned into a
leisure park*

Britain's pioneer 'leisure park', and still the market leader, Alton Towers is a unique combination of entertainments designed for the whole family. In the grounds of the ruined 19th-century stately home of the Earls of Shrewsbury are reconstructed streets (linked by cable-borne gondolas) and some of the most sensational fairground rides ever devised, including the gravity-driven Corkscrew. Very young children have their own small-scale but equally exciting fun-fair. If your tastes are more traditional, you will enjoy the magnificent gardens, well away from the hurly-burly. The park has its own comprehensive services, including shops, a bank and a medical centre.

IN EASY REACH There are pleasures of a more tranquil kind at the Hawksmoor Nature Reserve, 2 miles north-east of Cheadle, on the B5417. Four walks of varying length explore this moorland area above the River Churnet, with its rich birdlife. The walks also take in rail and canal history. On a minor road, 2 miles south of Alton, are the ruins of 13th-century Croxden Abbey, a Cistercian foundation. The impressive walls of the west front of the church hint at its former splendour.

152

BUXTON
DERBYSHIRE

Tourist Information Centre, The Crescent (01298) 25106.

Although the Romans discovered the mineral waters at Buxton, the town was virtually the creation of the 5th Duke of Devonshire from 1780 onwards. He was responsible for most of the fine Georgian architecture in the town, and the huge dome of the Royal Devonshire Hospital marks the site of his former stables. The railway started a second wave of development after 1867, which produced the Pavilion, the Pavilion Gardens and the splendid Opera House, which is now the centrepiece of the summer Buxton Festival. Much has been done in recent years to refurbish the town's best buildings, gardens and the thermal baths. There's an interesting museum of local history, with a collection of Blue John objects, and a unique 'micrarium', or exhibition of nature under the microscope, where you can select specimens such as snowflakes, fossils, crystals and flowerbuds for sensational enlargement.

IN EASY REACH Buxton Country Park, south of the town, includes the fine Grin Low woods, 'Solomon's Temple' (a folly which is a superb viewpoint), and Poole's Cavern, with illuminated stalagmites and stalactites. There is also an exhibition centre which displays archaeological finds from the cavern. North-west of Buxton, the woods and reservoirs of the Goyt Valley provide excellent walking. Look out for the sombre ruins of Erwood Hall, built by the Grimshawe family in 1830, but abandoned when the estate was depopulated prior to flooding.

153

CALEY MILL
NORFOLK

At Heacham, 3 miles south of Hunstanton on the A149.
Tourist Information Centre, The Green, Hunstanton (01455) 532610.

In July or August you'll find Caley Mill fields awash with mauve lavender in full flower, smelling delicious and ready for harvest. Watch Britain's largest lavender factory at its busiest, cutting, drying and distilling the flowers for making oils and delicate lavender waters. Tour the old mill gardens and see extraordinary numbers of different lavender varieties, many of them specially bred at Caley Mill. Then you can visit Heacham village, which is prettily arranged around a green. Inside the old church you'll discover the portrait of the romantic Red Indian princess, Pocohontas, wife of John Rolfe of Heacham Hall until her death in 1617.

IN EASY REACH North of the lavender farm, overlooking The Wash, is Hunstanton, an old fishing village and Victorian seaside resort. Here you will find sandy beaches, swimming and boating, a fun-fair, and the famous 60ft-high Hunstanton cliffs, brightly banded with coloured rock layers of white, red and brown.

South of Caley Mill, on the B1440, is Sandringham House, the royal country residence built in 1870. The house and its beautiful gardens are open in summer except when the royal family is there. Outside is lovely parkland, offering beauty and colour throughout the season, which is always open to the public. Within the grounds is a museum containing fascinating displays of royal memorabilia and an exhibition of the Sandringham Fire Brigade. Wolferton Station Museum, west of the A419 on the Sandringham estate, shows the royal retiring rooms where King Edward VII entertained guests arriving by rail for Sandringham.

King's Lynn is a pleasant old town just below the mouth of the River Great Ouse. It has an 18th-century gaol and a 17th-century Customs House by the quay. The beautiful 15th-century guildhall of chequered flint and stone is the largest surviving medieval guildhall in England, and is now used as an arts centre. The Lynn Museum covers the geology, archaeology and natural history of the area with Bronze Age weapons and relics from the medieval town of Lynn among the displays. The Town House Museum of Lynn Life shows the life of merchants, tradesmen and families who made King's Lynn a prosperous place, with costumes, toys and a working Victorian kitchen.

Buxton Festival

In 1979 the restored 900-seater Opera House in Buxton was re-opened and the Buxton Festival was founded. It takes place around mid-July to August, and one of the festival's highlights has always been the performance of neglected operas. Each year a fresh theme is chosen, concentrating on the influence of a creative artist on his own time and on subsequent generations, and the festival's major events are linked with this theme.

King's Lynn Festival

Late in July, the charming old town of King's Lynn stages its Festival of Music and the Arts, a regular event since 1951. Early, classical and avant-garde music are featured, with choral music, jazz, modern dance, mime, puppetry and children's entertainments, drama, film, poetry and arts and crafts.

154

CHATSWORTH
DERBYSHIRE

At Edensor, on the B6012, 4 miles east of Bakewell.
Tourist Information Centre, Old Market Hall, Bakewell (01629) 813227.

To call Chatsworth a house is rather like calling the *Queen Mary* a boat. The 'Palace of the Peak' has a massive splendour cunningly enhanced by its setting – one of 'Capability' Brown's greatest achievements. The 1st Duke of Devonshire set out in 1686 to enlarge an existing Tudor house, but 11 years later he was the owner of a vast classical mansion. A big stable block was added in the late 1750s, and a whole new north wing in the early 19th century. The visitor today passes through a succession of overwhelming rooms with rich furniture, priceless tapestries, painted ceilings and an astonishing collection of pictures and sculptures. The immense library is particularly impressive.

The grounds are the creation of several talents. The dramatic water cascade survives from the original design, but 'Capability' Brown, seeking a more 'natural' effect, did away with the first formal gardens. The sixth duke's head gardener, Joseph Paxton of Crystal Palace fame, restored them and also improved the view by moving the old village of Edensor and planning a new one.

IN EASY REACH Haddon Hall, 2 miles south-east of Bakewell, on the A6, is very different. Smaller than Chatsworth, it is a charming combination of medieval and Elizabethan styles, almost entirely free from 'improvement' and perfectly set on a sloping hill site. Five miles south of Chatsworth, near Birchover, is Stanton Moor, a gritstone plateau that contains a remarkable concentration of prehistoric sites, the best-known of which is the Nine Ladies stone circle. Another and much larger stone circle, the most important Neolithic site in Derbyshire, can be seen at Arbor Low, on a minor road off the A515 to the south-west of Bakewell.

In the opposite direction, north from Bakewell, is the small village of Eyam, famous for the courageous action of its villagers who, at the time of the Great Plague, put themselves in voluntary quarantine to prevent the disease spreading. Also north of Bakewell is Monsal Head, on the B6465 near Little Longstone, where you can walk along a footpath following the route of the old London to Manchester railway.

Plague Sunday Service

In a field near the church at Eyam are seven tombstones of members of the Hancock family – a poignant reminder of the heroism of the villagers in 1665, when plague struck this remote settlement in the Peak District. Led by the rector, William Mompesson, they decided not to flee, and so not to spread the infection to other villages. Eighty per cent of them died before the plague burnt itself out, including Catherine Mompesson, the rector's wife, whose grave is in the churchyard. The rector held services in the open air at a rocky spot which became known as the Cucklet Church. This is where the Plague Sunday Service is now held on the last Sunday in August every year (see right).

155

CONSTABLE COUNTRY
SUFFOLK AND ESSEX

Off the A12 and A137 in the Stour Valley.
Tourist Information Centres: Duchy Barn, Dedham (01206) 323447
(seasonal opening only) and 1 Queen Street, Colchester (01206) 712920.

The country in the valley of the Stour on the border of Suffolk and Essex was already known as 'Constable Country' in the painter's own lifetime. It was here, in the village of East Bergholt, that John Constable was born in 1776 and here that he found subjects for the well-loved paintings – among them the watermill at Stratford St Mary, Flatford Mill, Willy Lott's Cottage and Dedham Vale – which influenced every subsequent generation's idea of what the English countryside ought to look like.

At East Bergholt is the little cottage where the painter worked (his birthplace is no longer standing) and in the churchyard are the graves of his parents and Willy Lott. Also here are the church bells in a separate 16th-century bell-house. This is because the church tower was never finished: according to local tradition the Devil dismantled the work as fast as the builders could put it up. Nearby

Flatford Mill, on the River Stour, belonged to Constable's father and the artist worked there for a year

Flatford Mill, built in 1733, is now a field studies centre. Willy Lott's Cottage, scene of *The Haywain*, is here on the river bank, looking as it does in the picture, but smarter. Constable went to school in Dedham, Essex, a pretty village of timber-framed houses. Another celebrated artist, Sir Alfred Munnings, lived here, at Castle House, which is now a museum to him (limited opening only). The Constable Country is ideal territory for walking – through Dedham Vale; along the valley of the Stour to its estuary, to watch birds on the mudflats; or following the disused railway lines of the area. The local Tourist Information Centres should be able to provide leaflets and booklets to guide you.

— 156 —

COTON MANOR GARDENS
NORTHAMPTONSHIRE

Between the A50 and A428, 10 miles north-west of Northampton.
Tourist Information Centre, Mr Grant's House, 10 St Giles Square, Northampton
(01604) 22677.

The appeal of Coton Manor Gardens, dating from 1926, is the deceptive feeling that you could do something like it yourself. Although the grounds cover 10 acres, the garden areas on different levels have an attractively homely atmosphere, enhanced by the creative use of familiar trees, shrubs and roses. Clever use is made of a stream and a variety of water features that form a habitat for an impressive collection of flamingos and waterfowl. All in all, it's a delightful place for the ordinary gardener.

IN EASY REACH A few miles south, also between the A50 and the A428, are Holdenby House Gardens. There is something for everyone here, including an Elizabethan garden, a museum, rare livestock breeds, a falconry centre, a pets' corner and other attractions especially for children.

Althorp, not far away to the south, off the A428, has been adapted by the Spencer family since 1508, and now has an elegant 18th-century character. It is the home of Earl Spencer, the brother of the Princess of Wales. The interior has distinguished furniture and porcelain, and the walls are hung with fine pictures. For a change from gardens and houses, head north to Naseby, on the B4036. Here, the Civil War battlefield, where the Royalists under Prince Rupert were decisively defeated by Fairfax and Cromwell in 1645, is the subject of an interpretative display at the Farm Museum (limited opening only).

157

CROFT CASTLE
HEREFORD AND WORCESTER

Off the B4362, 5 miles north-west of Leominster.
Tourist Information Centre, 6 School Lane, Leominster (01568) 616460.

The Croft family have lived here almost continuously for about 900 years, and the present house reflects their successive changes of taste. The authentic 15th-century castle towers and walls survive, but now enclose a house which was modified in the three following centuries to produce an intriguing architectural mix. The most notable features of the mainly 18th-century interior are a splendid staircase in Georgian-Gothic and some exceptional ceilings of the same period.

The grounds form a country park with free access, and are worth visiting for the specimen trees and the famous avenue of Spanish chestnuts. Another attraction here is the hill-fort of Croft Ambrey on the edge of the park. At 1,000ft it commands fine views into Wales.

IN EASY REACH At nearby Lucton the 18th-century watermill (limited opening) has been restored. The three-storey mechanism is one-man-operated, and surprisingly it was working until the 1940s. Outside Kington (west of Leominster on the A44) are the nationally famous Hergest Croft Gardens – 50 acres of trees and plants collected from all over the world, and a rewarding experience for both the connoisseur and the casual visitor.

158

CROMER
NORFOLK

Tourist Information Centre, Bus Station, Prince of Wales Road (01263) 512497.

Fishing boats at Sheringham

Breezy, sandy-beached and unspoilt, Cromer is the nicest of Norfolk's seaside towns, an Edwardian resort surrounded by wooded hills. It is the home of the famous Cromer crab – don't leave without tasting some – and the even more famous lifeboat, whose coxswain from 1909 to 1949, Henry Blogg, was Britain's most decorated lifeboatman.

Cromer's cliffs tower over the beach. You can climb the windy, heather-tufted lighthouse cliff and pause to enjoy the view before touring the lighthouse, or stroll along the pier to inspect the lifeboat station before visiting the 15th-century church: its tower was once used as a lighthouse. Cromer Museum has local history, natural history and geology displays: best of all here are the displays of fossils found in the cliffs.

IN EASY REACH Felbrigg Hall, 2 miles south-west of Cromer off the A148, is a splendid high-chimneyed 17th-century house set in 1,700 acres of wooded park. Inside are elegant Georgian furnishings, pictures and a superb 18th-century library.

At Baconsthorpe Castle, off the A140 south-west of Cromer, you can see the impressive ruins of a fortified and moated manor house built in 1486 by the once powerful Heydon family: you'll find their monuments in the local church. Five miles west of Cromer is the North Norfolk Railway, whose lovely little steam trains chuff picturesquely through scenic countryside between Sheringham and Holt. Besides the ride on the railway, there is a museum of railway memorabilia, and an interesting display of historic locomotives and rolling stock.

Blickling Hall, a National Trust property south of Cromer and a mile north-west of Aylsham on the A140, is a great, red-brick Jacobean and 18th-century mansion. The state rooms are full of interesting furniture, pictures and tapestries, and the great gallery has a beautiful ornate plasterwork ceiling. Landscaped parkland and formal gardens surround the house.

●

Ely Folk Weekend

The Folk Weekend in Ely in July is principally concerned to present traditional folk song and folk dance, in an area of the country which was once a stronghold of these arts. Traditional English, Scottish, Welsh and Irish folk music, English country dancing and Scottish ceilidh dancing, and street theatre for children, are all featured.

●

159

ELY
CAMBRIDGESHIRE

Tourist Information Centre, 29 St Mary's Street (01353) 662062.

The best views of Ely Cathedral are from the south-east, along the A142, but from any angle it effortlessly dominates the flat fenland. The most impressive features are the central octagonal tower and the west front and tower, which are mainly Norman. Inside, Norman pillars support the long nave. Above the crossing is the astonishing octagon, 70ft across, which holds up 400 tons of wooden lantern 94ft above the floor. It was designed in the 1320s by a monk of Ely, Alan of Walsingham, who lies buried near the

west end of the nave. He also designed the choir and the lady chapel. The stained-glass museum in the cathedral is particularly strong on 19th-century glass, while Ely Museum, in the High Street, concentrates on the natural history and social history of Ely and the surrounding fenland. Standing in the shadows of the cathedral Oliver Cromwell's House gives visitors an insight into the domestic and political aspects of his life.

Racehorses off for early-morning exercise near Newmarket

IN EASY REACH The Fens, lying between Cambridge and Lincoln, have gradually been drained over the centuries since Roman times and are now rich farmland. Though flat, this is a haunting landscape, and man-made, as the ruler-straight dykes, neatly regimented rivers and pumping stations bear witness. To see what the fenland was once like, visit Wicken Fen (preserved by the National Trust), off the A1123.

Newmarket, in Suffolk, on the A142 south-east of Ely, is the capital of English horse-racing and breeding, and horses worth a king's ransom are exercised on Newmarket Heath. In the main street, next to the elegant red-brick premises of the Jockey Club, the lively and evocative National Horseracing Museum is well worth a visit. At Haddenham, 7 miles south-west of Ely on the A1123, the Farmland Museum covers rural life and bygones: limited opening here, though.

--------- **160** ---------

GREAT WITLEY CHURCH
HEREFORD AND WORCESTER

On the A443, 10 miles north-west of Worcester.
Tourist Information Centres: Guildhall, High Street, Worcester (01905) 726311 and Load Street, Bewdley (01299) 404740.

Great Witley church is most unusual and most rare. Its contents were bought by Lord Foley from the Duke of Chandos in 1747 and transferred from Edgware to Great Witley. The church interior is a Baroque extravagance with 23 Venetian ceiling paintings by Bellucci, and enamel painted windows by Joshua Price. Recent restoration work on the magnificent gilded stucco and the paintings cost £170,000 and Handel's gilded organ case now looks splendid. Rysbrack's largest marble monument, to Lord Foley, is in the south transept. Concerts are held on summer weekends.

It is a unique experience to explore the ruins of Witley Court, next door, with its huge foundations and remains of Nesfield's fine garden, all of which should be restored and working in the next few years. Formerly the home of the Earls of Dudley, the mansion was started by the Foleys (an iron-making family) in the 17th century. A permanent photographic exhibition of Nesfield's paintings can be seen in the Court.

IN EASY REACH Hartlebury Castle, to the north-east, near Kidderminster, is both the palace of the Bishops of Worcester (limited opening to the public) and the county museum, specialising in rural and domestic life. Canal enthusiasts will enjoy Stourport, on the A451, with its locks, basins, warehouses and inn built by James Brindley as the terminus of the Staffordshire and Worcestershire Canal. At nearby Bewdley, behind the handsome waterfront, is a fascinating museum of local life and industry housed in the old Shambles, and children will love the wild animals and spectacular amusements at The West Midland Safari and Leisure Park, just outside Bewdley.

161

KEDLESTON HALL
DERBYSHIRE

Off the A52, 4½ miles north-west of Derby.
Tourist Information Centre, Assembly Rooms, Market Place, Derby (01332) 255802.

Derbyshire is famous for its stately homes, but none outdoes the grandeur and elegant symmetry of Kedleston Hall, long the home of the Curzon family, and now in the hands of the National Trust. An immense portico fronts the main block, which is connected by curved walkways to substantial pavilions on each side. Robert Adam, the principal architect, created the sensational marble hall and a succession of splendid state rooms, finely furnished and housing an important collection of paintings. He also designed the breathtaking park with consummate skill. The most famous member of the Curzon family was Viceroy of India at the turn of the century, and visitors can see his memorial chapel in the 12th-century church, together with other family monuments, and a collection of his treasures.

IN EASY REACH Derby does not spring to mind as a tourist attraction, but it has much to offer the visitor (including the county show in May). The cathedral, for example, has an interior that combines 18th-century splendour with the best modern craftsmanship. The Museum and Art Gallery in the Strand has an enormous range of displays, including porcelain, coins, natural history, archaeology and folk exhibits, together with a collection of paintings by the important local artist Joseph Wright, while the former silk mill, off Full Street, now houses the Derby Industrial Museum, devoted to the history of local mining, quarrying and manufacturing, with special emphasis on Rolls-Royce and British Rail. You can see the porcelain industry at first hand at the Royal Crown Derby factory in Osmaston Road. Joseph Pickford's House, 41 Friar Gate, has been converted to a museum of domestic life.

Finally, there is a museum of a different kind, 5 miles south-east of Derby, at Elvaston Castle Country Park. Here the lifestyle, work and crafts associated with a country estate at the turn of the century are re-created. There are also formal gardens, and extensive topiary gardens.

162

THE MALVERN HILLS
HEREFORD AND WORCESTER

Tourist Information Centre, Winter Gardens, Grange Road, Malvern (01684) 892289.

Herefordshire Beacon, lying just to the east of Little Malvern, is one of the best viewpoints along the Malvern Hills

•

Malvern Spa Days and Three Counties Agricultural Show

In July the Victorian age comes back to life at Malvern. Some of the townspeople and shopkeepers dress in 19th-century Victorian costume, there is a Victorian craft fair, a polite garden party, musical entertainments, and an exhibition by the local quilters. Perhaps the most vivid item is a re-enactment of the full horrors of the water cure in the town's spa days. The month before sees the three-day Three Counties Agricultural Show (the counties being Worcestershire, Herefordshire and Gloucestershire) with prizes for cattle, sheep, pigs and poultry, plus show-jumping, a dog show, morris dancing, and motor cycle races to finish things off.

•

The 9-mile range of the Malverns rears up dramatically from the plain on the former border of Worcestershire and Herefordshire, providing panoramic views for those who take advantage of the easily accessible walks. Popular for many centuries, the hills were first celebrated by the medieval poet William Langland, who made them the setting for his poem *The Vision of Piers Plowman*.

The whole ridgetop walk is perfectly feasible for the active family, but most people prefer to aim for well-known landmarks like the Worcestershire Beacon, the highest point at 1,400ft, which can be reached by a path from Great Malvern. (The path passes St Anne's Well, one of the original sources of Malvern water.) The Herefordshire Beacon has a powerfully ramparted Iron Age hill-fort, with a car park conveniently close at Wynds Point, and there is another fort further south on Midsummer Hill.

It was the combination of bracing walks, and remarkably pure water that established Great Malvern as a Victorian spa, and the town retains much of the atmosphere of a respectable resort. The wide streets near the centre are full of splendidly varied 19th-century architecture, and many of the spa buildings survive in new guises in and around Belle Vue Terrace at the top of the town. Here, too, are the attractively landscaped Priory Park, the entertainment centre at the Winter Gardens and the magnificent Priory Church.

The Malvern Hills had a great influence on the life and music of Elgar and the simple graves of the composer and his wife can be seen in the churchyard of St Wulfstan's Roman Catholic Church at Little Malvern. Not far away, on the A4104, Little Malvern Court incorporates a fine 14th-century prior's hall, and the remains of the adjacent priory, used as the parish church, are well worth visiting. Four miles further south-west, on the A438, is Eastnor Castle, a massive castellated house in the Gothic style, built in 1814. The imposing interior contains collections of armour, tapestries and portraits, and there are fine grounds.

163

NEWSTEAD ABBEY
NOTTINGHAMSHIRE

Off the A60, 10 miles north of Nottingham.
Tourist Information Centre, 1-4 Smithy Row, Nottingham (0115) 9470661.

The Byron family acquired this 13th-century abbey in the 1540s and turned it into a private house, building round the original cloister. By the time Lord Byron, the poet, inherited it, Newstead had become so run down that he sold it to a man wealthy enough to have it restored, by the architect John Shaw. As a result the house is an odd but attractive mixture of medieval and modern, with some very old rooms around the courtyard and mainly 19th-century furnishing in the principal apartments above. The saloon and Great Hall are outstanding, but for most people the attraction will be the wealth of mementoes of the poet, including his bedroom. There is also an extremely beautiful park.

IN EASY REACH In the nearby village of Ravenshead is the Longdale Rural Craft Centre. In addition to the permanent craft museum, the centre caters for just about every traditional craft, with demonstrations during the holiday season. Four miles to the south, on the B683, is Papplewick Pumping Station – a very grand Victorian engine house set in fine landscaped gardens. The interior (which can only be seen weekends, by appointment) is richly decorated, with ornate columns and stained-glass windows, but the focus of attention is the pair of beam-engines built in 1884 by the James Watt company.

Not far away, across the M1 Motorway, is Eastwood, on the A610, the birthplace of D H Lawrence and the setting of his early novels, including *Sons and Lovers*. He was born at 8a Victoria Street, and occupied various other houses in the town. There's a detailed guide available for devotees of the author.

164

SOMERSBY CHURCH
LINCOLNSHIRE

Off the A158, 6 miles north-east of Horncastle.
Tourist Information Centre, New Market Hall, Louth (01507) 609289.

Remote and secluded in a hollow of the Lincolnshire Wolds, the hamlet of Somersby was the birthplace of Alfred Lord Tennyson. His father was rector here and the poet was born in the old rectory (not open). Across the road in the humble little 15th-century church of St Margaret is a bust of Tennyson by Thomas Woolner and a few personal relics of the poet – a quill pen and some clay pipes. His father's grave is in the churchyard.

IN EASY REACH The Wolds are low chalk hills, running some 40 miles north-west from Spilsby. In the 15th and 16th centuries they supported vast flocks of sheep. The A153 from Horncastle to Louth offers Wolds views, but they are best explored on the back roads.

A mile or so east of Somersby, Harrington Hall, the house in Tennyson's poem *Maud* ('Come into the garden, Maud') was destroyed by a fire in 1992, and is now being rebuilt. Further south-east, 6 miles from Somersby, the quiet market town of Spilsby was the birthplace of another famous figure, the Arctic explorer Sir John Franklin, whose statue stands in the marketplace. If you visit in mid-July, you may catch the Spilsby show. To the south-east again, on the coast, is the bleak nature reserve of Gibraltar Point, whose saltmarshes and sand dunes offer good birdwatching. Alford, on the A1104, 5 miles north-east of Spilsby, has a handsome church, a craft market and a folk museum.

There's a good sandy beach at Mablethorpe and a small zoo, the Mablethorpe Animal and Bird Gardens. Louth, on the A16, 11 miles north-west of Alford, is a handsome Georgian, Regency and Victorian town. The museum in Broadbank has collections of butterflies and moths, as well as local bygones.

Tennyson Memorial Service

The Tennyson Memorial Service is held in alternate years at Somersby and next-door Bag Enderby – the two villages of which the poet's father, the Reverend George Tennyson, was rector – on the first Sunday in August every year. Both these little churches date from the 15th century. The future Poet Laureate was baptised in the font in Somersby church and there are Tennyson connections also at Louth, where he attended the grammar school as a small boy. He detested it and persuaded his father to teach him at home. His first poems were published by a Louth bookseller in 1827.

The Stiperstones

●

Arts Festival

Church Stretton is an enjoyable little town, set in a valley among dramatically beautiful hills. The local population blends middle-class retired people with farmers and farm workers, and the Church Stretton and South Shropshire Arts Festival at the turn of July and August was started in the 1960s by a group of local enthusiasts to bring art of all varieties to both elements of the mix. It has moved from amateur performances to being entirely professional. Classical music, country and western, brass bands, jazz, photography, film, poetry and prose, drama and the visual arts are all included.

●

--- **165** ---

THE STIPERSTONES
SHROPSHIRE

South of Minsterley, off the A488, 18 miles south-west of Shrewsbury.
Tourist Information Centre, Church Street, Church Stretton (01694) 723133.

A dark folklore has always surrounded these dramatic quartz outcrops, jagged and broken after millions of years of hostile weather. On a bright day they are a cheerful place, with some of the best views in Shropshire, but in gloomy weather it is easy to understand the legends that tell of their creation by the Devil. Indeed, the highest point, at 1,700ft, is called the Devil's Chair. But don't be put off by the stories – the Stiperstones are a memorable place to walk. Around Snailbeach, at the northern end of the ridge, you can find many remains of the once-thriving lead-mining industry.

IN EASY REACH To the east of the Stiperstones lie the Church Stretton hills. You can take a car over the broad Long Mynd massif, with its prehistoric track called the Portway, and on foot explore the deep ravine known as Cardingmill Valley. The more energetic can follow the path from Church Stretton to the hill-fort on Caer Caradoc, east of the A49.

Five miles south of the village, off the A49, is the delightful Acton Scott Working Farm Museum, where the Victorian age of pre-mechanised farming has been revived. Machinery and rare breeds are on show, and there are regular craft demonstrations. Wenlock Edge can be reached by minor roads to the south-east of Church Stretton – the best views are at the northern end and include the famous precipice known as Major's Leap. Finally, it is well worth seeking out the remote and tranquil ruins of the 13th-century Acton Burnell Castle, 7 miles north-east of Church Stretton, where Edward I held a parliament.

--- **166** ---

TATTERSHALL CASTLE
LINCOLNSHIRE

On the A153, 4 miles south of Woodhall Spa.
Tourist Information Centre, Blackfriars Art Centre, Spain Lane, Boston (01205) 356656.

With walls up to 16ft thick, the castle keep at Tattershall is composed of some of the finest brickwork in all England, and inside is a wonderful winding brick staircase. The huge tower, 110ft high, is almost all that is left of the combined stronghold and stately home built in the 15th century by Ralph Cromwell, who was Lord Treasurer to Henry VI. Turreted and battlemented, it can be seen for miles across the Fens and there are stunning views from the top. The guardhouse inside the double moat now holds a small museum. Ralph Cromwell also built the light, airy church, in the local stone.

IN EASY REACH Near Tattershall Bridge on the A158 is the Dogdyke Pumping Station, where you can see the 1856 steam drainage engine – the last one in the Fens that still works – and the 1914 diesel engine that replaced it. Woodhall Spa, on the B1191 to the north, is a pleasant little place which thrived in the 19th century on its iodine-rich spring water. To the south-east of Tattershall is the busy town of Boston, famous for 'Boston Stump', the graceful 272ft tower of St Botolph's Church. Crowned by an octagonal lantern, it is a landmark for miles around. The 15th-century guildhall in the High Street is now a local museum.

167

WIMPOLE HALL
CAMBRIDGESHIRE

At New Wimpole, off the A603, 8 miles south-west of Cambridge.
Tourist Information Centre, Wheeler Street, Cambridge (01223) 322640.

Inside this gorgeous red-brick house, in the care of the National Trust, is one of the loveliest rooms in England, and also one of the oddest. Both were designed by Sir John Soane in the 1790s. The beautiful one is the yellow drawing-room, T-shaped under a noble dome. The odd one is the bathroom, where a tub which holds no less than 2,200 gallons of water (heated from a boiler underneath) is reached down an elegant flight of curving wooden stairs.

Built in the 17th century for a rich London merchant, the house was enlarged in the following century by James Gibbs. He bestowed on it a splendid library and a chapel, with astonishing *trompe-l'oeil* baroque effects by Sir James Thornhill. The church, next to the house, contains huge, grandiose monuments to the 18th-century Yorkes. In the park is the home farm, now a rare breeds centre, with a great black barn by Soane.

Rudyard Kipling's daughter, Mrs Elsie Bambridge, was a former owner of Wimpole Hall

IN EASY REACH Don't miss the Imperial War Museum's terrific assemblage of military and civil aircraft at Duxford Airfield, an old Battle of Britain fighter aerodrome on the A505 to the east; there are plenty of flying days and special events here, with a particular attraction being the Military Show in early August. Anglesey Abbey, 6 miles north-east of Cambridge, like Wimpole is another National Trust property, an Elizabethan manor house with sumptuous gardens and garden statuary. On the other side of Cambridge, at Madingley, the touching and dignified American Cemetery is the last resting place of thousands of American servicemen of World War II.

168

WORCESTER
HEREFORD AND WORCESTER

Tourist Information Centre, Guildhall, High Street (01905) 723471.

Every three years, in August, Worcester is host to the Three Choirs Festival, established in the 18th century and the oldest arts festival of all. It also has its own Carnival Week each year in late June or early July. Music, together with sauce, porcelain and gloves have made the city famous, although its older charms are less apparent following 1960s development.

However, there is still much to seek out and enjoy, and most people will start at the cathedral. The original foundation was Norman, and the magnificent crypt dates from this period. The graceful choir houses the tomb of King John (the marble effigy is the oldest royal effigy in the country) and the chantry tomb of Prince Arthur, eldest son of Henry VII.

Close to the cathedral is the Commandery, originally a medieval hospital and now a small museum housing exhibits relating to the Civil War. In nearby Severn Street you can visit the famous Royal Worcester porcelain factory to watch production, and to see the superb displays in the museum. Many of the city's surviving timber-framed buildings are in Friar Street, including the Tudor House Museum and the well-restored Greyfriars.

IN EASY REACH At Lower Broadheath, a few miles to the west of Worcester, is Elgar's birthplace, on Crown East Lane, an unassuming cottage, now a museum to the composer and packed with interesting memorabilia

Spetchley Park, on the A422, is 3 miles from the city centre in the other direction, and has 30 acres of very fine natural gardens with rare trees, a lake and a deer park. Further afield, Hanbury Hall, 3½ miles east of Droitwich, and for the Watney collection of porcelain figures. While you are in Hanbury it is also well worth looking in at the Jinney Ring Craft Centre on the B4091.

Three Choirs Festival and Festival of Busking

The Three Choirs Festival in August is held in turn in Worcester, Hereford and Gloucester cathedrals, and is Europe's oldest music festival. The choirs of the three cathedrals first joined together for two days each year in about 1715, the object being to raise money for the widows and orphaned children of clergymen in the three dioceses. The occasion gradually grew and by the middle of the 18th century Handel oratorios were regular features. Sir Edward Elgar took a prominent part in the festivals in his day and his music remains a major element of the occasion, together with music by Vaughan Williams, Bliss, Holst and other English composers.
To the north of Worcester, at Droitwich, a much newer annual event is the Festival of Busking, early in June, when buskers perform in the streets and the shopping precinct.

169

BIRMINGHAM
WEST MIDLANDS

Tourist Information Centres: 2 City Arcade 0121-643 2514. The Piazza, National Exhibition Centre 0121-780 4321 and Birmingham Airport 0121-767 7145.

Walsall Illuminations

Though not as famous as their counterparts in Blackpool, Walsall Illuminations draw no fewer than 300,000 visitors to the town every year in September and early October. The trees in Walsall Arboretum, which is the principal park, are hung with thousands of light bulbs, and large representations of aeroplanes or whatever – the theme changes each year – are fastened up and picked out with lights. The whole scene shimmers and sparkles after dark.

It may be difficult now to visualise Birmingham, Britain's second biggest city, as a village in open country, but you can see the evidence with your own eyes at Blakesley Hall in Blakesley Road, Yardley. Despite its important-sounding name, it is a 16th-century half-timbered farmhouse, now kept as a museum and furnished in 17th-century style. On a much grander scale is Aston Hall, in Trinity Road, Aston, the palatial country seat of the Holte family, completed in 1635. It, too, is now a museum (open till the end of October only), with period rooms from the 17th century to the 19th.

Birmingham made its first fortune turning out weapons for the Roundheads during the Civil War, but its major growth came with the Industrial Revolution as a manufacturing centre and a hub of communications for the coal and iron industries of the Black Country. In its day it was at the centre of the English canal network, and there are pleasurable cruises today from Gas Street Basin.

The city's history can be enjoyably examined at the Birmingham Museum and Art Gallery, Chamberlain Square, which also possesses one of the best collections of Pre-Raphaelite art in existence, along with excellent fine and applied arts material. The Museum of Science and Industry, Newhall Street, covers the Birmingham arms trade, with much else of interest.

IN EASY REACH At Bournville, to the south of the city centre, is Cadbury World, a 'must' for chocolate lovers. To the north-west, in Walsall, the Museum and Gallery, Lichfield Street, houses the Garman-Ryan collection of fine art formed by Lady Kathleen Epstein, the sculptor's widow, with art of all periods arranged by theme instead of chronologically. There is a local history gallery as well, and in Bradford Street is the Jerome K Jerome Museum, in the birthplace of the author of *Three Men in a Boat*.

170

THE BLACK COUNTRY MUSEUM
WEST MIDLANDS

In Tipton Road, Dudley, off the A4123.
Tourist Information Centre, 39 Churchill Precinct, Dudley (01384) 250333.

Buildings from the area have been re-erected at the Black Country Museum. Seen here are the premises of 38 Piper's Row, which stood at the junction with Tower Street in Wolverhampton.

Out of the grime of the old Black Country has come a whole range of leisure attractions in and around Dudley. The centrepiece is the Black Country Museum, a misleading name for an enjoyable reconstruction of a Victorian working village, complete with cottages, shops, pub, chapel, workshops, canal and pithead. You can take a tram ride to the Bottle and Glass pub, which is genuine right down to its fine real ale, and drop in on a glass-cutter, a chain-maker, a chemist, a baker and even a photographer.

Not to be missed is a trip on a canal boat into the Dudley Tunnel – an eerie underground journey, during which you emerge into two former basins and enter the 'Singing Cavern', a re-opened mine with an audio-visual display.

IN EASY REACH On a wooded hill in the centre of the town stands Dudley Castle. The ruins, especially of the Great Hall and chapel, are impressive, and the whole area is well-landscaped and an ideal place for a picnic. Around it is the long-established Dudley Zoo, laid out in an old limestone quarrying area, with a very extensive collection of wild animals.

The Stourbridge area has always been noted for fine crystal ware, and the Broadfield House Glass Museum not only explains the history and production methods of the industry, but shows off a vast range of the beautiful results. The museum has been set up in a handsome mansion in Barnett Lane, Kingswinford, to the west of Dudley. The glass industry is still very much alive in the area, and two of the largest firms welcome visitors: Royal Doulton at Amblecote north of Stourbridge and a little further north on the A461 at Royal Brierley Crystal in North Street, Brierley Hill visitors can go on factory tours, look round the museums and buy glass.

— 171 —
BURGHLEY HOUSE
CAMBRIDGESHIRE

Off the A1, 1½ miles south-east of Stamford. Only open till early October.
Tourist Information Centre, Stamford Arts Centre, Stamford (01780) 55611.

The famous Horse Trials in September attract thousands of visitors to 'Capability' Brown's huge park, which extends right up to the streets of Stamford. Burghley House is a modest name for what is in fact an Elizabethan palace built by William Cecil, Queen Elizabeth's chief minister. Of awe-inspiring size, three storeys high and with a roofscape that bristles with pinnacles, cupolas and paired chimneys, the house is, from the outside, one of the best examples of 16th-century architecture. But don't expect to find a restrained Tudor interior. The vast kitchen is original, but a complete refurbishment between 1681 and 1700 resulted in state rooms that are exuberantly baroque, with silver fireplaces, elaborate plasterwork and ceiling paintings by Antonio Verrio, whose virtuoso skill culminates in the Heaven Room with figures that seem to leap from the walls. The furniture and tapestries are superb, and every room abounds with paintings from the Marquess of Exeter's collection.

IN EASY REACH Stamford is a most elegant town of handsome stone buildings. Its five medieval churches are all of interest, but St Mary's is undoubtedly the grandest, with a soaring spire, a fine Corpus Christi chapel and a chancel beautifully restored in the Arts and Crafts tradition. The 15th-century Browne's Hospital is reckoned to be among the best medieval almshouses in the country with an outstanding chapel. The 'gallows' sign of the George Inn extends across the street, a reminder of Stamford's splendid Georgian heritage, seen at its best in the Barn Hill area. A preliminary visit to the museum in Broad Street is highly recommended, and don't miss the Steam Brewery Museum (open till the end of October only), where the entire Victorian equipment has been restored to sparkling condition.

The Wildfowl Trust at Peakirk (8 miles east of Stamford on the B1443) has well over 100 species of birds housed in a very attractive setting where visitors are encouraged to roam at will.

●

Horse Trials and Ashton Conker Knock-Out Championships

The first Three-Day Event in the Burghley House parkland was held in 1961 and was won by Anneli Drummond-Hay on a horse called Merely-a-Monarch. A three-day event combines a dressage contest with speed and endurance tests, including a cross-country marathon (see above), and the final day's show jumping. The Burghley event (held in early September) has established itself as the major autumn occasion in the horse trials calendar.

Another interesting sporting event in the district follows a month later. This is at Ashton, a village near Oundle, to the south of Stamford, where the World Conker Knock-Out Championships are held every year in October.

●

Burton Beer Festival

Real-ale addicts should flock to Burton upon Trent in September each year, when the local branch of the Campaign for Real Ale organises the Burton Beer Festival, which stays open to the public for three thirst-quenching days. Local, national and international breweries bring their beers, lagers and ciders to Burton Town hall.

172

BURTON UPON TRENT
STAFFORDSHIRE

Tourist Information Centre, Octagon Centre, New Street (01283) 516609.

The annual Beer Festival in September provides an excellent reason for visiting Burton, a town that is not otherwise high in the tourist league. It may be short on romance, but there is no lack of local pride in the brewing industry, and the famous firm of Bass runs an entertaining and informative museum in its old joiner's workshop in Horninglow Street. There are three floors of indoor exhibits on brewing history, very professionally housed, and outside you can see some unusual vehicles, including a 1917 steam lorry and an extraordinary Daimler van built as a replica of a bottle of beer. Among other attractions are a late-Victorian brewhouse, stables with shire horses, a steam locomotive and, of course, the beer.

Apart from several more giant breweries, the town of Burton has monuments of Victorian architecture in the old Midland Railway grain warehouse near the station, the splendid Gothic town hall and St Paul's Church, which has a notable iron screen. The gem of the town, however, is St Modwen's Church, built in 1726 in the very distinctive Gothic style of the period.

IN EASY REACH Tutbury, on the A50, to the north-west of Burton, is a market town noted for its crystal; visitors can watch craftsmen at work. Mary, Queen of Scots was imprisoned in the Castle, whose grim ruins include a 14th-century gatehouse and a high tower which provides fine views over the Dove Valley. In the main street of the town look out for the 16th-century Dog and Partridge Hotel. Further north-west, on the A50, 6 miles south-east of Uttoxeter, Sudbury Hall has what is probably the best Restoration interior of any house in England, with carving by Grinling Gibbons among others. The house is worth visiting for its staircase and long gallery alone. An outbuilding has been converted into an enjoyable museum of childhood.

One of the Bass Museum's prime exhibits is this Daimler Bottle Car. In the 1920s five chassis were bought from Daimler and turned into advertising vehicles by the brewery

173

CANNOCK CHASE
STAFFORDSHIRE

Between Cannock and Rugely, on either side of the A460.
Information Centre at Milford on the A513. Tourist Information Centres: The Ancient High House, Greengate Street, Stafford (01785) 40204 and Octagon Centre, New Street, Burton upon Trent (01283) 516609.

Kings and noblemen once hunted the stag and the wild boar where today oaks and silver birches, pines and gorse, bracken and heathland cover 17,000 acres of an Area of Outstanding Natural Beauty. At the highest point are the Iron Age ramparts of Castle Ring. There are birch woods, pools and streams at Seven Springs, fine views over the River Trent from Brereton Spurs, and wild deer in Sherbrook Valley and near Coppice Hill. The Staffordshire Way Footpath runs through the Chase and there are nature trails, picnic places and a 3-mile forest walk.

Besides its natural attractions, the Chase has particularly interesting World War I links. Between 1914 and 1918 a quarter of a million soldiers were trained here and the ruins of the army camps and the camp railway can be explored. The military cemeteries are a moving reminder of the cost of war. Near Pye Green is the Commonwealth Cemetery, and not far away 5,000 German servicemen who died in Britain in the two World Wars lie beneath plain grey headstones.

IN EASY REACH On the northern edge of the Chase, off the A513, is Shugborough Hall, the stately 18th-century residence of the Ansons, Earls of Lichfield, with mementoes of Admiral Lord Anson. The laundry, brewery and domestic quarters are specially worth seeing, as are the wondrous follies in the grounds, and a working farm with rare breeds.

Further south-east off the A51 at Longdon Green is Hanch Hall, attractive in red brick, with a thoroughly engaging collection of art objects, oddities and oddments gathered by the owners. The gardens are full of exotic wildfowl, so tame and lazy that you may have to step over them.

Abbots Bromley, to the north-east on the B5014, is an attractive village, best known for its Horn Dance held each September. It has an ancient buttercross, an unusual church, numerous inns, and a rich mixture of good buildings. Just to the west of Abbots Bromley is Blithfield Reservoir, a rewarding place for bird-watchers in autumn and winter.

174

THE DONINGTON COLLECTION
LEICESTERSHIRE

At Donington Park, 2 miles south-west of Castle Donington.
Tourist Information Centre, Assembly Rooms, Market Place, Derby (01332) 255802.

The Donington motor-racing circuit came to fame in the 1930s, when Grand Prix races were run there. It was reopened for racing in 1977 and is also home to the world's largest display of single-seater racing cars, some of them still run in events for historic machines. Lotuses and Ferraris are cheek by jowl here with BRMs and Brabhams, Maseratis and McLarens, and there are cars driven in their prime by such great names as Fangio, Nuvolari, Clark, Hill, Stewart and Mansell.

IN EASY REACH The 18th-century formal gardens of Melbourne Hall (limited opening only) are among the finest of their kind, and the modest house has a notable collection of furniture and pictures. It lies 8 miles south of Derby on the A514. Don't miss the impressive Norman church in Melbourne, with its remarkable nave arcade. Two other churches in the area are of great interest. At Repton, on the B5008, 5 miles west of Melbourne, there is a marvellously preserved crypt, designed as the resting place of Saxon kings, while the church at Staunton Harold in Leicestershire, off the B587, 3 miles south of Melbourne, boasts an astonishing wrought-iron screen and outstanding 17th-century woodwork.

175

GRIME'S GRAVES
NORFOLK

Off the A1065 from Weeting, north-west of Thetford.
Tourist Information Centre, 21 White Hart Street, Thetford (01842) 752599.

About 5,000 years ago, Neolithic miners hacked flint from the rock at Grime's Graves. In some places they mined opencast workings, in others they sank shafts up to 40ft deep to reach the stone. Over the 34-acre site nearly 400 shafts have been found, each with a series of radiating galleries below ground. One of the shafts is open and you can clamber down ladders to the bottom and peer along the stuffy little galleries, 5ft high and just wide enough for a man lying down to swing a deer-antler pickaxe.

IN EASY REACH North of Thetford lies the Breckland – wild sandy heathland where stone curlews nest, scattered pine trees grow and rabbits nibble the short matted grasses. It's ideal for walks: make for Weeting Heath Nature Reserve (summer only) or East Wretham Heath Reserve (open all year with nature trails). Further north, at Cockley Cley, south-west of Swaffham, a village of the Iceni tribe has been reconstructed. Thetford itself, once the seat of East Anglian kings, stands where the rivers Thet and Little Ouse meet. The castle mound is an impressive 80ft hill encircled by Iron Age earthworks (no traces of the fortress); the Ancient House Museum is an early-Tudor, half-timbered house with displays on local history and Breckland wildlife. The Charles Burrell Museum in Minstergate tells the story of this once world-famous manufacturer of steam engines.

Horn Dance

The annual Horn Dance at Abbots Bromley early in September is one of the oddest folk customs in the country. Six men dance through the village and the surrounding countryside carrying on their shoulders heavy reindeer antlers – kept in Abbots Bromley church the rest of the year – and accompanied by a Maid Marian (a man dressed as a woman), a hobby horse, a fool, a bowman, a triangle player and an accordionist (see above). How and why this dance began, no one knows, but it is believed to bring good luck to the parish. The earliest reference to it comes from 1686, but one set of reindeer horns has been carbon-dated to about 1100.

— 176 —

HARDWICK HALL
DERBYSHIRE

On a minor road off the A617, 5 miles north-west of Mansfield.
Tourist Information Centre, Low Pavement, Chesterfield (01246) 207777.

Festival of the Arts

The two-week Festival of the Arts at Mansfield (5 miles from Hardwick Hall) every year in the middle of October, was started in 1967 by the Borough Council and is now organised by the local arts association. The festival mingles professional and amateur performances in the areas of classical and popular music. British folk music, dance and ballet, plays, films, puppetry, literature and such crafts as ceramics, wood-carving and jewellery.

There is a jingle 'Hardwick Hall, more glass than wall', and certainly this house must have been considered avant-garde in the 1590s. A very low colonnade runs in front of the central section, which appears to be hung between tall towers, and the generous windows dominate the façade. But the most remarkable feature of the house is its internal construction, with low service rooms on the ground floor and the other two storeys increasing in height to provide a magnificent long gallery and great chamber on the top floor. It was built at great expense by 'Bess of Hardwick', widow of the 6th Earl of Shrewsbury, and her descendants had little interest in 'improving it', so the house and fine gardens have remained largely unchanged. The furniture, tapestries and plasterwork are splendid examples of their period.

IN EASY REACH Bolsover Castle, on the A632, 5½ miles east of Chesterfield, is less well-known but just as fascinating. It stands on a high ridge in coal-mining country, and includes a succession of state rooms and an attractive 170ft-long riding school – now used by Riding for the Disabled. This is another of the grand Cavendish houses in Derbyshire. Bess's second husband (she had four) was Sir William Cavendish, and her youngest son, Sir Charles, rebuilt the Norman remains of Bolsover Castle into a splendid romantic mansion in the early 17th century. Various monuments to the Cavendishes can be seen in Bolsover Church, where there is a chapel named after the family. A little further north-east again, off the A616, is the limestone gorge of Creswell Crags. The caves in the gorge are among the oldest homes in Britain, occupied by Neanderthal man far back in the Old Stone Age. There is a good visitor centre here with an exhibition and an audio-visual programme showing what life must have been like in those days.

— 177 —

IRON BRIDGE
SHROPSHIRE

In the centre of Ironbridge, on the southern outskirts of Telford.
Tourist Information near the site (01952) 432166.

An almost perfect semi-circle with a road deck supported on elaborate cast-iron tracery, the Iron Bridge is surely the most recognisable bridge in the world, and certainly one of the most photographed. Opened in 1781, the first major bridge ever to be constructed in previously unpredictable cast iron, it stands as a monument to the technical brilliance of Abraham Darby III and the architectural skill of Thomas Pritchard.

The River Severn has carved a deep gorge here, and it was discovered at a very early date that supplies of coal, iron, limestone and timber were all concentrated within this small area. When Abraham Darby I moved to nearby Coalbrookdale in 1708 and perfected a technique for smelting iron with coke rather than charcoal, he started an era which made the Severn Gorge the technological centre of the world and cradle of the Industrial Revolution.

The first iron rails, the first iron boat, the first iron-framed building and, of course, the first iron bridge were all made possible by the ironmasters of the gorge. Other industries established themselves too, and the area was particularly noted for decorative tiles and the famous Coalport china.

Industry gradually died out in the early 20th century and the area quietly decayed, but in the 1960s a Trust was formed to set up an industrial museum. What started as a small project now has many sites covering a wide area. You can visit the original Darby works at Coalbrookdale with its Museum of Iron, the vast Blists Hill site, which is being developed as a reconstruction of a Victorian working community, the Coalport Museum, with marvellous displays of fine china, and the Jackfield Tile Museum. The Museum of the River at Ironbridge is the best place to start, since it introduces the history of both the area and the museum. Apart from these major sites there are many subsidiary attractions, such as the Tar Tunnel at Coalport (a tunnel into the river bank) with the spectacular Hay Inclined Plane rising above it.

IN EASY REACH Buildwas Abbey, off the B4380 west of Ironbridge, was built in the 12th century and its ruins include the fine arcades of the church and an interesting chapter house with medieval tiles. Nearby are the vast cooling towers of Buildwas Power Station, one of Shropshire's most impressive modern sights. Other attractions in the area include the small town of Much Wenlock, with fine priory ruins and an interesting Guildhall, and back towards Ironbridge, the 16th-century Benthall Hall. This house (only open till the end of September), was owned by a Roman Catholic family and has an interior of outstanding interest, with decorated plaster ceilings and oak panelling, and a fascinating church in the grounds.

178

LAVENHAM
SUFFOLK

On the A134, north of Sudbury. Tourist Information Centre, The Caravan, Station Road, Sudbury (01787) 881320.

In the 15th century Suffolk sheep supported a wealthy wool industry and Lavenham was a prosperous centre for the merchants. Probably the prettiest small town in the county (and one of the most popular with tourists), Lavenham rejoices in beautiful timbered houses, decorated with carving and pargetting plasterwork. The spectacular 16th-century Guildhall of Corpus Christi, a National Trust property, is now a museum of local history with a delightful garden (only open till the end of October). For refreshment try one of the town's lovely old inns – the Angel Hotel with its 16th-century ceiling, for instance, or the Swan Hotel, with the old Wool Hall standing behind it.

IN EASY REACH Long Melford, 4 miles south-west of Lavenham on the A134, is another pretty, old Suffolk wool town. The main things to see here are the large and elegant church; Melford Hall (National Trust), a 16th century mansion in red brick, with fine pictures, furniture and porcelain, a Beatrix Potter display and gardens; and romantic Kentwell Hall, a moated red-brick Tudor house at the end of a long avenue of limes, with a rare breeds farm.

Cavendish and Clare are two exceptionally pretty villages on the A1092, west of Long Melford in the Stour Valley. Cavendish has thatched cottages around a green, the Sue Ryder Foundation Museum, and Nether Hall, a listed 15th-century manor house surrounded by its own vineyards (tour the house, taste the wines). Clare is noted for its beautiful pargeted houses, the remains of a 13th-century Augustinian priory and a ruined castle.

Designed by Thomas Pritchard of nearby Broseley, the sections of the Iron Bridge were cast at Coalbrookdale. Inset: a rather smaller example of cast-iron work the 'Boy and Swan' fountain was made in 1851

—— 179 ——

LICHFIELD
STAFFORDSHIRE

Tourist Information Centre, Donegal House, Bore Street (01543) 252109.

The 'Ladies of the Vale' – the three spires of Lichfield Cathedral – dominate a city that is in reality a small market town of unusual character. Large areas of swamp in the original settlement which grew up around St Chad's 7th-century chapel made close-set building impossible, so your first impression of Lichfield is likely to be of space and greenery, complemented by the Minster Pool (easily mistaken for a stretch of river) that still cuts off the cathedral area from the town.

The cathedral's isolated position has resulted in a remarkably complete group of ecclesiastical buildings, and The Close is a quiet and harmonious precinct of gracious houses, dominated by the deanery and the bishop's palace. The cathedral itself has needed much restoration over the centuries, but the impact of its famous west front remains as strong as ever – the elaborate and deeply etched carving has a dramatic effect, even though most of the large figures are Victorian. The interior is an equally striking vista of intricate vaulting stretching the full length of the building. As you walk towards the lady chapel you pass Francis Chantrey's sculpture of the 'Sleeping Children', commemorating two children who died in a fire in 1812.

Much of the compact city centre has been pedestrianised, so you can stroll at leisure to admire the handsome small-scale streets. Lichfield produced four celebrated men of the 18th century – the scientist Erasmus Darwin, the actor David Garrick, the essayist Joseph Addison and, of course, Samuel Johnson, whose birthday, 18 September 1709, is commemorated each year. A statue of him now sits on a pedestal in the Market Place, facing his house, which contains a museum of his life and work. James Boswell stands loyally nearby.

For the story of Lichfield itself, you should visit the former St Mary's Church, now preserved as a vivid heritage centre. Another famous Lichfield church, St Chad's, stands by Stowe Pool, well worth visiting for the view of the cathedral. Among the outstanding buildings in the city centre are the Georgian mansion called Donegal House and the 16th-century Lichfield House – both in Bore Street. Best of all, perhaps, is St John's Hospital, an almshouse of 14th-century foundation and still incorporating its chapel, recently enhanced by a magnificent John Piper window.

IN EASY REACH To the south-west of Lichfield, at Wall, are Roman remains including a posting station with bath house, and a fascinating museum of finds from the locality. Still close to Lichfield, but to the south-east, is the Staffordshire Regiment Museum at Whittington Barracks. Weapons, uniforms, medals and captured trophies are amongst the exhibits here.

Samuel Johnson's Birthday

Every year on the Saturday nearest to 18 September, the Mayor and Councillors of Lichfield, with representatives from the Johnson Society and pupils from the school which the great man attended, assemble at Samuel Johnson's statue. A wreath is laid on it and a local church choir sing hymns and a special Johnson song (see below). That evening there is a private dinner in the guildhall at which his favourite dishes are always served – steak and kidney pie and apple tart with cream.

— 180 —

NORWICH
NORFOLK

Tourist Information Centre, Guildhall, Gaol Hill (01603) 666071.

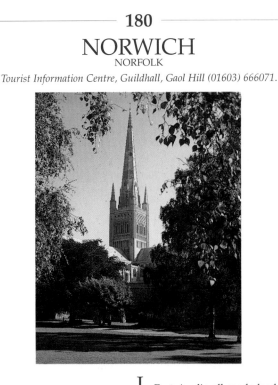

Norwich Cathedral

•

Norwich Festivals

The Norfolk and Norwich Festival, held in Norwich in October every year, is one of the oldest festivals in the country. First staged in 1821, it has been interrupted only by world wars. The festival traditionally centres on choral music and symphony concerts by a major orchestra, but of late it has broadened out to take under its wing the visual arts, plays and jazz, and even such events as fireworks and vintage car rallies. Norwich also holds a 10-day jazz festival in the autumn, and hosts the Royal Norfolk Show each June.

•

In East Anglia all roads lead sooner or later to Norwich, the region's capital. The city is tucked inside a fat loop of the River Wensum. At the neck of the loop, on a steep artificial mound, stands Norwich Castle, built in about 1100 and given a facelift in the 1830s. For nearly 700 years the castle was the county gaol. Public executions went on here until 1867 and special trains were laid on to bring spectators. In the dungeons you can observe ghastly instruments of torture and gruesome plastercasts of the heads of hanged murderers (made for phrenological study originally). To recover your equilibrium, try a breath of fresh air on the battlements before plunging into the richly enjoyable Castle Museum, one of the best in the country. Among much to savour, there is a delectable collection of Norwich School paintings, with pictures by Crome, Cotman and others, a particularly splendid Roman cavalry helmet, Norwich silver, a wonderful collection of teapots and the Norwich Snapdragons, which were carried in civic processions.

Norwich has almost 1,000 buildings listed as of historic and architectural interest, so there is not exactly a shortage of things to see. Not far from the castle is the tall-spired cathedral, one of England's loveliest. The view of it from the river bank across playing fields is deservedly famous. It is a marvellous example of Norman work, built of Caen stone which was brought from Normandy first by sea, then up the River Wensum and finally along a specially dug canal – traces of which can still be seen. The 315ft spire was added in the 15th century.

Outside again, in The Close, is King Edward's School, whose famous pupils included Horatio Nelson. Before you leave, you might like to search out the quiet spot outside the east end of the cathedral where Nurse Edith Cavell was buried, after being executed in 1915 by the Germans for helping Allied prisoners to escape to Belgium.

The 15th-century guildhall in Gaol Hill, built of Norfolk flint, has 15th-century stained glass and Nelson's sword, taken from a Spanish admiral after the Battle of Cape St Vincent. The Strangers' Hall, Charing Cross, a medieval merchant's house round a courtyard, is now a museum, with each of the 15 rooms furnished in a different style from Tudor to Victorian. The Bridewell Museum, in Bridewell Alley, was also a merchant's house, but later became the local 'bridewell' or prison for tramps and beggars: you can see the prisoners' graffiti in the courtyard. The flint wall of the museum facing St Andrew's Church dates from the 14th century and is perhaps the finest of its kind in the country. Inside are displays on the history of Norwich trades and industries, from boots and shoes to chocolate and mustard. For more about mustard, visit the charming Colman's Mustard Shop, also in Bridewell Alley.

Worth seeing, too, is the Churchman's House with its fine plasterwork and fireplaces, while in the outskirts of the city, on the university campus, the Sainsbury Centre for the Visual Arts houses notable collections of Art Nouveau, modern art and the art of native peoples.

Don't leave Norwich without visiting some of its old churches. St Peter Hungate, Princes Street, is now a museum of ecclesiastical art and a brass-rubbing centre, and St John Maddermarket also has interesting brasses. Most impressive of all is the great church of St Peter Mancroft, with its hammerbeam roof and Norwich glass. One more 'must' is a stroll through the Royal Arcade to enjoy the Art Nouveau architecture and browse in the shops. It leads to the busy marketplace, where 200 stalls under awnings are open every weekday.

— 181 —

NOTTINGHAM
NOTTINGHAMSHIRE

Tourist Information Centre, 1-4 Smithy Row (0115) 9470661.

•
Goose Fair

The three-day Goose Fair at Nottingham in October is one of Britain's greatest traditional fairs. Down into the 19th century thousands of geese were herded along the roads from Norfolk and Lincolnshire to Nottingham every year, their feet smeared with a mixture of sand and mud to protect them against the wear and tear of the journey. However, by the early years of the century, a fun-fair element had been added (see below), with the appearance of merry-go-rounds, Wombwell's wild beast show and a bearded lady. Nowadays, the fun-fair has taken over almost entirely, though traders do still man hundreds of stalls.
•

Nottingham has been extensively re-built, but the city has been successful in preserving its history. The castle for example, a 17th-century house built on the site of the medieval castle, has become a fine museum of ceramics, silver and glass, with an art gallery. The more ordinary bygones of local life are on display at the Brewhouse Yard Museum, a terrace of 17th-century houses at the foot of Castle Rock. A Georgian terrace in Castle Gate houses a museum of costume, while a 15th-century building is now used as a lace museum. Nottingham was a canal centre, too, and a Canal Museum has been set up in a former dock warehouse in Canal Street. Tales of Robin Hood, in Maid Marian Way, transports the visitor to medieval Nottingham and the glades of the greenwood.

Elsewhere in the city it is worth looking for two old inns, the Trip to Jerusalem and the Salutation, and among the major buildings you should not miss the superb Council House in the old Market Square, St Mary's Church, with its notable monuments, and the Roman Catholic cathedral, designed in the 19th century by Pugin.

IN EASY REACH Wollaton Hall, 2 miles west of the city centre, is one of the most spectacular of England's Elizabethan mansions, with an interesting interior that now incorporates a natural history museum. Outside are gardens and a deer park, and a stable block has been converted into a museum celebrating Nottingham's notable industrial history. On the other side of the city, at Radcliffe on Trent, is Holme Pierrepont Hall (limited opening times), with a castellated Tudor brick front hiding additions dating from the 17th and 19th centuries. The interior boasts fine woodwork and furniture, and there is a delightful courtyard garden. The country parks at Holme Pierrepont and Colwick lie side by side, forming a complex of lakes and pools that led to the establishment here of the National Watersports Centre. On the A60, 6 miles south of Nottingham, a Framework Knitters Museum has been set up in a unique group of 19th-century knitters' cottages.

182

RANWORTH BROAD
NORFOLK

Off the B1140, near South Walsham. Open April until October.
Tourist Information Centre, Guildhall, Gaol Hill, Norwich (01603) 666071.

Just to the north of little Ranworth village lie the marsh-edged waters of Ranworth Broad. Rich in habitats for broadland wildlife, the area is protected by the Norfolk Naturalists' Trust as a nature reserve. The quarter mile boardwalk trail leads through woodland and reed-beds to the Conservation Centre, a thatched floating building moored by the water's edge. Here you can see exhibitions on the history and natural history of the Broads and climb to the viewing gallery to look out over the water.

IN EASY REACH North-west of Ranworth, off the A149, lies Hickling, largest of the Broads and centre of an important National Nature Reserve covering 1,361 acres. Lapwings, redshanks, ringed plovers, sedge warblers and marsh harriers can be seen from the hides or the observation hut. Better still, the water trail, a 2 ½-hour trip in a traditional reed lighter, visits the best points of the reserve – including an unusual tree hide. Autumn is a good time to visit, with waders stopping off on their migration

The windmill at Horsey stands to the south of the village beside the Mere. Both belong to the National Trust

journeys. Connected to Hickling Broad by a channel is Horsey Mere. Here you'll find swallowtail butterflies in summer, marsh harriers, migrant wildfowl, birds of passage, the occasional swan and rare plants such as the holly-leaved naiad. There is no access to the mere itself without a permit, but a public footpath skirts the reed-beds on the northern edge.

183

SHREWSBURY
SHROPSHIRE

Tourist Information Centre, The Square (01743) 350761.

Almost completely encircled by a meander of the River Severn, with only a narrow neck a few hundred yards across linking it to land to the north-east, the ancient town of Shrewsbury had ideal natural defences. A castle was built on the neck of the meander by Roger de Montgomery soon after the Norman Conquest, but the oldest parts of today's castle date from 100 years or so later, and the building owes much of its appearance to 18th-century modifications by the architect and engineer Thomas Telford. Used as Council Chambers, the Castle also houses the regimental museums of the three Shropshire regiments.

Shrewsbury has many fine houses and bridges, the best known of the latter being the Welsh and English Bridges on respective sides of the town. The houses include Rowley's House Museum, containing Roman remains from nearby Wroxeter as well as local and natural history displays, and Clive House, an 18th-century town house now housing fine collections of Shropshire porcelain and paintings. Opposite the abbey the Shrewsbury Quest focuses on medieval life in the town and abbey.

IN EASY REACH To the south-east of Shrewsbury, on the B4380, is Viroconium, the Roman town at Wroxeter, a very important site which is still being investigated. The vast bath-house complex is particularly striking. A small museum on the site interprets the discoveries so far. In the same area, but on the B4380 at Atcham, is the magnificent 18th-century Attingham Park (open weekend afternoons only in October and closed November). The house consists of a central block with flanking pavilions, and features a picture gallery and staircase by John Nash.

Ploughing Championships and Agricultural Show

An enjoyable regular event at Shrewsbury is the annual Horse and Tractor Ploughing Championships of the British Isles, on the first Saturday of October. The championships are organised by the Cruckton and District Ploughing and Hedging Society and were first held in 1927. Hedging competitions were soon added and later so were sheepdog trials and clay pigeon shooting. The Society's 'Queen of the Plough', chosen at its annual dance, presides over the contests. Another big event at Shrewsbury is the Shropshire and West Midlands Agricultural Show, in May, one of the earliest and most prestigious occasions of its kind in the year. It also involves the finals of the Shropshire Tug-of-War.

184

STRATFORD-UPON-AVON
WARWICKSHIRE

Tourist Information Centre, 1 Bridgefoot (01789) 293127.

Don't believe people who tell you that Stratford is brash and commercialised – it is a handsome old market town with an attractive waterside, some fine buildings and a few discreet tourist attractions. Nevertheless, it is best enjoyed out of season, and if you choose October you might catch the Mop Fair, when the town traditionally lets its hair down.

However, you can't escape Shakespeare. The Birthplace in Henley Street gives a good idea of his home life and his later work. New Place in Chapel Street is an attractive garden on the site of his retirement house, and Nash's House next door has a small history museum. Hall's Croft in Old Town is the home of his son-in-law, but of more interest is the reconstruction of Dr Hall's dispensary.

In the Bancroft Gardens by the river you will find the famous Shakespeare Memorial statue and the attractive junction of the River Avon with the Stratford Canal. From here wide lawns lead to the Royal Shakespeare Theatre, where there are regular backstage tours. The surviving buildings of the old theatre next door house an interesting theatre exhibition.

For a change from Shakespeare the Teddy Bear Museum in Greehill Street is devoted to bears of all shapes and sizes.

IN EASY REACH Anne Hathaway's Cottage, the home of Shakespeare's wife, a mile west of Stratford at Shottery, is a fascinating example of a Tudor farmhouse, virtually a museum of 16th-century domestic life. Mary Arden's House at Wilmcote, 3 miles north-west of the town, was the home of Shakespeare's mother and is now a farming museum. Four miles to the east, on the B4086, is Charlecote Park (open until the end October), the home of the Lucy family. Originally Elizabethan, the house was rebuilt in the 1830s, but the interior is absorbing and you can picnic in the deer park.

185

SYMONDS YAT
HEREFORD AND WORCESTER

Off the A40, 5 miles north-east of Monmouth.
Tourist Information Centre, 27 Market Place, Coleford, Royal Forest of Dean,
Gloucestershire (01594) 836307.

For over 200 years the lower Wye Valley, with its wildly looping river and its dramatic cliff scenery, has been a magnet for tourists, and most of them have climbed to Symonds Yat. The sensational view from the Yat Rock is seen at its best in autumn when the leaves turn in the heavily wooded valley. From here there appears to be two parallel rivers, but they are in fact the two ends of one of the Wye's giant meanders.

IN EASY REACH On the B4228, 2 miles to the north, are the remains of Goodrich Castle, a moated stronghold of sandstone rising from solid rock above the Wye, with a 12th-century keep and an interesting chapel. The 13th-century Pembridge Castle, restored in 1914, lies 5 miles west of Goodrich near Welsh Newton, on the A466. The pleasant riverside town of Ross-on-Wye, to the north-east, benefited from the philanthropy of the remarkable John Kyrle, who died in 1724. Among his gifts was the Prospect, a fine viewpoint west of the church. His memorial is in St Mary's Church (look out also for the Rudhall tombs and the 'plague cross' in the churchyard) and his house is opposite the Town Hall. Brockhampton, north of Ross, off the B4224, has a remarkable thatched 'Arts and Crafts' church of 1902, with concrete vaulting and William Morris tapestries.

Mop Fair and Shakespeare's Birthday

Mop Fairs used to be occasions when young farm labourers and domestic servants hired themselves out for the next 12 months. A shepherd would carry his crook or a lock of wool at the fair to indicate his calling to prospective employers, a day labourer would carry a piece of plaited hay and maidservants would have mops or brooms. The usual date was 10 October, which was 'old' Michaelmas Day. At Stratford it was a cheerful gathering, with an ox roasted in the street and many stalls. A second fair called the Runaway Mop was held a week later, at which servants who found they had made a poor choice of master or mistress would try their luck again.

Another big day in the town of Stratford is Shakespeare's Birthday, celebrated on 23 April with a procession through the streets to lay a wreath on the Bard's tomb in the parish church.

A traditional cottage garden and orchard contribute to the charm of Ann Hathaway's cottage at Shottery. The oldest part dates back to the 15th century

---
186
ASHBOURNE
DERBYSHIRE

Tourist Information Centre, Market Place (01335) 43666.

Att the southern tip of the Peak District National Park, Ashbourne is isolated in an extensive rural area, so it has always had a vital role as a market town. It is also known for its Shrove Tuesday 'football match'. The town makes no attempt to be pretty, but the main streets are harmonious and there are some pleasant individual buildings. St Oswald's Church, surrounded by daffodils in the spring, stands out (literally) with its 200ft spire, and the impressive interior has some fine monuments, including a famous sculpted memorial to 5-year-old Penelope Boothby who died in 1793. In Church Street look out for the Elizabethan building that was once the grammar school and the fine 18th-century mansion opposite.

IN EASY REACH The pleasant village of Tissington, to the north of Ashbourne off the A515, is approached through gateposts and along a tree-lined drive. It is an estate village of the Fitzherbert family and has consequently been preserved from unsightly development. The Hall, church and village houses range through several centuries, and are grouped photogenically around the green and pond. Skirting round the edge of the village is the Tissington Trail, a foot and bridle-path along the former track of the Cromford and High Peak Railway. It joins the High Peak Trail at Parsley Hay and extends almost to Ashbourne. Dovedale, to the west, scarcely needs an introduction, for its dramatic scenery has been famous for centuries. The Dove, a redoubtable trout stream, has carved a twisting, narrow gorge through the limestone hills for a couple of miles. There are impressive caves and strangely weathered rock formations – the Twelve Apostles, the Lion's Head, and so on.

Shrovetide Football

Shrove Tuesday was the day preceding the long fast of Lent (beginning on Ash Wednesday) and it was marked by feasts and jollifications, which in some places included riotous games of football (see above). One of these has survived at Ashbourne. The two sides are the Up'ards and Down'ards, who live on opposite sides of the Henmore Brook, which runs through the town. The goals are 3 miles apart, each being a mill spindle on which the ball must be touched three times to score. There is no limit to the numbers involved on either team and the game is a free-for-all like a giant rugby scrum – locally called the 'hug' – which can go on for anything up to 8 hours.

187
BREDON HILL
HEREFORD AND WORCESTER

Between the A44 and A435, south-west of Evesham.
Tourist Information Centre, 19 High Street, Pershore (01386) 554262.

Inn the flat south Worcestershire countryside, Bredon Hill is a prominent landmark, although it stands at less than 1,000ft. One of A E Housman's favourite spots, it provides an extensive area of enjoyable walking, with paths leading up from the several villages that surround it. Elmley Castle is a good starting point for a stroll to the Iron Age hill-fort at the summit, to see the huge Banbury Stone and the dilapidated 18th-century tower known as Parson's Folly. There are excellent views up here over the Vale of Evesham and into Wales.

IN EASY REACH The village of Bredon lies on the south-western edge of the hill, a delightful place with a very grand church (look out for the Reed memorial) and one of the best tithe barns in England. Amongst the harmonious architecture of many centuries the Reed Almshouses are outstanding. All the Bredon villages have points of interest, but Overbury repays a leisurely visit to see the 'rustic' buildings designed by the Victorian architect Norman Shaw. There are some notable monuments in the church at Elmley Castle, and Great Comberton has England's biggest dovecot. The main attraction at Ashton under Hill is the 1½ acre private garden at Bredon Springs (check at the Tourist Information Centre for opening times).

--------- 188 ---------

BRIDGNORTH
SHROPSHIRE

Tourist Information Centre: The Library, Listley Street, Bridgnorth (01746) 763358 and Load Street, Bewdley, Hereford and Worcester (01299) 404740.

Bridgnorth is one of Britain's most fascinating towns. High Town is perched up on sandstone bluffs, while Low Town lies below, beside the Severn, and the two are linked by an unnervingly steep cliff railway. The keep of the Norman castle leans at an unbelievable angle and the adjacent church is an elegant creation of the great engineer Thomas Telford. The 17th-century Town Hall stands in the middle of the main street which is full of harmonious buildings.

IN EASY REACH Bridgnorth is situated at one end of the Severn Valley Railway, which remains open during weekends in winter as well as running Santa Specials in early December. In 1965 a small group of enthusiasts dreamed about reopening part of the Shrewsbury-Worcester railway line through an idyllic stretch of the Severn Valley. Today the SVR is the country's biggest private standard-gauge company, running a busy 16-mile line. The vast collection of locomotives and rolling stock is obviously a magnet for the railway buff, but for the ordinary visitor the appeal of a journey on the SVR lies in the very English countryside viewed through large windows from a comfortable seat – the SVR has proper big carriages with proper big engines. As a destination the handsome town of Bewdley (see also under Great Witley) is strongly recommended, and it is worth breaking your journey at the pretty riverside village of Arley, whose station, like the others, has been restored.

Another attraction for transport enthusiasts, but of interest to others as well, is the Midland Motor Museum at Stanmore Hall, 1½ miles south-east of Bridgnorth on the A458. The museum, which is housed in the converted stables of the Hall, has a collection of over 90 restored sports and racing cars and motor cycles. The surrounding grounds are very attractive.

South-east of Bridgnorth, 4 miles north of Kidderminster is the steep ridge called Kinver Edge; here (at Holy Austin's Rock) you can see cave dwellings inhabited as recently as 30 years ago and explore the heath and woodland.

--------- 189 ---------

CAMBRIDGE
CAMBRIDGESHIRE

Tourist Information Centre, Wheeler Street (01223) 322640.

The Christmas service of lessons and carols televised from King's College Chapel draws attention every year to one of the most breathtakingly beautiful buildings in England. With its superb fan-vaulted ceiling and magnificent stained glass, the chapel is one of the glories of Western civilisation.

There is much more to Cambridge, however, which is one of the most attractive and enjoyable cities in Britain. The university began to develop in the 13th century and the oldest of the colleges, Peterhouse, was founded in 1284. The colleges, with their courts and chapels, their libraries and gardens, are spread through the city and give it its special flavour: along with the presence of 10,000 students in term-time and the correspondingly ample supply of quality bookshops, museums and galleries, and lively theatre and cinema programmes.

One of Cambridge's great attractions is the river, the Cam or Granta, with the college lawns running down to it and a succession of charming bridges leading across to college gardens in the area known as 'the Backs'. Few things beat a punt trip on this stretch of water, and from April to October punts and rowing boats can be hired at Quayside, off Bridge Street and the Mill Pond, off Silver Street.

The largest of the colleges is Trinity, with about 900 students. Founded by Henry VIII, it is famed for its spacious Great Court, its library by Wren and its chapel with statues of famous past members, including Bacon, Newton, Macaulay and Tennyson. Next door is another 16th-century foundation, St John's , whose handsome Tudor gatehouse leads to a succession of courts and the Bridge of Sighs over the river, built in 1831 in imitation of the Venetian one.

Each of the other colleges has its own charms. Queens', for example, with its mellow buildings of red brick, rejoices in a wonderful 17th-century sundial. Pembroke has a chapel by Wren. Downing was built early in the 19th century by William Wilkins in all the classical grandeur of the Greek Revival style.

The oldest building in Cambridge is the Saxon tower of the church of St Bene't (short for Benedict). The tower of Great St Mary's commands a sweeping view of the city, and Holy Sepulchre is one of Britain's few round churches. The Botanic Garden on Bateman Street numbers a scented garden and a notable rockery among its attractions.

A wealth of museums is headed by the Fitzwilliam Museum, Trumpington Street, with a magnificent art collection and distinguished displays of ceramics, glass and silver, as well as objects from Ancient Egypt, Greece and Rome. The

Festival of Carols and Lessons

The service of nine lessons, interspersed with appropriate carols and other music, celebrated in King's College Chapel on Christmas Eve has become an accepted and familiar part of the Christmas season on radio, and more recently on television. It was first broadcast in 1928 and first held in the chapel 10 years before that. Services of this kind are now held in many places at Christmas time, but they are quite a modern invention, first introduced at Truro Cathedral in the 1880s.

King's College Chapel (seen here from the Backs) has a choir which still consists of 16 boys, as ordered by Henry VI, but today it is augmented by 14 adult male voices

Cambridge and County Folk Museum, Castle Street, bulges with domestic and country bygones. The Whipple Museum of the History of Science, in Free School Lane (navigational and astronomical instruments, pioneer electrical apparatus, etc) and the Scott Polar Research Institute, Lensfield Road are very rewarding, as is the Kettle's Yard Gallery of modern art, off Castle Street.

— **190** —

THE POTTERIES
STAFFORDSHIRE

Tourist Information Centres: Potteries Shopping Centre, Quadrant Road, Hanley, Stoke-on-Trent (01782) 284600 and The Ironmarket, Newcastle-under-Lyme (01782) 711964.

The sprawling city of Stoke-on-Trent was created in 1910 through a 'federation' of six towns. Inevitably this resulted in a rather shapeless conurbation which can be daunting to the visitor, but the excellent town trails available from the Information Centre in Hanley (in the centre of the city) provide an informative choice of routes for anyone interested in exploring the history of the Potteries on the ground.

Many museums and exhibitions illustrate the history of the ceramics and mining industries, and you can tour the factories. There are some distinguished names here. The Wedgwood Museum and Visitor Centre in Barlaston (in the south of the city) has a reconstruction of the original 18th century Etruria workshops and a centre demonstrating the skills of today's craftspeople, as well as a gorgeous display of Wedgwood products of all periods. The celebrated Minton ware can be studied (and purchased) at the Minton Museum in London Road, Stoke, while the Royal Doulton factory in Nile Street, Burslem, has the fine Sir Henry Doulton Gallery.

The atmosphere of a small Victorian pottery factory has been re-created at the Gladstone Museum of British Pottery in Uttoxeter Road, Longton. The museum is in fact a restored 'potbank', of the kind that produced common-or-garden household chinaware, and there are regular demonstrations.

Ford Green Hall, at Smallthorne, is a 17th-century farmhouse with 16th- to 19th-century furnishings. For a broader picture of Potteries history, go to the excellent City Museum and Art Gallery in Bethesda Street, Hanley, to see displays of social and natural history, archaeology and fine art, as well as one of the world's major ceramics collections. The adjoining borough of Newcastle-under-Lyme has its own Borough Museum and Art Gallery in The Brampton, with the emphasis on local history and the products of the Industrial Revolution.

The 'Portland' vase, a rare piece of Roman glassware with the figures carved in relief, was eventually acquired by the Duke of Portland – hence its name – and bought by the British Museum in 1945. Josiah Wedgwood was among many who copied the vase and his pieces made in Jasper ware were so successful that the vase became the Pottery's symbol

191

ST IVES
CAMBRIDGESHIRE

Off the A1123. Tourist Information Centre, The Library, Princes Street, Huntingdon (01480) 425831.

On the 15th-century bridge over the River Ouse at St Ives is a little chapel – a great rarity, one of only three of the kind in England. You can get the key at the Norris Museum of local history on The Broadway, which itself has interesting collections including local history, archaeology and lace-making. The riverside is attractive and there is a statue of Oliver Cromwell in the marketplace. Cromwell farmed at St Ives and attended All Saints church whose steeple soars up beside the river.

IN EASY REACH To the west along the Ouse is the charming village of Hemingford Grey, whose red-brick church has only the stump of its spire left: the rest was blown off in a gale in 1741. The much photographed 17th-century watermill at Houghton, on an island in the Ouse, is owned by the National Trust and is set working on open days.

Further on is Huntingdon, about 5 miles west of St Ives. Cromwell was born here and the old grammar school which he, and later Samuel Pepys, attended is now the Cromwell Museum. Just outside the town to the west, on the A14 (A604), the ancestral seat of the Cromwell family, Hinchingbrooke House, is now a school but is sometimes open to visitors.

To the south, 4 miles away on the A1 is Buckden. Administered by the Claretian Brotherhood it has a magnificent Tudor tower, a gatehouse and walls which can all be seen all year; the knot garden is being restored. Tours of the buildings by appointment. To the south-west, 5 miles from Huntingdon, the 2½ square miles of Grafham Water Reservoir constitute the biggest man-made expanse of inland water in the country: there is angling, sailing and birdwatching here. To the north-east of Huntingdon, on the B1040, the scant remains of Ramsey Abbey (limited opening only) are dominated by its 15th-century gatehouse, owned by the National Trust. Further north on the B1040, the brick-making town of Whittlesey is the scene of a peculiar winter custom, the Straw Bear Festival.

Straw Bear Festival

In January every year the nightmare figure of the Straw Bear (see above) – a man covered from head to foot in straw, with a straw tail – capers in the streets of Whittlesey on the Friday night and the Saturday before Plough Monday (which is the first Monday after Twelfth Night). He is accompanied by morris dancers and sword dancers. Money is collected for charity and there is general merrymaking on the Saturday night. This used to happen on Plough Monday itself or the day after, and the Straw Bear was led about on a chain, growling ferociously and going down on all fours.

— 192 —
SOUTHWELL MINSTER
NOTTINGHAMSHIRE

On the A612, west of Newark-on-Trent. Tourist Information Centre, The Gilstrap Centre, Castlegate, Newark-on-Trent (01636) 78962.

The plain and solid west front of the Minster, with its twin towers, capped by spires, has a severe Norman strength, and this impression is reinforced by the vista of massive pillars inside. But a closer look reveals superlative craftsmanship – every huge arch is subtly decorated, and the stone chancel screen has marvellously intricate carving. The stone-carver's art reaches a peak in the chapter house, where the exuberant decoration consists of foliage and flowers, carved in such crisp detail that they can be readily identified by the botanist. Occasional human and animal figures are woven in. It is a work of genius.

The Minster has been a cathedral since 1884. In the small town of Southwell itself, look out for the historic Saracen's Head Inn where, in 1646, Charles I spent his last night as a free man.

IN EASY REACH There is much to see at Newark, including the ruins of the castle where King John died, the big market square and fine 18th-century town hall by John Carr, and the impressive parish church of St Mary Magdalen, with a 250ft tower and spire, and splendid interior details. A walk round the town centre will reveal handsome 18th-century houses and interesting inns like the 14th-century Olde White Hart. Don't miss the Air Museum, 2 miles north-east of the town on the A46, with its comprehensive outdoor display of aircraft, or the dolls and costumes in the Vina Cooke Collection, at Cromwell, 5 miles north of Newark.

— 193 —
STOKE BRUERNE WATERWAYS MUSEUM
NORTHAMPTONSHIRE

Off the A508, 3 miles north-east of Towcester. Tourist Information Centre, 10 St Giles Square, Northampton (01604) 22677.

In an old grain warehouse on the banks of the Grand Canal is a marvellous collection of bygones of the canal age. The museum is not only for enthusiasts but for anyone interested in what life was like for a nomadic family living in the tiny cabin of a narrowboat. One of these claustrophobic spaces has been reconstructed and equipped with its traditional bits and pieces of furniture, crockery, brassware, and traditional art, and there is much more to see on the three floors of the building and outside. In summer a boat trip or towpath walk to Blisworth Tunnel, which runs for over a mile between Stoke Bruerne and Blisworth, is an attractive extra.

IN EASY REACH Standing in pleasant gardens just outside Stoke Bruerne are the delightful Stoke Park Pavilions (open summer only), believed to be the work of Inigo Jones. They are the only surviving features of a 17th-century house burned down in 1886.

Northampton is best known for boots and shoes, and the Central Museum and Art Gallery emphasises the footwear industry among its extensive local history collections, while the Museum of Leathercraft is entirely devoted to the subject of leather-working. To the east of Northampton is Earls Barton, where the church's formidable tower is one of the finest survivals of Saxon work in the country.

Sulgrave Manor, 10 miles west of Towcester, off the B4525, is a modest 16th-century manor house notable as the home of the ancestors of George Washington. Apart from its interesting kitchen and good furniture the house has a collection of Washington memorabilia (closed January and February).

Cradle Rocking

The village of Blidworth in Nottinghamshire, a few miles to the west of Southwell, is the scene of the charming Cradle Rocking custom on the Sunday nearest to Candlemas Day (2 February). An old wooden rocking cradle, decorated with flowers, is brought into the church and the baby boy who has been most recently baptised in the parish is put in the cradle and gently rocked for a little while during an afternoon service (see above). This old ceremony, commemorating the presentation of the child Jesus in the Temple, was revived at Blidworth in the 1920s. A list of all the babies rocked since then is on a board in the church.

Painted water cans such as these typify the Canal Art of the narrowboat people

Tin Can Band

In the village of Broughton, north-east of Northampton, a dreadful noise breaks out every year at midnight on the first Sunday after 12 December. This is the Tin Can Band, recruited from anyone who cares to turn up at St Andrew's Church. The band goes round the village beating dust-bin lids or watering-cans with sticks, rattling stones in tins and generally making as much of a racket as possible. This has been done since time out of mind, but no one any longer knows why.

*W*ales is visited for its mountains and river valleys, for its beaches and cliffs, for its menacing castles and 'great little trains', for the music of its choirs and its waterfalls. Any lingering impression of the Principality as an industrial wasteland – black with collieries and tips – is severely out of date. King Coal has been dethroned and in fact one of the interesting things to do in Wales today is to visit the valleys where he reigned and see what has been done to restore them.

The contrast between the remains of the industrial past and the wild beauty of untamed scenery is a piquant pleasure in Wales. You can sample it, for example, by driving down the A5 southwards from Bangor into the heart of Snowdonia and passing on the way the shattered, twisted, tortured landscape of the giant slate quarries near Bethesda – a landscape from Dante's Inferno. Among all the scenic splendours of the mountains at Blaenau Ffestiniog you can worm your way deep into the hillside to see how the slate was torn from the earth: or similarly at Llanberis, at the very foot of Snowdon itself.

Down in South Wales, there could hardly be a sharper visual contrast than between the smoke and steel of Port Talbot and the wooded valley of the Afan Argoed Country Park half a dozen miles away, itself a coal-mining wasteland not so long ago. Not a nugget of coal is mined in the Rhondda today, but at Blaenavon you can go down into the unused pit to see for yourself what coal mining was all about.

Three of the ten national parks are in Wales: Snowdonia, with 850 square miles of stupendous mountains, forests and lakes; the Brecon Beacons with high peaks and fine moorland scenery; and the Pembrokeshire Coast, with a 170-mile path hugging rugged cliffs and golden beaches. There is also marvellous coast and estuary scenery in Anglesey, in the Lleyn Peninsula, on Cardigan Bay and in the Gower Peninsula.

Tenby and Llandudno are perhaps the most likeable of the seaside resorts. For beautiful ruined abbeys, try Tintern, Llanthony and Strata Florida. The wealth of castles needs little trumpeting, but Caernarfon, Conwy, Kidwelly and Pembroke might chill the stoutest heart. In the Marches there are Powis, Chirk and Raglan. The 19th-century castles make a highly enjoyable group, led by Cardiff, Castell Coch and Penrhyn. Stately homes are not in as ample supply as in England, but you are most unlikely to be disappointed by Erddig or Nanteos, or Plas Newydd.

Among engaging oddities are the prison at Beaumaris, the Mediterranean-style village of Portmeirion and the Roman gold mines at Dolaucothi. The biggest camera obscura in the world is at Aberystwyth and perfumes are made from the local flowers by silent monks on Caldey Island.

Prehistoric remains are particularly thick on the ground in Anglesey and on the Preseli Hills. In the Roman legionary base at Caerleon you can see the amphitheatre where gladiators were butchered to make a Roman holiday. Fortunately, no one will need butchering to make you a holiday today in Wales.

Snowdon Mountain Railway – one of the many narrow-gauge railways for which Wales is famous. First built to transport slate and other raw materials, they are now one of the country's greatest delights

Wales

A special event, described in the text, occurs in the vicinity of the places marked with a star.

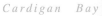

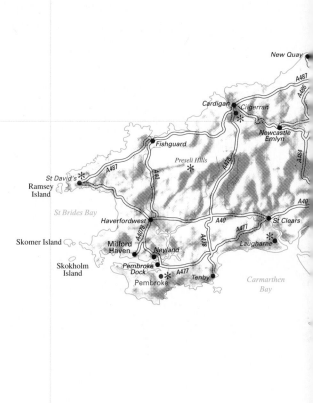

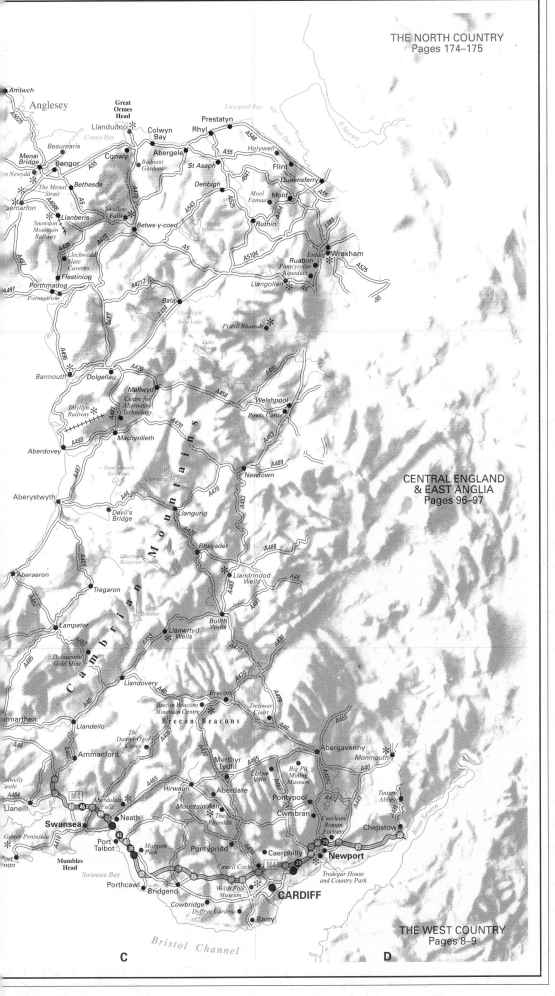

Liverpool Bay

R. Mersey

River Dee

Anglesey

Amlwch

Great Ormes Head

Llandudno

Colwyn Bay

Rhyl

Prestatyn

A548

Holywell

A55

Conwy Bay

Conwy

Bodnant Gardens

Abergele

St Asaph

Flint

Queensferry

A55

Beaumaris

Menai Bridge

Bangor

A55

Denbigh

A525

Moel Famau

Mold

A494

A483

Bethesda

The Menai Strait

Caernarfon

Swallow Falls

Betws-y-coed

Ruthin

Wrexham

A525

Erddig

Ruabon

Pontcysyllte Aqueduct

Llangollen

Snowdon Mountain Railway

Llanberis

A470

A5

A5104

Llechwedd Slate Caverns

Ffestiniog

Porthmadog

Portmeirion

A4212

Bala

Llyn Tegid or Bala Lake

Pistyll Rhaeadr

Lake Vyrnwy

A496

Barmouth

Dolgellau

Mallwyd

Centre for Alternative Technology

A458

A495

Welshpool

Powis Castle

Talyllyn Railway

A487

A493

Machynlleth

A470

A483

Aberdovey

Nant-y-moch Reservoir

Newtown

A489

Aberystwyth

A44

Devil's Bridge

Llangurig

A470

A44

Aberaeron

A485

Caerwys Reservoir

Rhayader

A488

Tregaron

Llandrindod Wells

A44

A483

A487

Lampeter

A482

Llyn Brianne

Llanwrtyd Wells

A470

A483

A488

Dolaucothi Gold Mine

Builth Wells

Teifi

A485

Cambrian Mountains

Llandovery

A40

Brecon

Carmarthen

Brecon Beacons Mountain Centre

Tretower Court

A40

A465

Abergavenny

Monmouth

Llandeilo

Brecon Beacons

A40

A465

The Dan-yr-Ogof Caves

Merthyr Tydfil

Big Pit Mining Museum

Tintern Abbey

Ammanford

A470

Ebbw Vale

A467

A40

A466

A449

Kidwelly Castle

A484

Hirwaun

Aberdare

Pontypool

A472

River Severn

Llanelli

M4

Aberdulais Falls

Mountain Ash

The Rhondda

Cwmbran

Caerleon Roman Fortress

Chepstow

46

44

Neath

A465

Swansea

41

Pontypridd

A470

Caerphilly

Newport

29

Port Talbot

39

Margam Park

Castell Coch

M4

Tredegar House and Country Park

Gower Peninsula

Mumbles Head

Swansea Bay

Porthcawl

Bridgend

Welsh Folk Museum

CARDIFF

Cowbridge

Dyffryn Gardens

Barry

Bristol Channel

C

D

Calendar of Events

Spring

MARCH

St David's Day
St David's Cathedral,
Dyfed
(1 March)

Newport Drama Festival
Newport, Gwent
(March – 3rd week)

EASTER

Easter Festival Parade
Rhyl, Clwyd
(Easter Saturday)

Easter Regatta
Bala Lake, Gwynedd
(Easter Bank Holiday
weekend)

Easter Arts Festival
Fishguard, Dyfed
(Easter week)

APRIL

**Wales and Border
Counties Game and
Country Fair**
Builth Wells, Powys
(early April)

Choir of Wales
Swansea, W Glamorgan
(mid-April)

**Working Breeds Dog
Show**
Builth Wells, Powys
(mid April)

Arts Festival
Holyhead, Gwynedd
(late April to early May)

MAY

**Wrexham Maelor Arts
Festival**
Wrexham, Clwyd
(May – whole month)

Old May Day Fair
Welsh Folk Museum,
St Fagans, S Glamorgan
(1 May)

Victorian Extravaganza
Llandudno, Gwynedd
(May Day Bank Holiday
weekend)

Victorian Fayre
Holywell, Clwyd
(May Day Bank Holiday)

Welsh Rugby Cup Final
Cardiff Arms Park,
S Glamorgan
(early May)

Classic Car Club Show
Pencoed,
Mid Glamorgam
(mid May)

**Isle of Anglesey Vintage
Rally**
Llanedwen, Anglesey,
Gwynedd
(May – 3rd weekend)

City of Swansea Show
Swansea, W Glamorgan
(late May)

Common Walk
Laugharne, Dyfed
(Whitsun – 1996 and every
3rd year)

Newport Spring Festival
Newport, Dyfed
(late May)

Cathedral Festival
St David's, Dyfed
(late May to early June)

Beaumaris Festival
Beaumaris, Anglesey,
Gwynedd
(late May to early June)

Vintage Rally
Canellefaes Ganol, Dyfed
(end of May)

Summer

JUNE

**Festival of Music and
Drama**
Llantilio Crossenny,
Gwent
(June – 2nd week)

World Harp Festival
Cardiff, S Glamorgan
(mid June)

**Aberystwyth
Agricultural Show**
Aberystwyth, Dyfed
(June – 2nd week)

**Man Versus Horse
Marathon**
Llanwrtyd Wells, Powys
(June – 2nd week)

Drovers Walk
Llanwrtyd Wells, Powys
(June – 3rd week)

**Welsh Game and
Country Pursuits Fair**
Gelli Aur Country Park,
Carmarthen, Dyfed
(June – 3rd week)

**Barmouth to Fort
William Three Peaks
Yacht Race**
Barmouth, Gwynedd
(late June)

Ceiriog Valley Fair
Chirk Castle, Clwyd
(late June)

**Festival of Music and
the Arts**
Criccieth, Gwynedd
(late June to early July)

**Gwyl Gregynog
Festival**
Newtown, Powys
(June – 4th week)

**Flower and Music
Festival**
Trellech, Gwent
(June – 4th week)

Chepstow Festival
Chepstow, Gwent
(late June to early July)

JULY

**Aberconwy Vintage
Vehicle Rally**
Llanwrst, Gwynedd
(early July)

**Celtic Traditional Music
Festival**
Llandysul, Dyfed
(early July)

Jazz Festival
Aberystwyth, Dyfed
(early July)

**North Wales Bluegrass
Festival**
Trefriw, Gwynedd
(early July)

**International Musical
Eisteddfod**
Llangollen, Clwyd
(July – 1st week)

**International Snowdon
Race**
Llanberis, Gwynedd
(mid-July)

Gower Festival
Gower Peninsula, W
Glamorgan
(July – 2nd half)

**Drystone Walling
Competition**
Betws-y-Coed
Gwynedd
(July – 3rd week)

**Llyn Padarn Long-
Distance Swimming
Championships**
Llanberis, Gwynedd
(July – 3rd week)

**Royal Welsh
Agricultural Show**
Builth Wells, Powys
(July – 3rd week)

**Mid Wales Festival of
Transport**
Welshpool, Powys
(mid July)

The Welsh Proms
Cardiff, S Glamorgan
(mid July)

*The Royal Welsh Show,
held at Builth Wells
every July*

Barry Horse and Horticultural Show
Barry, S Glamorgan
(July – 3rd week)

Conwy Festival
Conwy, Gwynedd
(July – 4th week)

Fishguard Music Festival
Fishguard, Dyfed
(July – 4th week)

Pembrokeshire Vintage Car Club Annual Show
Scolton Manor Country Park, Spittal, Dyfed
(late July)

Power Boat Grand Prix
Cardiff Bay,
S Glamorgan
(late July)

Tywyn Festival
Tywyn, Gwynedd
(late July)

Menai Strait Regattas
Menai Bridge and other locations, Gwynedd
(late July to early August)

Monmouth Festival
Monmouth, Gwent
(late July to early August)

AUGUST

Annual Game Fair
Scolton Manor Country Park, Spittal, Dyfed
(August – 1st week)

Llanwrtyd Wells Festival
Llanwrtyd Wells, Powys
(August – 1st week)

Royal National Eisteddfod
Various locations
(August – 1st week)

Anglesey County Show
Anglesey, Gwynedd
(August – 2nd week)

Victorian Week
Talyllyn Railway,
Gwynedd
(August – 2nd week)

River Festival
Conwy, Gwynedd
(August – 2nd week)

Historic Festival
Caergwrle, Wrexham,
Clwyd
(mid August)

Eglwysbach Agricultural Show
Colwyn Bay, Clwyd
(mid August)

Vale of Glamorgan Agricultural Show
Penllin Castle Grounds,
Cowbridge,
S Glamorgan
(mid August)

Welsh National Sheepdog Trials
Llandeilo, Dyfed
(mid August)

United Counties Show
Carmarthen, Dyfed
(mid August)

Brecon Jazz Festival
Brecon, Powys
(mid August)

Victorian Festival
Llandrindod Wells,
Powys
(mid to late August)

Cilgerran Coracle and Aquatic Sports
Cilgerran, Dyfed
(August – 3rd week)

Gwyl Machynlleth Festival
Machynlleth, Powys
(August – 3rd week)

Race the Train
Tywyn, Gwynedd
(August – 3rd week)

Tydfillians Roman Run
Brecon, Powys
(on or near 23 August)

Vale of Glamorgan Festival
St Donat's Art Centre,
Llantwit Major, S
Glamorgan
(August – 4th week)

Beca Mountain Race
Mynachlog-ddu,
Dyfed
(late August)

Caerleon Carnival
Caerleon, Gwent
(late August)

Dolgellau Farming Festival
Dolgellau, Gwynedd
(late August)

*Contestants
in the International
Snowdon Race*

World Bog Snorkling Championships
Llanwrtyd Wells,
Powys
(late August)

Mid Wales Festival of Opera
Newtown, Powys
(late August to early September)

Presteigne Music Festival
Presteigne, Powys
(late August to early September)

Autumn

SEPTEMBER

Annual Raft Race
Monmouth, Gwent
(early September)

South Wales Country Fair
Margam Park, W
Glamorgan
(early September)

Betws-y-coed Wales Festival
Betws-y-coed,
Gwynedd
(September – 1st week)

Newport Show
Tredegar House,
Newport, Gwent
(September — 1st week)

Arts Festival
Barmouth, Gwynedd
(early and mid-September)

Usk Show
Usk, Gwent
(September – 2nd week)

Welsh Mounted Games Championships
Builth Wells, Powys
(mid September)

Cardiff Festival
Cardiff, S Glamorgan
(mid September to early October)

Annual Vintage Car Rally
Tredegar House,
Newport, Gwent
(around 18 September)

Swansea Festival of Music and the Arts
Swansea,
W Glamorgan
(late September and October)

OCTOBER

Arts Festival
Caernarfon, Gwynedd
(early October)

Michaelmas Fair
Pembroke, Dyfed
(early October)

Llandudno Festival
Llandudno, Gwynedd
(mid October)

Ffair y Borth (traditional fair)
Menai Bridge, Anglesey,
Gwynedd
(late October)

NOVEMBER

Mid Wales Beer Festival
Llanwrtyd Wells,
Powys
(November – 2nd and 3rd week)

Winter

DECEMBER

Royal Welsh Winter Fair
Builth Wells, Powys
(early December)

Christmas Swim
Porthcawl, Mid
Glamorgan
(25 December)

Nos Galan Midnight Race
Mountain Ash, Mid
Glamorgan
(31 December)

JANUARY

Mari Lwyd
Various places in
Glamorgan and Dyfed
(January – 1st week)

LAND OF SONG

Welsh traditional folk customs are thin on the ground these days. Their survival rate is far lower than in England – partly as a consequence of the powerful hostility of the Methodist chapels in the 18th and 19th centuries. The great storehouse of Welsh folk tradition today is the Folk Museum at St Fagans, near Cardiff.

A service used to be held in Welsh churches at dawn on Christmas Day, hence called *plygain* (cockcrow). People would come through the night for miles to sing carols in Welsh, bringing their own candles with them to light the proceedings. The local poets wrote new carols each year on the traditional themes and the local chandlers sold special thick candles, proof against church draughts. The *plygain* service almost died out, but is now reviving again in Mid Wales: for example, at Mallwyd and Llanymawddwy, close to the borders of Gwynedd and Powys. It is held in January nowadays, and in the evening, but the central feature is still the singing of carols in Welsh.

What has survived, in other words, is the Welsh enthusiasm for singing, poetry and music – an enthusiasm which is extremely old. All of 800 years ago, the Norman churchman Gerald of Wales, who was born in Manorbier Castle and knew South Wales well, commented on the aptitude the Welsh had for part singing.

Today's great Welsh choirs are a direct legacy of the 19th century, of the Industrial Revolution which created communities large enough to mount a substantial choir and sing Mendelssohn's *Elijah*, and of the chapels, which encouraged singing. The middle of the 19th century saw the development of 'singing school' after the evening services on Sundays and the growth of hymn-singing festivals. Besides the chapels, collieries and quarries produced their choirs.

Today, listening to a choir is one of the special pleasures of a visit to Wales: at Aberystwyth's ruined castle on a summer night, perhaps, or in St John's Church in Llandudno on summer Sunday evenings, or at chapel services and concerts all across the country.

Marvellous singing by the crowd is a well-known feature of international rugby matches in Cardiff. In Elizabethan times in Wales (as in England) a ferocious brand of primitive football was played by hundreds of people at a time, struggling to force a stout wooden ball into their opponent's territory. Whole parishes used to challenge each other to this game, a spiritual ancestor of modern Welsh rugby which, though introduced

Members of the Gorsedd of the Bards with the Archdruid (far right) at the 1986 National Eisteddfod, which was held at Fishguard that year

directly from England, has become a significant component of Welsh national feeling.

Probably the most important single factor in Welsh national awareness and separateness has been the survival of the Welsh language. A leading factor in that survival has been the national eisteddfod and its lesser brothers and sisters – the little local eisteddfodau which were highlights of the year in the days before radio or television had penetrated the Principality.

An eisteddfod, or 'session', is a meeting at which poets, story-tellers and musicians (and nowadays choirs) compete. Meetings of this sort on a grand scale, attracting competitors from a sizeable area and by tradition proclaimed a year and a day in advance, were held in Wales in the Middle Ages and on into the 16th century. By the 18th century they had died out, and the Welsh country gentry were by this time completely Anglicised in their outlook.

Late in the 1700s, a powerful, romantic and nationalistic revival of interest in Welsh culture and traditions – starting among Welsh exiles in London and at first opposed by the chapels – injected new life into the national eisteddfod, along with the belief that the medieval Welsh bards had inherited the lore of the ancient Druids. A national eisteddfod was organised at Corwen in 1789, and more followed. In 1819 the Druidical ritual of the *gorsedd* (throne) of bards was grafted onto the occasion. In 1858 a committee was appointed to organise the national eisteddfod every year, and in 1880 the National Eisteddfod Association was founded.

The Royal National Eisteddfod is now held annually in the first week of August, at a different place each year. The proceedings, entirely in Welsh, are presided

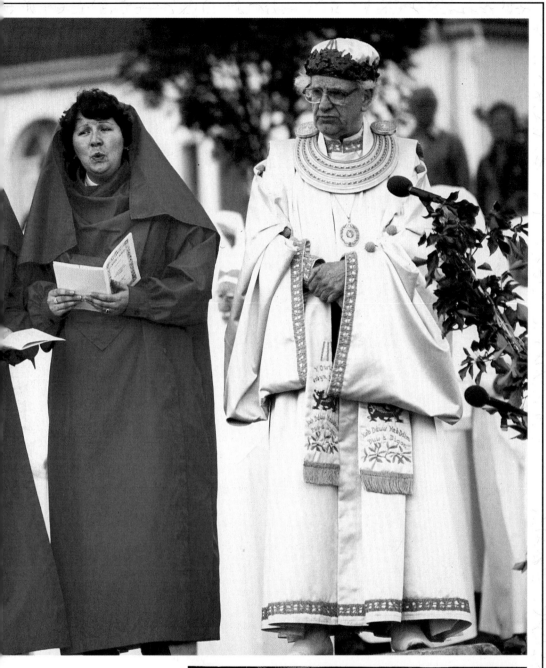

over by the Archdruid with his white robes, gold crown, sceptre and neck ring. He is supported by the bards in the white, blue and green robes which the 19th century deemed suitable to their dignity. (Another product of the same movement, incidentally, is the steeple-hatted 'national costume' beloved of the tourist authorities.)

In every town where the national eisteddfod meets a bardic circle of stones is erected. Travellers in Wales will often see these mute testimonials to the Welsh passion for the spoken and musical arts.

The BBC Welsh Symphony Orchestra and Eisteddfod Choir performing The Messiah *at Rhyl in 1985*

Beaumaris, like Conwy, was designed by James of St George

Din Lligwy's burial chamber – perhaps 5,000 years old – where the remains of 30 people were found

The dramatic 90ft-high lighthouse on South Stack was built in 1808

•

Vintage Rally

The island of Anglesey's first major event of the year comes on the third weekend in May: the two-day Vintage Rally at Llanedwen, near Llanfair P. G. It has been going since 1977 and traction engines, stationary engines, vintage cars and motorcycles assemble to show themselves off to their admirers. There's a vintage fairground, equipped with steam roundabouts and other old-style attractions, as well as modern fairground rides, and also a vintage rifle range. Plenty of trade stalls round off what is claimed to be the biggest event of its kind in Wales.

•

194

ANGLESEY (Beaumaris)
GWYNEDD

On the A545. Tourist Information Centre, Station, Llanfair P. G. (01248) 713177.

One of the main tourist attractions in this Anglesey town is Beaumaris Castle, the shell of a romantically moated stronghold built for Edward I in the 1290s. With its 15ft-thick curtain wall and elaborate defences, no one ever ventured to assault it.

Beaumaris's other 'attraction' is its prison (open May to September), which was built in 1829 to designs by Joseph Hansom, better known as the inventor of the hansom cab. It has now been turned into a museum, where you can see the cells, including the condemned cell, the wooden treadmill which could accommodate six convicts at once, and the final route to the scaffold.

IN EASY REACH Further north-east along the Anglesey coast, 4 miles from Beaumaris, are the ruins of Penmon Priory. The church of St Seiriol here dates from the 12th and 13th centuries, and there is a fine dovecot, big enough for 1,000 birds, built much later (about 1600) for a local landowner. A path from the church leads to St Seiriol's Well. The puffin population of Puffin Island, which can be seen from Penmon Point, was seriously depleted in the 19th century when pickled puffin was a popular local snack.

Following the coast westwards from Penmon Point, you come to the broad sandy stretch of Red Wharf Bay, with the resort of Benllech. Further on still is Din Lligwy, a British village of the Roman period, on a hill north of the A5025. The boundary wall, dated to the 4th century AD, encloses the remains of stone huts.

195

ANGLESEY (Holy Island)
GWYNEDD

On the A5. Tourist Information Centre, Marine Square, Salt Island Approach, Holyhead (01407) 762622.

Thomas Telford's A5 road and Robert Stephenson's railway line reach Holy Island across Telford's ¾-mile causeway, now dominated by a giant aluminium smelting plant. At the western end of the causeway is the Penrhos Nature Reserve which offers plenty of opportunities for birdwatching. The reserve is situated, on the shore of the narrow arm of the sea which cuts Holy Island off from the rest of Anglesey.

Holyhead is the port for the Irish ferries, and regular mail boats have plied between here and Ireland since the 1570s at least. The walls of the Roman fort of Caer Gybi are still standing and inside them is the parish church, which was rebuilt about 1500. It has windows by Burne-Jones and William Morris.

Spectacular cliffs and seal-haunted coves line the northern shore of the island. The earthworks of an Iron Age fort crown Holyhead Mountain, 720ft high, from which, on an exceptional day, you can see the Mountains of Mourne in Ireland. To the south-west are the huts of a settlement of the Roman period. On South Stack, the most westerly point of the island, is a lighthouse built by the architect of Dartmoor prison, and the RSPB reserve here is home to rare red-legged choughs as well as puffins and multitudes of other seabirds.

196

ANGLESEY (Plas Newydd)
GWYNEDD

On the A4080, south-west of Llanfair P. G.
Tourist Information Centre, Station, Llanfair P. G. (01248) 713177.

Idyllically set on the Menai Strait, the house at Plas Newydd was rebuilt at the turn of the 18th and 19th centuries by the 1st Earl of Uxbridge. There are splendid classical-style rooms, Paget family portraits and fine furniture. Rex Whistler was a friend of the family in the 1930s and examples of his work include a superb *trompe-l'oeil* fantasy on the dining-room wall. In the military museum are relics of the 2nd Lord Uxbridge, including his wooden leg! He led the British cavalry at Waterloo, where his leg was shattered by grapeshot, and he was afterwards created Marquess of Anglesey.

IN EASY REACH The 90ft Anglesey Column to the gallant marquess is on the A5 between Menai Bridge and Llanfair P. G. Off a side road, 2 miles south-west of Llanfair, is Bryn Celli Ddu, an impressive Stone Age tomb beneath a mound. Near Brynsiencyn on the A4080, the Anglesey Sea Zoo has Wales's largest aquarium, with a special tank in which you can handle live lobsters and other denizens of the deep. Further on westwards, the Newborough Warren Nature Reserve once home to rabbits in hundreds of thousands, is a desert of sand dunes rich in bird life, toads and lizards.

The Pin Mill standing at one end of Bodnant's canal pool was built as a summerhouse. Later it was used as a pin 'factory', and then as a tannery. It was brought to Bodnant in 1939 and restored as a garden feature

— 197 —

BODNANT GARDENS
GWYNEDD

At Tal-y-Cafn, off the A470, 8 miles south of Llandudno.
Tourist Information Centre, Station Road, Colwyn Bay, Clwyd (01492) 530478.

In springtime there's a fairyland of rhododendrons in every possible hue here, together with azaleas and magnolias, but the gardens at Bodnant are among the most beautiful in Britain all year through. In summer they have been described as 'a poem in greens' and in autumn they blaze with colours from yellow to red. Formal terraces, built before World War I, descend a hillside above the Vale of Conwy, with fine views of the Snowdonian mountains. There is a profusion of roses, and reflected in a lily canal is an 18th-century summerhouse, used at one time as a mill for manufacturing pins and brought here from Gloucestershire in 1938.

The garden was laid out in the 1870s by a rich Lancashire industrialist named Henry Pochin, who built Bodnant Hall (not open). His daughter married a Scots politician and businessman who became Lord Aberconway. Lady Aberconway was a notable gardener and she and her son and grandson enlarged and developed the gardens, which were given to the National Trust in 1949.

IN EASY REACH A little way to the north of Bodnant, on the A470, the restored water-powered flour-mill of Felin Isaf is open to visitors, while further north-east is Colwyn Bay, an 1860s-vintage seaside resort with 3 miles of sandy beach. Perched up in the south-western outskirts of the town, and looking out to sea, is the Welsh Mountain Zoo, which has an excellent collection of birds of prey, and flying displays by falcons and eagles. For the younger members of the family there is a special 'children's zoo', and they will also no doubt be enchanted by the sea lions.

--- **198** ---

THE DAN-YR-OGOF CAVES
POWYS

At Craig-y-nos, on the A4067, 10 miles south of Sennybridge.
Tourist Information Centres: at the caves (01639) 730284 (seasonal opening only), and
Cattle Market Car Park, Brecon (01874) 622485.

It is a marvellous experience to walk round this vast complex of limestone caverns, the biggest yet opened up in Britain. They were discovered early this century and further explored in the 1930's, and although there is probably more to be revealed the present spectacular display is certainly enough to be going on with. Two cave systems are open, skilfully lit to display some beautiful and often awe-inspiring natural rock formations. In addition to the vast 'cathedral', there are underground lakes, stone bridges and elaborate stalagmites and stalactites. Walking is easy, and you won't need special clothing. Other attractions here include a museum, craft shop, dinosaur park, shire horse centre and a recreated blacksmith's shop.

IN EASY REACH A little further down the A4067, Craig-y-nos Castle is a mansion built in 1842 to a severe 'castle' design. It was later bought by the famous soprano, Adelina Patti, who lived here until her death in 1919. The most famous feature of the house is Patti's private theatre, which was maintained after the house became a hospital. Visitors can tour the house and theatre by appointment. The grounds have been turned into a country park with enjoyable riverside and woodland walks. The country park is used for sheepdog and gun-dog displays, demonstrations of country crafts, drystone walling and sheep-shearing. A mile south of Craig-y-nos, a road runs to the south-east to the Henrhyd Falls in a ravine owned by the National Trust.

--- **199** ---

ERDDIG
CLWYD

Off the A525, 2 miles south of Wrexham.
Tourist Information Centres: Lambpit Street, Wrexham (01978) 292015 and Craft
Centre, Park Road, Ruthin (01824) 703992.

•

Wrexham Maelor Arts Festival

In May every year the month-long Wrexham Maelor Arts Festival brings concerts and art exhibitions to the Wrexham area. The name may seem curious, but Wrexham Maelor is a new-fangled administrative district, set up in 1974, which includes what used to be called the Part of Flint. The Part was an anomaly created by Edward I in 1284. It was separated entirely from the main body of the old county of Flintshire and protruded from the right bank of the River Dee, sandwiched between Cheshire and Shropshire. Known for centuries as Maelor Saesneg (Saxon Maelor), it is now included with the towns of Wrexham and Ruabon on the other side of the Dee.

•

Erddig is a house where the atmosphere of a kindly and sometimes eccentric family still survives powerfully. The square house that forms the centre of the façade was built in the 1680s, and two rather undistinguished wings were added in the 1720s. It passed to the Yorke family in 1733, and they owned it until 1973, by which time it was collapsing through subsidence. A heroic restoration effort by the National Trust has now left the house as far as possible in the state it was in when last occupied.

The centre of interest of Erddig is downstairs in the maze of domestic quarters and estate workshops, which have been restored with remarkable completeness. The Yorkes took an obsessive interest in this aspect of the house, and one result is a unique gallery of paintings and photographs of servants from the 18th century onwards, sometimes accompanied by doggerel verse. The formal gardens, which include old varieties of fruit, are also justly famous.

IN EASY REACH Wrexham's character as a market town has largely been dispelled by sprawling suburbs and town-centre development, but the parish church of St Giles should not be missed. The noble iron gates, made in 1720 by the Davies brothers of Bersham (who also supplied the gates for Chirk Castle, 8 miles to the south) lead to a splendid church with a superbly decorated 16th-century tower and an unusual chancel formed by turning the original east window into an arch.

Just to the west of Wrexham is the village of Bersham, where an interesting Industrial Heritage Centre has been set up to commemorate the work of John Wilkinson,whose iron-foundries dominated the neighbourhood in the 18th century. After seeing the exhibitions in the centre, you can obtain a set of information pamphlets to enable you to explore a whole chain of notable industrial sites along an 8-mile trail.

--- **200** ---

HOLYWELL
CLWYD

On the A55, 12 miles north-west of Mold.
Tourist Information Centres: Town Hall, Earl Street, Mold (01352) 759331 (seasonal
opening only) and Craft Centre, Park Road, Ruthin (01824) 703992

The small town of Holywell hides some unusual attractions. The one which gave the place its name is St Winefride's Well, a famous healing shrine. It is on the site where, according to legend,

St Winefride's head fell to the ground when it was cut off by a disappointed suitor. The basin and bathing pool have their own elegant little chapel, and there is a much larger 15th-century chapel overhead.

Another attraction is the Greenfield Valley Heritage Park, a reclaimed industrial area that includes the ruins of 12th-century Basingwerk Abbey, a farm museum and industrial and wildlife trails.

IN EASY REACH Two castles to the south-east of Holywell are well worth visiting. At Flint, on the A548, the site was chosen to command the estuary of the Dee, and an unusual feature is the detached circular keep which is separated by a moat, to be used as a final defensive position. Flint castle was started by Edward I in 1277. The less conspicuous castle at Ewloe, further south-east and just off the A55, was built by the Welsh. Part of the Welsh Tower in the upper ward still stands to its original height, and there is a well in the lower ward. The interesting remains are pleasantly sited in low-lying woodland.

A few miles further south-east, Hawarden (pronounced 'Harden') was the home of W E Gladstone, who moved into the new battlemented 'castle' in the 1860s. The house is not open, but the original 13th-century castle nearby can be visited. The statesman and his wife are commemorated by an imposing monument in the Gladstone memorial chapel in the parish church, and by St Deiniol's Library, a residential study centre which benefited from many thousands of Gladstone's own books.

201

KIDWELLY CASTLE
DYFED

At Kidwelly, off the A484.
Tourist Information Centres: Lammas Street, Carmarthen (01267) 231557 and Pont Abraham Services, junction 49 M4, near Cross Hands (01792) 883838.

The grim gatehouse of one of the most impressive castles in Wales rears up above the River Gwendraeth. Inside it are dungeons and an oubliette (in which unfortunate prisoners were left to rot forgotten). You can walk along the top of the curtain wall which joins the castle's towers. In the inner ward are the remains of the hall, chapel and kitchen, and in the outer ward a later hall, of about 1500. Most of what you see was built in the 13th and 14th centuries, but the castle was originally built about 1130 by a bishop of Salisbury, who founded a priory here.

The priory church is in the town of Kidwelly on the other side of the river. A colliery winding engine, locomotives, machinery and equipment are preserved in an old tin-plate factory, now the Kidwelly Industrial Museum.

IN EASY REACH South of Kidwelly are the sand dunes and nature trails of the Pembrey Country Park. To the north, 10 miles away along the A484, is Carmarthen, on the River Towy, the county town of Dyfed. In legend it is closely linked with Merlin, the great magician, who was born here, but today is mainly remarkable for its large covered market.

The Carmarthen County Museum is at Abergwili, 2 miles to the east on the A40, occupying what was once a palace of the Bishops of St David's, set in a fine park. You can browse here among prehistoric and Roman antiquities, local history and natural history, costume and folk life. If a ride in a steam train appeals, make for Bronwydd, 3 miles north of Carmarthen on the A484, where the Gwili Railway runs trains on a section of the old line from Carmarthen to Aberystwyth (no trains until Easter, and then infrequently except during July and August).

The stronghold of Kidwelly was a bone of contention between the Welsh and the invading Normans. One attack, in 1136, was led by a Welsh princess who was defeated, captured, then beheaded

LAUGHARNE
DYFED

*On the A4066. Tourist Information Centres:
Lammas Street, Carmarthen (01267) 231557 and Pont Abraham Services, junction 49
M4, near Cross Hands (01792) 883838.*

●

The Common Walk

*Beating the Bounds was
a medieval way of
making sure that
everyone in a town or
parish knew exactly
where the boundaries lay.
The precise geography
was firmly etched on the
minds of the young by
beating them, dragging
them through hedges or
ducking them in streams
or pools at significant
points along the way.
Nowadays the beatings
are only of a token kind,
as at Laugharne, one of
the few places in Wales
where the custom is kept
up. In May every third
year the Portreeve
(equivalent of the mayor)
leads a party of banner-
bearers, guides and locals
on the Common Walk, a
20-mile peregrination of
the town's boundary (see
right).*

●

Pronounced 'Larn', this small town on
the River Taf grew up around its ruined castle. It seems a quiet place to be linked
with the boisterous genius of Dylan Thomas, who lived here and lies buried
here, in St Martin's churchyard. The poet wrote *Under Milk Wood* and many of
his other works in his home in an old boat-house, at the end of Cliff Road,
looking out over the 'heron priested' shore of the broad Taf Estuary. The house is
now a museum to him, with the original furniture in the parlour, the old garage
he used as a writing shed, photographs and an audio-visual presentation about
his life and work, as well as an art gallery displaying work by local artists.

IN EASY REACH To the south are the Pendine
Sands, six golden miles of them, where both Sir Malcolm Campbell and J G
Parry-Thomas attacked the world land speed record in the 1920s. It was also
from here that Amy Johnson and her husband flew the Atlantic in 1933.

Heading north from Laugharne, you come to the small town of St Clears
which now only has a castle mound and a few earthworks in Priory Park as a
reminder of its former importance in the Middle Ages. To the west along the A40
is the market town of Whitland, famous as the place where Hywel Dda in the
10th century AD prepared the codex of the ancient Welsh laws. A mile or so
outside the town is the ruin of the once great Cistercian Whitland Abbey. More
impressive, perhaps, are the grim ruins of Llanstephan Castle, on the B4312
south-east of St Clears, which glare across the estuary of the Towy back towards
Laugharne.

—— 203 ——

LLANDUDNO
GWYNEDD

Tourist Information Centre, Chapel Street (01492) 876413.

Known for its mild climate, Llandudno
is set along 2 miles of curving sandy beach between a pair of cave-pocked
headlands, Great Orme and Little Orme. The local landowners, the Mostyns,
who developed the resort in the 19th century, kept a check on commercial
excesses and the town has managed to preserve a good deal of its Victorian
charm and dignity. There is a fine pier of 1883 and a pleasant park called Happy
Valley, with rock gardens and an open-air theatre. From here a cable car will lift
you effortlessly to the summit of Great Orme, for marvellous sea and mountain
views. Alternatively, there is a 5-mile nature trail to the summit on foot, or it can

be reached by tramway or by car from Marine Drive, a scenic route round the headland opened in 1878. There are also boat trips to view the caves and cliffs.

IN EASY REACH Three miles to the south of Llandudno, at Conwy, are two bridges of exceptional interest. The tubular railway bridge was built by Robert Stephenson in 1848. Beside it is a graceful suspension bridge by Thomas Telford, dating from 1826. Both bridges were designed to harmonise with the dramatic bulk of Conwy Castle, built by Edward I in the 1280s to command the river crossing here. Even more spectacular are the town walls, in effect an outwork of the castle. Swooping up and down hills, 6ft thick and 30ft or so high, they are studded by 21 round towers and three great gates. Other attractions in the town include medieval Aberconwy House, the only 14th-century merchant's house to have survived the turbulence, the fire and the pillage of this frontier town for nearly six centuries. An audio-visual presentation here shows daily life in the house at different periods in its history. A tiny house on the quayside, only 10ft high and 6ft wide, claims to be the smallest house in Britain.

Victorian Extravaganza

The annual Victorian Extravaganza in Llandudno on May Day Bank Holiday weekend takes the town back to its early days as a resort, from the 1850s on, when dignified Victorian fathers brought their wives and children for decorous enjoyment of the sea-air and the sands. Today there are parades in 19th-century costume, and carriage rides. Meanwhile theatre groups perform suitable melodramas, fairground organs groan and traction engines wheeze, and street buskers help to recapture a vanished age.

204

LLECHWEDD SLATE CAVERNS
GWYNEDD

At Blaenau Ffestiniog.
Tourist Information Centres: High Street, Blaenau Ffestiniog (01766) 830360 (seasonal opening only) and Oriel Pendeitsh, Caernarfon (01286) 672232.

One of the most exciting industrial sites in the country lies where the A470 runs north from Blaenau Ffestiniog towards the Crimea Pass in the Snowdonia National Park. In the Llechwedd Slate Caverns visitors are carried deep into the mountain on a tramway through a tunnel dug in 1846 and into a series of vast caverns where the slate was quarried. The conditions of Victorian times have been re-created and there are displays of slate splitting. Another trip takes you down a steep gradient into the 'deep mine' for a walk to an underground lake. On the surface are more displays and exhibitions, a craft workshop, a pub and a restaurant.

A little further up the road, the Gloddfa Ganol Mine was at one time the largest slate mine in the world. Here you can see slate-splitting displays, machinery, 19th-century cottages and a museum, and you can explore miles of chambers and tunnels by Land Rover. Blaenau Ffestiniog is also the inland terminus of the narrow-gauge Festiniog Railway (see under Portmeirion).

IN EASY REACH The technology of more recent times is on view the other side of Blaenau Ffestiniog. To the south on the A496 are the Tan-y-Grisiau Reservoir and the Ffestiniog Power Station, a gigantic electricity generating station which is open to visitors. A drive up to Stwlan Dam yields a dramatic prospect of Snowdonia. Further south, on the A470, a nature trail runs round Trawsfynydd Lake, where Britain's first inland nuclear power station is open to groups by arrangement.

205

MARGAM PARK
WEST GLAMORGAN

Off the M4 and A48, south-east of Port Talbot. Tourist Information Centre: Sarn Services, junction 36 M4, near Bridgend (01656) 654906.

More than 800 acres of gracious parkland, with nature trails, a boating lake, pony rides, and a herd of fallow deer, make a contrast to the industrial scenery of Port Talbot. There are modern sculptures in the open air, and an elegant and unusually large orangery of 1790 (now used for classical music concerts) is set among gardens. Margam Castle is a mock-Tudor residence, dating from the 19th century, but in the Stones Museum you can see evidence of the Celtic monks who settled here long before, in the Dark Ages. There is a fine collection of Celtic crosses and carved stones, with gravestones and memorials of later centuries. In the 12th century Cistercian monks established themselves here. The ruined chapter house can still be seen, and part of their abbey church is now the nave of the parish church. Special events held in the Park include the Margam Abbey Fayre in August.

IN EASY REACH To the south-east of Margam are the Kenfig Sands, which swallowed up most of the town of Kenfig 600 years ago. A nature trail explores the burrows, which form a Site of Special Scientific Interest. Further south-east is Porthcawl, a popular seaside resort with a pleasure park, busy beaches and a giant caravan park.

Going north-east from Margam Park, the A4107 provides a scenic route to the Afan Argoed Country Park, the local 'little Switzerland', with its countryside centre and walks in the pine forest. This is a 19th-century industrial area which has been reclaimed, and its past is recaptured in the Welsh Miners Museum in the park.

--------- **206** ---------

PISTYLL RHAEADR
CLWYD

On a minor road, 5 miles north-west of Llanrhaeadr-ym-Mochnant, itself 12 miles west of Oswestry. Tourist Information Centres: Mile End Services, Oswestry, Shropshire (01691) 662488 and Town Hall, Llangollen (01978) 860828.

This 240ft waterfall on the border of Clwyd and Powys, is the highest in Wales and is seen at its most impressive after heavy rain or when the winter snows are melting. You get to it by a narrow minor road which climbs out of Llanrhaeadr and runs deep into the Berwyn mountains, and ever since the intrepid George Borrow reached the fall in the mid-19th century, it has been a tourist attraction. The stream falls in a sheer drop impeded only by a natural rock arch, and a bridge at the foot provides a good viewpoint

IN EASY REACH The Berwyn mountains are little known and much underrated. There is excellent walking on this high range of broad uplands, provided you have the Ordnance Survey map. The range runs south-west from Llangollen and the highest point (at 2,713ft) is Moel Sych, 2 miles to the north of the waterfall. Accessible starting points for the Berwyns are Llanrhaeadr itself and Llangynog, a few miles to the west, on the B4391.

Ten miles south-west of Llanrhaeadr is the vast and beautifully landscaped Lake Vyrnwy, on the B4393, a reservoir 4 miles long, constructed in the 1880s to supply water to Liverpool. It holds more than 12 million gallons. The visitor centre at one side of the imposing dam provides a 'trail' for a circular drive and details of tranquil walks in an almost Scandinavian landscape.

From Lake Vyrnwy a minor road runs north through lovely moorland scenery to the attractive small town of Bala, once famous for its knitted woollen stockings. Bala Lake (Llyn Tegid in Welsh) is the biggest natural expanse of inland water in Wales, almost 4 miles long. It is home to a rare salmon-like fish, the gwyniad, which is found nowhere else, and legends have the lake as a resting place of Noah's ark or alternatively as drowning a town whose inhabitants were punished for their wicked ways! The Bala Lake Railway runs steam trains on a narrow-gauge line along the eastern bank of the lake.

Easter Regatta

Bala Lake is one of Wales's major sailing centres and the Easter Regatta, held over the Bank Holiday weekend, enables colourful flocks of sailing dinghies to wheel and swoop and show their paces on the water. The event is open to dinghies up to 18ft long and to entrants from outside the local sailing club, and attracts about 150 boats each year.

--------- **207** ---------

PORTMEIRION
GWYNEDD

Off the A487, 1 mile south of Minffordd.
Tourist Information Centre, High Street, Porthmadog (01766) 512981.

Looking up towards The Dome – used as the town hall – in Portmeirion. The statue in the foreground is Hercules, demonstrating his strength by supporting the globe. He was a popular figure in Roman mythology – appropriate in this Italianate village

In 1926 a young Welsh architect named Clough Williams-Ellis bought an early Victorian house and estate looking out over a romantically beautiful bay on the Welsh coast, on the estuary of the River Dwyryd. Here, over the next 40 to 50 years, he created an extraordinary Italian-style Shangri-La, or retreat from the world, which was also a last home for old, unwanted buildings or bits of them: a Gothic colonnade from a house outside Bristol and the ballroom from a Welsh stately home. The main house itself is a hotel and the other buildings include the town hall, the tall campanile, the museum, a restaurant, craft shops and a pottery whose products have gained a high reputation. The village is set in lovely, rhododendron-studded grounds with miles of paths.

IN EASY REACH Porthmadog, 3 miles to the west of Portmeirion, is reached across a 1-mile embankment, The Cob, built in 1811 across the mouth of the River Glaslyn. Once the outlet for the slate quarries at Blaenau Ffestiniog inland, the town is now a holiday and boating centre. The Gwynedd Maritime Museum, on one of the old wharfs, has displays on the history of the port. The steam trains on the narrow-gauge Festiniog Railway make the 13 and a half mile trip to Blaenau Ffestiniog in an hour, through gorgeous mountain, forest and lake scenery. The line was originally built to carry the slate from the quarries, and the museum in the station at Porthmadog covers its history.

To the south, on the A496, Harlech Castle on its rock ridge is one of the best preserved of the chain of fortresses built by Edward I in the 13th century to hold down the conquered Welsh. The fortress's resistance to a long siege during the Wars of the Roses inspired the march *Men of Harlech*. The gatehouse is especially impressive, and there are magnificent views of Snowdonia and Tremadog Bay.

208

POWIS CASTLE
POWYS

Just south of Welshpool on the A483.
Tourist Information Centre, The Flash, Salop Road, Welshpool (01938) 522043.

Don't be deceived by the solid, battlemented bulk of Powis Castle – behind the forbidding exterior is a most elegant stately home. It has been lived in for 500 years, mainly by the influential Herbert family, although the title Earl of Powis was revived in the 1804 after the son of Clive of India married into the family. The story of the occupants is complex, and so is the architectural history of the castle. Six centuries are represented in the buildings, which include a beautiful Elizabethan long gallery, a 17th-century state bedroom and an early 19th-century ballroom. There was much Victorian restoration and alteration, but the results were outstandingly successful in producing a treasure-house of fine furniture, painting, wood-carving and plasterwork. An additional attraction is the profusion of works of Indian art collected by Robert Clive. The extensive gardens and deer park are reckoned to be among the best in Britain.

IN EASY REACH Welshpool is a bustling market town with a handsome main street. The social history of the area is portrayed at the Powysland Museum at the canal wharf, while part of that history has been re-created in the Welshpool and Llanfair Light Railway, which has an astonishing variety of engines and rolling stock. Eight miles to the south, on the B4385, the old county town of Montgomery is a delightful Georgian miniature, with the ruins of its castle perched dramatically on a cliff that commands panoramic views.

209

ST DAVID'S
DYFED

Tourist Information Centres: 4 Hamilton Street, Fishguard (01348) 873484
and Pont Abraham Services, junction 49 M4, near Cross Hands (01792) 883838.
National Park Information Centre, City Hall, St David's (01437) 720392 (seasonal opening only).

The smallest and sleepiest city in Britain is little more than a village, and owes its status to its cathedral, on the site where St David founded a monastery in about AD550. The largest church in Wales, it was built in the 12th century, altered in the 14th, and restored in the 18th and 19th, and lies deep down in the valley of the River Alun. The west front is by John Nash. Inside is the Norman nave with its pillars leaning outwards at a distinctly alarming angle and apparently only held together by the beautiful 16th-century ceiling. Other points of special interest are the 14th-century rood screen, the medieval bishop's throne and the misericords in the choir. Outside the cathedral stand the substantial remains of the 14th-century bishop's palace.

IN EASY REACH Close to the city, to the west, are the great cliffs of St David's Head, the sands of Whitesand Bay and the stacks of Ramsey Island, with its seals and seabirds. The magnificent scenery is all part of the Pembrokeshire Coast National Park, with a coast path running, altogether, 168 miles, from the Teifi Estuary right round to Carmarthen Bay and offering rambles of any length you like along one of Britain's most breathtaking shorelines. Visit the National Park Information Centre at St David's for leaflets covering the area and, indeed, the whole of Pembrokeshire.

●

St David's Day

On 1 March, St David's Day, a special service in the cathedral honours the saint who by the 12th century was regarded as the patron saint of Wales: the only Welsh saint to be accepted officially by the Roman Catholic Church. The custom of wearing a leek on St David's Day was already an ancient tradition in Shakespeare's time, but how the connection between the saint and the vegetable arose is a mystery.

●

210

TENBY
DYFED

*Tourist Information Centres: The Croft (01834) 842402, Pont Abraham Services,
junction 49 M4, near Cross Hands (01792) 883838 and Kingsmoor Common, Kilgetty
(01834) 813672 (seasonal opening only).*

*Castle Hill splits Tenby's
sandy beach in two –
South Beach looks
towards Caldey Island,
and North Beach
towards the Gower
Peninsula*

Tenby is a charming seaside resort and holiday base, with sandy beaches, a picturesque harbour, and quay, and narrow old streets. Part of the medieval town wall is still standing, protecting the place from attack from the landward side. The Tudor Merchant's House, Quay Hill, dating from late in the 1400s, recalls Tenby's past as a prosperous port, and the town museum on Castle Hill, covers the local history and the town's development as a resort in the 19th century, as well as the geology and archaeology of Pembrokeshire.

IN EASY REACH From Tenby there are boat trips along the magnificently scenic coast, and to Caldey Island, with its old churches and bird sanctuary. The Trappist monastery here is open Monday to Friday between May and September (to male visitors only), and the monks sell perfumes made from the island's wildflowers.

Fine cliff walks lead from Tenby through the scenery of the Pembrokeshire Coast National Park: if you head northwards you reach Saundersfoot, 5 miles away, another seaside resort, with its 19th-century harbour crammed with jostling small boats. From Kilgetty, inland on the A477, a coalfield trail explores the area's industrial past.

West from Tenby on the B4318, near St Florence, Manor House Leisure Park has a small zoo and attractive gardens. To the north-west, on the A477, is Carew Castle, a medieval stronghold which was turned into a Tudor mansion. Near the entrance is a striking Celtic cross, 13ft high, which was erected in the 11th century as a monument to a ruler of Dyfed. Also here is a rarity, a working tidal mill.

211

TREDEGAR HOUSE AND COUNTRY PARK
GWENT

*Off the A48, 2 miles west of Newport, Tourist Information Centre, Museum and Art
Gallery, John Frost Square, Newport (01633) 842962.*

*Events in and around
Newport*

*The Dolman Theatre in
Newport is the scene of
an enjoyable occasion in
March every year, the
week-long Newport
Drama Festival. The
festival is for amateur
dramatic companies,
performing full-length
plays in English. During
the first week in
September, Tredegar
House is host to the
Newport Show, and
around 18 September the
biggest crowd of the year
gathers here for the
annual vintage car rally.*

The powerful Morgan family lived at Tredegar in the Middle Ages, and an early range of buildings survives, but their 'new' house, dating from the 1660s, is the finest of its period in Wales. It was built in pleasant red brick to form two sides of a courtyard, and its formal façades are relieved by decorated doorways and pediments. The local council has done much to restore the house and its sumptuous state rooms, with their painted panels, elaborate carving and decorated ceilings, while the grounds boast a fine stable block and orangery, a bird garden, craft workshops, a boating lake and plenty of opportunities for family walks in the adjacent country park.

IN EASY REACH The charms of Newport are limited, but the Museum and Art Gallery, in John Frost Square, has an outstanding archaeological exhibition, as well as displays of more recent history, and a fine collection of English watercolours. On the western outskirts of the town, off the A467, the Fourteen Locks Picnic Site has been established on a section of the old Monmouthshire Canal. As the name suggests, the locks are the main attraction, and you can walk along them with an informative leaflet from the interpretation centre.

—————— 212 ——————

ABERYSTWYTH
DYFED

Tourist Information Centre, Terrace Road (01970) 612125.

The principal town on Cardigan Bay, Aberystwyth was developed as a seaside resort after the arrival of the railway in the 19th century, by promoters who touted it as 'the Brighton of Wales'. Its two shingle beaches lie on either side of a headland, on which stand the ruins of the much fought-over medieval castle. At the northern end of the town, perched 400ft up on top of Constitution Hill, and reached by a Victorian electric railway which proceeds at a decorous 4mph, is the largest camera obscura in the world, providing a view of an enormous area of landscape, including the Snowdonian mountains. Down below in the town, the Ceredigion Museum in the old Coliseum Theatre in Terrace Road covers folk life and farming in Cardigan.

On Penglais Hill, close to the north-eastern edge of the town, the National Library of Wales holds the biggest collection in existence of books in Welsh and about Wales, and a superb collection of ancient and beautiful manuscripts: these include the 12th-century Black Book of Carmarthen, the oldest surviving Welsh manuscript. On a similar theme, prints, book illustrations and photographs are on view at the Catherine Lewis Gallery of the University of Wales.

IN EASY REACH On the eastern edge of Aberystwyth, there are Celtic crosses in the 13th-century church of Llanbadarn Fawr, while the seaside resort of Borth, to the north of Aberystwyth, commands 4 miles of sandy beach. A nature trail explores the sand dunes of Ynyslas nearby. At Tre'r-Ddôl, inland on the A487, 10 miles north of Aberystwyth, is Yr Hen Gapel, a museum of Welsh 19th-century religious life, appropriately housed in a former Methodist chapel. To the south-east, 3 miles from Aberystwyth on the B4340, Nanteos is the great Georgian house of the Powell family, Wagner is said to have composed part of *Parsifal* in the glitteringly beautiful rococo music room, whose gilded mirrors reflect each other in endless perspectives.

—————— 213 ——————

BARMOUTH
GWYNEDD

Tourist Information Centre, Station Road (01341) 280787 (seasonal opening only).

The fishing village of Barmouth, with its 2 miles of sandy beach where the beautiful Mawddach Estuary runs out into Cardigan Bay, turned into a seaside resort late in the 19th century, and is popular with swimmers, surfers and wind-sailors. As a result of the expansion a new church was built in the 1890s, dedicated to St John and set dramatically against a cliff. Up on the hilltop looking out over the bay is a piece of land called Dinas Oleu, the first property acquired by the fledgling National Trust, in 1895. An attractive panorama walk climbs the hill from near the railway bridge.

IN EASY REACH The broad Mawddach Estuary is framed enticingly by wooded hills, with legend-haunted Cader Idris looming above it to the south. Gold for royal wedding rings is mined at nearby Bontddu and there are many enjoyable walks in the area. The railway bridge across the estuary has a footpath beside it with a tremendous view. There is also a ferry from Barmouth, met on the opposite shore by the comic little steam engines of the Fairbourne Railway – the gauge is only 15 inches – which haul passengers the 2 miles into Fairbourne itself, another popular family holiday resort with a sandy beach. Going the other way, miles of sand stretch away up the coast north of Barmouth.

Three Peaks Yacht Race

The annual Three Peaks Yacht Race in June is a testing event which starts from Barmouth and requires the competitors not only to race from Barmouth (see left) to Fort William in Scotland, but to scramble up and down the three mountain peaks of Snowdon, Scafell Pike and Ben Nevis on the way. Putting the three mountains together, the climbing adds up to a total height of 11,174ft, or altogether more than 4 miles straight up and down.

• •

Tydfillians Roman Run

This cross-country run over the Brecon Beacons from Brecon to Merthyr Tydfil involves close to 20 miles of tough going on the route which Roman legionaries used between their forts on either side of the high moors. The run is held on the Saturday nearest 23 August, which is St Tydfil's Day. She was martyred in the 5th century and left her name to Merthyr Tydfil.

214

BRECON BEACONS MOUNTAIN CENTRE
POWYS

At Libanus, off the A470, 5 miles south-west of Brecon.
Tourist Information Centre, Cattle Market Car Park, Brecon (01874) 622485.

Do not be put off by the term 'mountain centre' – the National Park Visitor Centre here is a comfortable place that welcomes any kind of visitor interested in finding out more about the area. You can look at the displays, consult maps and reference books and use the centre as an ideal base for a day's exploration. On the other hand, nobody minds if you just drop in to relax in the big lounge, have a cup of tea and admire the views. Picnickers are welcomed and there are easy walks, suitable for families, nearby on Mynydd Illtud Common.

IN EASY REACH Most of the National Park area lies at over 1,000ft. The terrain is open moorland with high rocky outcrops of Old Red Sandstone, and there is a tremendous feeling of space with splendid views. An active family can enjoy quite ambitious walks, with no steep scrambling involved armed with the Mountain Centre literature and a map, but heed the warnings about clothing and footwear – the Beacons can look deceptively gentle. An alternative way of getting around is pony-trekking, and there are plenty of centres in the area catering for it. Brecon itself is a town of great character. The excellent Brecknock Museum in the former Shire Hall will enhance your knowledge of the area, and the small cathedral has an interesting Cordwainers' Guild chapel and a fine chancel. Home of the South Wales Borderers, Brecon also has a good military museum where there is an impressive display of items depicting the Regiment's past glories.

215

CARDIFF
SOUTH GLAMORGAN

Tourist Information Centre, Bridge Street (01222) 227281.

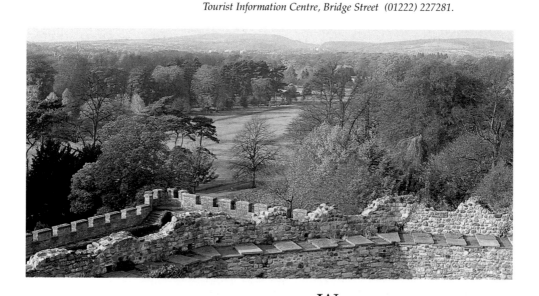

Glorious views over Bute Park from the Norman keep at Cardiff Castle

Wales's capital is an enjoyable place to visit, for operas and concerts, rugby football, attractive Victorian shopping arcades, quality museums, an impressive civic centre and, in Cardiff Castle, one of the most remarkable buildings in Britain. Also close to the city are Castell Coch and the Welsh Folk Museum at St Fagans (see separate entries).

The town grew up around its Norman castle, on the site of an earlier Roman fort, but modern Cardiff is largely the creation of the 2nd Marquess of Bute, the local landowner, who built the docks and transformed a moribund little harbour into, what was in 1913, the world's greatest coal port.

His son, the 3rd Marquess, was one of the richest men in Britain and used some of his immense wealth to restore and rebuild Cardiff Castle. His architect was a brilliant eccentric with a taste for opium and the Middle Ages, William Burges. Starting in the 1860s, the two men turned the fortress into an intensely romantic, larger-than-life medieval fantasy of Wagnerian opulence. Outside, lions and other creatures in stone snarl and stare at passers-by from the top of the surrounding wall, and the beautiful 150ft clock-tower soars above the city streets, while inside is a riot of imaginative decoration and superlative craftsmanship – wall paintings, tiles, stained glass, tapestries, coats of arms, bulging chimney-pieces, gorgeously carved and painted animals, birds, butterflies and fishes, statues and carvings of knights and damsels, angels and saints. Also to be seen here are stretches of Roman wall 10ft thick, the formidable 12th-century keep of the old castle, and the Black Tower home to the military museums of the Royal Regiment of Wales and Queen's Dragoon Guards.

A stroll in Bute Park on the bank of the River Taf will yield good views of the castle. Immediately to the east, in Cathays Park, is the Civic Centre, which has taken shape since the 1890s. Among many dignified buildings in white Portland stone are the City Hall of 1906, the Welsh National War Memorial of 1928 and the National Museum of Wales. The museum has notable collections in the fields of painting (especially Welsh artists and French Impressionists), geology, archaeology, zoology, botany and the industrial history of Wales.

Further south you will find the Victorian market and the elegant 19th-century shopping arcades. To the west from here is Cardiff Arms Park, the citadel of Welsh rugby, with the National Stadium. Bute Street leads south to the docks, now the Cardiff Bay Redevelopment Area, and the Welsh Industrial and Maritime Museum, with its engines, boats and steam locomotives and Techniquest – Britain's largest hands-on science centre.

— 216 —

CASTELL COCH
SOUTH GLAMORGAN

At Tongwynlais, off the A470, north of Cardiff.
Tourist Information Centre, Central Station, Central Square, Cardiff (01222) 227281.

Castell Coch's domed drawing room ceiling, adorned with painted birds and carved butterflies, astonishes the visitor. The lower part of the walls have wood panelling in dark green and gold inset with flower paintings. Above are murals of scenes from Aesop's Fables. Portraits of members of the Bute family hang from painted ribbons with a background of cranes, foxes, cats, monkeys and flocks of wild birds set among golden apples amid green foliage

On the side of a steep, wooded hill, the conical towers of Castell Coch (Red Castle) rise among the trees like something from a fairy-tale or *The Prisoner of Zenda*. The castle has, in fact, frequently appeared in films. It was created by the two men responsible for the present appearance of Cardiff Castle, the architect and designer William Burges and his patron, the 3rd Marquess of Bute. They started work in the 1860s and constructed the castle on the foundations of a ruined 13th-century stronghold on the site.

The castle has three round towers crowned by pointed roofs. It also has a working drawbridge and portcullis, and probably looks very much as a small fortress of its period and type would actually have done. Inside, however, the rooms are decorated in the same spirit of inventive and exuberant fancy as at Cardiff Castle, with superbly executed murals, statues and carvings. The bedroom designed by Burges for Lady Bute, with its domed ceiling on the theme of Sleeping Beauty above the bed, is particularly memorable (though it is hardly surprising that she never ventured to sleep in it).

IN EASY REACH At Caerphilly, 7 miles north of Cardiff, stand the awe-inspiring ruins of the second largest castle in England and Wales (Windsor is the largest), built in the 13th and 14th centuries with elaborate defences including two moats.

Lying to the east of Caerphilly is the Rudry Forest, with waymarked walks. Further north, the 7-mile Scenic Forest Drive starts from Cwmcarn on the A467. Organised by the Forestry Commission, it commands wonderful prospects of the Brecon Beacons.

●

CILGERRAN
DYFED

On a minor road, between the A478 and A484, 2 miles south of Cardigan.
Tourist Information Centre, Terrace Road, Aberystwyth (01970) 612125.

Coracle Races

Coracles are prehistoric portable boats, little changed since before the Romans came, and until quite recently still widely used to catch salmon and trout on the Rivers Teifi, Taf and Towy. They would fish in pairs, by stretching a net between two boats, and required skilful handling. Roughly oval in shape, a coracle was made by stretching animal skins (nowadays canvas) over a frame of hazel, willow or ash rods. They still race over a course of 100yds through the rocks and eddies of the Teifi at Cilgerran (see right) every August, and there are canoe races too, as well as swimming and diving competitions.

●

The coracles still race at Cilgerran each August, in the deep wooded gorge of the River Teifi, below the castle. There is a fine romantic view of the castle ruins from the waterside. A favourite subject with painters, on its high rock, it was frequently attacked, damaged and rebuilt again as Norman warlords and Welsh princes contended for mastery. Most of what remains today dates from the 13th century.

IN EASY REACH Cardigan, on the Teifi, is a pleasant but unremarkable town. Across the river in St Dogmaels are the ruins of a Benedictine abbey, and a working watermill, Y Felin, where you can see how the corn is ground and buy some of the flour if you like – no one will press you. The B4546 from here leads to Poppit Sands, where the Teifi flows out to sea and the Pembrokeshire Coast Path clambers up to 550ft-high Cemaes Head. Take the B4548 north-east of Cardigan to Gwbert-on-Sea and the Cardigan Island Coastal Farm Park and Waterfowl Centre, located right on the cliff tops opposite Cardigan Island. Going eastwards from Cardigan, the A484 follows the Teifi to Cenarth, with its spectacular rapids. The unusual Fishing Museum with exhibits associated with the area is housed in Felin Geri, another working flour mill, at Cwmcoy, close by. Staying on the A484, a side road 4 miles east of Newcastle Emlyn will take to you to the Museum of the Welsh Woollen Industry at Drefach Felindre. Here you can see a working mill, machinery and tools from the 18th century on, and follow a factory trail.

DOLAUCOTHI GOLD MINE
DYFED

Near Pumsaint, off the A482, 7 miles south-east of Lampeter. Tourist Information
Centre, Canolfan Owain Glyndwr, Machynlleth, Powys (01654) 702401.

South-east of the village of Pumsaint, the hillside is pock-marked with the workings of a gold mine efficiently exploited by the Romans, worked again briefly in the late 19th and early 20th centuries, and now looked after by the National Trust. Even before the Romans arrived, the native Britons had begun mining here, but the Romans ran operations on an altogether larger scale and brought water to the site by an aqueduct whose course can still be seen. The mine shafts are dangerous to explore, but marked trails lead past all the main features and there are guided underground and surface tours during the summer. The Roman entrance tunnels were cut to the shape of a workman with a loaded basket on his head. While in the area you can also explore the National Trust's estate with its acres of woodland and farmland.

IN EASY REACH Southwards from Pumsaint on the B4302 are the lakeside ruins of Talley Abbey. Founded by a Welsh prince in the 12th century, this was the only Premonstratensian monastery in Wales: the monks wore white habits like the Cistercians and followed a similar rule. To the north-east, Lampeter, on the A482, is a pleasant market town on the River Teifi. The artificial mound of a vanished Norman castle stands in the grounds of St David's College, whose buildings were designed in the 1820s by C B Cockerell.

219

DYFFRYN GARDENS
SOUTH GLAMORGAN

Near St Nicholas on a side road off the A48, about 6 miles west of Cardiff.
Tourist Information Centres: Central Station, Central Square, Cardiff (01222) 227281
and The Triangle, Paget Road, Barry Island, Barry (01446) 747171.

Wales's 'secret garden' is hidden away in green and pleasant country west of Cardiff and not visited as much as it deserves. The estate here was bought in 1891 by John Cory, a rich Cardiff coal magnate, who built Dyffryn House (not open), and he and his family developed the gardens. They cover 55 acres and combine a wild grassland area and arboretum – with rare cucumber trees and Chinese maples – and formal gardens, with a palm house and conservatories for carnivorous plants, cacti and rampageous ferns. Yew hedges divide part of the garden into separate 'rooms' or areas, including a Roman garden and a begonia garden.

IN EASY REACH Half a mile south-west of St Nicholas, Tinkinswood Burial Chamber is a Stone Age tomb, with a 40-ton capstone. To the west , off the A48, the ruins of Beaupré Castle are at St Hilary, south of Cowbridge. Down on the coast to the south is Barry, a popular holiday resort and sailing centre, which was formerly a thriving coal port. A special attraction is the Welsh Hawking Centre in Weycock Road. Here over 200 birds of prey can be seen, and flying demonstrations are held daily. Immediately to the west of Barry, in the Porthkerry Country Park, a beautiful wooded valley crossed by a 19th-century railway viaduct, runs down to the sea.

220

GOWER PENINSULA
WEST GLAMORGAN

Tourist Information Centres: Oystermouth Square, The Mumbles (01792) 61302
(seasonal opening only) and Singleton Street, Swansea (01792) 468321.

This official Area of Outstanding Natural Beauty, a peninsula 15 miles long and up to 8 miles across, protrudes into the Bristol Channel from Swansea. It has a remarkable variety of attractions in quite a small area, including dramatic cliffs and rock formations, fine bays and golden beaches, roaming ponies, wooded valleys and fortified medieval churches.

At the peninsula's eastern end, The Mumbles (from the French *mamelles*, 'breasts') are strictly speaking two small islands offshore, but the name is now used for the whole popular resort area along the sands, with a pier, a lighthouse, steamer trips, and the ruins of Oystermouth Castle. Heading west along the south coast, the National Trust owns the narrow Bishopston Valley, with its disappearing river, running down to the sea, and there are fine views from ruined Pennard Castle. Behind Oxwich Bay is the 500-acre Oxwich Burrows Nature Reserve, where a sand trail runs across the dunes at high-tide level.

The headland of Port-Eynon Point is also National Trust land. A curiosity here is Culver Hole, a great gash in the cliffs, walled up by someone unknown in the 15th century who gave it circular and rectangular 'windows' – possibly a giant dovecot? There are enjoyable cliff walks from here westwards, and caves which have yielded human remains from as long as 18,000 years ago as well as bones of hippos and elephants, mammoths and lions.

At the western end of the peninsula is the magnificent sandy beach of Rhossili Bay, with good surfing, and behind it is Rhossili Down, rising to above 600ft, commanding wonderful views, and giving even better views to hang-gliders. At the southern end of the bay the island of Worms Head, accessible when the tide is low, has a seabird sanctuary and there are sometimes seals to be seen. At the other end of the bay the island of Burry Holms, with its remains of an Iron Age hill-fort and a medieval chapel, can also be reached around low tide. Beyond is another nature reserve, at Whitford Burrows, before one reaches the strikingly different northern coast – a world of marshes and saltflats.
Along at the eastern end, Penclawdd is noted for cockles and laver bread (edible seaweed).

●

Gower Festival

The simple old churches of the Gower Peninsula, small and battlemented against medieval foes, today provide sanctuary and a welcoming setting for chamber music groups, singers and solo recitalists during the annual Gower Festival in July. Their acoustics are admirably suited to music of a small-scale, intimate kind – whether classical or folk – and this is what the festival concentrates on. The performances are entirely professional and of a high standard.

●

Rhossili Bay at the western end of the Gower

LLANGOLLEN
CLWYD

Tourist Information Centre, Town Hall (01978) 860828.

International Musical Eisteddfod

For one week in July every year 12,000 and more performers from 30 and more countries gather in Llangollen for the International Musical Eisteddfod, which has been held since soon after World War II. They come as members of choirs, folk-singing and dance groups, to compete during the day and enjoy concerts by previous years' winners in the evenings. Events include the Choir of the World Competition.

Llangollen squats between high hills in a narrow stretch of the Dee Valley and is probably best known for its world-famous Eisteddfod. But even outside Eisteddfod week there is still much to enjoy here. The old Dee bridge, with the river foaming below, is a magnet for visitors. Below the bridge the former station is the centre of a preserved steam railway, and on the canal bank nearby is an interesting small waterways museum, with boat trips. The church of St Collen is noted for its finely timbered roof and for a memorial of Sarah Ponsonby and Lady Eleanor Butler, the 'Ladies of Llangollen'. This eccentric Irish couple became almost a cult at the turn of the 18th century, attracting celebrities like Scott, Wordsworth and the Duke of Wellington to Plas Newydd, their picturesque mock-Tudor house above the town. It is open to visitors now and well worth the climb.

IN EASY REACH Castell Dinas Bran, the ruins of a 13th-century castle set in picture-book fashion on a summit overlooking Llangollen, makes an excellent target for a walk with splendid views. For a less strenuous walk, follow the canal towpath to the pleasant Horseshoe Falls, the weir on the Dee built by Telford to divert water into the canal. A short drive northwards on the A542 will bring you to the imposing ruins of the Cistercian abbey of Valle Crucis, the 'Valley of the Cross'. The cross in question is on Eliseg's Pillar near the main road, reputed to be a 9th-century memorial to a local ruler, although the inscription has now been eroded. From here the A542 goes on to climb through the Horseshoe Pass and the striking mountain scenery at the southern end of the Clwydian Range.

LLANWRTYD WELLS
POWYS

Tourist Information Centre, The Old Town Hall, Memorial Gardens, Llandrindod Wells (01597) 822600.

Victorian visitors were drawn to this tiny spa (claimed to be the smallest town in England and Wales) partly by the sulphur-laden waters but also by its setting in the broad Irfon Valley among rolling hills. The area has long been popular with pony-trekkers, and gentle exploration of the countryside, on horseback or foot, is still the main attraction. The town itself, built around its charming bridge, has an appealing mixture of architecture, and in the summer you can stroll to the Pump Room for tea.

IN EASY REACH Just outside the town, on the A483 to Builth, is the Cambrian Factory, established in 1918 to employ disabled ex-servicemen. You can see high-quality tweeds being made and browse in the attractive shop. To the north-west of Llanwrtyd there are picnic places and waymarked walks in the Towy Forest and around Llyn Brianne reservoir. A mile below the Llyn Brianne dam, near Ystradffin, the Dinas Nature Reserve is signposted from the road. Pamphlets are available on the trails and the birds to be seen here and in the nearby Gwenffrwd reserve (they include buzzards, kestrels and the rare red kite), and you can walk to the cave hideout of Twm Sion Cati, an amiable 17th-century thief, the Welsh equivalent of Robin Hood, who later became a respected citizen.

Odd Events at Llanwrtyd Wells

If the idea of the World Bog Snorkling Championships causes you to boggle, spare some pity for the contestants in this event, held in late August, who must snorkle for 100yds along a channel cut in a black bog near Llanwrtyd Wells. This is not the only odd event that goes on in this Victorian spa town. In June they hold a ferocious Man Versus Horse Marathon, in which runners, horses and cyclists compete over a 22-mile course in the surrounding mountains. Later in the month comes the gentler but taxing Drovers Walk, along a route the drovers used to take driving cattle and sheep to market.

LLEYN PENINSULA
GWYNEDD

Tourist Information Centres: Y Maes, Pwllheli (01758) 613000 (seasonal opening only) and High Street, Porthmadog (01766) 512981.

The 'Land's End of Wales' is an official Area of Outstanding Beauty, a peninsula (*lleyn* means 'peninsula' in Welsh) 25 miles long and up to 10 miles across, reaching down into the Irish Sea from the north-western corner of Wales. The Lleyn has sandy beaches and 1,800ft mountains – the highest being triple-peaked Yr Eifl, 1,849ft – and a Christian history stretching far back into the 5th century, when a Breton missionary, St Cadfan, is said to have founded a monastery on remote Bardsey Island, 2 miles off the peninsula's tip. The island became a major place of pilgrimage and today's visitors tread in the footsteps of thousands of medieval pilgrims who walked the length of the peninsula to visit 'the island of 20,000 saints'.

One of the pausing places on the pilgrim route was the shrine of Clynnog-fawr (on the north-east coast) where St Beuno was buried. The great church here

Looking towards the Lleyn Peninsula, which in turn commands superb views in all directions – including parts of Ireland and the Pembrokeshire Coast National Park 70 miles away to the south-west

today dates mainly from the 15th and 16th centuries, and beside the road (the A499) is St Beuno's Well, to which sick people came to be healed. Further west, on the easternmost peak of Yr Eifl, a great earthen rampart still stands up to 13ft high, protecting the unusually well-preserved Iron Age village of Tre'r Ceiri (Town of Giants), reached from the B4417.

Aberdaron, close to the western end of the peninsula, was where the pilgrims took to boats for Bardsey Island, and still is. The island is now a nature reserve, and the Bird and Field Observatory is open to visitors.

Heading east, along the southern coast, you come to the seaside resort of Pwllheli. To the east of the town, off the A497, is Penarth Fawr, a 15th-century 'hall house', meaning that it virtually consisted of one big room. Further east still is Llanystumdwy, the boyhood home of David Lloyd George, who was orphaned at an early age and lived with his uncle's family here. He went to the village school and it was at his house in Llanystumdwy, Ty Newydd, that he died in 1945. The Lloyd George Memorial Museum in the village contains photographs, cartoons and numerous mementoes of this spell-binding orator and politician, who became a Member of Parliament in 1890, Chancellor of the Exchequer in 1908 and Prime Minister in 1916. Sir Clough Williams-Ellis designed his grave, which stands beside the river. Criccieth, 2 miles east again, is another pleasant little seaside resort, with a ruined 13th-century castle.

Thomas Telford's Pontcysyllte Aqueduct, the longest in the United Kingdom

--- **224** ---

PONTCYSYLLTE AQUEDUCT
CLWYD

Off the A5 at Froncysyllte, 5 miles east of Llangollen.
Tourist Information Centre, Town Hall, Llangollen (01978) 860828.

At the turn of the 18th century the Pontcysyllte Aqueduct was regarded as the engineering miracle of the age, and it is still an astonishing sight to see boats crossing a deep valley high up in a narrow iron trough, less than 12ft wide, carried on a stone aqueduct 1,000ft long and 120ft above the river, supported on 19 slender arches. Completed in 1805, it was Thomas Telford's solution to the problem of getting the Ellesmere Canal across the River Dee on its way to the Mersey. Nowadays the aqueduct carries the canal feeder channel from the Dee at Llangollen, and it is a popular waterway. Crossing the aqueduct in a boat or walking across it on the towpath is a highly memorable experience, provided you have a good head for heights.

IN EASY REACH Telford built another splendid aqueduct 3 miles to the south at Chirk, to carry the canal across the Ceiriog. Somewhat older, the squat, grey, 14th-century castle at Chirk, erected by Edward I, has been modified internally over hundreds of years to provide an outstanding long gallery and a series of gracious state rooms with fine furniture, tapestries and pictures. It has been continuously occupied since 1595 by the Myddleton family, whose monuments can be seen in the parish church, and is now owned by the National Trust. The formal gardens are delightful, and as you drive into the park you see the magnificent iron gates, made locally in 1719 by the Davies brothers, Robert and John, famous for their superb ironwork.

Below right: Pentre Ifan burial chamber in the Preseli Hills

—————— **225** ——————

PRESELI HILLS
DYFED

South-east of Fishguard.
Tourist Information Centre, 4 Hamilton Street, Fishguard (01348) 873484.

•

Events in and around the Preseli Hills

Late in August near Mynachlog-ddu in the eastern Preseli Hills, the Beca Mountain Race commemorates the Rebecca Riots. The race is up and down a mountain and the first few runners home hastily put on women's clothes. The first to dress then chops down a wooden gate with an axe. The gate represents the toll-gates on the roads which aroused the ire of rioters in 1843. Dressed as women, under leaders called 'Rebeccas', they smashed the gates which were making life more expensive for pedlars and travelling traders, and so for their customers. Events at Scolton Manor, near Spittal, include the Pembrokeshire Vintage Car Club's annual show in July – with veteran, vintage and classic cars on display – and the Annual Game Fair in August, with shooting, riding and archery contests.

•

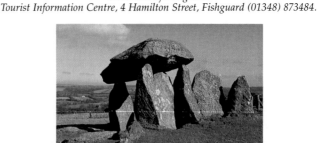

Grazed by mountain sheep and ponies, the often mist-shrouded Preseli Hills have an uncanny quality about them, packed as they are with prehistoric remains – stone circles, standing stones, tombs and cairns. This was sacred land, and it was from here that the 'blue stones' were taken with enormous labour to build Stonehenge, 4,000 years ago. The most striking single monument to be seen today is the Pentre Ifan burial chamber with its 16ft capstone, on a side road 3 miles south-east of Nevern. Other tombs lie along the Bronze Age track – part of the ancient trade route between Salisbury Plain and Ireland – which runs some 8 miles from Bwlch Gwynt on the B4329 eastwards to Crymych on the A478, through the heart of the moors and close to their highest point at Preseli Top, 1,760ft.

IN EASY REACH The church of St Brynach at Nevern, just north of the hills, is of special interest for its carved stones, which include the Great Cross, 13ft high and elaborately decorated in the 10th century. Near it is a stone inscribed in both Latin and Ogham (an ancient Celtic system of writing), and there are more stones of interest inside the church. One of the churchyard yews here was long an object of special reverence as people believed it 'bled' for Christ's death.

To the south-west of the hills, on the B4329, Scolton Manor, among its pleasantly landscaped grounds, has been turned into a regional museum, with material on local history and rural crafts. Nearby, the A40 runs through the Treffgarne Gorge, with Iron Age earthworks crowning the hilltops on either side. The Nant y Coy Mill here has a collection of local Victorian furniture and household objects.

—————— **226** ——————

SNOWDON MOUNTAIN RAILWAY
GWYNEDD

Starts from Llanberis, on the A4086.
Tourist Information Centre, Oriel Eryri, Llanberis (01286) 870765.

•

Endurance Tests

Events in and around Llanberis in the summer include some notable endurance tests. One is the International Snowdon Race in July, which is a race from Llanberis to the summit of Snowdon and back. A few days later, 100 or more competitors assemble for the long-distance swimming races on the waters of Llyn Padarn.
There is a 2-mile race for contestants aged 12 to 16, and a 4-mile race for their elders.

•

Britain's only narrow-gauge rack-and-pinion railway takes an hour over the 4½-mile journey from the starting point in Llanberis to the 3,560ft summit of the highest mountain in England and Wales. It has been clambering up the ascent since 1896 and still uses the original Swiss-built steam locomotives. On the way are views of peaks and precipices, tarns and waterfalls, broad valleys and deep gorges. The summit itself, if not shrouded in cloud (which it frequently is), commands majestic prospects of the surrounding mountains and lakes, the Menai Strait and Anglesey, and great stretches of sea. An efficient bus service operates round Snowdon (mainly in summer), and if you prefer to make the ascent on foot there are six main tracks, starting from various points in the surrounding terrain. The path from Llanberis is regarded as the least taxing, but also the least inspiring of them.

IN EASY REACH Snowdonia's natural riches are explored in the Oriel Eryri environmental centre in Llanberis. The town itself owes its existence to the 19th-century Snowdonia tourist boom and to the great Dinorwic Quarry, the world's largest producer of slate, which reached its peak of activity in the 1890s, when it employed 3,000 men. It closed in 1969, but the workshops, the machinery and much of the atmosphere have been preserved in the Welsh Slate Museum.

Slate for export was sent by a specially constructed railway to Port Dinorwic on the Menai Strait. Two miles of its tracks now carry the steam trains of the Llanberis Lake Railway through the Padarn Country Park along the shore of Llyn Padarn. Between it and the next lake to the south-east, Llyn Peris, stand the ruins of Dolbadarn Castle, built about 1200.

227

SWALLOW FALLS
GWYNEDD

Off the A5, 2 miles west of Betws-y-Coed.
Tourist Information Centre, Royal Oak Stables, Betws-y-Coed (01690) 710426.

Rising on one of the great peaks of Snowdon, Carnedd Llewellyn (3,484ft), the River Llugwy runs eastward to the holiday centres of Capel Curig and Betws-y-Coed. Before reaching the latter it tumbles in a cataract down the rocky Swallow Falls, long one of the most visited beauty spots in all Wales. At one time the income from visitors to the falls gave Betws-y-Coed the lowest rates in Britain. The falls lie in the 20,000-acre Gwydyr Forest, managed by the Forestry Commission, which has waymarked numerous attractive walks in this area. One runs through the gorge below the falls for a couple of miles past some of the finest trees in the forest.

IN EASY REACH On the outskirts of Betws-y-Coed, Thomas Telford's Waterloo Bridge, of 1815, which carries the A5 over the River Conwy, is admired for its beautiful decorative ironwork. The A470 runs south-west from Betws-y-Coed to Dolwyddelan, 5 miles away, and the dramatic 12th-century keep of Dolwyddelan Castle, high on a ridge above the road. According to tradition, this was the birthplace of Llewellyn the Great, the last Welsh prince to rule virtually the whole of Wales. Going the other way, north from Betws-y-Coed, the A470 runs 3 miles to Llanrwst on the River Conwy, where the church of St Grwst is worth seeing for the magnificent wooden rood screen and the monuments of the Wynne family of Gwydir Castle, just outside the town. The once magnificent castle is now being restored, and open to the public. Close by is Gwydir Uchaf Chapel, built in the 17th century, with a tremendous painted ceiling.

Drystone Walling Competition

There is a fascinating event at Betws-y-Coed in July every year, when the Snowdonia National Park Society holds its drystone walling competition. This is now a firmly established occasion, which draws entrants from a wide area. If you want to see how the experts build a durable wall simply by fitting stones together, without any mortar to hold them, this is the place to be.

The Snowdon Mountain Railway, operated by vintage steam and modern diesel locomotives

• 228 •

TALYLLYN RAILWAY
GWYNEDD

Tourist Information Centres: High Street, Tywyn (01654) 710070 (seasonal opening only) and Canolfan Owain Glyndwr, Machynlleth, Powys (01654) 702401.

Race the Train

Racing the train along the Talyllyn Railway on an August day is not quite as impossible a challenge as it may sound. The event started in 1984 and raises money for charity. The runners keep as close to the railway line as the terrain permits, and cover a distance of 7 miles out from Tywyn and 7 miles back again. They are assisted by the fact that the train takes some time to turn round at the far end, and of some 500 runners every year, 100 or so are likely to beat the train. The record time for the 14-mile distance so far is 1 hours 22 minutes (the train takes 1 hours 45 minutes).

The earliest of the 'great little trains' of Wales to be rescued from closure and managed by volunteers, the steam trains of the narrow-gauge Talyllyn Railway run from the Cardigan Bay coast at Tywyn 7 miles inland up the Fathen Valley into the southern parts of the Snowdonia National Park and the village of Abergynolwyn. The gauge is 27 inches and the one-way trip takes the best part of an hour. On the way you can pause to admire the falls at Dolgoch or stroll in the forest at Nant Gwernol.

The museum at Abergynolwyn depicts the life of a slate-mining village, for the railway was originally built in the 1860s to carry slate from Abergynolwyn quarry. It was when the quarry closed in 1947 that the railway was threatened. At the other end of the line, the museum at the Tywyn station covers the narrow-gauge railways in general.

IN EASY REACH Tywyn was developed as a seaside resort in the 19th century by John Corbett, better known as the 'salt king' who created Droitwich Spa. In the church of St Cadfan is a stone of the 7th or 8th century, on which is inscribed the oldest known piece of written Welsh. Bees are on view at the Holgates Honey Farm, which is celebrated for its honey ice-cream.

The church of Llanegryn, off the A493, 2 miles north of Bryncrug, has a superb 16th-century rood screen. In the other direction, south of Tywyn, Aberdyfi (or Aberdovey) is a peaceful seaside, sailing and golfing resort on the beautiful estuary of the River Dovey, famous for its bird life and its mountain views. On the front, the Outward Bound Museum concentrates on sailing, with model ships and lifeboat gear.

229

TRETOWER COURT
POWYS

On the A479, 10 miles north-west of Abergavenny.
Tourist Information Centre, Cross Street, Abergavenny, Gwent (01873) 857588 (seasonal opening only).

The attractive village of Tretower is noted for one of Britain's best-preserved fortified manor houses. Tretower Court dates from the 14th century, but later additions, built around a courtyard, were designed to change it from a refuge into a comfortable home for the powerful Vaughan family. The early Great Hall is impressive, but the charm of the house lies in the family apartments, with their external gallery. Close by is a separate 13th-century castle, where 'Picard's Tower' rises above the defensive walls.

IN EASY REACH To the north-west of Tretower, near the B4560, Llangorse Lake, the second largest natural lake in Wales, offers boating and fishing, and the Victorian church at Llangasty-Talyllyn on the southern shore is worth visiting. The Black Mountains, which rise sharply to the east of Tretower, are fairly inhospitable on this side, but the Sugar Loaf peak near Abergavenny can be approached by car.

Perhaps the best Black Mountains experience is the ride through the Vale of Ewyas. You take the B4423 at Llanfihangel Crucorney (6 miles north of Abergavenny on the A465), where the old manor house, Llanfihangel Court, with its famous 17th-century staircase, is occasionally open in the summer. The minor road takes you past the imposing ruins of Llanthony Priory, a 12th-century foundation that had a chequered history. It never prospered as a monastery, and after the Dissolution it fell into private hands with a succession of owners including the poet Walter Savage Landor, who tried unsuccessfully to develop an estate here. A shooting box was incorporated into the ruins and is now a small hotel. The road finally reaches the summit at the Gospel Pass, a superb viewpoint from which you can descend into Hay-on-Wye.

230

ABERDULAIS FALLS
WEST GLAMORGAN

On the A465, 3 miles north-east of Neath. Tourist Information Centres: Aberdulais Basin, near Neath (01639) 633531 (seasonal opening only) and Singleton Street, Swansea (01792) 468321.

This miniature Niagara among the trees on the River Dulais, where it joins the River Neath, is not only a beauty spot painted by Turner and admired by thousands of visitors since his time, but also an important site in the industrial archaeology of South Wales, as an early metalworking centre. In the 1580s copper-smelting started here under the eye of an expert German smelter named Ulrich Frosse, whose arrival set the whole South Wales copper industry in train. In the late 1600s iron was forged here and in the 19th century tin plate was rolled on the site.

IN EASY REACH Not far from the falls is the Aberdulais Basin, where the Tennant Canal of 1824 joined the Neath Canal of 1795. Both canals were constructed to carry coal from further north in the valleys down to the coast. The basin has been rescued from decay and you can explore the routes. Nearer to Neath, along a towpath, or off the B4434, are the Tonna barge-building workshops and a visitor centre with material on the history of the canals. On the A4109, looking out over Aberdulais from the mountainside, are the animals and birds of the Penscynor Wildlife Park – chimpanzees and marmosets, penguins, deer and the rest. A little way further north, the Cefn Coed Colliery Museum tells the story of mining in the Dulais Valley.

The city of Swansea, to the south-west of Aberdulais, has some lively museums. Modern art is on show in the Glynn Vivian Art Gallery, Alexandra Road, and the Maritime and Industrial Museum, with its ships, locomotives and working woollen mill, is in South Dock, near the marina. Not far away, the Swansea Museum in Victoria Road deals with local history.

Swansea Festival

Held since 1948, the Swansea Festival of Music and the Arts in late September and the first half of October is the principal professional arts festival in Wales. It centres on orchestral concerts in the Brangwyn Hall (which contains the British Empire war memorial paintings by Sir Frank Brangwyn). The picture above shows the Borodin String Quartet playing here. There are also art exhibitions in the Glynn Vivian Gallery and plays in the Grand Theatre. Since 1981 there has also been a fringe festival, which features nationally known alternative comedians, cabaret and theatre companies, as well as providing opportunities for local performers.

231

BIG PIT MINING MUSEUM
GWENT

At Blaenavon, off the B4248, 6 miles north of Pontypool.
Tourist Information Centres: Swan Meadow, Cross Street (01873) 857588 (seasonal opening only) and Museum and Art Gallery, John Frost Square, Newport (01633) 842962.

If you have ever wanted to go down a coal mine, Big Pit is the place to do it. The mine closed in 1980, and very little artificial reconstruction was needed to provide an authentic experience for visitors. On the underground tour (you need warm clothes and sensible shoes) you do what every miner did – put on your helmet, hand over your matches, descend 294ft in the cage and then walk through the galleries. The surface attractions include a miner's cottage, the winding engine, pithead baths and colliery workshops. Under-fives cannot go down the pit.

IN EASY REACH The Big Pit is one of several imaginative projects designed to interpret the rich social history of the area. In the elegant stable block of Pontypool Park, Valley Inheritance offers a vivid picture of local life and industry over the centuries. For the rural equivalent, go to the Gwent Rural Life Museum in Usk, on the A472, where the Malt Barn has been turned into a storehouse of fascinating bygones. There are further agricultural exhibits and rare livestock breeds at the farm park on the shore of the vast Llandegfedd Reservoir, 4 miles west of Usk. The lake is a fine place for a picnic, and boats can be hired.

Now not much more than a shell, Caernarfon Castle is at its most impressive seen towering above the quay on the River Seiont

●

Caernarfon Arts Festival

The two-day arts festival at Caernarfon early in October every year started in 1981 and is primarily a celebration of Welsh folk dancing. Other aspects of the arts which may get a look in however, range from jazz and country and western, to mime, drama, films, poetry and prose, the visual arts and photography.

●

— 232 —

CAERNARFON
GWYNEDD

Tourist Information Centre, Oriel Pendeitsh (01286) 672232.

Caernarfon, the largest and most important of Edward I's Welsh castles, with its massive walls and its unusual polygonal towers and courses of coloured stone, may have been designed deliberately in imitation of the walls of Constantinople, to exploit the tradition that Constantine the Great was born here, in the nearby Roman fort of Segontium. James of St George was the architect, and the castle is traditionally the place where the Princes of Wales are proclaimed: Prince Charles was invested here in 1969. The Queen's Tower houses the regimental museum of the Royal Welch Fusiliers, whose history goes back to 1689: eight VCs are on display.

The town walls of Caernarfon run for about half a mile and in Castle Square is an impressive statue of David Lloyd George, who was the local Member of Parliament for more than 50 years. On the A4085, south-east of the castle, are the remains of Segontium, an important Roman military base for 300 years. The small museum contains finds from the site and displays about the Romans in Wales.

IN EASY REACH On a side road off the A4086 near Llanrug, 4 miles east of Caernarfon, is Bryn Bras Castle (limited opening). 'Medievalised' in the 1830s, the romantic gardens provide lovely woodland and mountain walks and afford wonderful views of Snowdonia. At the south-western end of the Menai Strait, Fort Belan (view from outside only) was built to keep Napoleon's forces at bay. Sandy beaches line the shore of Caernarfon Bay where various regattas and sailing events take place during the summer.

— 233 —

DEVIL'S BRIDGE
DYFED

On the A4120, 10 miles east of Aberystwyth.
Tourist Information Centre, Terrace Road, Aberystwyth (01970) 612125.

Three bridges are stacked on top of each other at this celebrated beauty spot where the Mynach joins the Rheidol among spectacular waterfalls in a deep, dark, densely wooded gorge. The oldest and lowest one is 'the bridge of the Evil One', traditionally the Devil's own handiwork, but perhaps actually built by the monks of nearby Strata Florida Abbey, and apparently in place here as early as 1188. Above it is a stone bridge constructed in 1753 and above that again is an iron bridge of 1901. Paths wind their way about the gorge, with views of the Mynach and Gyfarllwyd Falls.

Close by is the terminus of the Vale of Rheidol narrow-gauge railway, whose trains run through lovely country between Aberystwyth and Devil's Bridge. With a gauge of 23½ inches, this is the last steam line on British Rail. The journey takes an hour each way.

IN EASY REACH To the north-east of Devil's Bridge are the bleak moorland fastnesses of Plynlimon, 2,468ft, where the Severn and the Wye rise within a mile or two of each other. Nearer to Devil's Bridge in the same direction, the Llywernog Silver-Lead Mine, at Ponterwyd on the A44, closed down in the 1880s, but is now a museum (limited opening in autumn). The great waterwheels are turning again and you can see the machinery and a mass of photographs and records, and penetrate along a section of cramped mine tunnel underground. Also off the A44, at Capel Bangor, the hydroelectric Rheidol Power Station and its fish farm are open to visitors.

To the south of Devil's Bridge, on a minor road off the B4343, are the evocative ruins of Strata Florida Abbey, a 12th-century Cistercian house which was a notable centre of learning in the Middle Ages. The great 14th-century poet Dafydd ap Gwilym is believed to have been buried here and there is a memorial to him. South again on the B4343, a nature trail probes the primaeval peat bog of Cors Caron, just north of the market town of Tregaron, with its wealth of birds and flowers.

234

LLANDRINDOD WELLS
POWYS

Tourist Information Centre, Old Town Hall, Memorial Gardens (01597) 822600.

Llandrindod Wells always surprises the visitor with its imposing 19th-century architecture set in the thinly populated Radnorshire countryside, and so much of the old Victorian spa town has survived here that you can still appreciate what attracted the thousands who came here to take the waters – the big hotels, wide streets, grand terraces, lawns and flower beds, the quaint Rock Park with its Pump Room and the huge artificial lake complete with sedate rowing boats. The small museum, situated next to the Town Hall, has good local history displays as well as an interesting collection of dolls.

IN EASY REACH The most spectacular attraction nearby is the Elan Valley, to the north-west of Llandrindod. You reach it by way of the B4518 from Rhayader, a small, grey market town which in recent years has become a busy holiday centre in its own right. The chain of reservoirs and impressive dams supplying much of Birmingham's water are set in magnificent scenery. A visitor centre (open Easter to October) at the first of the dams explains the workings of the scheme and gives information about walks and the wildlife in the area. Five miles north of Llandrindod, off the A483, are the ruins of Abbey Cwmhir, a Cistercian foundation in a typically remote and peaceful spot. A memorial marks the traditional resting place of Llywelyn ap Gruffydd.

235

THE MENAI STRAIT
GWYNEDD

Tourist Information Centres: Theatr Gwynedd, Bangor (01248) 352786 (seasonal opening only) and Station Site, Llanfair P.G. (01248) 713177.

Fourteen miles long and up to a mile wide, the Menai Strait separates the Isle of Anglesey from the mainland. For centuries it was crossed by ferries, and cattle were swum across, but in the 1820s Thomas Telford slung across it his pioneering 1,000ft suspension bridge, 100ft above the water, the longest bridge in the world at that time (it was widened in 1941). A mile to the west, Robert Stephenson built his great tubular railway bridge in 1850. It was badly damaged by fire in 1970 and was rebuilt as a combined road and rail bridge.

There are good views of the Telford bridge from the A5 and from the town of Menai Bridge at the Anglesey end. The Tegfryn Art Gallery here, in Cadnant Road, is a private gallery standing in its own grounds. Paintings by contemporary artists are exhibited, and pictures may be purchased.

On the mainland side of the Strait, Bangor has a much-rebuilt cathedral with a garden of plants mentioned in the Bible. In the Museum of Welsh Antiquities, in the Old Canonry, is material from prehistoric times onwards, and the city's 1896 pier has been restored to its pristine glory. But the 'must' in this area is Penrhyn Castle, a mile or two east of Bangor. This gigantic 'Norman' robber baron's stronghold was erected by Thomas Hopper in the 1830s for a local slate magnate. This explains the carved slate staircase, which took 10 years to complete, and the one-ton slate bed.

A few miles further east on the A55 is the village of Aber. To the south is the Coedydd Aber Nature Reserve, with its mixed woodland of oaks and alders, birches and hazels. Here the Aber Falls drop 120ft down a precipice.

Victorian Festival

The nine-day Victorian Festival in Llandrindod Wells every August is a delightful and nostalgic celebration of the spa town's past and an important tourist magnet in this sparsely populated area of Wales. It was first held in 1981 to mark the re-opening of the Victorian Pump Room and was so enjoyable that it has gone on ever since. The whole town is involved, with the townspeople and shopkeepers dressed in Victorian costume (see left). Cars are banned from view and a mass of events from 19th-century soirées to concerts, Welsh and English folk dancing, traditional jazz, street theatre and brass bands culminate in a grand ball.

Ffair y Borth and Menai Strait Regattas

The Ffair y Borth at Menai Bridge in October was formerly a cattle and pony show, but nowadays is an affair of sideshows and fairground rides and amusements. Earlier in the year, late July or early August brings the formidable Menai Strait Regattas. The waters of the Strait are alive with sailing boats as a round dozen regattas are organised by 12 clubs and committees based in Bangor, Beaumaris, Caernarfon, Menai Bridge and Port Dinorwic. More than 100 yachts compete every day and there is a 17-mile race for sailing dinghies from Beaumaris Pier to Traeth Bychan Bay, near Llanallgo, on Anglesey's east coast.

•

Raft Race

About 200 rafts turn out every year in early September for the annual raft race down the River Wye, organised for charity by Monmouth Conservatives and first staged in 1964. The course is 6 miles, from the boat-house in Monmouth to Tump Farm, Whitebrook. The fastest rafts do the distance in 1 hour 10 minutes or so, while the slowest may take 4 hours or longer over it. Some of the contestants wear fancy dress and there is always a prize for the best-dressed raft.

236
MOEL FAMAU
CLWYD

Off the A494, north-east of Ruthin.
Tourist Information Centre, Craft Centre, Ruthin (01824) 703992.

Moel Famau is the highest point of the Clwydian Range at 1,820ft, and its broad, heather-covered slopes positively invite the keen walker to make the gentle climb from the car park at the foot to the Jubilee Tower on the summit. This tower was an imposing memorial of George III's Golden Jubilee, but it soon collapsed, and is now truncated and shapeless. Nevertheless, it is one of the best viewpoints in this part of the world, commanding a panorama that takes in the Vale of Clwyd, Snowdonia and (on the right sort of day) the Isle of Man.

IN EASY REACH The high moorland of the Clwydian Range makes for exhilarating walking, and the best way to experience it is to take the Offa's Dyke long-distance footpath, which runs along the top. The finest stretch is probably from Moel Famau to the village of Bodfari, 8 miles to the north. For lower-level walking the Loggerheads Country Park is ideal. It lies off the A494 further to the east, and its riverside paths pass through pleasant woodland with steep limestone cliffs.

Ruthin, to the west of the Clwydian Range, is a most attractive small hilltop town, with a handsome architectural mix that repays a leisurely stroll with the town trail. St Peter's Church is noted for the superb carved woodwork of its 16th-century roofs. Not much remains of the town's original castle, but it is attractively set in a park which also houses a Victorian hotel. The castle ruins at Denbigh to the north-west are also slight, apart from the impressive gatehouse, but there is a very rewarding view from the site, as well as a bonus in the form of a small museum commemorating the explorer H M Stanley. The town has some interesting Victorian buildings and a main street with unusual arcades.

237
MONMOUTH
GWENT

Tourist Information Centre, Shire Hall, Agincourt Square (01600) 713899.

This bustling old town, just within Wales, is squeezed by the Rivers Wye and Monnow. The main streets reveal an agreeable mixture of styles with some good Georgian and Victorian buildings, and they radiate from Agincourt Square, a reminder that this was the birthplace of Henry V. His effigy on the Shire Hall is rather overshadowed by the statue of another local hero, Charles Rolls, of Rolls-Royce fame. The distinctive feature of Monmouth is the tall 13th-century gatehouse on the Monnow bridge, and you should also find time to visit the Grecian-style Market Hall in Priory Street, which now contains a good local history museum and an interesting collection of memorabilia of Lord Nelson. Nelson and other admirals are commemorated by the 'Naval Temple' on a hill a mile east of the town called The Kymin, highly recommended as a viewpoint.

This bronze statue of Charles Stewart Rolls stands outside Shire Hall in Monmouth. He was the third son of Lord Llangattock, who had a country estate at Rockfield to the north-west. Rolls acquired fame as an aviator and partner of Rolls-Royce, and there is a section devoted to him in the town museum

IN EASY REACH Raglan Castle, on the A40, 7 miles south-west of Monmouth, is one of the great medieval castles of Wales, and the ruins are very impressive indeed, with a moated Great Tower and the remains of a splendid house built round two courtyards. The much earlier castle at Skenfrith, 6 miles north-west of Monmouth on the B4521, has a round keep set within an imposing fortified curtain wall. It stands in an attractive riverside village noted for its old mill and unusual church. Abergavenny, on the A40, to the west, is an unpretentious market town. Its castle grounds contain a pleasant 19th-century folly housing a local history museum.

238
PEMBROKE
DYFED

Tourist Information Centres:
Old Bridge, Haverfordwest (01437) 763110 and Pont Abraham Services, junction 49
M4, near Cross Hands (01792) 883838.

Glowering over the town of Pembroke from its rocky ridge, protected on three sides by water, is one of the most powerful fortresses in the kingdom. Most of it was built in the 13th century by the redoubtable soldier and statesman William Marshal, Earl of Pemboke, and the five sons who succeeded him one after the another. Henry VII was born here in 1457. During the Civil War the Roundheads besieged the castle for 48 days before starving it into surrender. The circular keep is 75ft high and the walls are

19ft thick at the base. Down underneath in the rock is a huge cavern called the Wogan, where stores were kept.

The town of Pembroke still has some of its medieval walls and gates. At the Castle Hill Museum, on Westgate Hill, a pleasant domestic setting provides an opportunity to view some of the objects that have been part of everyday life over the past three hundred years (open May to September). From nearby Pembroke Dock you can take a boat trip on Milford Haven, a magnificent natural harbour used today by both yachts and giant oil tankers.

IN EASY REACH To the north-west the Dale Peninsula, with its fine cliffs and sandy beaches stretching out to the west, is claimed to be the sunniest area in Wales. There are boat trips in summer from Martin's Haven to Skomer Island and Grassholm Island, with their bird sanctuaries, while a nature trail explores the shoreline at Marloes.

To the north, 4 miles south-east of Haverfordwest at Rhos, is Picton Castle (open Easter to September only), distinguished for its important collection of work by Graham Sutherland. Haverfordwest itself is a handsome town, best explored on foot, with its impressive castle ruins now housing a museum, art gallery and record office. The parish church is also worth visiting.

———— **239** ————

TINTERN ABBEY
GWENT

Beside the A466, 5 miles north of Chepstow. Tourist Information Centres: Bridge Street, Chepstow (01291) 623772 (seasonal opening only) and Shire Hall, Agincourt Square, Monmouth (01600) 713899.

During the 18th century Tintern Abbey was considered to be the highlight of the Wye Tour – a fashionable boat trip between Ross-on-Wye and Chepstow that attracted, among others, many eminent artists and writers

On an autumn day, when the crowds have thinned and the thick woodland provides a subtly coloured backdrop, it is still possible to recapture the melancholy splendour that has attracted visitors to Tintern Abbey for well over 200 years. The monastery was rich, and after its foundation in 1131 it continued to expand well into the 15th century, but at the Dissolution most of the ancillary buildings disappeared, leaving the shell of the great church. Remarkably, the magnificent west window and the soaring arches of the crossing have survived to convey the scale of the building, and the fine detail of doors and windows has been well preserved. An exhibition in the grounds gives an insight into the life and work of the monks here.

IN EASY REACH The lower Wye Valley became a popular attraction in the 18th century, and the grandeur that entranced those early visitors can still be appreciated by anyone willing to leave the car. The Lower Wye Valley Walk runs from Chepstow to Monmouth, the Offa's Dyke Path follows a course above the eastern side of the river, and the Forestry Commission has established many short walks in Tintern Forest (information at the former Tintern Station). There are spectacular views at Symonds Yat, Wynd Cliff and Wintour's Leap.

Chepstow itself has many attractions, including a huge, sprawling castle, a long 13th-century defensive wall, a church with impressive Norman work, a museum, and some very handsome streets. Eight miles north-west of Chepstow, off the B4293, the craft centre and folk museum at Wolvesnewton is housed in an interesting 18th-century 'model' farm, and is packed with vastly entertaining domestic bygones.

Michaelmas Fair

Within living memory the traditional early October four-day Michaelmas Fair in the long main street of Pembroke attracted crowds of people from the surrounding country and numerous traders who sold china, linen and a wide range of goods. Nowadays, like so many other fairs, it has turned almost entirely to amusements and rides. The fair is a legacy of Pembroke's important position as the capital of 'Little England beyond Wales,' a district so strongly influenced by the English for so many centuries that even the local Welsh dialect contains many English words.

240
CAERLEON ROMAN FORTRESS
GWENT

*On the northern outskirts of Newport. Tourist Information Centre, Ffwrrwm Art &
Craft Centre, High Street, Caerleon (01633) 430777.*

Carleon ranked with Chester and York as an important Roman military headquarters. Established in about AD75, it was developed over the next hundred years to accommodate a legion of 5,600 men, and within the boundary of the 500-yd-square fortress you can see the foundations of their barrack lines and part of the defensive ramparts. The remains here include the cookhouses and a latrine building, and work continues on revealing the baths. Rather more stirring to the imagination is the nearby amphitheatre, the best of its kind in Britain. The town's Legionary Museum, an attractive Victorian building, houses a fascinating display of excavated artefacts and inscribed stones.

IN EASY REACH At Caerwent, 5 miles east of Newport on the A48, are more Roman remains. The town of Venta Silurum sits incongruously in suburban surroundings, but the long stretch of high defensive wall is still imposing, and excavation has revealed the footings of two Roman houses and a small temple. Many of the finds are on display in museums at Newport and Caerleon. *En route* to Caerwent from Caerleon you might like to stop off at Penhow Castle (open Wednesdays only in winter), where a stocky Norman tower was added to, in later centuries, to form an interesting house. The enterprising owner has carried out much restoration, and you can tour the castle with a personal headset instead of the usual leaflet. Caldicot Castle, to the south-east of Caerwent on the B4245, is more conventional – a carefully restored 13th-century structure with a circular keep and a fine gatehouse with flanking towers, The castle (open March to October) houses a small but interesting local history museum and exhibitions, and stands in a country park where herons and other water-loving birds may be seen.

241
CENTRE FOR ALTERNATIVE TECHNOLOGY
POWYS

*Off the A487, 3 miles north of Machynlleth.
Tourist Information Centre, Canolfan Owain Glyndwr, Machynlleth (01654) 702401.*

On a day when your winter fuel bills are looming large, a visit to the Centre for Alternative Technology is an eye-opening experience. Back in the days when self-sufficiency was the new watchword, a group of enthusiasts established themselves in an abandoned slate quarry here, to explore natural sources of energy and a simple lifestyle that would not deplete the earth's resources. What may have seemed a cranky enterprise at the time has grown into an extremely impressive demonstration of alternative living methods, including gardening techniques, small-scale farming, waste recycling and various methods of energy production and energy saving. There is a windmill, a display of solar heating systems and a house specially designed to conserve energy. A bookshop and a vegetarian restaurant are added attractions.

IN EASY REACH A little further up the A487, waymarked walks start from the picnic site in the Forestry Commission's Tan y Coed Forest. A little further on still is the straggling mountain village of Corris, where railway enthusiasts will enjoy a visit to the small museum (limited opening) devoted to the former slate quarries railway that came through here on its way down to Machynlleth. In the other direction, Machynlleth itself, with its curious battlemented clock-tower of 1872, is a pleasant shopping and market centre and useful base for exploring this beautiful part of Wales.

242
THE RHONDDA
MID GLAMORGAN

*The two valleys of Rhondda Fawr and Fach run north-westwards from Porth.
Tourist Information Centre, Bridge Street, Pontypridd (01443) 402077.*

On the eve of World War I, more than 600 mines were operating in the South Wales coalfield. Today there are fewer than a tenth of that number. A hundred years ago 'the valleys' were thin black strips of crowded houses, collieries, ironworks and railways, with tips and slag heaps looking over them, but today land reclamation on a huge scale has been brought into action to restore the valleys to their original natural beauty.

Nos Galan Race

Mountain Ash, a coal-mining town a few miles from Aberdare, is the scene of the Nos Galan Midnight Race, held by torchlight every year on New Year's Eve. The race was first held in 1958 over a course of 4 miles down the mountainsides to the town. There was a long suspension in the 1970s because of badly behaved crowds, but the event was revived in the 1980s, over a distance of 6 kilometres (about 3 3/4 miles), with a winning time of around 16 minutes. Runners from many clubs in Wales and England take part.

The effects can be seen and admired in the twin valleys of the River Rhondda and the surrounding country: at Gilfach Goch, for example, on the B4564, in the valley which was the setting for Richard Llewellyn's *How Green Was My Valley*. You can also explore the past here on a special industrial trail. Treorchy, on the A4061, is the home of a particularly famous male voice choir, the oldest one in Wales. Further north is the Blaenrhondda Waterfalls Walk in moorland scenery sparkling with streams and waterfalls.

IN EASY REACH At Aberdare, on the A4059, the canal nature reserve is a sanctuary for herons. To the west of the town the trees of the Dare Valley Country Park grow on what not so long ago was a wasteland of collieries and tips. Merthyr Tydfil, to the north-east, has displays on the industrial and earlier history of the area at Cyfartha Castle. An ironmaster's home, built in 1825, it is now the town museum and gallery.

243

WELSH FOLK MUSEUM
SOUTH GLAMORGAN

At St Fagans, between the M4 and the A48, west of Cardiff.
Tourist Information Centre, Central Station, Central Square, Cardiff (01222) 227281

At this old buildings' retirement home, covering 100 acres or so outside Cardiff, farmhouses, cottages, barns and all sorts of other constructions which illuminate the past have been brought from all over Wales to be lovingly re-erected, stone by stone, and preserved. They range from a timber-framed Clwyd farmhouse of the late 15th century which the family shared with their cows, to an 18th-century circular Glamorgan pigsty and a single-room cottage from Snowdonia built of bulky glacial boulders. There is an 18th-century cock-pit from the yard of a Denbigh inn, working woollen and corn-mills, an oak-bark tannery, a smithy, an austere Unitarian chapel of about 1800, and a school (in which Victorian lessons are re-created for visiting school parties).

The indoor part of the museum contains an exhaustively, fascinating assemblage of objects which vividly recall life in Wales in past centuries. They include costumes from about 1700 on, farm implements and machinery, and exhibits on such themes as cookery, laundering, dairying, lighting, folk beliefs, heraldry, games, weapons, law and order, medicine and dentistry, education and music. Keep your eyes peeled for the Welsh harps, the Welsh dresses and the charming love spoons, which young men made for their sweethearts.

At the eastern end of the complex is St Fagans Castle, an Elizabethan mansion which belonged to the Earls of Plymouth, who donated it to the National Museum of Wales in the 1940s. It has been restored to its 17th-century appearance and visitors can see the long gallery and the family rooms, nursery and kitchen. Outside are 18 acres of gardens.

The Grey Mare

In the first week of January in South Wales you can no longer depend on seeing the Mari Lwyd, or 'grey mare', the weird hobby horse which used to make the rounds of houses in the period after Christmas. It was made of a horse's skull mounted on a long pole and carried by a man concealed under a sheet (see below), who would make the horse's jaws snap frighteningly. Bits of bottle glass were put in the empty eye sockets, ears of black cloth were sewn on, and ribbons were attached to the head. The 'horse' was accompanied by mummers and singers, who were rewarded with money, food and kisses. The Mari Lwyd is rarely seen today but can be viewed in the Welsh Folk Museum, which has more than one of them.

No region in England outdoes the North in beauty of landscape. It is only necessary to mention the Lake District, with its spectacular mountain scenery, the Yorkshire Dales and the North York Moors, Teesdale in County Durham and the Cheviots in Northumberland to make the point. In terms of sea coast the North offers everything from the popular beaches of Blackpool, Scarborough and the Isle of Man, to the vast and gleaming sandflats of Morecambe Bay and the towering cliffs of Flamborough Head.

In towns and cities, too, the North has nothing to concede. There are notable cathedrals and churches in Durham and York, Beverley and Liverpool, Selby and Hexham. There are tremendous Victorian town halls to relish, in the classical style in Leeds and Bolton, in the Gothic at Bradford, Manchester and Rochdale. There are delightful walks on the old city walls at Chester and York, and a wonderful array of bridges across the Tyne in Newcastle.

Hadrian's Wall is the most impressive Roman monument in the country and there are particularly good Roman collections in museums in Chester, Carlisle and Newcastle. Castles include frowning Border bastions like Raby, Warkworth and Alnwick. The colossal grandeur of Castle Howard must make it the stateliest of stately homes, but not far behind are the 18th-century splendours of Harewood House and Nostell Priory, the red-brick warmth of Newby Hall, and the black-and-white charm of Little Moreton Hall. Even the briefest list of famous people and places must include Wordsworth and Ruskin in the Lake District, the Wesleys at Epworth, Captain Cook around Middlesborough and Whitby, and the Brontës at Haworth. And there are families which have been part of the countryside for centuries: Leghs at Lyme Park and Adlington Hall, for example, Fittons at Gawsworth Hall.

A touch of the offbeat is always welcome. You can follow a Dracula trail in Whitby or a silk trail in Macclesfield, tour the galaxy at Jodrell Bank or see prehistoric wild cattle at Chillingham, chug over Coniston Water in a 19th-century steam yacht or hear the unearthly singing of whales in the Town Docks Museum in Hull. You can learn about liquorice in Pontefract and toffee in Halifax, and Manchester United Football Club has its own museum.

There is naturally a wealth of industrial archaeology, with the former textile towns vying for the visitor's attention — places like Blackburn, Bolton, Burnley and Halifax. The machines still clatter and pound at Quarry Bank Mill near Wilmslow, in the Abbeydale Industrial Hamlet in Sheffield and in the Stott Park Bobbin Mill in the Lake District, and working life in the North-East around the turn of the century is richly revealed at the the Beamish Open-Air Museum near Durham.

Nor is it all machines. Any visit of a few days which took you to the Lady Lever Art Gallery in Port Sunlight, the Walker Art Gallery in Liverpool, the Ferens Art Gallery in Hull, the Bowes Museum at Barnard Castle and the Oriental Museum in Durham would leave you speechless. And that would be only a taste of the vast array of riches to enjoy.

Britain's first Long Distance Footpath, The Pennine Way, traverses some 60 miles of the Yorkshire Dales on its way up through northern England. The views across Swaledale are among the Way's finest

Swaledale, North Yorkshire

The
North Country

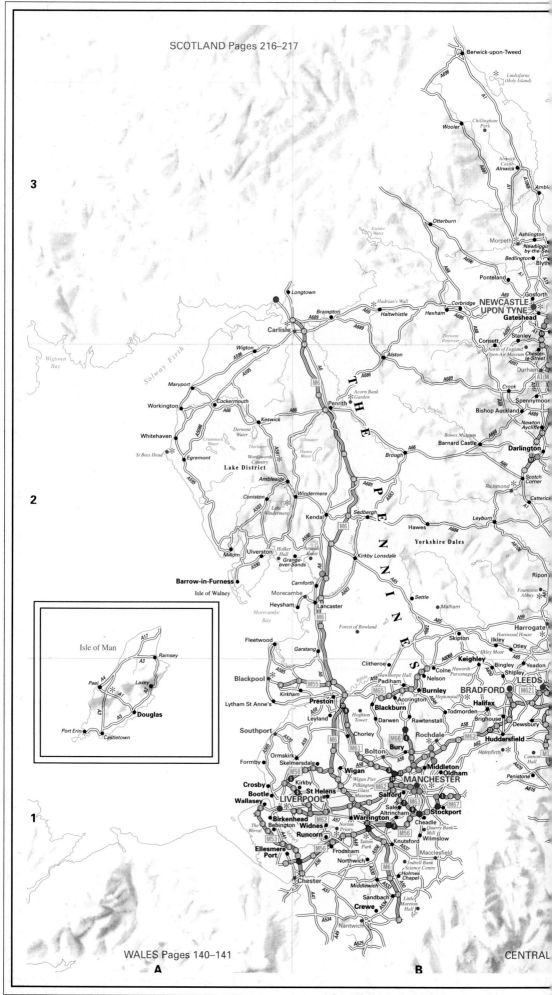

SCOTLAND Pages 216–217

Berwick-upon-Tweed
Lindisfarne (Holy Island)

Chillingham Park
Wooler

Alnwick Castle
Alnwick
Amble

Ashington
Morpeth
Newbiggin-by-the-Sea
Bedlington
Blyth

Otterburn
Kielder Water

Ponteland
Gosforth

3

Longtown

Brampton
Haltwhistle
Hexham
Corbridge
Hadrian's Wall
NEWCASTLE UPON TYNE
Gateshead
Stanley
Consett
North of England Open-Air Museum
Chester-le-Street
Durham

Carlisle
Wigton
Alston

Maryport
Cockermouth
Workington
Keswick
Penrith
Acorn Bank Garden
Crook
Spennymoor
Bishop Auckland
Newton Aycliffe

Whitehaven
Crummock Water
Derwent Water
Thirlmere
Ullswater
Hawes Water
Brough
A66
Barnard Castle
Bowes Museum
Darlington

St Bees Head
Egremont
Lake District
Wordsworth Country
Ambleside
Windermere
Teesdale
Richmond
Scotch Corner
Catterick

2

Coniston
Lake Windermere
Kendal
Sedbergh
Hawes
Leyburn

Ripon

Millom
Ulverston
Holker Hall
Grange-over-Sands
Arnside Knott
Kirkby Lonsdale
Yorkshire Dales
Fountains Abbey

Barrow-in-Furness
Isle of Walney
Carnforth
Settle
Malham

Morecambe
Heysham
Lancaster
Forest of Bowland
A65
Harrogate
Harewood House
Ilkley
Otley

Fleetwood
Garstang
Skipton
Ilkley Moor
Yeadon

Clitheroe
Colne
Haworth Parsonage
Keighley
Bingley
Shipley
LEEDS

Blackpool
Padiham
Nelson
Gawthorpe Hall
Burnley
BRADFORD

Kirkham
Preston
Accrington
Heptonstall
Halifax
Dewsbury

Lytham St Anne's
Leyland
Blackburn
Darwen
Rawtenstall
Todmorden
Brighouse
Huddersfield

Hoghton Tower
Chorley
Rochdale
M62
Holmfirth
Cannon Hall

Southport
Bolton
Bury
Middleton
Oldham
Penistone

Formby
Ormskirk
Skelmersdale
Wigan
MANCHESTER
Stockport

Isle of Man

Ramsey
Laxey
Peel
Douglas
Port Erin
Castletown

Crosby
Bootle
Wallasey
Kirkby
St Helens
Salford
Sale
Altrincham
Cheadle

1

LIVERPOOL
Birkenhead
Bebington
Widnes
Warrington
Wilmslow
Quarry Bank Mill

The Wirral
Runcorn
Norton Priory
Knutsford
Tatton Park
Macclesfield

Ellesmere Port
Frodsham
Northwich
Jodrell Bank Science Centre

Chester
Middlewich
Holmes Chapel

Sandbach
Little Moreton Hall
Crewe

Nantwich

WALES Pages 140–141

A   B   CENTRAL

A special event, described in the text, occurs in the vicinity of the places marked with a star.

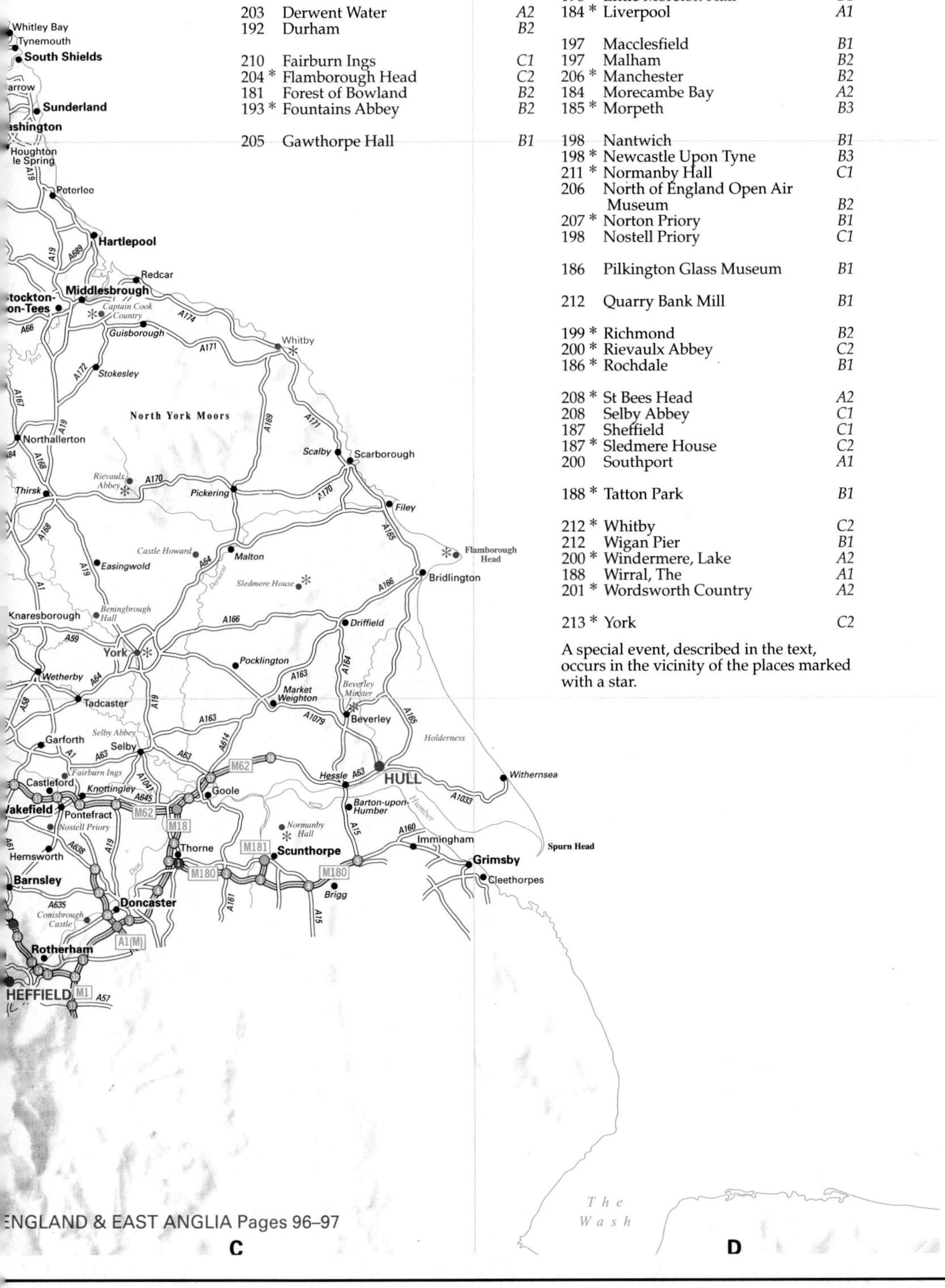

ENGLAND & EAST ANGLIA Pages 96–97

C

D

The Wash

Calendar of Events

Spring

MARCH

Kiplingcotes Derby
South Dalton, Humberside
(March – 3rd Thursday)

North of England Head of the River Race
Chester
(mid-March)

City of Leeds College of Music Festival
Leeds, W Yorkshire
(mid or late March)

EASTER

Midgley Pace Egg Play
Calder Valley,
W Yorkshire
(Good Friday)

Maritime Festival
Lancaster Maritime Museum, Lancashire
(Good Friday to Easter Monday)

Nutters Dance
Bacup, Lancashire
(Easter Saturday)

Northumbrian Gathering
Morpeth,
Northumberland
(week after Easter)

APRIL

Boaters Gathering
Boat Museum, Ellesmere Port, Cheshire
(early April)

Grand National Meeting
Aintree, Merseyide
(April – 2nd Saturday)

Spring Flower Show
Harrogate, N Yorkshire
(late April)

MAY

Riding the Bounds
Berwick-upon-Tweed,
Northumberland
(1 May)

Folk Festival
Holmfirth, W Yorkshire
(early May)

Lancaster Literature Festival
Lancaster
(early May)

Royal May Day Celebrations
Knutsford, Cheshire
(May – 1st Saturday)

Mary Wakefield Westmorland Festival
Kendal, Cumbria
(May – 2nd week)

Sheffield Chamber Music Festival
Sheffield, S Yorkshire
(May – 2nd and 3rd weeks)

Early Music Festival
Beverley, Humberside
(mid-May)

Jazz Festival
Keswick, Cumbria
(May – 3rd week)

Chester Regatta
Chester
(late May)

Manchester Air Show
Barton Aerodrome,
Manchester
(late May)

Northumberland County Show
Corbridge,
Northumberland
(late May)

Spring Boat Festival
Boat Museum, Ellesmere Port, Cheshire
(late May)

Coniston Water Festival
Coniston, Cumbria
(late May to early June)

Northern International Arts Festival
Kendal, Cumbria
(late May to early June)

Swaledale Festival
Richmond , N Yorkshire
(late May to early June)

TT Races
Isle of Man
(late May to early June)

Summer

JUNE

Mersey River Festival
Liverpool, Merseyside
(June - most of month)

Manchester to Blackpool Veteran and Vintage Car Run
Manchester
(early June)

The Isle of Man TT Races

Morecambe Carnival
Morecambe, Lancashire
(June – 1st week)

Durham Regatta
Durham
(June – 2nd week)

Appleby Horse Fair
Appleby-in-Westmorland,
Cumbria
(June – 2nd Tuesday and Wednesday)

Victorian Weekend
Silloth, Cumbria
(mid June)

Whitby Festival
Whitby, N Yorkshire
(June – 2nd and 3rd weeks)

Beverley Folk Festival
Beverley, Humberside
(mid-June)

Grassington Festival
Grassington, N Yorkshire
(mid-June to early July)

Scarborough Fair
Scarborough, N Yorkshire
(June – 3rd week)

The Hoppings
Newcastle upon Tyne,
Tyne & Wear
(June – last full week)

Alnwick Fair
Alnwick, Northumberland
(late June to early July)

Filey Edwardian Festival
Filey, N Yorkshire
(late June to early July)

Mananan Festival of Music and the Arts
Isle of Man
(late June to early July)

JULY

Humber Grand Prix
River Humber/Hull
Marina, Hull
Humberside
(early July)

Tynwald Day
St Johns, Isle of Man
(5 July)

Ambleside Rush-bearing
Ambleside, Cumbria
(July – 1st Saturday)

Chester River Carnival and Raft Race
Chester
(July – 2nd Sunday)

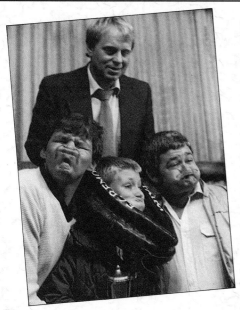

'Gurning' winners at the Egremont Crab Fair, Cumbria, held in September

Hull Festival
Hull, Humberside
(July – 1st half)

Great Yorkshire Agricultural Show
Harrogaate, N Yorkshire
(July – 2nd week)

Kilburn Feast
Kilburn, N Yorkshire
(July – 2nd week)

Lancaster Carnival and Big Parade
Lancaster
(July – 2nd week)

Redcar Folk Festival
Redcar, Cleveland
(July – 2nd week)

Durham County Agricultural Show
Chester-le-Street, Durham
(mid-July)

Wirral Show
New Brighton, Merseyside
(mid-July)

Tweedmouth Salmon Feast
Tweedmouth, Northumberland
(Sunday after 18 July)

Cumberland Show
Carlisle, Cumbria
(July – 3rd week)

Penrith Agricultural Show
Penrith, Cumbria
(July – 3rd week)

Ambleside Sports
Ambleside, Cumbria
(late July)

Leeds Championship Dog Show
Harewood House, W Yorkshire
(late July)

Harrogate International Festival
Harrogate, N Yorkshire
(late July to early August)

Ryedale Festival
Helmsley, N Yorkshire
(late July to early August)

St Wilfrid's Procession
Ripon, N Yorkshire
(late July or early August)

AUGUST

Grasmere Rush-bearing
Grasmere, Cumbria
(Saturday nearest 6 August)

Lakeland Fell Pony Show
Penrith, Cumbria
(August – 1st week)

Hull Regatta
Hull, Humberside
(early August)

Leyland International Children's Festival
Leyland, Lancashire
(early August)

Lake District Summer Music Festival
Ambleside, Cumbria
(August – 1st half)

Royal Yorkshire Yacht Club Regatta
Bridlington, Humberside
(August – 2nd week)

Morecambe International Folklore Fiesta
Morecambe, Lancashire
(August –3rd week)

Southport Flower Show
Southport, Merseyside
(August – 3rd week)

Grasmere Sports
Grasmere, Cumbria
(Thursday nearest 20 August)

Burning of Bartle
West Witton, N Yorkshire
(Saturday nearest 24 August)

Carlisle Great Fair
Carlisle, Cumbria
(late August)

Kendal Folk Festival
Kendal, Cumbria
(late August)

Rochdale Festival of Live Entertainment
Rochdale, Greater Manchester
(late August)

Autumn

SEPTEMBER

Blackpool Illuminations
Blackpool, Lancashire
(early September to early November)

Manchester Festival
Manchester, Greater Manchester
(varies from year to year)

Scarborough Cricket Festival
Scarborough, N Yorkshire
(early September)

Victorian Weekend
Kirkby Lonsdale, Cumbria
(early September)

Westmorland County Show
Kendal, Cumbria
(early September)

St Leger Meeting
Doncaster, S Yorkshire
(September – 2nd week)

Nidderdale Show
Pateley Bridge, N Yorkshire
(mid September)

Egremont Crab Fair
Egremont, Cumbria
(Saturday nearest 18 September)

Great Autumn Flower Show
Harrogate, N Yorkshire
(mid-September)

OCTOBER

Border Shepherds Show
Alwinton, near Morpeth, Northumberland
(October – 2nd week)

Hull Fair
Hull, Humberside
(October – 2nd week)

International Film Festival
Leeds, W Yorkshire
(October – 3rd week)

Antrobus Soul Caking Play
Antrobus, Cheshire
(31 October and during 1st two weeks of November)

NOVEMBER

Contemporary Music Festival
Huddersfield, W Yorkshire
(late November)

Winter

DECEMBER

Greatham Sword Dance
Greatham, Cleveland
(26 December)

Allendale Tar-barrel Ceremony
Northumberland
(31 December)

JANUARY

Haxey Hood Game
Haxey, Humberside
(5 or 6 January)

Plough Stots Service
Goathland, N Yorkshire
(early January)

FEBRUARY

Jorvik Viking Festival
York, N Yorkshire
(February – whole month)

SHROVETIDE

Shrovetide Skipping
Scarborough, N Yorkshire
(Shrove Tuesday)

MONASTIC LIFE

A tour of the North which concentrated on its treasure-trove of abbeys and priories would cover most of the region: from Norton Priory in Cheshire north to Lancaster, on to Furness Abbey and Lanercost Priory in Cumbria, eastwards to Northumberland's Hexham and Lindisfarne, and then south again past Jarrow and Whitby to the haunting ruins of the great Cistercian houses of Yorkshire – Fountains, Rievaulx and Jervaulx. Many of the sites are in surroundings of the utmost loveliness, and much can be gleaned from them about the lives of the monks.

Monks took vows of poverty, chastity and obedience, and lived under discipline and within a strict routine, which centred on the worship of God at eight church services a day. The day began at about 2 or 2.30 in the morning, when the monks got up for matins by candle-light in the cold and dark of their church. Another service, lauds, followed before dawn, and prime was at daybreak. As the day wore on, three more services were held: tierce, sext with High Mass, and none. Vespers was said at sunset and compline before bedtime.

The church was the heart of the monastery and always the grandest building in it. Some abbey and priory churches survived the Dissolution of the Monasteries because they were used as parish churches (Lancaster, Hexham and Bridlington are cases in

Cuthbert, the 7th-century saint who spent most of his life on Lindisfarne and the Farne Islands

point). At sites like Fountains and Rievaulx, Lindisfarne and Whitby, however, it is the ruins of the church that dominate the scene – the massive walls and columns, the soaring arches, the delicate tracery of the windows.

The main domestic buildings of a monastery were usually ranged round three sides of a quadrangle, or cloister, with the church making the fourth side. The monks ate together in the frater, or refectory, with the kitchen close by. Near the door was a stone trough for cold water, in which they washed their hands

The illumination of manuscripts was one of the chief occupations in a monastery

before meals: there are good examples at Fountains, Rievaulx and Kirkham Priory near Castle Howard. The first meal of the day was dinner, at about 4 in the afternoon. There was a frugal supper in the evening, but this was omitted during Lent and on fast days.

The monastery would have its own bakehouse and brewhouse, and substantial storerooms where food, ale and all necessary supplies were kept. The monks slept in the dormer, or dormitory, on an upper floor, from which there might be stairs to the church for use at night (as at Hexham). Other buildings would include the latrines and the infirmary, where sick and aged monks were cared for (there is an enormous one at Fountains). The monastery would have its own herb garden and make its own medicines, and the monastery infirmaries set the pattern for modern hospitals.

An important building was the chapter house, where the monks assembled every morning, to hear notices given out, the rules recited and punishments announced. Calder Abbey in Cumbria, Furness Abbey, Easby Abbey near Richmond, and Kirkstall Abbey in Leeds all have substantial chapter-house remains. At Kirkstall you can also see the guesthouse. One of the important functions of a monastery was to provide travellers with a safe lodging for the night. They also cared for the poor who would come for a 'dole' of food.

Besides worship, the other main daily activities of monks were private prayer and meditation, and work of some kind – in the fields or the garden, or copying manuscripts or craftsmanship in wood, metal or stone. Monasteries had to support themselves and they

acquired large estates and business interests. They ranched sheep and ran farms and mines. Fountains Abbey was the biggest wool producer in the North and Rievaulx, Jervaulx, Furness and Easby were all rich in sheep. The farming work was often done by lay brothers, who also staffed the outlying farms, or granges, which might be several days' journey away.

The business of the monastery was run by those of its senior brethren who showed aptitude for the task. At their head was the abbot (or the prior in a priory), a powerful figure with an influence extending far beyond his abbey's walls as a major landowner and political force. The Abbot of Furness, for instance, ruled the whole Furness peninsula. The abbot would have separate quarters in the monastery, with his own hall for entertaining important guests: as can be seen at Roche Abbey, the Cistercian house near Rotherham.

All this was ended in the 1530s, when the monasteries were closed down. The monks were driven out, the more recalcitrant abbots were hanged, valuables were seized by the king and the estates were given to neighbouring landowners. The buildings were left to crumble away and to be pillaged by the locals for stone. Today they stand quiet and solitary, still with something separate and otherworldly about them.

The agricultural estates of Byland (right) and Rievaulx (below right) were largely run by the 'conversi', the lay brethren of the Order. Mount Grace Priory (below) is renowned for its hermit cells

— 244 —

ARNSIDE KNOTT
CUMBRIA

One mile south of Arnside, which is on the B5282.
Tourist Information Centres: 29 Castle Hill, Lancaster, Lancashire, (01524) 32878 and
Station Buildings, Morecambe, Lancashire (01524) 582808.

The National Trust owns most of this wooded hill above the sandy estuary of the River Kent. The flat, 520ft summit is a platform for magical views of Morecambe Bay, the Lake District mountains, Shap Fell and the Forest of Bowland. The Knott is geologically interesting, with limestone pavements, glacial erratic boulders, screes and fossils, and botanically exciting for its wildflowers, which include six species of orchid. Among the shrubs and trees are spindle, juniper and rowan, and walks laid out through the woods are liable to yield sight or sound of red squirrels and deer, owls and woodcock. This is also a favourite spot for butterflies and glow-worms.

IN EASY REACH There are attractive walks in the area between Arnside and the village of Silverdale, just over the Lancashire border to the south and once a port for Morecambe Bay steamers, though now 4 miles inland. On the eastern edge of Silverdale is the RSPB reserve of Leighton Moss, a reed-swamp which is home to bitterns and bearded tits, warblers, ducks and gulls, as well as otters and deer. Close by is Leighton Hall (open May to September), near Yealand Conyers, rebuilt in the 18th century with a Gothic front fastened on to it in 1800. The home of the Gillow family, it contains notable examples of Gillow furniture and has a gallery with resident artist. Outside a large collection of birds of prey can be seen, and there are exciting flying displays with trained eagles and falcons. To the south, 3 miles away on the A6, the Steamtown Railway Museum in Carnforth has an outstanding collection of steam locomotives, including the *Flying Scotsman*.

— 245 —

BEVERLEY MINSTER
HUMBERSIDE

Tourist Information Centre, The Guildhall, Register Square (01482) 867430.

Beverley Minster – one of the town's two magnificent churches

Music Festivals in Beverley

Strains of Mozart and Bach, Vivaldi and Handel, sound sweetly in Beverley during May in a new venture for the town, the annual Early Music Festival. The festival concentrates on medieval music, an elastic expression which enables the organisers to include anything suitable down to the 18th century. There are concerts, workshops and displays of early instrument making. The Minster choir joins in, too. In June more up-to-date sounds come to Beverley during the Folk Festival, with high-quality folk music, dance and song, which has been running since 1983: there are workshops and plenty of events for children.

The best views of the Minster are from the west. By common consent one of the most beautiful churches in Britain, 'a symphony in stone', it outdoes not a few cathedrals in size and splendour. Begun after the Norman Conquest and taking many centuries to complete, it is famed especially for the loveliness of its 13th-century work and the graceful glory of its twin-towered west front.

Not content with one magnificent church, Beverley has another, St Mary's with its 15th-century west front and 16th-century tower. On the chancel ceiling are portraits of English kings and the delightful carvings include a rabbit said to have inspired the White Rabbit in *Alice in Wonderland*.

Beverley was the county town of the old East Riding of Yorkshire. The main square, Saturday Market, has a fine 18th-century market cross, and North Bar is the sole survivor of the medieval town gates. The art gallery, in the Champney Road, has local history material and work by a local artist, Fred Elwell, who died in 1958. You can climb aboard some of the lorries and vehicles in the Museum of Army Transport, Flemingate, as well as look at them, and the museum covers the transport of British troops by road, rail, sea and air, mainly from World War II onwards.

IN EASY REACH To the south-east, about 10 miles from Beverley, Burton Constable Hall is a residence of tremendous grandeur, as befits the seat of the Lords Paramount of Holderness. It was built in the 16th century, with interiors by Robert Adam and James Wyatt, and has a chapel converted from a billiard room, and an 18th-century Chinese room. There are sumptuous grounds by 'Capability' Brown, stables, vintage motorbikes, boats and a model railway, all in all providing masses to do.

246

BOWES MUSEUM
CO DURHAM

At Barnard Castle. Tourist Information Centres: 43 Galgate, Barnard Castle (01833) 690909 and 4, West Row, Darlington (01325) 382698.

Ten thousand beautiful objects the Bowes Museum claims, and a ravishing display of elegance and glittering luxury they make. There's a famous El Greco, *The Tears of St Peter*, and paintings by Goya, Tiepolo, Boucher, Canaletto and others. There are statues, porcelain, furniture, tapestries, embroideries, Napoleonic items and automata, including a magnificent 18th-century silver swan which gobbles up a fish. Everything is beautifully displayed, French decorative arts of the 18th and 19th centuries are strongly represented, and the rooms are a walk-through history of styles.

The collection was formed in the 1870s by a rich mine owner, John Bowes, and his wife, Josephine, and installed in a handsome château-style building specially constructed for it, in attractive grounds. More has been added since their time. Also of interest in Barnard Castle is the ruined castle itself, rearing up high above the swirling River Tees.

One of the most amazing exhibits at the Bowes Museum is this silver swan which, operated by a clockwork mechanism, catches a fish from the moving water. Mark Twain saw it at the 1867 Paris Exhibition and was so impressed by its beauty and realism that he later referred to it in Innocents Abroad. John Bowes bought the swan five years later, in Paris, for £200

IN EASY REACH The ruins of Eggleston Abbey lie a couple of miles to the south, off the B6277, and another mile or two further on is a celebrated beauty spot where the River Greta joins the Tees. North-east of Barnard Castle, at Staindrop on the A688, is the grim bulk of Raby Castle (limited opening in Spring), a formidable stronghold of the Nevilles in the Middle Ages. Rebuilt by John Carr in the 18th century and surrounded by velvety parkland, it still looks ominously ready to bite. Inside are impressive 18th- and 19th-century interiors and a medieval kitchen. There are impressive monuments to the Neville family in Staindrop Church.

247

FOREST OF BOWLAND
LANCASHIRE

*To the east of the M6 and A6.
Tourist Information Centres: 5 Dalton Square, Lancaster (01524) 32878 and 12-14 Market Place, Clitheroe (01200) 25566*

An official Area of Outstanding Natural Beauty, this former royal hunting forest lost most of its trees long ago, but remains an unspoiled, sparsely populated, wild region: much of it is accessible only on foot or on horseback. Lying between the scenic valleys of the Lune in the north and the Ribble in the south, it is a country of high fells and open moorland, bracken-covered slopes, tree-lined rivers and rocky streams, secluded villages and solitary stone farmhouses – with the hen harrier and the merlin hovering overhead. A minor road crosses the Forest from Lancaster south-east through a 1,000ft pass, the Trough of Bowland, to Dunsop Bridge and on down to Clitheroe.

On the south-western edge of the area, near Claughton, a country park centres on Beacon Fell, an old beacon site with commanding views, circled by a scenic drive. A nature trail explores Brock Valley close by. To the east, Browsholme Hall, 5 miles north-west of Clitheroe, was built early in the 16th century. This is the ancestral home of the Parkers, the hereditary Bowbearers of Bowland (a Parker was originally an official in charge of the deer in a hunting forest). Members of the family show visitors round though there are only a limited number of days during the year when it is open.

● Midgley Pace Egg Play

Pace-egging was once a common custom in the North, when children went round begging for eggs at Eastertime: 'pace' is a corruption of the Latin for Easter, Pascha. Nowadays, boys from Calder High School perform the Midgley Pace Egg Play on Good Friday at Midgley (see right), Hebden Bridge and various locations in the Calder Valley. It's a traditional mumming play, with such characters as St George, the Fool, the Bold Slasher and the Black Prince of Paradine, in red smocks with rosettes on them, and with decorated mortarboards on their heads. Another character is Toss Pot, a tramp-like figure in clothes too big for him, and there's also a bugler.

248

HEPTONSTALL
WEST YORKSHIRE

*Heptonstall is on a minor road, 1 mile north-west of Hebden Bridge.
Tourist Information Centre, 1 Bridge Gate, Hebden Bridge (01422) 843831.*

The gritstone houses and narrow ginnels of this Pennine weaving village cling to the high moor above beautiful Calder Valley. The grammar school, built in 1771 and used until 1889, is now a small but evocative museum of village life. Besides the battered desks, with the inevitable carved initials of generations of boys and the headmaster's throne, you can see old photographs of village folk and all sorts of country objects – clogs, tools, toys and games. There are also items from the all-purpose village shop.

IN EASY REACH On the moor a mile or so to the north is the National Trust's beauty spot of Hardcastle Crags, where the Hebden Water runs in a narrow valley below rocky outcrops. To the south-east, Hebden Bridge is a mill town of character. Walkleys, a working clog factory is here, and Automobilia in Billy Lane, has pre-war Austins and Morrises. To the east of Hebden Bridge, on the A646, lies Halifax, a great cloth town in its day and full of interest. Don't miss the splendid Piece Hall, where cloth was traded. Next door is the Calderdale Industrial Museum, with working machinery in a 19th-century mill (subjects include toffee wrappings, and cats-eyes on roads). Bankfield Museum, Akroyd Park, covers local history, local artists, textiles and costume, whilst Shibden Hall houses the West Yorkshire Folk Museum.

249

HOLDERNESS
HUMBERSIDE

Tourist Information Centres: 75 Newbegin, Hornsea (01964) 536404 (seasonal opening only) and Central Library, Albion Street, Hull (01482) 223344.

Holderness is the name given to the flattish district along the North Sea coast in what used to be the East Riding of Yorkshire. It is also the 'South Riding' of Winifred Holtby's much-loved novel, and is known for its fine churches. The grandest of them, the 'king of Holderness', is St Augustine's at Hedon on the A1033, 6 miles east of Hull, with its 130ft tower dominating a small town which, long ago before the rise of Hull, was the major port on the Humber. The 'queen of Holderness' is 7 miles further east on the A1033, at Patrington, where the 14th-century church of St Patrick pierces the sky with its spire, nearer the ground are some horrible gargoyles.

The district's southernmost extension is the Spurn Peninsula, which grows longer by about two inches a year as sand and shingle wash up on it from the eroding cliffs further north. It pokes a skinny, curling finger, 4 miles long, down into the North Sea, to end at Spurn Head, where there is a nature reserve and bird sanctuary among the desolate saltmarshes, mudflats and sand dunes.

Further north, on the coast, Hornsea is known for the Hornsea Pottery, which welcomes visitors, and Hornsea Mere, which welcomes birds. There is an RSPB reserve on this large lake and a colony of reed warblers inhabits the reed-swamp at the western end. The North Holderness Museum of Village Life, at 11 Newbegin, is housed in an 18th-century farmhouse, and has period rooms of a century back and old photographs and postcards of the area.

—— 250 ——
ILKLEY MOOR
WEST YORKSHIRE

The moor is part of Rombalds Moor, south of Ilkley.
Tourist Information Centre, Station Road, Ilkley (01943) 602319.

The moor to the south of the town of Ilkley is famous for the song, and also for the mysterious patterns cut into rocks here far back in prehistoric times, when this was apparently a sacred area. The Swastika Stone has a swastika inscribed round a group of hollows in the shape of a cross. Other stones have 'cups' or hollows, rings and ladder patterns on them, presumably of religious and magical significance. Also on the moor are numerous other prehistoric remains, including earthworks and stone circles of which the best known is the Twelve Apostles.

Prehistoric carved stones, brought down from the moor, can also be seen in the gardens opposite St Margaret's church, and in All Saints church are three Anglo-Saxon cross shafts. Ilkley, however, is mainly a Victorian town, a successful spa in the 19th century. You can discover the local history in the Manor House Museum and explore the cold water baths at White Wells on Ilkley Moor.

IN EASY REACH Ilkley is a good base for exploring the beauties of Wharfedale. Six miles to the north, on the B6160, is Bolton Priory in a lovely setting on the Wharfe. There are stepping stones across the river here. The nave of the priory church was preserved as the parish church, but the choir and transepts fell into picturesque decay. To the west is Skipton where the castle belonged to the powerful Clifford family, whose impressive tombs are in the nearby church. The town also has the Craven Museum, with exhibits dealing with folk life, lead mining and the early inhabitants of the area.

—— 251 ——
JODRELL BANK SCIENCE CENTRE
CHESHIRE

Off the A535, 4 miles north-east of Holmes Chapel.
Tourist Information Centre, Council Offices, Toft Road, Knutsford (01565) 632611.

Driving along the A535 between Holmes Chapel and Chelford, you may be surprised to see an enormous circular space-age object towering up among the green fields and placid cows of the Cheshire Plain. The object is the Mark 1 radio telescope built for Manchester University in 1957, the largest in the world. Near it are four smaller dishes. The telescopes are the pride and joy of the Science Centre here, which has astronomy displays and space models in a large exhibition hall, with telescopes you can steer and an infinity of mirrors. In the planetarium you can take a 'whistle-stop tour of the galaxy'. After wandering among the stars, you can return to earth to ramble in the 35-acre arboretum around the Centre.

IN EASY REACH To the east of Jodrell Bank, the giant telescope is an eye-catching sight from Capesthorne Hall (limited opening only), off the A34. This Victorian pile contains fine pictures and furniture, and special collections of vases and Americana.

The Mark 1 telescope at Jodrell Bank. Its 250ft metal dish picks up radio waves from outer space and can be turned to track satellites

Peover Hall (open May to September only) at Over Peover (it's pronounced to rhyme with 'weaver') is 4 miles south of Knutsford off the A50. In 1944 General Patton had his headquarters here in this lovely Elizabethan brick mansion, owned for generations by the Mainwaring family. There is elaborate plasterwork in the luxurious 17th-century stables, and peaceful gardens with topiary work. Further west is the town of Northwich, in what was once a salt-mining district. The Salt Museum, in London Road, tells the story. Also in the area, at Anderton on the A533, is the remarkable 1875 boat lift, which used to pick up boats in water tanks from the River Weaver and transfer them bodily to the Trent and Mersey Canal.

—————— 252 ——————

LEEDS
WEST YORKSHIRE

Tourist Information Centre, 19 Wellington Street (0113) 2478301/2478302.

On the north-west edge of Leeds stands ruined Kirkstall Abbey. It was here, in medieval times, that the city's mighty cloth industry was born, when a group of Cistercian monks decided to dabble in the wool trade. The abbey itself is worth seeing for its beautifully preserved 12th-century architecture. Church, cloisters and chapter house all survive, making it the best early monastic site in Britain. In the grounds there is an interesting geological garden and in the restored gatehouse is the Abbey House Museum, with folk collections including three re-created life-size streets.

Back in the city centre you can see the later results of the monks' early trading ventures. Cuthbert Brodrick, in the 1850s, created the town hall, a great classical building, with a 225ft tower housing a 4-ton bell. He also built the city's Corn Exchange. As you explore the arcades of the city shopping centre look out for the clock with rotating figures modelled on characters from Scott's *Ivanhoe*.

Museums not to be missed include Temple Newsam, in the eastern outskirts of Leeds, off the A63, a Tudor-Jacobean house with Georgian rooms, furniture, paintings, ceramics and silver; Leeds City Museum and Art Gallery; and Armley Mills, in Armley to the west of the city centre, one of the world's largest woollen mills, built on an island in the River Aire and now a museum of Leeds' industrial history. More recent attractions include the gardens at Tropical World, Roundhay Park and Tetley's Brewery Wharf, The Waterfront, which tells the story of the English pub.

—————— 253 ——————

LIVERPOOL
MERSEYSIDE

Tourist Information Centres: Clayton Square Shopping Centre 0151-709 3631 and Atlantic Pavilion, Albert Dock 0151-708 8854.

The Grand National

Early in April every year all eyes turn to Aintree racecourse on the northern outskirts of Liverpool, where the world's most famous steeplechase is run over a course of some 4½ miles and 30 fences, some of them bywords for size, difficulty and danger – Becher's, Valentine's, The Chair. The first Grand National specifically so named was run in 1847, but it is generally accepted that its direct ancestry goes back to the Grand Liverpool steeplechase, first run in 1839. This race was won, appropriately enough, by a horse named Lottery, and it was on this occasion that the dashing Captain Becher fell into the brook ever afterwards known by his name.

In the Middle Ages a port for Ireland, Liverpool began to trade with the New World in the 17th century and grew apace in the 18th on the back of the slave traffic to overtake Bristol as Britain's major west-coast seaport. With booming prosperity, the city was largely rebuilt in the 19th century and now rejoices in public buildings of exceptional grandeur, in addition to its two magnificent cathedrals.

The centre of Liverpool is surveyed with eagle eye by the great Duke of Wellington on his noble 115ft column in Lime Street. Down below is St George's Hall, completed in 1854, majestically classical with Corinthian columns 60ft high and equestrian statues of Queen Victoria and Prince Albert in front. Close by is the Walker Art Gallery, famed for its early Italian and Flemish paintings.

The waterfront, which can be seen to advantage from the Mersey ferries, is dominated by the Royal Liver Building of 1910, on whose twin 295ft towers perch the mythical 'liver birds' after which the city is supposed to be named. The massive brick warehouses of the Royal Albert Dock of 1845 have been handsomely refurbished for shopping, exhibitions and conferences. Here you will find Animation World, a permanent exhibition of cartoon and animation; The Beatles Story, a magical history tour for all the family; the Museum of Liverpool Life which explores the history of Liverpool and its people; and a branch of London's Tate Gallery. The Merseyside Maritime Museum covers the history of the port and the days when millions of emigrants left Liverpool for new lives in America and Australia (9 million between 1830 and 1930).

—————— 254 ——————

MORECAMBE BAY
LANCASHIRE

Tourist Information Centres: Station Buildings, Central Promenade, Morecambe (01524) 582808 and 29 Castle Hill, Lancaster (01524) 32878.

Wildfowl in huge numbers cluster to feed on the sandflats and saltmarshes of Morecambe Bay, where the receding tide leaves a vast expanse of sand glistening under an awesomely enormous sky. Mallard and shelduck, wigeon and oystercatcher, merganser and grebe in turn provide food for the peregrine falcons which wheel and swoop above them. When the tide is in, the birds roost in their thousands north of Morecambe. The sands are highly dangerous, because the returning tide races in so fast, but there are walks across them at the right state of the tide, led by official guides.

Morecambe has a 4-mile promenade along the bay shore. With Heysham to the south, a ferry port for the Isle of Man, it offers all the popular seaside attractions, including Frontierland theme park and a leisure park. The observation tower of the Heysham nuclear power station is also open to the public.

Safely over – for some – at a Grand National race. Aintree was the first course to hold regular steeplechases

IN EASY REACH Lancaster, 4 miles inland on the A589, is a historic town with handsome Georgian and Victorian buildings and much to see. The medieval castle, dramatically altered about 1800, contains grim relics of its day as a prison. A path leads down to St George's Quay on the River Lune, where the maritime museum in the 18th-century Customs House surveys Lancaster's past as a port trading with the West Indies. The city museum and the museum of the King's Own Royal Regiment are in the old town hall in Market Square. In the Judge's Lodging, Castle Hill, you can enjoy the museum of childhood and the furniture collection, concentrating on Gillow's the famous Lancaster firm. Finally, don't miss Lancaster's equivalent of the Taj Mahal, the Ashton Memorial which rises high above the town in Williamson Park and was built in 1909 by Lord Ashton in memory of his wife.

255

MORPETH
NORTHUMBERLAND

Tourist Information Centre, The Chantry, Bridge Street (01670) 511323

Nestling in the arms of the River Wansbeck, Morpeth is an attractive old town. The ruins of the medieval castle are put in the shade by the battlemented tower built in 1822 by John Dobson, the Newcastle architect, as a combination police station, court-house and gaol. The bridge over the Wansbeck is by Thomas Telford and there is 14th-century stained glass in St Mary's Church, where there is also an 1830s watch-house keeping a wary eye out for body-snatchers in the graveyard. In the Bagpipe Museum, Bridge Street, you are provided with a cordless headset, and as you go round you hear the sounds of the various types of pipes in your headphones.

IN EASY REACH Wallington House, 12 miles west of Morpeth on the B6343, is a National Trust showplace with superb rococo plasterwork, notable 19th-century decorations, dolls' houses and a Victorian nursery among its attractions, as well as beautiful gardens and a park with nature trails. On the A696, 6 miles south-east, English Heritage owns Belsay Hall, which dates from the early 1800s. There is a 14th-century tower house and castle in the grounds, and many rare and exotic plants – mostly labelled – in the gardens.

Northumbrian Gathering

The Northumbrian Gathering at Morpeth, during the week after Easter every year, was founded in 1968 with the aim of preserving the heritage of Northumberland and bringing it to the attention of a wider public. Lasting for three days, the gathering embraces competitions in traditional aspects of Northumbrian life ranging from music and dance to language, literature and crafts There are contests for Northumbrian, Border and Highland pipes. Prose, verse and plays must be on Northumbrian themes and in some classes must be written in Northumbrian dialect. There's 'rapper' sword dancing in the Northumbrian style and Northumbrian and Durham clog dancing.

---------- 256 ----------

PILKINGTON GLASS MUSEUM
MERSEYSIDE

In St Helens, on the Prescot Road (A58). Tourist Information Centres: Merseyside Welcome Centre, Clayton Square Shopping Centre, 0151-709 3631 and Municipal Buildings, Cherryfield Drive, Kirkby 0151-443 4025/4026.

An array of glitteringly beautiful objects awaits the visitor to the museum in the Pilkington works, where the evolution of glass-making techniques from Ancient Egypt onwards is efficiently and enjoyably revealed. There is glass plain and glass coloured, glass clear and glass opaque, glass cut, engraved and patterned. There are holograms and mirrors (with an 'infinity box'), window glass and stained glass, and a small Egyptian oil bottle that has somehow miraculously survived for more than 3,000 years. There are early glass beads from Persia and China, Roman urns, 19th-century cameo vases, a family tree of English wine bottles, paperweights and perfume flasks, and an optic from an Irish lighthouse. The modern industrial use of glass is not neglected, and you can use a do-it-yourself periscope for views across the lake.

St Helens has been a great glass-making centre since the 1770s. The town has some striking Victorian buildings and a good local museum and art gallery, in College Street, which covers local industry, including Beecham's pills: Sir Thomas Beecham was born here.

IN EASY REACH The outskirts of Liverpool offer a rich harvest to the trawling visitor. West of St Helens is the Knowsley Safari Park at Prescot, in the grounds of the ancestral home of the Earls of Derby, now roamed by lions, tigers, African elephants and white rhinos. Prescot also has a museum of clock and watchmaking. Further west is Croxteth Hall and Country Park, with Edwardian room settings in the former home of the Earls of Sefton, rare breeds of farm animals and an enjoyable park. To the south, priests' holes and ghosts seem to be in about equal supply at Speke Hall, a very fine half-timbered manor house of the 15th century, on the Mersey's north bank.

---------- 257 ----------

ROCHDALE
GREATER MANCHESTER

Tourist Information Centres: The Clock Tower, Town Hall, Rochdale (01706) 356592 and 84 Union Street, Oldham 0161-678 4654.

●

Bacup Nutters Dance

On Easter Saturday, the town band of Bacup, to the north of Rochdale, plays for the Britannia Coconut Dancers, a morris troupe which dances and clatters its way through the streets in outlandish costumes. The dancers' faces are blackened and they wear white hats, heavy black woollen jerseys, white aprons with red frills on them, black knee breeches, white stockings and clogs (see right). They carry hoops or 'garlands', covered with red, white and blue paper. The 'nuts' with which they set up a complicated, clattering rhythm as they go, are actually wooden discs on their hands, wrists and knees. This custom is believed to have started in Bacup in 1857, but where the dance and the costumes came from, no one knows.

●

Rochdale is Gracie Fields' territory, and you'll find material on the singer in the town museum in Sparrow Hill, as well as much else about local history and industry. Near by are the parish church of St Chad at the top of 122 steps, and the grand Victorian-Gothic town hall, with its 190ft clock-tower. Rochdale is also the place where the Co-operative Movement was born, in a little grocery shop in Toad Lane, in 1844. In the shop now is the Rochdale Pioneers Co-operative Museum (closed every Monday), where the story is told, in an appropriate setting of cobbled streets and gas lamps.

IN EASY REACH To contemplate Constable and Crome, Turner and Epstein, head west for the art gallery in Bury. There is also a transport museum (limited opening only) here, as well as the regimental museum of the Lancashire Fusiliers. North of Rochdale is the old Forest of Rossendale, and the Rossendale Museum in Rawtenstall is rich in portraits of local textile kings and shoe magnates, and local natural and social history.

To the south-east of Bury and Rochdale, Oldham also has an art gallery and a local interest centre. At Uppermill, further east is the Saddleworth Museum, which explores local history and customs in an old cotton mill. The local-interest trails around the former cloth-making villages in this area are good value, and there is stunning Pennine scenery along the Lancashire – Yorkshire border. Right on the border, at Blackstone Edge on the A58 is, what is considered to be, the best-preserved stretch of Roman road in Britain, a marvellous piece of engineering getting on for 2,000 years old.

258

SHEFFIELD
SOUTH YORKSHIRE

Tourist Information Centre, Peace Gardens (0114) 2734671.

It is hardly surprising that the 1890s town hall has a 7ft statue of Vulcan, the Roman god of smiths, on top of its grandiloquent 210ft clock-tower, for the city of Sheffield was long a byword for steel, cutlery and plate. Splendid displays of cutlery and Sheffield plate can be seen in the City Museum in Weston Park, together with local ceramics, guns, clocks and watches and sundials. For a lively view of Sheffield life and work, yesterday and today, try the Industrial Museum, Alma Street, in a former generating station, where there are cutlery craftsmen at work. In the southern outskirts on the A621, the Abbeydale Industrial Hamlet is an old scytheworks, where you can watch the waterwheels turning and the great tilt hammers rising and thudding down, and explore the workers' houses and the manager's house for a glimpse of how people lived.

At the junction of the Don and the Sheaf, Sheffield is the largest town in Yorkshire. Besides its industrial archaeology, it is distinguished for its art galleries and its controversial post-war architecture, including the huge high-rise estates above the Sheaf. The Mappin Art Gallery in Weston Park is noted for British paintings and sculptures, while The Graves Art Gallery, Surrey Street, concentrates on 20th-century British works, with French Impressionists and also Oriental and Islamic art. On no account however, leave Sheffield without visiting the exceptionally rewarding Ruskin Gallery, 101 Norfolk Street, where John Ruskin's own collection is displayed as he intended, to teach us how to see.

The 15th-century church of St Peter and St Paul has been a cathedral since 1914 and has a modern chapter house, tower and entrance. Inside are stained-glass windows by Christopher Webb, and the tombs of the Earls of Shrewsbury, the principal local landowners from the 15th to the 17th centuries.

259

SLEDMERE HOUSE
HUMBERSIDE

Sledmere is at the junction of the B1251, and the B1253, 8 miles north-west of Great Driffield. Open May to September. Tourist Information Centres: 25 Prince Street, Bridlington (01262) 673474 and Old Town Hall, Market Place, Malton, North Yorkshire (01653) 600048 (seasonal opening only).

This house in its 'Capability' Brown park has an Edwardian atmosphere. It was originally built in the 1750s for the Sykes family, who have lived here and dominated the area for well over 250 years, and was altered by Sir Christopher Sykes, the great agricultural improver, in the 1780s. A fire in 1911 destroyed most of it, but everything from inside was saved and the house was rebuilt from the evidence of plans and pictures, as well as memory, for Sir Mark Sykes by a York architect, Walter Brierley. He added the chapel and the remarkable Turkish room, copied from one in an Instanbul mosque. The beautiful 18th-century interiors were reproduced and the magnificent library runs the whole length of the south front.

In the grounds are follies, monuments and the parish church, rebuilt in 1898 and much admired. In the village there is a remarkable war memorial to the Yorkshire Waggoners (a regiment raised by Sir Mark Sykes) decorated with war scenes in relief.

IN EASY REACH From the 120ft-tower in memory of Sir Tatton Sykes on Garton Hill, 2 miles south-east of Sledmere, there is a fine view of the rolling country of the Yorkshire Wolds. To the west, off the B1248, just south of Wharram le Street, the ruined church of Wharram Percy stands sentinel over the earthworks of a deserted medieval village. South-west from here, on the other side of the A166, is the attractive Wolds village of Bishop Wilton, and south again at Pocklington, on the B1246, are the lakes and waterlilies of Burnby Hall Gardens, with a museum of sporting trophies.

●

Kiplingcotes Derby

Britain's oldest horse-race, the Kiplingcotes Derby, is run at South Dalton, about 12 miles south of Sledmere, on the third Thursday in March. It dates back to 1519 and was organised on a regular basis by the local gentry a hundred years later. There is no racecourse in the modern sense and order is kept by a solitary official, the clerk of the course, whose office has been handed down through several generations of the same family. The course is about 4 miles, along country roads and over fields. The winner gets a cup and a cash prize, but the rider who comes in second gets the entry money, which is always more than the winner receives. As a result there have sometimes been complicated manoeuverings for second place.

●

Below right: the Japanese Gardens at Tatton Park

●

Knutsford Royal May Day

Knutsford, on the first Saturday in May, is one of the few places where you can still see a traditional Jack in the Green, in the past a familiar and uncanny figure in springtime and summer customs (he is the 'green man' of church bosses and inn signs). Covered with leaves, he parades through the town as part of a grand procession, with the Royal May Queen and her attendants in carriages, the town crier, troupes of morris dancers, several bands and hundreds of children in all sorts of

costumes. In due course the May Queen is solemnly crowned and there is dancing round the maypole. She has been 'royal' since 1887, when the Prince of Wales, the future Edward VII, attended the ceremony. In a curious custom before the procession begins, dyed sand is used to spell out inscriptions and draw patterns on the ground in front of public buildings, shops and the May Queen's house (see above).

●

— 260 —
TATTON PARK
CHESHIRE

Off the A50, north of Knutsford.
Tourist Information Centre, Council Offices, Toft Road, Knutsford (01565) 632611.

There is something for everyone at Tatton. The grand house of the Egertons, rebuilt at the turn of the 18th and 19th centuries by Samuel and Lewis Wyatt, has a beautiful dining room and library, Gillow furniture, family portraits, fine glass, silver and porcelain. In one capacious hall are the trophies of the last Lord Egerton, a big-game hunter who shot his last tiger in India at the age of 81.

Outside are 50 acres of delightful gardens, with terraces, designed by Sir Joseph Paxton and a Japanese garden, walled rose garden, Victorian fernery, orangery, beech maze and pools. Deer and rare sheep roam the enormous park and there is also a 1930s working farm on the estate. Other attractions include a forestry walk and wartime and medieval village trails, and there is also riding, carriage rides, a garden centre, a gift shop, a restaurant and picnic places.

IN EASY REACH Knutsford is the 'Cranford' of Mrs Gaskell's 19th-century novel, and she is buried in the Unitarian graveyard, but the town is best known for its spectacular May Day celebrations. To the other side of Tatton Park, off the A56, stands a handsome 18th-century house, Durham Massey, enlarged shortly before World War I. Outside there is a deer park and a working Elizabethan mill.

— 261 —
THE WIRRAL
MERSEYSIDE AND CHESHIRE

Tourist Information Centres: Woodside Ferry Terminal, Merseyside 0151-647 6780 and Clayton Square Shopping Centre, Liverpool 0151-709 3631.

A low-lying, oblong peninsula of land, with the River Mersey on one side and the River Dee on the other, the Wirral is historically part of Cheshire, but since 1974 has been shared with Merseyside. In the Middle Ages it was a wild and dangerous wasteland. Today, besides its seaside town and the links at Hoylake, it has several worthwhile attractions.

One of them is Port Sunlight, just off the A41, and named after Sunlight soap, a model company suburb of the 1890s and 1930s. It was built for his employees by William Hesketh Lever, the dynamic Lancastrian soap king who founded Unilever and became the first Lord Leverhulme. There is an attractive brick church (in which Leverhulme and his wife are both buried), a good garden centre and a statue of the founder atop a tall column. The heritage centre in Greendale Road fills in the background. However, the star of this particular show is certainly the Lady Lever Art Gallery, built for Leverhulme's fabulous art collection.

Further south, the dispiriting streets of Ellesmere Port mercifully fail to conceal the Boat Museum in Dockyard Road, at the terminus of the Shropshire Union Canal. Here there is a large collection of canal boats, working steam engines, restored workmen's houses and material on life on the canals, with trips in a horse-drawn narrowboat.

Also well worth a visit are Ness Gardens, outside Neston off the A540. These are the botanical gardens of Liverpool University, with many exotic trees and plants, and notable among other things for flowering cherries.

— 262 —
ACORN BANK GARDEN
CUMBRIA

Near Temple Sowerby, on the A66, 6 miles south-east of Penrith.
Tourist Information Centres: Robinson's School, Middlegate, Penrith (01768) 67466
and The Moot Hall, Boroughgate, Appleby-in-Westmorland (017683) 51177.

Blackroot and skunk cabbage, baneberry and wild indigo, together with more familiar names like mint, tansy, borage and elecampane, are among the 250 varieties in the National Trust's garden at Acorn Bank, the biggest collection of medical and cooking herbs in the North. The garden is quite small, occupying only 2½ acres, but it is also worth seeing for the flower and shrub borders and for the fruit trees in the walled orchards. The 18th-century house is open on application.

IN EASY REACH Penrith is an old market town, veteran of years of Border warfare and raiding, with narrow streets, a ruined castle and a group of ancient crosses and tombstones making up 'the Giant's Grave' in the churchyard. The story of the Eden Valley is told in the town museum in Middlegate. To the north-west of Penrith, 6 miles along the B5305, is Hutton-in-the-Forest, a house which has grown by stages on to an old pele tower, with pictures, china and furniture from 450 years past. Another pele tower is the nucleus of Dalemain, 3 miles south-west of Penrith on the A592, with a beautiful deer park, a countryside museum in the 16th-century cobbled courtyard, and material on the Cumberland and Westmorland Yeomanry. Appleby, the old county town of Westmorland 13 miles away to the south-east, off the A66, is the scene of a celebrated horse fair in June. Its castle was rebuilt in the 17th century, and in the grounds are rare breeds of British farm animals, ornamental waterfowl and unusual birds.

●

Appleby Horse Fair

Early in June every year the biggest gathering of gypsies in Britain takes place at the horse fair in Appleby (see left). In the fair's great days as many as a thousand brightly painted caravans would cluster close to Gallows Hill, and there was music and dancing until dawn. The fair was given a royal charter in 1685 by James II and is still a notable occasion. Large crowds come to enjoy the colour and sparkle of the fair, as horses are watered in the River Eden close to the town bridge, and put through their paces to be sold. There are hotly contested trotting races as well.

●

— 263 —
ALNWICK CASTLE
NORTHUMBERLAND

Tourist Information Centre, The Shambles, Northumberland Hall (01665) 510665.

A frowning 15th-century barbican guards the entrance to the Duke of Northumberland's great towered and battlemented fortress, stronghold of the Percy dynasty in the turbulent Border country. Dating back to the 12th century, it was restored in the 1760s, and at this point the statues of armed men were installed on the battlements. The interiors were remodelled in the 1850s for the fourth duke by Anthony Salvin, and contain magnificent paintings, furniture, china, manuscripts and books. There is a dungeon, a state coach of 1825 and an impressive museum of antiquities.

The Hotspur Gate is all that remains of the medieval walls of the grey, narrow-streeted town of Alnwick (pronounced 'Annick'). The Lion Bridge dates from 1773 and the 83ft Percy Tenantry Column, topped by the Percy lion, was erected in 1816 by farmers grateful for a reduction in rents.

IN EASY REACH North-east of Alnwick, 7 miles away on the coast, the fishing village of Craster is known for its kippers, and on a rocky headland a few miles north from here rise the romantic ruins of Dunstanburgh Castle.

Going inland from Alnwick, there is a bird sanctuary and hospital (viewed by appointment only) at the World Bird Research Station at Glanton, off the A697. To the south, just outside Rothbury, on the B6341, the National Trust owns 19th-century Cragside House, a tremendous mansion with Pre-Raphaelite paintings and a pioneering electric-light system, in a magnificent park.

—————— 264 ——————
BENINGBROUGH HALL
NORTH YORKSHIRE

Off the A19, 8 miles north-west of York
Tourist Information Centres: De grey Rooms, Exhibition Square, York (01904) 621756
and York Railway Station, Outer Concourse, York (01904) 643700

Beningbrough, built around 1716 by John Bourchier and now in the hands of the National Trust, is a fitting home for the permanent exhibition of 100 pictures from the National Portrait Gallery in London. Perhaps the finest feature of the house is the great staircase, built of oak with wide parquetried treads and delicate balusters carved to imitate wrought iron. The servants' exhibition and the restored Victorian laundry, which has original stoves, drying racks and other equipment, shows the other side of country house life. Outside are formal gardens (guided garden walks most weekends), a conservatory and, for the children, a wilderness play area.

IN EASY REACH North-west on the B6265 is Aldborough, a pretty village which occupies the site of the northernmost civilian Roman town in Britain. Remains revealed through excavation include tessellated pavements and a variety of coins, pottery and artefacts which are on display in the small site museum. Just a little further on, to the west of Boroughbridge, are three large monoliths known ominously as the Devil's Arrows. The largest is over 22ft, and it is thought that the group date from the Bronze Age.
Sutton Park is on the B1363 north-east of Beningbrough. The early Georgian house is only open to parties, but the grounds are well worth a visit for the superb terraced gardens, lily pond and delightful woodland walks.

—————— 265 ——————
BOLTON
GREATER MANCHESTER

Tourist Information Centre, Town Hall (01204) 364333.

Cumberland Show

Crowds gather in July every year by the idyllic River Eden for the Cumberland Show, a venerable event which goes back to the 1830s. Besides spectators, you'll see lumbering Clydesdale horses, Friesians and Holsteins, Jerseys, Guernseys and a few Ayrshires among the dairy cattle, Hereford and Aberdeen Angus bulls, and sheep which include Cheviots and Suffolks, Border Leicesters and the shaggy Herdwicks from the Lake District. No classes are held for pigs, which are easily upset by crowds, but there are jumping and dressage classes, plus prizes for cookery, home brewing and wine-making, needlework and flower arranging. All the fun of the traditional county show, in fact, as well as bands, entertainment and a spectacular show by the Red Devils or a motorbike team.

Bolton was a premier cotton-spinning town in its time and some of the machines which made its fortune are preserved in the Tonge Moor Textile Museum: they include Arkwright's water frame, Hargreave's spinning-jenny and Crompton's spinning-mule. Arkwright and Crompton were both Bolton men. Stationary steam engines from Lancashire textile mills can be admired in the Steam Museum (open weekends and bank holidays only), and you can glean more of the local history at the museum in the old town hall in St George's Street. The newer town hall in Victoria Square is a noble product of 1870s civic prosperity and pride, in the classical manner – you step much further back into history at Bolton's oldest inn, Ye Old Man and Scythe, said to date from 1251. Local textiles are amongst the exhibits at the Bolton Museum and Art Gallery, Le Mans Crescent, which has an aquarium and an interestingly varied collection, including 18th-century watercolours.

IN EASY REACH On the track of Samuel Crompton, be sure to visit Hall i' th' Wood which is situated on the northern outskirts of Bolton. This vivid black-and-white 15th-century house, where he invented his spinning-mule in 1779, is now a museum dedicated to him, and is furnished in 18th-century style. Also on the northern fringes of the town is Smithills Hall, another venerable half-timbered house, now furnished in the manner of the 16th and 17th centuries.

—————— 266 ——————
CARLISLE
CUMBRIA

Tourist Information Centre, Old Town Hall, Green Market (01228) 512444.

You can buy local delicacies, Cumberland sausage and rum butter, in the Victorian covered market in Carlisle. The town was fought over by English and Scots for centuries and is appropriately dominated by its grim castle, above the River Eden. It may have been the Scots who built the formidable keep. Inside you can see the graffiti scratched by unhappy prisoners, and the museum of the Border Regiment, formed in 1680. Down beneath today's city is the Roman military base and town of Luguvallium, and the Carlisle Museum and Art Gallery in Tullie House, Castle Street, has particularly good prehistoric and Roman collections, along with much else to enjoy. The cathedral is substantially smaller than it would have been if the Scots had not knocked a good deal of the nave down in 1645. Inside, be sure to see the superb east window and the 15th-century choir stalls with misericords. In the half-timbered guildhall, in Green Market, are local items including the town pillory and stocks.

IN EASY REACH A minor road leads west beyond Burgh-by-Sands to the Solway Firth. There is good walking along the shore here, with enormous numbers of birds and views across to Scotland. Going the other way take the A69 11 miles to Brampton, where St Martin's Church was built by Philip Webb in the 1870s and has dazzling Burne-Jones windows.

Two miles south-east from here are the pleasant lake and woods of Talkin Tarn Country Park. North from Brampton, a minor road leads to Lanercost Priory in the valley of the Irthing. Dating from around 1166 the nave of the church has survived and is still used, and makes a strange contrast with the ruined priory buildings around. There are also stretches of Hadrian's Wall in this area, with a Roman fort at Birdoswald, off the B6318.

Inset: Chester's famous Rows – a unique feature of the city

The town crier, who can be hired to publicise various events, is seen here in the company of the Cheshire Cat during Chester's Alice in Wonderland Festival

---
267

CHESTER
CHESHIRE

Tourist Information Centres: Chester Visitor Centre, Vicars Lane (01244) 351609/318916 and Town Hall, Northgate Street (01244) 317962.

The way to see Chester is to walk the circuit on top of the old city walls. Punctuated by towers and gates of various periods, the walls are mainly medieval in date, but go back ultimately to the Romans. They provide an enjoyable, traffic-free walk of a little under 2 miles, with splendid vistas of one of Britain's most attractive and most civilised cities. Some of the towers contain small museums. Inside the walls, Chester's star attraction is its central set of two-decker shopping streets called the Rows. On top of the street-level tier of shops runs a wooden gallery, reached by flights of stairs at intervals, off which opens an upper tier of shops.

Chester started life as a major Roman base. Outside the walls is the 7,000-seater Roman amphitheatre and part of the Roman quay can be seen where the old Roodee racecourse is now. The memorials to Roman soldiers and their families in the Grosvenor Museum, Grosvenor Street, somehow cross the centuries and bring them affectingly close. The later history of the town is covered in the museum too.

A rhapsody in black and white, Chester is celebrated for its gorgeous panoply of half-timbered buildings. The most famous one, the God's Providence House in Watergate Street, is dated 1652, but was rebuilt, bigger and better than before, in 1862. Bishop Lloyd's House in the same street, with its carved monsters and grotesques, was restored in 1899. Chester Cathedral, though Norman in origin, is also a Victorian building in large part, so thoroughly was it restored by Sir George Gilbert Scott. Outside is an unusual and striking feature, a detached 85ft bell-tower, faced with grey slate and built in the 1970s.

A few fragments of Chester's important medieval castle survive, but today the main buildings, where the museum of the Cheshire regiments is housed, are in the Greek Revival style of the early 19th century. Chester Zoo, actually 2 miles outside the city, at Upton, is noted for its gardens as well as its animals.

●
River Events in Chester

Chester's riverside takes on a carnival air on the second Sunday in July every year. Beside the Dee there are bands, musicians, sideshows, charity stalls and children's amusements. On the water, meanwhile, 40 or so rafts entered by various groups and business firms race over a course of about half a mile near the old Dee bridge. Earlier in the year, in March, the river between Eccleston Ferry and the boat-house of the Chester Rowing Club is the scene of the North of England Head of the River Race, and in late May there's the Chester Regatta.

●

268

CHILLINGHAM PARK
NORTHUMBERLAND

Chillingham is 4 miles south-east of Wooler, on a minor road.
Tourist Information Centre, Bus Station Car Park, High Street, Wooler (01668) 81602.

The cattle of Chillingham are believed to be descendants of a herd trapped within the park in 1220. Visits are only possible between April and October

From the warden's house near Chillingham Castle (not open), the ancestral seat of the Earls of Tankerville, visitors are escorted in batches to gaze cautiously (binoculars are recommended) at a rare and remarkable sight – the wild cattle which are believed to have been roaming the park here for 700 years and which, not interbred with any other herd, are as close to prehistoric wild oxen as you will see. Fairly small, they are white with black muzzles and black-tipped horns, and are ruled by their king bull. The wardens bother them as little as possible, but try to make sure they survive: the herd was almost wiped out in the ferocious winter of 1947 and again in a foot-and-mouth epidemic in 1966.

IN EASY REACH Close by to the east, the National Trust owns Ross Castle, a prehistoric earthwork on a 1,036ft hill, commanding wide-ranging views. To the west are the Cheviot Hills and the Northumberland National Park, 398 square miles of rolling hills and deep forests stretching down to Hadrian's Wall, almost entirely unpopulated and largely without roads. There is an information centre at Ingram off the A697 to the south-west of Chillingham.

Close to the northern edge of the park is the Iron Age hill-fort on top of Yeavering Bell, 1,182ft, north-west of Wooler, off the B6351. This is another commanding viewpoint, which looks over the battlefield of Flodden to the north and the monument to 'the brave of both nations' near Branxton church, on the spot where James IV of Scotland was killed in the battle in 1513.

269

DURHAM
CO DURHAM

Tourist Information Centre, Market Place 0191-384 3720.

Towering majestically above a loop in the River Wear Durham Cathedral, with the castle close by, makes an unforgettable picture of Norman splendour. The steep wooded banks of the river provide lovely walks

Britain has few sights more thrilling than the view of Durham Cathedral from the train pulling in from the south over the long railway viaduct. The huge church stands on its towering rock above a horseshoe bend of the River Wear, at the point where in AD995 a party of wandering monks finally decided to deposit the remains of St Cuthbert. However, Durham's most famous view of all is perhaps the one across the river to the old fulling-mill (now an archaeology museum), with the cathedral almost standing on top of it,

The church on the cliff-top today was begun in 1093 and is an overwhelming monument to Norman power and pride. Going in by the north porch, you confront the bronze lion's head door-knocker, which was used by fugitives claiming sanctuary. In the nave is a black line on the floor, and in the past women were not allowed to approach any closer than this to the shrine of St Cuthbert beyond the high altar. The tomb of the Venerable Bede, historian and biographer of St Cuthbert, is in the Galilee chapel, and fragments of Cuthbert's coffin can be seen together with his pectoral cross in the cathedral treasury.

Next to the cathedral is the castle, which is now part of the university. Also part of the university is the Oriental Museum in Elvet Hill, where objects of the most exquisite beauty are installed: Buddhas, jade carvings, figures of Chinese, Japanese and Hindu deities, Tang figurines, and Tibetan copper teapots. Also well worth seeing is the Durham Light Infantry Museum, Aykley Heads, where the history of this famous regiment is vividly brought to life.

When tired of city streets, there are pleasant walks along the River Wear in both directions from Durham, and the ruins of Finchale Priory, 4 miles to the north, stand in a delightful riverside setting.

270

FOUNTAINS ABBEY
NORTH YORKSHIRE

On a minor road off the B6265, 3 miles west of Ripon.
Tourist Information Centre, Minster Road, Ripon (01765) 604625
(seasonal opening only).

The wealth of Fountains Abbey grew on the backs of its sheep. In its heyday the monks were the biggest producers of wool in the North and, for all their austere Cistercian principles, the profits paid for the impressive buildings whose grey and haunting ruins stand in the lovely valley of Skell. The oldest buildings are the nave and transepts of the abbey church, built in the 1130s and 1140s. The tower was added shortly before the monastery was dissolved in 1539 and the last abbot was hanged. Close to the river are the remains of the other monastery buildings, including the refectory and kitchen, the warming house and the infirmary.

The ruins stand at the western end of one of the most satisfying pieces of large-scale landscape gardening in the country, on the Studley Royal estate, which was laid out in the 18th century with water features and follies as well as artfully contrived 'views'. Like the abbey ruins, it now belongs to the National Trust. A bonus here is a fascinating 1870s church by William Burges, rich in symbolism.

IN EASY REACH Ripon is arranged round its handsome market square with a 90ft obelisk in the middle, the town hall of 1800 and the medieval Wakeman's house, built for the town's principal official and now a local history museum. The small cathedral has fine 15th-century choir stalls and the crypt goes right back to the 7th century when it was the church built here by St Wilfrid. Punishments and policing are the themes of the Prison and Police Museum in St Marygate.

Norton Conyers, the Jacobean house which is thought to have given Charlotte Brontë the idea for *Jane Eyre*, is 3 miles north of Ripon on a side road off the A1. Four miles south-east of Ripon, off the B6265, is Newby Hall, splendid in William-and-Mary red brick, with its elegant Robert Adam interiors, its gallery of classical sculptures, its beautiful gardens and grounds, and another Burges church.

271

HAREWOOD HOUSE
WEST YORKSHIRE

On the A61, 8 miles north of Leeds.
Tourist Information Centre, 19 Wellington Street, Leeds (0113) 2478301.

John Carr did the outside, Robert Adam did the inside, Sir Charles Barry made alterations in the 1840s, and between them they and an army of craftsmen created one of England's most palatial houses for the Lascelles family, Earls of Harewood. The Robert Adam rooms are unrivalled essays in elegance, and the great house bulges with Chippendale furniture, superb ceiling paintings and plasterwork, Sèvres and Chinese porcelain, glittering mirrors and luxurious carpets, and a gallery of priceless paintings. Outside are formal gardens by Barry and a park by 'Capability' Brown, now embellished with a 4-acre walk-through bird garden. There are impressive tombs in the church, and the village was rebuilt by John Carr.

IN EASY REACH Not far to the east, near the junction of the A64 and the A1, is another piece of theatrical grandeur, the gardens of Bramham Park. They were laid out in the 18th century in the French style, with ornamental ponds, glittering cascades, long vistas to obelisks and temples, and straight avenues running between beech hedges. There is a dramatic stable block, with classical columns and a clock turret. The house itself is a delightful Queen Anne mansion, with a good collection of pictures, china and furniture.

●

Ripon Customs

On the Saturday before the first Monday in August every year a procession of floats passes through the streets of Ripon. On the floats are scenes from the city's history, and at the head of the procession, on a white horse and amply bearded, is a man dressed as a bishop, with mitre and crook (see below). He represents St Wilfrid and is greeted at the west door of the cathedral by the Dean and clergy, after which there is a service of thanksgiving. The original St Wilfrid was abbot of the monastery at Ripon in the 7th century. Afterwards appointed Bishop of York, he was buried in Ripon where he died in 709.

Another Ripon custom of formidable antiquity, is the sounding of a horn in the market square every night at nine o'clock. This is said to go back to the year 886, when the town was given a charter by King Alfred. The blowing of the horn is a signal that the night-watch has been set, to guard the citizens during the hours of darkness.

●

— 272 —
HOGHTON TOWER
LANCASHIRE

At Hoghton, on the A675, 5 miles east of Preston. Limited opening only.
Tourist Information Centres: The Guildhall, Lancaster Road, Preston (01772) 253731
and King George's Hall, Northgate, Blackburn (01254) 53277.

Entertained at Hoghton Tower in 1617, James I of England jovially knighted a particularly appetising loin of beef and so coined the word 'sirloin', or so the story goes. This battlemented house (pronounced 'Horton') looks out over miles of country from its hilltop above the River Darwen. It was built in the 1560s by Thomas Hoghton. His nephew, Sir Richard Hoghton, had the king to stay in 1617 and the cost almost bankrupted him. The tower from which the house takes its name was blown up in a Roundhead attack during the Civil War. Sir Henry de Hoghton restored the house in the 1860s and today you can enjoy the splendid banqueting hall, the underground passages, the dolls' houses, and the old English rose garden.

IN EASY REACH In Preston you will find the Harris Museum and Art Gallery, Market Square, with a distinguished art collection, ceramics and glass. Leyland, to the south of the M6, is a famous name in heavy vehicles, and the British Commercial Vehicle Museum, King Street, covers the history of buses and lorries since the horse age.

Ghost fanciers should congregate at Chingle Hall, north of Preston on the B5269 near Goosnargh, one of the most haunted houses in Britain. Older ghosts perhaps hover at Ribchester, to the east on the B6245, where the River Ribble runs by the remains of a major Roman fort. South-east of here on the A677 is Blackburn, once the greatest cotton-weaving town in the world. To find out all about the industry, visit the Lewis Textile Museum, Exchange Street. The museum and art gallery in Museum Street has engagingly wide-ranging collections, including coins, books and manuscripts, and icons.

— 273 —
HOLKER HALL
CUMBRIA

On the B5278, west of Grange-over-Sands.
Tourist Information Centres: Victoria Hall, Main Street, Grange-over-Sands
(015395) 34026 and Coronation Hall, Ulverston (01229) 57120.

The 7th Duke of Devonshire laid out the gardens of Holker Hall – a mixture of formal and informal planting. Fallow deer roam the 120-acre park which is used for balloon flights and vintage rallies

This house goes back to the beginning of the 17th century, but its main feature is the imposing Victorian west wing, built after a severe fire in 1871. The work was done by local craftsmen and there's fine wood-carving, a superb cantilevered oak staircase and panelling in oak from the park. Holker Hall was the favourite home of the 7th Duke of Devonshire and his bedroom has been preserved with his tent bed and coronation robes. The house is occupied by his descendants and has a 'lived-in' atmosphere, with furniture, paintings, photographs and Cavendish family items. Other attractions are a motor museum with a replica of Sir Malcolm Campbell's Bluebird, a display of bygone kitchen appliances, a craft and countryside museum and, for the children, an adventure playground.

IN EASY REACH In the nearby village of Cartmel are the beautiful church and gatehouse of Cartmel Priory. To the north, at Haverthwaite on the B5278, are the headquarters of the Lakeside and Haverthwaite Railway, which runs steam trains on a scenic route along the Leven Valley to the foot of Lake Windermere. Don't miss the working mill at Stott Park, just outside Finsthwaite, which made bobbins from 1835 to 1971. The machinery turns over still, under the eye of English Heritage.

ISLE OF MAN

Tourist Information Centres: Harris Promenade, Douglas (01624) 686766, also in all main towns and at the airport.

Ruled by the Queen, but with its own parliament, money and stamps, the Isle of Man is not part of the United Kingdom. It has a long semi-independent history under its own 'kings' and 'lords' – viceroys for the Viking rulers of Dublin and from the 14th century, for the English Crown. Placed like a stepping stone half-way between England and Ireland, it is easily reached in an hour by plane from London and other British airports, in up to 4 hours by ferry from Liverpool or from Heysham and Fleetwood in Lancashire, or by catamaran in the summer.

The capital, and the largest and liveliest town on the island, is Douglas on the east coast, the port to which the ferries run. Its solid Victorian terraces look down on 2 miles of sandy beach, with horse-drawn trams plying on the promenade. In the Manx Museum, Crellins Hill, there are displays on Manx history, geology, natural history and country life, with impressive Celtic and Viking collections.

Going north, the Electric Railway will take you up the coast to Laxey and Ramsey, and you can hop off here and there for strolls in enticing glens. Manx tartans are woven in Laxey, which is famous for its huge water-wheel, at 72 ½ft in diameter, the world's biggest. From Laxey the Mountain Railway starts on its 5-mile journey to the top of Snaefell, at 2,036ft the island's highest peak.

Ramsey is a sailing and seaside resort. The Grove Rural Life Museum, Andreas Road, delightfully preserves the flavour of Victorian family life. To the west along the A3 road is the Curraghs Wildlife Park, with the native four-horned Loghtan rams, as well as deer, monkeys, penguins, waterfowl and gambolling otters. Going on down the west coast, the A3 comes to Peel, where the frowning battlements of the castle enclose the ruined cathedral of St German's.

Dramatic cliffs mark the south-western end of Man. Off the tip, the small island called the Calf of Man, reached by boat from Port Erin, is a nature reserve teeming with nesting seabirds. Near Port St Mary are the thatched, whitewashed houses of the Cregneash Folk Museum, where the lifestyle of Manx crofters and fishermen early in this century is illustrated. East again is Castletown, the capital of Man until the 1860s, where the island's most impressive fortress, Castle Rushen, rises above the crowded harbour. The nautical Museum in Bridge Street has an 18th-century armed yacht and a display of nautical bygones, and serves as a reminder that the island takes its name from the Celtic god of the sea.

The island's famous motorcycle festival takes place every year during the two weeks straddling May and June. The race, covering 37¼ miles of public highways, is considered to be the most exciting motorcycle road race in the world and attracts top-class international competitors

●

Tynwald Day

In Viking times the freemen of the Isle of Man met in an assembly which developed into the island's parliament, the Tynwald. On 5 July, which is 'old' Midsummer Day, a colourful ceremony is held on Tynwald Hill, a prehistoric man-made mound in the village of St Johns, near Peel. The Manx sword of state is borne point upwards before the Lieutenant Governor, clergy, judges and other dignitaries, who proceed along a path strewn with rushes. New laws are announced in both Manx and English, and officials for the coming year appointed and sworn in. The formal proceedings are enlivened by a traditional fair.

●

275

LINDISFARNE (HOLY ISLAND)
NORTHUMBERLAND

A bonus at Lindisfarne's fairy-tale castle is the small garden designed by Lutyen's contemporary, Gertrude Jekyll

Reached by causeway from Beal, off the A1. Tide tables at each end of the causeway. Tourist Information Centres: Seafield Road, Seahouses (01665) 720884 and Castlegate Car Park, Berwick-upon-Tweed (01289) 330733.

The causeway to the island can be crossed only at lowish tide, which reinforces the air of sanctity and specialness proper to one of the oldest Christian centres in Britain. St Aidan founded a monastery here in 635, St Cuthbert became bishop in 684, and the Lindisfarne Gospels (now in the British Museum in London) were produced here by the end of the 7th century. After the Norman Conquest a Benedictine priory was established on the site, whose evocative ruins can be seen here today. In the small museum are pre-Christian carved stones. The 16th-century castle was restored early this century by Sir Edwin Lutyens, and now belongs to the National Trust. Much of the island is a National Nature Reserve.

IN EASY REACH Ten miles to the south, Bamburgh Castle rears up in grandeur on its crag above the shore. In the churchyard is the grave of Grace Darling, heroine of a famous rescue off this coast in 1838, and opposite is the Grace Darling Museum. Further down the coast is Seahouses, with boat trips to the Farne Islands and their seal colonies.

Going the other way, northwards, the A1 comes to Tweedmouth. Worth seeing here are the Elizabethan town walls and the early-18th-century barracks, where you can find out about life in the infantry, with the museum of the King's Own Scottish Borderers and the town museum and art gallery.

Tweedmouth Salmon Feast

One of the pleasures of a visit to Berwick is to watch the salmon fishermen at their age-old task in the Tweed during the season, from mid-February to mid-September. They drop their nets into the water from a boat, and then return to the shore to haul them in with the catch. The traditional type of boat used is a coble, a flat-bottomed craft, with a square stern, 20ft or so long. The port for the fishing fleet is Tweedmouth, on the river's southern bank, where in July the traditional Salmon Feast is held and the Salmon Queen is crowned. The custom was revived in 1945 after a gap of a good many years, and combined with a carnival, athletics and a dance. It happens on the Sunday after St Boisil's Day, 18 July. St Boisil, an Irishman, was Abbot of Melrose in the 7th century, and Tweedmouth is one of only two churches in the country dedicated to him.

276

LITTLE MORETON HALL
CHESHIRE

On the A34, 4 miles south-west of Congleton. Tourist Information Centre, Town Hall, High Street, Congleton (01260) 271095.

Riotously striped and patterned, with richly carved gables, this archetype of black-and-white Cheshire 'magpie' building leans perilously out over its moat, looking as if it might tumble into it at any moment. Inside is prodigious panelling, a long gallery running the full length of the building, and 16th-century wall paintings. There is a massive kitchen, full of pewter and with an ox-sized fireplace, and there is also a secret room, so easily spotted behind a chimney that is may have been a deliberate cover for the real secret hidey-hole, concealed down under the moat.

IN EASY REACH North of Congleton, on the A536, is another beautiful and romantic half-timbered house. Gawsworth Hall was the home of the Fittons for centuries, and Mary Fitton, maid of honour to Elizabeth I, is a candidate of the 'dark lady' of Shakespeare's sonnets. There are lakes, a tiltyard and an open-air theatre in the grounds.

Notable buildings in Congleton itself include three half-timbered inns and an 18th-century church. Three miles to the east of the town is a National Trust hill called The Cloud, which juts up suddenly 1,000ft to provide extensive views.

---- 277 ----

MACCLESFIELD
CHESHIRE

Tourist Information Centre, Council Offices, Town Hall (01625) 504114.

Until fairly recently, what Macclesfield mainly did was make silk, and today a self-guiding trail will pilot you round the town's substantial heritage of silk mills and workshops. The first mill was opened in 1756. The last to close was Paradise Mill, in Park Lane, where the last handloom shop in the town shut down in 1981 and the last handloom weaver went into retirement. It is now a museum, concentrating on the 1930s period in its history. At the heritage centre, in Roe Street, you can learn more about the story of the town and, unusually, about the history of the Sunday School movement. The West Park Museum in Prestbury Road has Egyptian antiquities, English 19th-century paintings and some work by Charles Tunnicliffe, the brilliant animal and bird artist, who was born in Macclesfield.

IN EASY REACH Going north from Macclesfield you come to Adlington Hall, home for centuries of the Legh family, where the house's 16th-century black-and-white half-timbering marries happily with its 18th-century brick south front. The scars of a Roundhead attack during the Civil War are still visible. Among the treasures inside are family portraits, the 15th-century Great Hall and an organ that Handel played.

Back to the south-east of Macclesfield, there is impressively wild country to explore among the Pennine foothills, in what was once an outlaw-haunted forest. Guided walks are available during the summer at Tegg's Nose Country Park, and good walking and birdwatching around the reservoirs in the Bollin Valley.

---- 278 ----

MALHAM
NORTH YORKSHIRE

On a minor road, off the A65.
Tourist Information Centres: 9 Sheep Street, Skipton (01756) 792809 and Town Hall,
Cheapside, Settle (01729) 825192.

Magnificent views can be enjoyed from the top of the great cliff of Malham Cove. Its dissected surface is the result of rain water gradually widening fissures in the limestone. These channels are known as grikes, and the blocks left in between as clints

The Malham area is a honeypot for geographers and geologists, both amateur and professional, and one of the main attractions, Gordale Scar, is reached by a footpath, 2 miles north-east of the village. It is a narrow, almost vertical gorge bisecting a 300ft limestone cliff, into which the Gordale Beck tumbles in a picturesque waterfall (provided the weather has not been unduly dry). There is a second fall called Janet's Foss, at the mouth of the gorge. A mile or so to the west is another great limestone cliff, Malham Cove, curving round to form an amphitheatre. Aeons ago the River Aire thundered over it in a fall to outdo Niagara, but today a stream issues meekly, if mysteriously, from the foot of the cliff. On top of Malham Cove is a weird 'moonscape' area of cracked and fissured limestone pavement. Further north lies Malham Tarn, a quiet 150-acre lake owned by the National Trust, with a nature trail along its shore. From here Settle is 5 miles to the west over the moors, or there is a fine moorland walk eastwards along the old drove road called Mastiles Lane, 6 miles to Kilnsey.

IN EASY REACH There is an information centre for the Yorkshire Dales National Park in Malham, and another visitor centre is to the east, at Grassington, on the B6265. The National Park embraces 680 square miles of marvellous walking and driving country, with more than 1,000 miles of footpaths traversing the high moors and their scenery of drystone walls, stone barns, isolated farms and secluded villages, their spectacular caves and waterfalls, and the major dales themselves: Swaledale, Wensleydale, Wharfedale and Ribblesdale.

---------- 279 ----------

NANTWICH
CHESHIRE

Tourist Information Centre, Beam Street (01270) 623914.

If you want to find out all about farmhouse Cheshire cheese and its making, head for the local museum in Pillory Street, Nantwich, as the town is at the centre of a prosperous dairying district. The museum will also tell you about Nantwich's past history as a leading salt-producing town (it still has a brine swimming pool) and about the catastrophic fire of 1583 which, fanned by a fierce west wind, burned down almost the entire place to the ground. Much to our advantage today, the town was promptly rebuilt by public subscription, so it is packed with black-and-white Elizabethan half-timbered buildings. There is good Georgian architecture as well, and the 2-mile town trail provides a chance to view a hundred or more buildings of interest.

IN EASY REACH Just to the north at Henhull, is the Hire Cruiser Base of the British Waterways Board. Here you can hire a narrowboat for cruising on the historic Shropshire Union Canal, which runs north to the canal museum at Ellesmere Port, and south by Audlem and Market Drayton to link up with the West Midlands canal network.

Just to the south-east of Nantwich, on the A51, are Stapeley Water Gardens, which claim to be the largest water garden centre in Europe. Stocked with landscaped pool layouts, fountains, aquatic plants and ornaments, and goldfish by the thousand, it has a lavish aquarium and a musical fountain with synchronised water patterns. Further on along the A51, 6 miles from Nantwich, Bridgemere Garden World is another gardening colossus, with the biggest display of house plants in Europe and 25 acres of trees, shrubs and borders, while in Bridgemere Wildlife Park it is tigers, wolves, monkeys, parrots and birds of prey you admire.

---------- 280 ----------

NEWCASTLE UPON TYNE
TYNE AND WEAR

Tourist Information Centres: Central Library, Princess Square 0191-261 0691, Central Station, Neville Street 0191-230 0030 and Newcastle Airport, Woolsington, Northumberland 0191-271 1929.

Newcastle's pride and joy is its quiver of bridges over the Tyne: the Tyne Bridge of 1928, whose single arch soars 190ft above high water; the Swing Bridge of 1876; Robert Stephenson's High Level Bridge of 1849; and the King Edward Bridge of 1906. The latest one carries the Metro rapid-transit system. The Victorians drove their railway smack through the castle (whose battlements command a marvellous view) to the handsome station, by John Dobson. Dobson was also the principal architect in the redevelopment of the city centre in the 1830s, which created the noble Regency curve of Grey Street. At the top is a high column to Lord Grey of the Reform Bill. The church of St Nicholas, made a cathedral in 1882, has a glorious 15th-century crown spire. Worthwhile galleries and museums include the Laing Art Gallery, Higham Place, with paintings by John Martin in a fine collection of British 19th- and 20th-century art, as well as silver, glass and pottery; the University Museum of Antiquities and the Hancock Museum, which has natural history displays and fossil collections. Newcastle Discovery, in Blandford Square, is also well worth a visit.

IN EASY REACH At Jarrow on the south bank of the Tyne, 7 miles east from Newcastle, is St Paul's Church, lonely and remote, with a Saxon window of 681 containing the oldest stained glass in Europe. Bede lived and worked in the monastery here, and there is a model of it and finds from the site at Bedes World up the hill. Other monastic ruins can be seen at the mouth of the Tyne, 9 miles east of Newcastle on the A1058. Here the remains of Tynemouth Castle and Priory overlook the resort of Tynemouth.

The Hoppings

Visitors to Newcastle late in June can enjoy the fun of the largest travelling fair in Europe, with all the usual rides and stalls, a big wheel, dodgems and the rest, on the Town Moor. The fair begins on the day of the Lord Mayor's Parade, when decorated floats process through the city streets. It is called The Hoppings – hopping being an old English word for a country festival or dance – and has a very unusual origin. It was started in 1882 as the North of England Temperance Festival, by local temperance organisations worried about the ill health, crime and violence caused by indulgence in alcohol. The idea was to demonstrate that people could enjoy themselves and have a thoroughly good time without any need to drink, and you still can't buy alcohol at The Hoppings.

---------- 281 ----------

NOSTELL PRIORY
WEST YORKSHIRE

On the A638, 6 miles south-east of Wakefield.
Tourist Information Centre, Town Hall, Wood Street, Wakefield (01924) 295000/295001

In 1733 an inexperienced architect only 19 years old was commissioned to build a new house for the wealthy Winn family. Seven years later young James Paine had produced one of the most magnificent stately homes in West Yorkshire – a tremendous Georgian pile of a house. Today Paine's façade is still intact, as are some of his gorgeously decorated rooms. Others are later additions by Robert Adam. Furnishings in the house are sumptuous and there is a wonderful collection of Chippendale furniture made specially for Nostell Priory. Paintings on show include works by Holbein, Brueghel, and Hogarth.

The 25-acre grounds have three lakes and a deer park, and on the edge you'll find Wragby church, opposite the site of the original 12th-century priory. Look inside at the beautiful 16th- to 18th-century Swiss glass.

IN EASY REACH Visitors to Wakefield can see and admire its handsome high-spired 15th-century cathedral, its 14th-century Bridge Chapel perched on the graceful medieval bridge which crosses the River Calder, its City Museum of local history, and its Art Gallery, which houses an important collection of 20th-century art. At Horbury, south-west of Wakefield on the A642, you can see the classical 18th-century church built and paid for by John Carr who was born in the town and is buried in its church. The hymn *Onward Christian Soldiers* was written by a curate of Horbury and was first sung here.

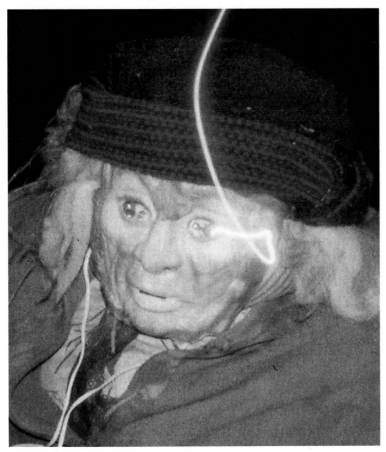

Burning of Bartle

*O*n the Saturday nearest 24 August, which is St Bartholomew's Day, a large and ugly effigy of 't'owd Bartle'. a gruesome object with eyes that light up (see left) is carried roud the village of West Witton, 10 miles south-west of Richmond. At intervals a verse is chanted, beginning, 'At Pen Hill crags he tore his rags, at Hunter's Thorn he blew his horn' and ending, 'at Grassgill End he made his end'. The effigy too, duly comes to its end, burned on a bonfire in Grassgill Lane. Who 't'owd Bartle' is supposed to be is not clear – a robber, a giant or a forest spirit according to various explanations – nor is the connection with St Bartholomew understood.

─── 282 ───

RICHMOND
NORTH YORKSHIRE

Tourist Information Centre, Friary Gardens, Victoria Road (01748) 850252.

The ruins of Richmond Castle pose dramatically above the swift River Swale on a high crag. The keep, 100ft high, dates from the 1170s, but the oldest parts of the fortress go back a century earlier and the Great Hall, dated about 1080, is one of the oldest surviving of its kind in the country. The town, which grew up under the castle's wing, is itself high above the river. There are attractive 18th- and 19th-century buildings, and you can see the home of the original 'sweet lass of Richmond Hill'. The Georgian Theatre Royal, built in 1788, is one of the two oldest in Britain. The history of the area is explained in the Richmondshire Museum, Ryder's Wynd, and in the former Holy Trinity Church is the museum of one of the oldest and most distinguished regiments in the British army, the Green Howards.

IN EASY REACH Richmond is an excellent base for exploring Swaledale, and delightful walks from the town include one to the ruins of Easby Abbey on the river's bank. Constable Burton Hall, to the south on the A684, was built by John Carr in the 1780s. At Middleham, a few miles further south on the A6108, the great Norman keep of Middleham Castle rises in grandeur: this was a favourite home of Richard III. The romantic ruins of Jervaulx Abbey are 4 miles east from here, also on th A6108.

Kilburn Feast

At Kilburn, to the south-west of Rievaulx, in July each year a boisterous four-day sport gala and general revel occurs. Events include races for children, a long-distance race over 4 ½ miles, and games of quoits, which is still a popular Yorkshire pastime. There is also an open-air service on the Sunday. The final evening sees a survival of what was once the widespread custom of electing a mock mayor, to make fun of authority. The 'lord mayor' of Kilburn is wheeled about in a handcart, arbitrarily fining people for any offences that occur to him, while his 'lady mayoress' – a man in woman's clothes – chases the women and kisses as many as he can catch.

283

RIEVAULX ABBEY
NORTH YORKSHIRE

Off the B1257, 2 miles west of Helmsley.
Tourist Information Centres: Sutton Bank (01845) 597426 and Thirsk Museum, 16
Kirkgate, Thirsk (01845) 522755.

Perhaps the most enchanting of England's ruined abbeys, Rievaulx sleeps in lonely Ryedale: a place, as its third abbot St Aelred, said, of peace, serenity and 'a marvellous freedom from the tumult of the world'. The shrine of the first abbot, St William, can be seen in the church. Thirteen Cistercian monks from France settled here in 1132, and in 15 years their number grew to 140, but when the abbey was dissolved in 1538 there were only 22. Much of the church is still standing, with substantial remains of the chapter house and refectory. To the south, and in the hands of the National Trust, is a long terrace constructed in 1758 by a local landowner to provide heart-wrenching views of the abbey and the dale. A classical temple stands at each end.

IN EASY REACH To the west and north are the Hambleton Hills and the Cleveland Hills, in the North York Moors National Park. The Cleveland Way Long Distance Footpath starts from Helmsley, which has an impressive ruined castle. West along the A170 is Sutton Bank, with a sweeping view across the Yorkshire Plain to the distant Pennines. There is a National Park Information Centre here. Off to the south is the village of Kilburn, known for its woodworking workshop, whose products are 'signed' with a mouse. On the hillside above is the 18th-century Kilburn White Horse. To the south-east and in close proximity to one another are the ruins of Byland Abbey; the delightful and little-changed house, Shandy Hall, in Coxwold, where Laurence Sterne lived in the 1760s and wrote part of *Tristram Shandy*; and Newburgh Priory, where the headless body of Oliver Cromwell is said to be kept in secret by his descendants.

284

SOUTHPORT
MERSEYSIDE

Tourist Information Centre, 112 Lord Street (01704) 533333.

Since the 1820s, tree-lined Lord Street with its smart shops, gardens and fountains has been the centrepiece of Southport, which is also equipped with miles of sandy beach, an amusement park, a zoo and a battery of distinguished golf courses led by Royal Birkdale. British art from the 18th century can be seen in the Atkinson Art Gallery, Lord Street, and there are special events when engines are in steam at the Southport Railway Centre in Derby Road. In the botanic gardens in Churchtown there is an interesting little museum specialising in the history of Southport and the Victorian period.

IN EASY REACH To the south are miles of tangled sand dunes and the Ainsdale Nature Reserve, home to the rare natterjack toad and sand lizard, while 10 miles south-east of Southport, off the A570 and across the Lancashire border, the Wildfowl Trust owns a bird reserve at Martin Mere. Further east, off the A59, lies Rufford Old Hall, owned by the National Trust, and glamorous in its ornate black-and-white timbering. It dates from the 16th century, with a 17th century wing, and has a remarkable Great Hall with a hammerbeam roof, arms and armour, and fine oak furniture.

Ambleside rush-bearing

Up until the 19th century the floors of churches were generally of beaten earth or stone flags, covered over with rushes. Fresh rushes were brought in once a year, often with considerable ceremony and merry-making, on the day of the saint to whom the church was dedicated. As wooden floors were installed in churches in Victorian times, the custom was abandoned, but it has survived in a few places. One of them is Ambleside, where, on the first Saturday in July, garlands of rushes and flowers, fastened to frames in various shapes, are carried through the town in a procession of grown-ups and children accompanied by the town band. The garlands are taken to the church, where a special service is held. The children, by tradition, are rewarded with gingerbread.

285

LAKE WINDERMERE
CUMBRIA

Tourist Information Centres: The Glebe, Bowness-on-Windermere (015394) 42895, The
Gateway Centre, Victoria Street, Windermere (015394) 46499 and Old Courthouse,
Church Street, Ambleside (015394) 32582.

England's largest lake is the starting point of most visits to the Lake District. Windermere is 10½ miles long from north to south, with a ring of mountains rising majestically above its northern end, and only a little over a mile across at the widest point. In summer the water swarms with boats and water-skiers. Far and away the best method of seeing it is by steamer from Lake Side, Bowness or Waterhead, taking about 2½ hours for a complete journey along the lake and back again.

The A592 runs up the eastern side of the lake, through Bowness, essentially a Victorian resort with quaint narrow streets which are busy in the summer with anglers, sailors, holidaymakers and walkers. The Windermere Steamboat Museum, Rayrigg Road, has a unique display of Victorian and Edwardian steamboats, many of which are still afloat and in working order.

Keeping on the A592 and going north, you can veer away from the lake to Troutbeck, to visit Townend, a 17th-century farmhouse occupied for generations by the Browne family. Its original furnishings and family possessions open a window on old-style lakeland life.

Taking the other fork, the A591 stays closer to the lake. There is a lovely view of it from the Lake District National Park Visitor Centre at Brockhole, set among waterside gardens and with full information about the park. The A591 goes on north to Ambleside, where there's a memorial chapel to Wordsworth in the Victorian church. Off the road here is Stagshaw (limited opening only), a beautiful hillside garden belonging to the National Trust.

286

WORDSWORTH COUNTRY
CUMBRIA

Around Grasmere, off the A591, north-west of Ambleside.
Tourist Information Centre, Red Bank Road, Grasmere (015394) 35245.

Dove Cottage – William Wordsworth's home for nine years

●

Grasmere Sports

Traditional Cumberland and Westmorland wrestling bouts (see below) are among the attractions of the 'Old English Games' at Grasmere, which bring thousands of spectators to the area every August. The games certainly date back to 1852, and may well be a great deal older, though whether they go all the way back to Viking times, as is sometimes claimed, is open to question. Besides the wrestling, there is a fell race to the top of Butter Crag and back again (up in 10 arduous minutes or so, down in a flying three minutes), hound and puppy trails, and numerous other races, track events and cycle races, with money prizes for the winners.

●

William Wordsworth was born in the Lake District, at Cockermouth in 1770, went to school there at the 16th-century Hawkshead grammar school, spent most of his adult life there, died there in 1850, and is buried there, in Grasmere churchyard. This beautiful area inspired much of his poetry. A tireless walker, he ranged it ceaselessly on foot and wrote a pioneering guidebook to the Lakes, which is still of interest.

Grasmere and Rydal Water are the two lakes most closely associated with the poet. Grasmere he called 'the loveliest spot man ever found', and his home at Dove Cottage, where he lived from 1799 to 1808, with his sister Dorothy and his wife Mary, is now the principal shrine to him. Many of his possessions are preserved here, and there is a Wordsworth Museum close by.

In 1813 the Wordsworths went to live, for the rest of their lives as it proved, at Rydal Mount, a couple of miles away (off the A591). This is a delightful house, with many family belongings, and you can enjoy the great man's garden and share the view he loved of tranquil Rydal Water, at the foot of 2,000ft Rydal Fell. The graves of all three Wordsworths and the poet's much-loved daughter Dora are in Grasmere churchyard.

There is scenery of an epic grandeur in all directions. North of Grasmere, the A591 runs through high fells to Thirlmere, below Helvellyn. From Ambleside westwards the A593 and B5343 penetrate the beautiful valley of Langdale with the great wall of the Langdale Pikes towering above it. South-west , the A593 runs to the high lake of Tarn Hows and on to Coniston Water, dominated by Coniston Old Man which rises to 2,633ft.

287

BLACKPOOL
LANCASHIRE

Tourist Information Centres: 1 Clifton Street (01253) 21623, 87a Coronation Street (01253) 21891, Terminal Building, Blackpool Airport (01253) 343434 and The Square, Lytham St Anne's (01253) 725610.

The Illuminations and other Blackpool events

There is nothing shy or retiring about Blackpool and they don't do things there by halves. From early September to early November close to 500,000 light bulbs go on every night as the famous Illuminations clothe the whole promenade and the Tower – for a long time the tallest construction in Britain – with ribbons of shimmering light, tableaux and moving figures and scenes, all reflected in the water of the silent sea. Lively events earlier in Blackpool's season include various dance festivals, bowls competitions and early in June, the Manchester to Blackpool run for veteran and vintage cars.

Eighteen million visitors a year flock to the 'fun city' of the North, to revel in its 7 miles of sandy beach, its seafront trams and its brash and cheerful abundance of piers, ballrooms, theatres, night-spots and amusement parks. From donkey rides to roller-coasters, from the circus to the zoo, from the waxworks to the 'indoor seaside' of the Sandcastle leisure pool (just in case of rain), Blackpool has the lot. After the coming of the railways in the 1840s which made it possible for the people of the northern industrial towns to reach the seaside, Blackpool developed and equipped itself with no less than three piers and the famous 518ft-high Blackpool Tower. Built in 1894, it has staggering views from the top and a circus and ballroom at the base.

The quieter side of the town can be enjoyed in the gardens of Stanley Park, famous for roses and chrysanthemums, or in the Grundy Art Gallery, Queen Street, with British paintings and a collection of ivories.

IN EASY REACH A stone's throw to the south on the A584, is the quieter resort of Lytham St Anne's, with sandy beaches and dunes, pleasant parks and a notable clutch of golf courses. There are steam galas at the Motive Power Museum, which displays engines, aeroplanes and cars.

288

CASTLE HOWARD
NORTH YORKSHIRE

Off the A64, 5 miles south-west of Malton.
Tourist Information Centres: Old Town Hall, Market Place, Malton (01653) 600048 (seasonal opening only) and De Grey Rooms, Exhibition Square, York (01904) 621756.

When his house burned down in 1693, Charles Howard, Earl of Carlisle, engaged a successful playwright of his acquaintance to build him a new one. The playwright, who had no previous experience as an architect, was John Vanbrugh, and the house is one of the most spectacularly palatial in Britain: domed, pillared and porticoed in colossal Baroque splendour, festooned with urns, statues and amazing fountains, and familiar from *Brideshead Revisited* on television. The marble entrance hall, lit by the dome, is 70ft high and 52ft square, and the wings are big enough to be grand mansions by themselves. The house contains a wealth of paintings, statues, tapestries, furniture and porcelain, and is set in a superb 1,000-acre park, with avenues 5 miles long, obelisks and other eye-catchers. The stables, designed by John Carr, are home to one of the best costume collections in the country.

IN EASY REACH Castle Howard is idyllically placed between two beautiful areas of countryside, the Howardian Hills to the west and the Yorkshire Wolds to the east. At Sheriff Hutton to the south-west, off the A64, are the ruins of a 14th-century castle with Richard III associations. Off the other side of the A64 are the ruins of Kirkham Priory. Finally, back in Malton, the museum in the town hall has a good prehistoric and Roman collection.

289
CONISBROUGH CASTLE
SOUTH YORKSHIRE

Off the A630, 5 miles south-west of Doncaster.
Tourist Information Centre, Central Library, Waterdale, Doncaster (01302) 734309.

One of the jewels in English Heritage's crown, the great white circular keep of Conisbrough rears up spectacularly above the River Don, with sweeping views of the surrounding mining and industrial area. It was built about 1190, for Hamelin Plantagenet, the illegitimate half-brother of Henry II, and Sir Walter Scott brought it fame in *Ivanhoe*. Much of the church of St Peter in the village was built at the same time as the castle. Inside the church is a remarkable Norman tomb-chest which is covered with patterns and scenes.

IN EASY REACH Doncaster's delight is the Mansion House in the High Street, a handsome classical construction of 1748 by James Paine. The imposing church of St George, with its 170ft tower, was built in the 1850s by Sir George Gilbert Scott. The St Leger is run at Doncaster and the town museum in Chequer Road has material on horse-racing, as well as a good Roman collection, Yorkshire pottery and Dutch paintings. The industry, agriculture and social history of the area are illuminated at the Museum of South Yorkshire Life in Cusworth Park on the northern outskirts of town.

290
DERWENT WATER
CUMBRIA

Tourist Information Centre, Moot Hall, Market Square, Keswick (017687) 72645.

Bordered by woods and crags, with the great bulk of Skiddaw shouldering into the sky to the north, island-studded Derwent Water is one of the loveliest stretches of water in Britain. There are boat trips on the lake, and you can walk right round it: it's 3 miles long by a mile wide. The National Trust protects most of the land here, including two good viewpoints near the north-eastern bank. One is Friar's Crag, with a memorial to John Ruskin and a nature trail. The other is Castle Head, a wooded 500ft hill just to the east of the B5289, which runs close to the lake's eastern shore.

To the east of Keswick, a minor road off the A591 leads to the Castlerigg Circle, an eerie prehistoric stone circle in a setting of magical beauty. On the western shore of Derwent Water, south of Portinscale, Lingholm Gardens nestle among the woods. South of the lake is the lovely valley of Borrowdale – beyond its spectacular gateway the Jaws of Borrowdale – with Scafell to the south.

Northwards, the A591 runs up close to Bassenthwaite Lake, which can be seen to advantage from the grounds of Mirehouse, a 17th-century manor house with many relics of Wordsworth, Tennyson and Southey. West of the lake, the A66 runs to Cockermouth, where Wordsworth's birthplace is open to pilgrims.

Near the head of Derwent Water, Keswick is a Victorian town which makes a useful base for exploring the northern Lake District. The museum in Fitz Park is strong on geology and on famous writers of this area, and there is a National Trust Visitor Centre in Packhorse Court. Keswick is well known for making pencils, and one 7ft long can be seen in the Pencil Museum, Greta Bridge.

Derwent Water – often referred to as the Queen of the Lakes. A scheduled boat service operates on the lake from Easter to November. Round trips take just under an hour and there are seven stop-off points en route

FLAMBOROUGH HEAD

HUMBERSIDE

Off the B1255, 4 miles north-east of Bridlington.
Tourist Information Centres: 25 Prince Street, Bridlington (01262) 673474 and St
Nicholas Cliff, Scarborough, North Yorkshire (01723) 373333.

The cliffs at Flamborough Head. They mark the northernmost point at which chalk occurs in Britain

●

Events in Scarborough

As the cricketing season draws to its autumn close, lovers of the game can watch it take an enjoyable final fling in Scarborough, where the Cricket Festival in September brings together the Yorkshire side and visiting teams for matches in the spirit in which the game ought to be played. The festival started over a century ago in 1871, with a match between Lord Londesborough's XI and The Visitors, and became firmly established in the calendar largely as a result of the support of Lord Hawke, then the leading figure in Yorkshire county cricket and afterwards captain of the Yorkshire county side and President of the MCC.

Round at the other side of the year, hundreds of people gather at Scarborough to skip on the promenade on Shrove Tuesday. This is a survival of an old custom, when the local fishermen used to bring long ropes and swing them while people skipped over them.

●

The spectacular chalk cliffs which tower up 400ft and more above the sea from Flamborough Head northwards towards Bempton provide a home for England's largest seabird breeding colony, culminating in the RSPB reserve at Bempton Cliffs. The only mainland colony of gannets is here, but they are dwarfed in numbers by thousands upon thousands of kittiwakes and herring gulls. Guillemots, shags and puffins may also be seen, and corn buntings nest on top of the cliffs, where the wildflowers grow. Flamborough itself was a fort in the Iron Age, defended by an earthwork. In Flamborough church, 2 miles inland, interesting monuments include a gruesome one to Sir Marmaduke Constable, who died in 1520, his heart allegedly eaten away by a toad he had swallowed.

IN EASY REACH Bridlington is a seaside resort with a sandy beach, an old priory church and a local history museum in Bayle Gate. Between Flamborough and Bridlington is Sewerby Hall, which dates from 1720 and stands in 500 acres of gardens. In the house is a room dedicated to the memory of Amy Johnson, the flyer.

Going north from Flamborough, across the border into North Yorkshire, is Filey, another sandy-beached resort, with splendid coastal views from the reef called Filey Brigg. Seven miles further north on the A165, Scarborough is the principal resort on Yorkshire's coast. The ruined castle is perched up on a rocky bluff between the two main beaches and the town is known for its wealth of attractive parks and gardens, and its theatres and lively amusement park. The history of this spa turned bathing resort can be explored in the Rotunda, Vernon Road and Millenium on the harbourside. Other local attractions include mementoes of the Sitwells in their former home at Wood End, The Crescent, and the art gallery with work by Lord Leighton, who was born here.

292

GAWTHORPE HALL
LANCASHIRE

At Padiham, 3 miles west of Burnley.
Tourist Information Centre, Manchester Road, Burnley (01282) 455485.

The house as it stands today is largely the creation of Sir Charles Barry and A W Pugin (who worked together on the Houses of Parliament in London), and the principal rooms have been restored as closely as possible to their 1850s state. Some fine plasterwork and panelling remains from the original house, built early in the 17th century for the Shuttleworth family, and there is a magnificent 100ft long gallery at the top of the house, where portraits on loan from the National Portrait Gallery are hung. Be sure to see the delightful objects from the textile collection, from waistcoats to bonnets. The 17th-century stables, and estate buildings have been adapted to house craft workshops and a gallery, shop and restaurant.

IN EASY REACH From the windows of the house looking northwards you can see Pendle Hill, a conspicuous landmark and viewpoint, associated with the Pendle witches, executed in Lancaster in 1612. In Burnley you can experience Queen Street Mill at Harle Syke, with its hundreds of clattering looms in a preserved steam-powered cotton mill, and the Canal Tollhouse Heritage Centre, Manchester Road, on the Leeds and Liverpool Canal. Both these attractions close at the end of September. Also of interest are the period rooms, interior decoration and art objects at Towneley Hall, on the A671 to the south of the town. In Accrington, close by to the south-west, the Haworth Art Gallery in Manchester Road has an unusual collection of Tiffany glass.

293

HARROGATE
NORTH YORKSHIRE

Tourist Information Centre, Royal Baths Assembly Rooms, Crescent Road
(01423) 525666.

In the 18th and 19th centuries and up until the 1930s, Harrogate was the queen of the northern spas and a smart holiday resort. It is still much enjoyed for its civilised atmosphere, its shops and hotels, its gardens and sumptuous flower shows. You can try the water of the old Sulphur Well in the Royal Pump Room of 1842, which is now a museum, and admire antiquities from Greece, Rome and Egypt in the Mercer Art Gallery in Swan Road. A mile or so out on the B6162 are Harlow Carr Botanical Gardens.

IN EASY REACH Three miles north-west on the A61, Ripley Castle is an engaging place with a priest's hole and Civil War armour, the home of the Ingilbys since the 14th century. To the north-east of Harrogate is Knaresborough, sited in the gorge of the River Nidd, with the 14th-century castle ruins (limited opening in the autumn) looking down on the town and the railway viaduct striding across. There is England's oldest chemist's shop in the market place, walks and boating along the river, and caves to explore.

294

HOLMFIRTH
WEST YORKSHIRE

Tourist Information Centre, 49/51 Huddersfield Road (01484) 687603.

Few places have been made a star by television as remarkably as this scraggy Yorkshire town on the River Holme, the setting for *Last of the Summer Wine*. Coachloads arrive now to tread the narrow streets in the footsteps of Foggy, Clegg and Compo, to eye Sid's Cafe and Nora Batty's house on the 'Summer Wine' trail, and to explore the craft and antiques shops which have sprung up to meet the demand. An engaging attraction here is the nostalgic Postcard Museum in the public library. The cards include the naughty seaside type and many ingenious novelties.

IN EASY REACH Viewers of the television series will know that there is fine scenery to explore in this area on the Peak District's edge, with walks by the Digley, Ramsden and Brownhill Reservoirs near Holme, or on the Marsden Moors. At Marsden, just off the A62, the Canal and Countryside Centre on the old Huddersfield Narrow Canal recalls canal life.

Huddersfield itself is 7 miles to the north-east on the A62, a hilly town, distinguished for its famous choral society and its huge and magnificent railway station in the classical style. There are marvellous views from the Jubilee Tower on Castle Hill, a worthwhile collection in the art gallery in Princess Alexandra Walk, and local material in the Tolson Memorial Museum, Ravensknowle Park.

Floral Extravaganzas

Harrogate thinks of itself as 'Britain's floral town;' and justly prides itself on its parks and flower gardens, in ironic contrast to its earlier reputation as 'the stinking spa' because of the infernal smell of its sulphur-laden springs. Fitting in with the town's modern image are the annual floral extravaganzas, one of which is the Great Autumn Flower Show in September, when leading nurseries create breathtaking spectacles of dahlias and chrysanthemums, gladioli and carnations, roses, begonias and cacti. There is an equally spectacular Spring Flower Show at the end of April, and events in the town during the summer include the Great Yorkshire Agricultural Show in July and the International Festival of music and the arts at the turn of July and August.

Musical Events in Huddersfield and Holmfirth

An unusual and challenging occasion is the 10-day Contemporary Music Festival at Huddersfield in November. Held yearly since 1978, the festival has established itself as one of the leading international arenas for new music, and includes lectures, discussions and exhibitions. There is usually a special workshop and concert for children.

Earlier in the year, in May, there is something rather more light-hearted in Holmfirth - the festival of folk music and folk dance. This has been going on since 1979, with concerts, ceilidhs, dance displays and workshops. About a quarter of the events are open to amateur performers.

295

HULL
HUMBERSIDE

Tourist Information Centres: Central Library, Albion Street (01482) 223344, King George Dock, Hedon Road (01482) 702118 and (01482) 223559.

Officially Hull is the name of the little river which joins the mighty Humber here, and the city is Kingston upon Hull, but whatever you call it, the place is rich in unexpected attractions. A busy port, it has an engrossing and taxing maritime heritage trail through a history which goes back to the 13th century. Rising in majesty in the old town area is the 150ft tower of Holy Trinity Church, one of the largest parish churches in England.

The haunting singing of whales in the deep echoes through the whaling galleries of the Town Docks Museum, Queen Victoria Square, which provides a fascinating account of Hull's involvement in whaling, trawling and ship-building, and has one of the world's best collections of scrimshaw (pictures on whalebone). Close by, you can steep yourself in another aspect of Hull's maritime past, in the Ferens Art Gallery, whose beautifully displayed treasures include marine paintings by John Ward and other artists of the Hull School. In the Wilberforce Museum, High Street, there are displays on the slave trade in the house where William Wilberforce was born in 1759. Also in High Street is Streetlife Museum of Transport – Hull's newest and noisiest museum which covers over 150 years of transport. The displays include a recreation of a Georgian courtyard, Britain's oldest tram, and Bicycle City which explores the city's strong cycling tradition.

A little way to the west of the town, but also worth visiting because it is so impressive is the huge and graceful Humber Bridge. Opened in 1981, this carries the A15 across the Humber and is 1,410 metres long.

296

MANCHESTER
GREATER MANCHESTER

Tourist Information Centres: Town Hall Extension, Lloyd Street 0161-234 3157 and Manchester International Airport 0161-436 3344.

Britain's most famous pub. (The Rovers', for those not familiar with Coronation Street)

●

Manchester Festival

Manchester's festival has been an annual occasion only since 1985, and before that happened every other year. With a carnival which draws a crowd of 80,000 people, the festival, in early September, features a lively range of classical and popular music, folk music and jazz, folk dance, comedy and cabaret, drama, mime, puppetry, film and the visual arts. Four out of five of the performers are professionals, but one of the festival's aims is to encourage local artists.

●

Covering some 45 square miles at the hub of a jumble of congested industrial districts, Manchester is essentially a great Victorian city, the metropolis of the Lancashire cotton industry. The opening of the Ship Canal in 1894 made Manchester, though well inland, an important port. It was also a major cultural and intellectual centre in the 19th century and a powerhouse of radical political ideas.

The parish church near the River Irwell, was made a cathedral in 1847 and is famous for its superb canopied choir stalls. There are masses of other beautiful things to see among Manchester's wealth of museums and galleries, headed by the City Art Gallery in Mosley Street. Designed in Greek Revival style by Sir Charles Barry in the 1820s, it is rich in British paintings and has outstanding sculpture, ceramics, glass, silver and furniture. Ranking second only to it is the Whitworth Art Gallery in Oxford Road, with its English watercolours, drawings and prints, and a superlative textile collection. Also in Oxford Road is Manchester Museum with dinosaurs, Egyptian mummies and Japanese material.

The Greater Manchester Museum of Science and Industry, Liverpool Road, housed in the world's first passenger railway station, is an exciting storehouse of things which actually work and steam and turn: ranging from steam locomotives and giant mill engines through textile and paper-making machines to cars and computers. For those who prefer books, there is the John Ryland Library in Deansgate, while devotees of the 'soaps' can stroll down Coronation Street and even into the Rovers' on a Granada Studios Tour.

All this hardly requires you to leave the city centre. If you have time to spare, the suburbs have many fine museums too. They range from a Jewish Museum at Cheetham Hill Road to a football museum at Manchester United's Old Trafford grounds, and from costumes at Platt Hall, Rusholme, to buses at the Museum of Transport in Boyle Street, Cheetham.

297

NORTH OF ENGLAND
OPEN-AIR MUSEUM
CO DURHAM

At Beamish, off the A693, near Chester-le-Street.
Tourist Information Centres: Market Place, Durham 0191-384 3720 and Central Library, Prince Consort Road, Gateshead, Tyne and Wear 0191-477 3478.

From liquorice all-sorts to Cherry Blossom shoe polish to trams and a stuffed champion whippet, the Beamish museum vividly recaptures the feel and flavour of ordinary people's everyday life in the north-east of England 50 to 100 years ago. Part of a town has been reconstructed. There is a park with a Victorian bandstand and drinking fountain, a 19th-century terrace of houses – you can explore one which has been fitted up as a dentist's – and shops, including a Co-op stocked with goods of the 1920s. There's a splendid pub, the Sun, brought here from Bishop Auckland, and stables where giant Clydesdale brewery horses can be admired. Elsewhere in the museum's 200 acres are a working farm with animals, a row of miners' cottages furnished in typical styles from the 1890s on, a country railway station of about 1910 and a colliery of the same period. You travel around by tram and there's plenty for the whole family to enjoy in one of Britain's most rewarding museums.

IN EASY REACH Across the border into Tyne and Wear is Gibside Chapel, off the A694 near Rowland's Gill. An avenue of oaks leads to the 18th-century chapel, designed by James Paine and now owned by the National Trust. In Washington, on the A1231, the Trust also owns Washington Old Hall (limited opening in autumn), a 17th-century manor house which was earlier the home of George Washington's ancestors, and near here, at Middle Barmston Farm, is the Washington Wildfowl Trust Park, with viewing hides. The imposing Greek temple outside Penshaw, on the A183, was erected in 1844 in memory of the 1st Earl of Durham, High Commissioner for Canada.

298
NORTON PRIORY
CHESHIRE

Off the A533 on the eastern outskirts of Runcorn.
Tourist Information Centre, 57/61 Church Street, Runcorn (01928) 576776.

Generations of 'black canons' lived, prayed and worshipped in the Augustinian priory at Norton in the four centuries of its existence. The only building still standing is the 12th-century undercroft, but in the 1970s one of the biggest archaeological digs of recent years uncovered the foundations of the buildings and much of the detail of the brethren's lives, from the bones of the beef joints they ate to a beautiful 11ft statue of St Christopher carrying the infant Christ on his shoulder. The modern museum displays the finds and illuminates the life of the priory.

The gardens of a house which stoood on the site until 1928 run down to the Duke of Bridgewater's pioneering canal, which cut through the grounds here in 1775, to the displeasure of the owners. There is a delightful stream glade, attractive summerhouses, and a Victorian rock garden.

IN EASY REACH Across the Mersey, Widnes is at the heart of an area given over to the giant tanks and twining pipes of huge chemical plants – an extremely impressive spectacle. The Catalyst Museum, Mersey Road, offers a unique insight into the industry and its effect on everyday life. You can follow this up nearby at Spike Island, on an industrial trail beside the Mersey.

East of Norton Priory, off the A56, is the village of Daresbury, where in 1832 a baby boy was christened Charles Lutwidge Dodgson. He is better known as Lewis Carroll, and there is an intriguing memorial window to him in All Saints' Church, showing the White Rabbit, the Mad Hatter and other Wonderland characters. Further east again, off the A559, is Arley Hall (closed after early October), an early Victorian house with exceptionally fine gardens. The twin herbaceous borders here are among the first ever planted.

●

Antrobus Soul Caking Play

*A*ll through the Middle Ages and down into modern times, the last night of October, Hallowe'en, was the night when the dead came back to visit their old homes. In some areas children used to go round begging for 'soul cakes', and in Cheshire groups of men, 'soulers' acted a mumming play in which there was a combat between good and evil. St George or King George was the hero and there was also a hobby horse involved, a man with a horse's skull, called Wild Horse or Dick. The custom is kept up by the soulers of Antrobus, a village off the A559 east of Runcorn, who act the play around the neighbourhood on Hallowe'en and during the next two weeks.

●

The delightful memorial window to Lewis Carroll (Charles Dodgson) in Daresbury's church. His father held the living there from 1827 to 1843

We have heard the children say Gentle children, whom we love | Long ago, on Christmas Day, Came a message from Above.

Egremont Crab Fair

The most celebrated and most extraordinary feature of the traditional Michaelmas Crab Fair at Egremont in September is the World Championship Gurning contest. Gurning is the ancient art of pulling faces through a horse collar, and the horrible contortions achieved by contenders of world class have to be seen to be believed. Cumberland wrestling, hound trails and terrier races, a greasy pole (see below), children's sports and street races also contribute to this ancient fair. Apples are thrown to the crowd, as a reminder of the largesse which the lord of Egremont used to bestow on his people in times

long gone by. They used to be crab-apples, which then tended to be used as ammunition in impromptu free-for-alls.

299

ST BEES HEAD
CUMBRIA

On the B5345.
Tourist Information Centres:12 Main Street, Egremont (01946) 820693 and Market Hall, Market Place, Whitehaven (01946) 695678.

From the red sandstone cliffs of this double headland on the Cumbrian coast you can see as far as the Isle of Man on a clear day. Closer at hand are views of thousands of wheeling and screaming kittiwakes and herring gulls, razorbills and guillemots, in one of the largest seabird colonies on the west coast. Puffins and rare black guillemots with red legs may be spotted in the RSPB reserve, or you may see ravens and stonechats. The village of St Bees, with its sandy beach and Norman priory church, is the starting (or finishing) point for the coast to coast walk, which goes all the way across England to Robin Hood's Bay on the Yorkshire shoreline.

IN EASY REACH Whitehaven, 4 miles north, has a past as a flourishing port, explored in the museum in the civic hall. A little way inland from St Bees is Egremont, with its romantic ruined castle high above the River Ehen and its famous Crab Fair in September. Going south on the A595, Ravenglass is on the Esk Estuary. The Ravenglass and Eskdale Railway runs steam trains here along a scenic 7-mile route, and there is also a railway museum.

300

SELBY ABBEY
NORTH YORKSHIRE

Tourist Information Centre, Park Street, Selby (01757) 703263.

Like a giant but beautiful cuckoo in the nest of the quite small town of Selby, the abbey church soars up in a glory of towers and pinnacles above its screen of trees. It has survived more than one disaster in 900 years: the central tower collapsed in 1690 and there was a disastrous fire in 1906. Each time it has been lovingly repaired.

The Benedictine abbey here was founded in 1069 by a runaway French monk, who brought with him a stolen finger of St Germain of Auxerre. Work on the church began about 1100 and went on for 250 years, and you can see the style changing from the simpler to the more elaborate. There are fine Norman doorways on the north and west sides. The great 14th-century east window still has some of its original glass. A new south transept was built in 1912 and the west towers were raised in height in 1935.

IN EASY REACH Huge power stations pouring out their smoke tend to dominate the views in this part of Yorkshire, and very impressive they are too. To the west of Selby, there are pleasant walks and picnic spots in Bishop Park. Lotherton Hall, on the B1217, about 11 miles west, is a delightful Edwardian house of charm and character, set among attractive gardens of the same period, and with a bird garden close by. An odd, rambling place, with a peculiar 'flying' staircase that shoots off in all directions, it contains a most engaging collection of High-Victorian furniture, paintings, modern furniture and ceramics, and a special collection of Chinese ceramics.

301

BRADFORD
WEST YORKSHIRE

Tourist Information Centre, National Museum of Photography, Film and TV, Pictureville (01274) 753678.

When the mills roared and sooty slums smothered the valley, Bradford was the greatest woollen market in the world. Today the old industries have decayed, the back-to-backs have vanished, and Bradford is promoting itself as a heritage centre for industrial Yorkshire.

High points of a Bradford tour must include the grand old Victorian City Hall, the marvellous Gothic-style Wool Exchange and the 14th- to-15th-century parish church which was transformed into a 20th-century cathedral in 1951. There are plenty of interesting museums, too – the National Museum of Film and Television, with its amazing Imax Cinema, the largest film screen in Britain; the Industrial Museum, with its four-storey mill and restored mill manager's house furnished in Edwardian style; Bolling Hall, a mainly 17th-century manor house with a medieval pele tower, and the Cartwright Memorial Hall, with its collection of paintings, drawings, sculptures and model engines.

IN EASY REACH Saltaire village, north-west of Bradford on the A650, is itself a fascinating little piece of industrial history. It was built in the 19th century by a Victorian industrialist and philanthropist Sir Titus Salt. Sir Titus had discovered a method for making alpaca fabric and he set up the first manufacturing plant as a model factory and created a workers' village.

302

CANNON HALL
SOUTH YORKSHIRE

*At Cawthorne, off the A635, 5 miles west of Barnsley.
Tourist Information Centre, 56 Eldon Street, Barnsley (01226) 206757.*

Glass rolling-pins and a 1930s Mabel Lucy Attwell teaset are ugly ducklings among the swans in this dignified 18th-century country mansion by John Carr. He remodelled it for the local squire, while the grounds were attractively landscaped in the 'Capability' Brown manner. Today it is a museum for Barnsley's collection of fine furniture, glass and ceramics, with Wedgwood and Doulton, Parian ware, and some delightful Art Nouveau pewter. Upstairs is the museum of the 13th/18th Hussars, two distinguished cavalry regiments which were amalgamated in 1922.

IN EASY REACH Barnsley is at the centre of the South Yorkshire coalfield and there are monuments here to the victims of pit disasters. The Cooper Art Gallery, Church Street, has a good collection of British watercolours. Worsborough Mill Museum, 2 miles to the south off the A61, has two working cornmills in a pleasant country park. The ruins of medieval Monk Bretton Priory are in the other direction, 2 miles to the north-east off the A628. Finally, you can see modern sculptures in an open-air setting at the Yorkshire Sculpture Park, north-west of Barnsley on the A637 at West Bretton, where the artists represented include Barbara Hepworth and Elisabeth Frink.

303

CAPTAIN COOK COUNTRY
CLEVELAND

Tourist Information Centre, 51 Corporation Road, Middlesbrough (01642) 2454532.

The great explorer was born in 1728, in a cottage at Marton, which is now part of Middlesbrough. The cottage is no longer there, but the Captain Cook Birthplace Museum, in Stewart Park close to the site, tells the story of his life and marks the start of the Captain Cook heritage trail. Displays include a mock-up of his cabin in the *Endeavour*, in which he sailed to New Zealand and Australia, and there is material from the places he explored on voyages which took him to the Americas and Africa, as well as the South Seas, where he was killed in Hawaii in 1779. In 1736 Cook's family moved to Great Ayton, a village south of Middlesbrough on the A172, and there is another museum in the school which he attended, and a monument to him up on Easby Moor. There are more museums and memorials in Whitby (see separate entry).

IN EASY REACH There is a particularly good railway museum in Darlington, 15 miles west of Middlesbrough on the A66. Housed in the North Road Station, which was built in 1842, its exhibits include the original *Locomotion No 1*, built by Robert Stephenson's company in the 1820s. Preston Hall Museum on the A135, 3 miles south of Stockton-on-Tees, also focuses on the 19th-century, with a reconstructed street and a blacksmith's forge.

●

Greatham Sword Dance

Sword dancing is an old tradition in the North-East and Yorkshire, often occurring at Christmas time and early in January, around Plough Monday. In Northumberland and Durham the traditional dance is the 'rapper' kind, which involves spectacularly rapid steps, intricate figures and short swords. At Greatham in Cleveland, on Boxing Day, the sword dancing is combined with a mumming play of the old kind, in which one of the characters is killed and brought back to life again: apparently symbolising the 'death' of nature in the winter and the promise of life returning in the new year ahead. The performance is put on at pubs and other places in the town.

●

304

FAIRBURN INGS
WEST YORKSHIRE

Off the A1, 2 miles north of Ferrybridge.
Tourist Information Centre, Town Hall, Wood Street, Wakefield (01924) 295000.

This must be Britain's most unusual nature reserve, run by the RSPB since 1976. The 'Ings' are flooded mining subsidence pits, and the reserve is surrounded by the smoke and clatter of collieries, power stations and railways. However, Fairburn Ings lies under a major flypath for migrating birds and attracts about 165 different species every year. In September an army of swallows assembles here. In winter the whooper swans arrive and in spring there are terns.

IN EASY REACH Close by to the south-west, off the M62, Castleford is a mining town, and the birthplace of sculptor Henry Moore. The museum in the public library has a small but select display of Casteleford pottery and glass, together with Roman finds, for there was once a Roman base here. At Pontefract, 3 miles south-east on the A639, are the ruins of the castle where Richard II was murdered in 1400. The museum in Salter Row has interesting material on the castle and the town, including the liquorice industry.

305

HADRIAN'S WALL
NORTHUMBERLAND

Tourist Information Centres: Hill Street, Corbridge (01434) 632815 (seasonal opening only) and Manor Office, Hallgate, Hexham (01434) 605225.

Still standing 6ft high in places, the Roman Wall is an imposing and evocative sight, especially where it swoops roller-coaster fashion over the crags of the Whin Sill ridge near Housesteads. It originally stood 20ft high to the top of the parapet, was 7½ ft thick, and ran for 73½ miles, with a ditch in front of it and military roads and another ditch behind.

The Wall is best seen one mile east of Housesteads Fort where there are substantial remains; in most places just the line of the Wall is visible with visitor centres, museum, forts and turrets along its entire length. At Corbridge, on the A69, are the remains of the garrison town of Corstopitum with a good museum of finds. Chesters is a fine example of a Roman cavalry fort and the museum here displays sculptures and Roman inscriptions. Hexham, although 14 miles from the actual Wall at Housesteads, is a popular base for visitors and has 14th-century Moot Hall and a beautiful priory church.

306

HAWORTH PARSONAGE
WEST YORKSHIRE

Tourist Information Centre, 2/4 West Lane (01535) 642329.

Haworth village huddles on the edge of grey moorland, a church, an inn and the famous parsonage gathered around an old churchyard with blackened headstones, and a steep, narrow road leading down to the houses in the valley. At the gloomy parsonage you can catch a taste

---

Allendale Tar-barrel Ceremony

As midnight draws near on New Year's Eve the guizers in fancy costumes parade through Allendale (to the south-west of Hexham), led by the town band. Each carries on his head a blazing 'kit' - part of a barrel, filled with tar and wood shavings, and soaked with paraffin before being set alight

(see above). The barrels are carried rapidly to the market-place, where they are thrown onto a large bonfire which has been got ready, to set it on fire. Then the guizers go off to first-foot it merrily through the night. This ceremony has been going on since 1860, at least, and no doubt has its roots in a much older ritual hailing the rebirth of light with the coming of the hew year.

Hadrian's Wall, recently designated a World Heritage Site

of the strange isolated life of the Brontë family. The house is full of their personal belongings, furniture, writings and odd little items.

Down in the valley is Haworth station, a stop on the preserved Keighley and Worth Valley Railway line. Here you can watch engines in steam, and take a ride along the old branch line with its beautifully restored stations and rolling stock.

IN EASY REACH Haworth is a good base to explore Brontë country, with its bleak landscapes of heath and gritstone. Stroll west to find the Brontë bridge and waterfall, and then on to the remote ruined farmhouse at Top Withens, probably the original Wuthering Heights. Further west towards Colne is Wycoller Hall (Ferndean Manor in *Jane Eyre*) and Wycoller Country Park.

Keighley's Cliffe Castle Museum is worth a visit, too, for its natural history and folk collections, its craft workshops and its art gallery. Finally, don't leave the area without seeing Bingley Five Rise Lock, which carries barges 59ft up hill on their way along the old Leeds and Liverpool Canal.

--- 307 ---

NORMANBY HALL
HUMBERSIDE

Off the B1430, 4 miles north of Scunthorpe.
Tourist Information Centre, Central Library, Carlton Street, Scunthorpe (01724)
860161.

The Sheffields were squires of Normanby from 1589 and rose to a peak of social eminence with John Sheffield, Duke of Buckingham, who rewrote Shakespeare's *Julius Caesar* and married an illegitimate daughter of James II: there is a splendid Kneller portrait of her in the house. In 1815 Sir Robert Sheffield decided to pull the old mansion down and build a new one. His architect was Sir Robert Smirke, and the result is solid, four-square and dignified, with elegant rooms and a handsome double staircase. The main block has been impressively fitted out by the Scunthorpe museum service with fine furniture, paintings, ornaments and costume displays. Outside there are enjoyable trails through the 350-acre park, as well as an aviary, a countryside centre and riding stables.

IN EASY REACH Along minor roads to the north is the village of Alkborough, with views over the Trent and the Humber. There is a famous turf maze here, near the church, and a replica of it in the church porch. In the other direction, the Scunthorpe Borough Museum and Art Gallery in Oswald Road covers the area's archaeology, industry and social history.

To the west across the Trent, is the area called the Isle of Axholme – fens which were drained by Dutch engineers in the 1620s. Its main town is Epworth, on the A161, where the Old Rectory is a Queen Anne house, the boyhood home of John Wesley and his brother Charles, the prolific hymn-writer. The house is now a Methodist shrine (open by appointment only in winter).

Haxey Hood Game

A peculiar game is played in Haxey, in the south-west corner of Humberside, every year on 6 January (unless it's a Sunday). The main part of it involves a scrum of men heaving and swaying for an hour or more to carry the 'hood' to one or other of the local pubs (see below). The Sway Hood is a cylinder of leather, with a piece of rope inside. Earlier, several lesser hoods, made of canvas, have been played for, with individual players trying to carry them off, against the opposition not only of the other players but of special characters called boggins (led by the King Boggin), who can make a hood 'dead' by touching it. Earlier still, the Fool appears and is smoked over a fire while making a traditional speech exhorting the players to take part in the right spirit.

308

QUARRY BANK MILL
CHESHIRE

At Styal, on the B5166, 1 mile north of Wilmslow. Tourist Information Centre, Town Hall Extension, Lloyd Street, Manchester 0161-234 3157.

The solidly handsome 18th-century cotton mill on the River Bollin, and the village which the mill owners, the Gregs, built for their workpeople, make up one of the most fascinating Industrial Revolution sites in Britain. In the care of the National Trust, the millhands' cottages, the chapels and shops have survived largely unaltered, together with the house where the young pauper apprentices lived. The mill, built in 1784 by Samuel Greg, has been put back into working order. The giant iron waterwheel is turning again, and you can watch the spinning and weaving machines which it powers – and buy the cloth they make, in the shop. However, it is not all industry at Styal. On the contrary, there are miles of woodland paths in the country park here, and a walk by the Bollin in its deep ravine to Wilmslow church.

IN EASY REACH To the north-east of Styal and near Cheadle Hulme is Bramhall Hall, an attractive black-and-white manor house, late medieval and Tudor in date. Set in a landscaped park, it has medieval wall paintings, Elizabethan plasterwork, and furniture by Pugin. Further east is Lyme Park, which was given to the National Trust in 1947 by the Legh family, who had owned it for six centuries. The Elizabethan long gallery has survived inside and there is fine furniture and glass to be admired, with carvings attributed to Grinling Gibbons, and a Velazquez showing one of the famous Legh breed of mastiffs. The house, with its formal Dutch garden, orangery and lake, is set in a 1,300-acre park, grazed by red and fallow deer.

●

Goathland and Plough Stots Service

Plough Monday was the day when work started again on the farm after the Christmas festivities. Or if work did not actually start, it soon would, and groups of young men used to dress up, dance and pull a decorated plough about.

Today something of this tradition survives at Goathland on the North York Moors. The Blessing of the Plough takes place at St Mary's church on the first Sunday after 12th Night (or the following Sunday if 12th night falls on Sunday). Teams of sword dancers in costumes and caps of pink and blue perform traditional 'longsword' dances round the village on the following Saturday.

●

309

WHITBY
NORTH YORKSHIRE

Tourist Information Centre, Langborne Road (01947) 602674.

The stars and contrasting attractions of Whitby are the beautiful ruined abbey and the Dracula trail, which leads you up and down the town in the wake of the vampire who, according to Bram Stoker, first trod English soil here. Whitby stands on cliffs where the River Esk cuts through to the sea, and St Mary's Church is at the top of no fewer than 199 steps. It has kept its 18th-century box-pews and galleries, and its three-decker pulpit. A statue of Captain Cook stands on the West Cliff, at the end of the promenade, and the house in Grape Lane where he lodged as an apprentice is a museum to him. There is more about him in the town museum in Pannett Park, which also has a splendid collection of Whitby jet ornaments, as well as fossils and good archaeology and geology displays.

Gaunt on their 200ft cliff are the ruins of the medieval abbey church. The monastery, for both monks and nuns originally, was founded by the redoubtable St Hilda in the 7th century, and it was here in 664 that the decision was taken which gave England to Roman Catholic rather than Celtic Christianity.

IN EASY REACH The picturesque old fishing village and smugglers' haven of Robin Hood's Bay is on the B1447, 7 miles to the south. Inland from Whitby stretches the North York Moors National Park, which can be observed in nostalgic comfort from the steam trains of the North Yorkshire Moors Railway on the scenic line between Grosmont and Pickering. (The railway is open from April to October, and there are 'Santa Trains' in December.) The main visitor centre for the park is at Danby, 16 miles west of Whitby.

310

WIGAN PIER
GREATER MANCHESTER

At Wigan, on the A49. Tourist Information Centre, Trencherfield Mill, Wigan Pier (01942) 825677.

Once a music-hall joke, now a successful tourist attraction, the 'pier' at Wigan is actually a wharf on the Leeds and Liverpool Canal, where coal used to be loaded onto barges. After mouldering away for years, the wharf and its handsome warehouses have been given a facelift, to reappear as a museum of life and work in the area in about 1900. Actors take the roles of teachers in a school and the public can play the children, and there is also a miner's cottage and other reconstructed settings. In a former cotton mill you can see the largest working steam-powered mill engine in the world, and other textile, colliery and rope-making machines in operation. There are also canal-side walks, a waterbus, a restaurant and a pub.

IN EASY REACH A mile or so to the north-east, Haigh Hall was the home of the Earls of Crawford. The house is not open, but there is a nature trail in the spacious grounds. Further north-east, off the A673, are the Rivington Reservoirs, which supply Liverpool with water. They lie at the foot of Rivington Pike, a celebrated viewpoint crowned by an 18th-century tower. There is a delightful park here.

311

YORK
NORTH YORKSHIRE

Tourist Information Centres: De Grey Rooms, Exhibition Square (01904) 621756 and York Railway Station, Station Road (01904) 643700.

York Minster, with Gray's Court in the foreground, from the city walls. Gray's Court belongs to the Minster and at present is being used by the College of Ripon and York St John

Viking Festival

Visitors may be bewildered at first by the number of things to see and the many-sidedness of the city: there is church York, Roman York, Viking York, the York of the medieval guilds, Georgian York, riverside York, railway York, chocolate York (Rowntree/Nestlé, Terry's and Craven's). The best way to get a preliminary impression is to walk along a section of the medieval wall. The city's position on the River Ouse, with sea-going ships coming inland from the Humber, made it the North's wealthiest and most important town until the coming of the Industrial Revolution, which passed it by.

York was the principal Roman base in the North, and the headquarters of the Sixth Legion (or what's left of it) is underneath York Minster. When you go down into the undercroft of the Minster today, you are inside the Roman headquarters and you'll see Roman finds on display, although the main collection of Roman material is in the Yorkshire Museum, Museum Gardens.

In the 9th century York became the capital of a Viking kingdom, Jorvik. To see what Jorvik was like, go to the Jorvik Viking Centre and travel in a moving pod through a reconstruction which brings to life the sights and sounds, and even the smells, of the time.

York Minster is essentially a medieval creation: 534ft long, with a 198ft central tower and two slightly lower western towers, it is one of the largest churches in Europe. It is celebrated especially for its medieval stained glass, and the great 15th-century east window is the size of a tennis court. There are many other medieval churches in the city, a row of medieval houses in Goodramgate, and the halls of the medieval merchant guilds.

From the 17th and 18th centuries, you should try to see the Treasurer's House (situated behind the cathedral and open April to October only), and Fairfax House, in Castlegate, by John Carr. He also built the dignified classical buildings opposite the castle mound, now partly occupied by the exceptionally lively and interesting Castle Museum, a treasure-house of Yorkshire bygones which no visit to the city should omit. The National Railway Museum, Leeman Road, is also exceptional value, housing the biggest collection of railway relics in the country.

Viking times return to York with a bang in February each year - a literal bang as the Viking Festival begins with a grand fireworks display on the outskirts of the city. Other events in the festival, which has been running since 1985 and is organised by the people who run the Jorvik Viking Centre, include a longships race on the River Ouse, Viking feasts with authentic food and drink, combats, folk dancing and a ceilidh, the acting out of one of the Viking sagas, and displays of such traditional crafts as barrel-making, knotting and the making of jewellery. The whole thing ends in style with a procession by torchlight (see above) and the burning of a replica Viking longship.

Geography divides Scotland into three or perhaps four parts. Across the south run the rolling, solitary Border hills. North of them lie the Lowlands, between the Firth of Clyde and the Firth of Forth, containing both Glasgow and Edinburgh. This is much the most heavily populated region, with 75 per cent of the people in 15 per cent of the total area, and also much the most heavily industrialised.

Further north again, the Highland Boundary Fault runs diagonally from Helensburgh, on the Firth of Clyde, to Stonehaven, on the east coast below Aberdeen. Beyond are the Highlands, Britain's least inhabited area. The Highlands themselves, however, are split in two by the Great Glen, scored as if by a giant cleaver from Fort William to Inverness. To the east the Cairngorms rear up in snow-capped majesty above the valleys of the Spey and the Dee. On the other side of the line lie the rugged peaks and deep green glens of the Western Highlands, the mist-hung precipices and lonely corries and lochans, the glimmering sea-lochs and all the magic of the remote and beautiful Isles.

Besides the entrancing loveliness of its scenery, Scotland is distinguished by the romance and the violence of its past. In the south are the ruined abbeys of Dryburgh, Jedburgh and Melrose (where the heart of Robert the Bruce was buried) which were looted and smashed by English invasions. Here too are memories of incessant Border raiding and blood feuds. In the north are echoes of the fiery cross, of treachery and murder, the lament of the pipes, the war-galleys of the Lords of the Isles scouring the western seas.

Scotland is rich in grim castles with atrocious dungeons – Border holds like Hermitage and Threave, Lowlands fastnesses like Hailes and Dirleton. There are sea-girt castles on impregnable cliffs, like Tantallon and Dunnottar, and castles crouched on unscaleable crags like Stirling and Edinburgh. Or there are castles which look like the product of an inspired collaboration between Walt Disney and the Brothers Grimm – Craigievar and Crathes, for example. And there are other castles which are really stately homes, crammed with elegant treasures – Culzean and Drumlanrig, Fyvie and Floors.

There is no lack in Scotland of fine art and architecture: the ravishing Burrell Collection in Glasgow and the Georgian streets of Edinburgh's New Town alone could give the lie to that. Nor are the odd and offbeat absent: the Loch Ness Monster Centre, say, or the weird echo in the Hamilton Mausoleum, or Glasgow's city of the dead. But in Scotland again and again the visitor is drawn back to the enchantment of the past.

In the grounds of Scone Palace is the place where the Kings of Scots from time immemorial were enthroned on the Stone of Destiny. At Falkland and Edinburgh, Loch Leven and Craigmillar, are memories of the beautiful and ill-fated Mary, Queen of Scots. At Glenfinnan is the spot where the Young Pretender raised his standard, and in the Highland glens and 'over the sea to Skye' are the places where he hid with a huge price on his head and was never betrayed.

Edinburgh Castle and Princes Gardens. As one of Europe's finest cities, Scotland's capital attracts thousands of visitors, not least because of the famous festival of art, music and drama held every summer

Scotland

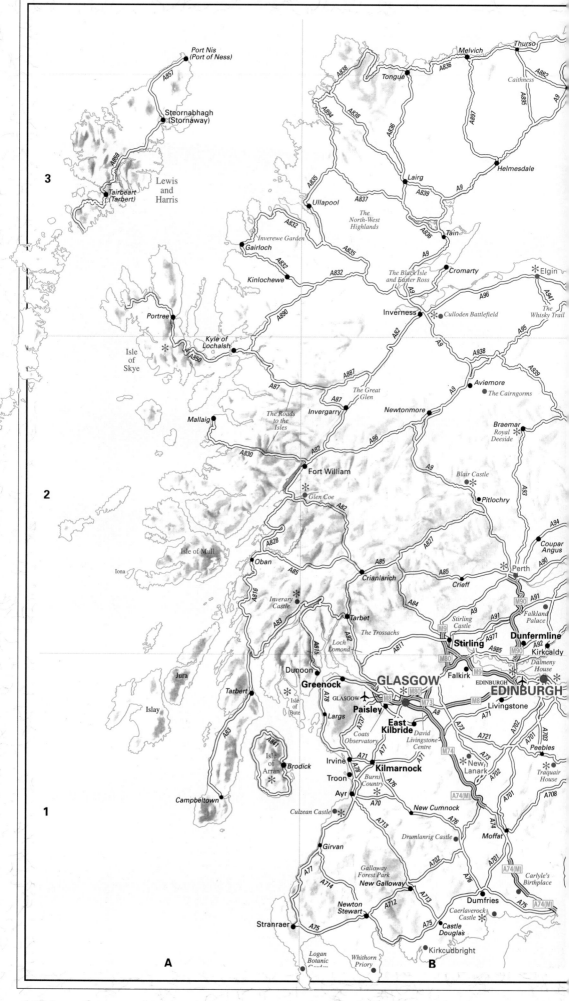

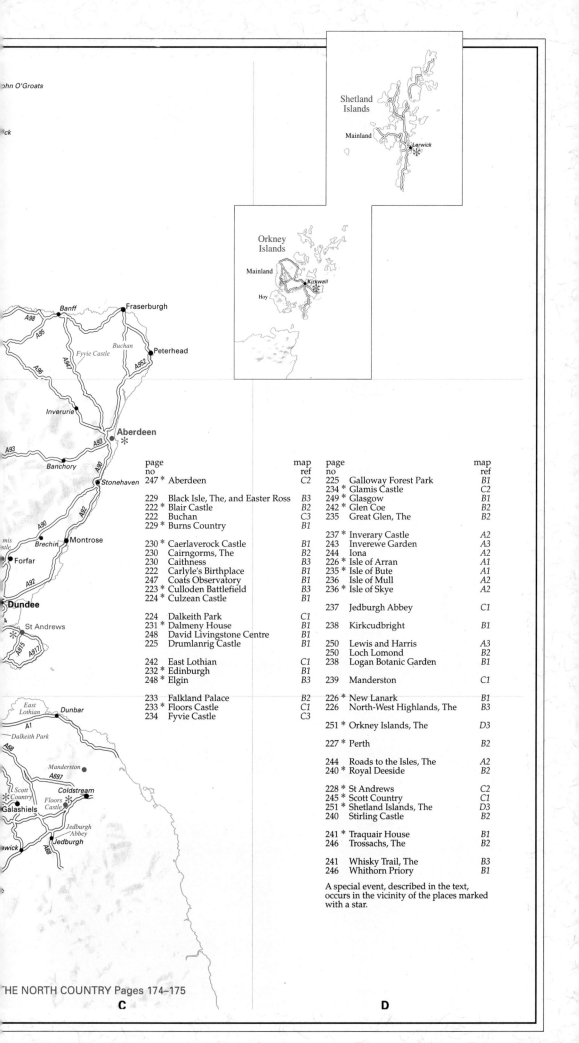

A special event, described in the text,
occurs in the vicinity of the places marked
with a star.

THE NORTH COUNTRY Pages 174–175

C

D

217

Calendar of Events

Spring

MARCH

Whuppity Scoorie
Lanark, Strathclyde
(1 March)

International Festival of Food and Wine
St Andrews, Fife
(March - 2nd and 3rd weeks)

Tobermory Drama Festival
Isle of Mull, Strathclyde
(March – 3rd week)

EASTER

Inverness Folk Festival
Inverness, Highland
(Easter weekend)

APRIL

Family Fun Run
Culzean Country Park, nr Maybole, Strathclyde
(mid April)

Traditional Music Festival
Isle of Mull, Strathclyde
(April – 3rd week)

St Andrews Golf Week
St Andrews, Fife
(mid April)

Shetland Folk Festival
Lerwick, Shetland Islands
(late April to early May)

Traditional Folk Festival
Girvan, Strathclyde
(late April or early May)

MAY

Pitlochry Theatre Festival
Pitlochry, Tayside
(early May to early October)

Goat Fell Race
Brodick, Isle of Arran, Strathclyde
(May – 2nd or 3rd Saturday)

Orkney Traditional Folk Festival
Stromness, Orkney Islands
(May – 3rd week)

Perth Festival of the Arts
Perth, Tayside
(May – 3rd and 4th weeks)

Angus Agricultural Show
Arbroath, Tayside
(late May)

Atholl Highlanders Parade
Blair Atholl Castle, Tayside
(May – last Saturday)

Dumfries and Galloway Arts Festival
Dumfries, Dumfries & Galloway
(late May and early June)

Summer

JUNE

Ayrshire Arts Festival
Ayr, Strathclyde
(early June)

Carrick Lowland Gathering
Girvan, Strathclyde
(June – 1st week)

Stewarton Bonnet Guild
Stewarton, near Kilmarnock, Strathclyde
(June – 2nd week)

Border Union Dog Show
Kelso, Boders
(mid-June)

Selkirk Common Riding
Selkirk, Borders
(mid-June)

Beltane Festival
Peebles, Borders
(June – 3rd week)

Royal Highland Show
Ingliston, Edinburgh, Lothian
(June – 3rd week)

St Magnus Festival
Kirkwall, Orkney Islands
(June – 3rd week)

Guid Nychburris Week
Dumfries, Dumfries & Galloway
(June – 3rd and 4th week)

Cairngorm Hill Race
Glenmore, Grampian
(June – 4th week)

Dunkeld and Birnam Arts Festival
Dunkeld, Tayside
(late June)

Highland Traditional Music Festival
Dingwall, Highland
(late June)

Braw Lads Gathering
Galashiels, Borders
(late June to early July)

JULY

Dumbarton District Festival
Dumbarton, Strathclyde
(July – 1st 3 weeks)

Caithness Highland Gathering and Games
Thurso, Highland
(early July)

Elgin Highland Games
Elgin, Grampian
(early July)

Riding of the Marches
Annan, Dumfries & Galloway
(early July)

Duns Summer Festival
Duns, Borders
(July – 1st week)

Jethart Callants Festival
Jedburgh, Borders
(July – 1st week)

New Galloway Gala Week
New Galloway, Dumfries & Galloway
(July – 1st week)

Jedburgh Border Games
Jedburgh, Borders
(July – 2nd week)

Scottish Week
Peterhead, Grampian
(July – 2nd week)

Transport Extravaganza
Glamis Castle, Tayside
(July – 2nd week)

Annual Dundee Shinty Games
Dundee, Tayside
(July – 2nd Saturday)

Kelso Civic Week
Kelso, Borders
(July – 2nd or 3rd week)

Tartan Festival
Stirling, Central
(mid-July)

Cromarty Raft Race
Fortrose, Highland
(July – 3rd week)

Inverary Traditional Highland Games
Inverary, Strathclyde
(July – 3rd week)

Trossachs Highland Festival
Kinlochard, Central
(July – 3rd week)

Traditional Highland dancing

Kirkcudbright Summer Festivities
Dumfries & Galloway
(July – 3rd week, to early August)

Dufftown Gala Week
Dufftown, Grampian
(July – 4th week)

Border Union Show
Kelso, Borders
(late July)

Langholm Common Riding
Langholm, Dumfries & Galloway
(late July)

Lochaber Highland Games
Fort William, Highland
late July)

Nairn Sheepdog Trials
Nairn, Highland
(late July)

Skye Folk Festival
Portree, Isle of Skye
(late July)

Coldstream Civic Week
Coldstream, Borders
(late July to early August)

AUGUST

Culzean Pursuits Weekend
Culzean Country Park, nr Maybole, Strathclyde
(early August)

Lammas Fair
St Andrews, Fife
(early August)

Skye Highland Games
Portree, Isle of Skye
(early August)

Berwickshire Agricultural Show
Duns, Borders
(August – 1st week)

Silver Chanter Piping Competition
Dunvegan, Isle of Skye, Highland
(August – 1st week)

Stirling District Festival
Stirling, Central
(August – 1st and 2nd weeks)

Arran Horticultural Show
Lamlash, Isle of Arran, Strathclyde
(August – 2nd week)

Bute Agricultural Society Summer Show
Rothesay, Isle of Bute
(August – 2nd week)

The Burry Man Festival
Queensferry, Lothian
(August – 2nd Friday)

Dundee Water Festival
Dundee, Tayside
(August – 2nd and 3rd weeks)

Marymass Festival
Irvine, Strathclyde
(August – 2nd and 3rd weeks)

Borders Country Fair
Ayton Castle, Borders
(mid August)

Edinburgh Festival
Edinburgh, Lothian
(mid August to early September)

Bute Highland Festival
Rothesay, Isle of Bute
(late August)

Cowal Highland Gathering
Dunoon, Strathclyde
(late August)

Deeside Steam and Vintage Club Annual Rally
Banchory, Grampian
(late August)

Peebles Arts Festival
Peebles, Borders
(late August to early September)

Autumn

SEPTEMBER

Kirriemuir Traditional Music Festival
Kirriemuir, Tayside
(September – 1st week)

Ben Nevis Race
Fort William, Highland
(September – 1st Saturday)

Braemar Royal Highland Gathering
Braemar, Grampian
(September – 1st Saturday)

Kelso Ram Sales
Kelso, Borders
(September – 2nd Friday)

Annual Fiddle Festival
Elgin, Grampian
(September – 2nd week)

OCTOBER

Border Festival
Galashiels area, Borders
(October – 1st half, alternate years)

NOVEMBER

Border Canary Association Annual Show
Galashiels, Borders
(early November)

St Andrew's Day Celebrations
St Andrews, Fife
(19-30 November)

Winter

DECEMBER

Annual Hogmnay Bonfire
Biggar, Strathclyde
(31 December)

Fireball Ceremony
Stonehaven, Grampian
(31 December)

The Edinburgh Festival

Flambeaux Procession
Comrie, Tayside
(31 December)

JANUARY

Ba' Games
Kirkwall, Orkney
(1 January)

Burning of the Clavie
Burghead, Grampian
(11 January)

Up Helly Aa
Lerwick, Shetland Islands
(January – last Tuesday)

FEBRUARY

St Andrews Festival of the Arts
St Andrews, Fife
(mid-February – 1989 and alternate years)

SHROVETIDE

Jedburgh Ba' Games
Jedburgh, Borders
(Shrovetide)

ROMANTIC SCOTLAND

Among the pleasures of a visit to Scotland are the Highland Gatherings, with kilts and clan badges much in evidence, and tossing the caber, massed pipe bands and Highland dancing all harking back to romantic traditions of the past. Hotels stage ceilidhs, or literally 'visits' in Gaelic, from a time when people in remote areas visited their neighbours to make their own entertainment of music, song and story.

Along the Borders, meanwhile, the common ridings follow each other from June well into August. These are a mixture of beating the bounds and commemorations of far-off history. From Coldstream, for instance, the ride crosses into England to Flodden Field, where the flower of Scots chivalry was cut down in battle in 1513 and at Hawick a skirmish of 1514 is celebrated.

That Scotland's past, and in particular the traditions of the Highlands, should be kept alive in this way would have seemed out of the question 200 years ago or so, when the clans seemed to have made their last gallant, hopeless charge against the modern world at Culloden. After the battle the government set out to destroy the clans' way of life and it was actually made illegal to play the bagpipes or wear the tartan. The English at this time regarded the Highlanders with contempt as primitive aborigines.

Dr Johnson spoke of 'savage clans and raving barbarians'. Nor was it only the English. Lowland Scots had viewed Highlanders with fear and disapproval for generations.

The new modern image of 'romantic Scotland' began to form in the later 18th century. The tide of the Romantic movement in literature and art was beginning to flow and a new appetite was growing for mountain scenery and wild nature. An enthusiasm for noble savages in a setting of peaks, rocks and foaming torrents was stimulated in the 1760s and 1770s by the Highland schoolmaster James Macpherson's 'translations', or forgeries, of Gaelic poems by the legendary bard Ossian. At the same time a pioneer travel writer, Thomas Pennant, toured Scotland on horseback and published a guidebook to the country. In 1781 the first piping contests were held, at Falkirk, and in the following year the law which banned the pipes and the tartan was repealed.

The scene was now set for the appearance of the principal architect of 'romantic Scotland'. Sir Walter Scott was the greatest publicist Scotland has ever had. His pride in his own Border family, the Scotts of Buccleuch, interested him from an early age in the history and poetry of Border raids and feuds, and in 1802 he published a collection of Border ballads. Then his eye moved north to the Highlands. His poem *The Lady of the Lake*, published in 1810, was hugely popular and visitors started going to see the beautiful Trossachs area in Perthshire for themselves. Already in 1820 a local landowner, the Duke of Montrose, drove a road north from Aberfoyle to make access to the lochs and glens easier and so encourage a profitable tourist trade which has continued to this day.

In a series of best-selling novels starting with *Waverley* in 1814, Scott brought vividly to life the colour and romance, customs and attitudes of the Highlands of the past. In 1818 it was Scott who inspired the successful search for the Honours of Scotland – the crown and royal regalia of the Kings of Scots – which had been tucked away in a vaulted chamber in Edinburgh Castle after the Act of Union and forgotten. In 1822 Scott stage-managed King

The Honours of Scotland – crown, sword and sceptre – can be seen today at Edinburgh Castle

George IV's state visit to Edinburgh at which the panoply of the clans came back to life.

Ironically, in the Highlands of real life, chiefs were evicting their clansmen from the land and replacing them with sheep, but visitors found what they came looking for and failed to see what was changing.

One of the visitors was Edwin Landseer, who made his first Scottish trip in 1824 and returned

year after year, entranced by the picturesque scenery and people, the deer and the stalking. Pictures like *The Monarch of the Glen* helped to fasten the new impression of the Highlands firmly into place and a royal seal of approval was stamped on it by Queen Victoria. She and the Prince Consort fell in love with Deeside and in the 1850s built their own Highland palace at Balmoral, so lavishly beplaided inside that people said it suffered from 'tartanitis'.

The Queen adored the Highlands and Highlanders, in whom she found courtesy combined with a welcome absence of servility. Her enthusiastic approval authorised a love-affair with 'romantic Scotland' that draws visitors to the country to this day.

Background: Glen Coe, epitome of the wild, brooding scenery that became so popular in the late 1700s

Below: art and literature of the Romantic movement – Jeanie Deans from Scott's Heart of Midlothian *and Landseer's* Monarch of the Glen

Tartan sprang into vogue under Scott's influence, and today there is a huge array of plaids which have no connection at all with the clan system. Seen here are two 'genuine' tartans – the Stuart (left) and the Campbell 'Cawdor'

●

Atholl Highlanders Parade

*W*hen Lord George Murray at the head of a Jacobite army bombarded his own home, Blair Castle, with red-hot shot, it was because the castle was held against him by government troops. Nowadays, on the last Saturday afternoon in May, the Duke of Atholl formally inspects his own troops on parade. The Atholl Highlanders, 80-strong, brawny, suitably kilted and equipped with bagpipes and a cannon, are mostly workers on the duke's estate. A picturesque sight, they are the only private army in Britain and exist by special permission of Queen Victoria, who visited the castle in 1844.

●

— 312 —
BLAIR CASTLE
TAYSIDE

Off the A9, 8 miles north-west of Pitlochry.
Tourist Information Centre, 22 Atholl Road, Pitlochry (01796) 472215.

*O*verlooking the village of Blair Atholl is Blair Castle (open April to October), gleaming white and suitably battlemented. This great house of the Murrays, Dukes of Atholl, guards a strategic route into the Highlands. This was the last castle in Britain to be besieged: in 1746, when a Jacobite army invested it under the command of Lord George Murray, younger brother of the second duke. The oldest part of the house goes back to the 13th century, but the castle was rebuilt in both the 18th and 19th centuries. Inside there are handsome 18th-century interiors, paintings by Lely, Raeburn and Landseer, serried ranks of antlers as mute testimony to the family's shooting prowess, fine china, embroidery and lace, Jacobite relics and Masonic regalia, and one of the best collections of weapons in the country. The duke's 80-man private army is the last one left in Britain. In Blair Atholl, there is the Atholl County Collection, a museum portraying local life since the middle of the last century.

IN EASY REACH Three miles away west of Blair Atholl, just off the A9, a footpath leads to spectacular waterfalls on the River Bruar. Here also is the museum of Clan Donnachaidh, which covers the history of a group of related families, including the Duncans, Robertsons and Reids. Half-way between Blair Atholl and Pitlochry, just off the A9, is the Pass of Killiecrankie, where an English army was defeated in 1689: here there is a good National Trust for Scotland visitor centre which will supply the historical details.

From Killiecrankie the A9 continues south for 3 miles to Pitlochry, a popular base for exploring the area, with the additional cultural attraction of a theatre festival in summer. Off to the south-west of Pitlochry, at Weem in the Tay Valley, off the A827, Castle Menzies is a Z-plan fortified house of the 16th century. It contains the Clan Menzies Museum.

— 313 —
BUCHAN
GRAMPIAN

Tourist Information Centres: 54 Broad Street, Peterhead (01779) 71904 and Saltoun Square, Fraserburgh (01346) 28315 (both seasonal opening only).

*T*his area on Scotland's north-east shoulder was once dominated by the Comyns, implacable foes of Robert the Bruce. There are sandy beaches and crumbling castles along the coast and the fishing towns here have gained a boost from North Sea oil. South of Peterhead, legions of seabirds wheel and scream round towering cliffs. One particularly spectacular spot is the Bullers of Buchan, off the A975, where the cliff path teeters along the edge of a gaping chasm, into which the sea thunders through a rock arch, creating what James Boswell described as 'a monstrous cauldron'. A little further south at Cruden Bay are the dramatic ruins of Slains Castle, built by the Hays, Earls of Erroll, and believed to have inspired Bram Stoker, author of *Dracula*, who used to holiday here.

Peterhead was founded by the Keiths, Earls of Marischal. It was once Scotland's premier whaling port and the story of whaling and fishing here is told in the Arbuthnot Museum. Ten miles inland, on the A950, are the ruins of Deer Abbey, a Cistercian house founded by one of the Comyns in the early 13th century. Between the abbey and Mintlaw, off the A950, is the Aden Country Park where there are pleasant walks through the woods. Here there is also a good agricultural heritage centre.

Fraserburgh is another fishing port. It is situated 18 miles north-west of Peterhead on the A952. From Fraserburgh the B9031 runs westwards along a coast studded by cliffs, ruined fortresses and picturesque harbours.

— 314 —
CARLYLE'S BIRTHPLACE
DUMFRIES AND GALLOWAY

At the Arched House, Ecclefechan, off the A74, 6 miles south-east of Lockerbie.
Tourist Information Centres: Gateway to Scotland, M74 Service Area, Gretna (01461) 38500 and The Old Headless Cross, Gretna (01461) 37834 (seasonal opening only).

A man full of energy, whose prose was much admired, Thomas Carlyle was highly respected in Victorian Scotland as a local poor boy who had made good. The plain, sturdy house in Ecclefechan's main street in which he was born in 1795 is today cared for by the National Trust of Scotland. It was built by his father, a stonemason and a stern Calvinist. As a little boy, Thomas Carlyle was taught to read by his father; his mother taught him arithmetic. Later he went to the village school, and then at the age of 11 – 'a lang, sprawling, ill-put-together thing', according to his mother – he was sent to Annan grammar school, which he hated. The rooms in the house have been restored to their 19th-century appearance, and contain furniture belonging to the Carlyle family. There are also letters, personal belongings and photographs, all of which help to bring Carlyle's career to life.

IN EASY REACH Ecclefechan is in Annandale, one of the main routes through the Border hills into Scotland since prehistoric times. Gretna Green, 9 miles to the south-east of Ecclefechan on the M74, enjoys romantic fame for the marriages performed for runaway couples by blacksmiths over their anvils. The Old Smithy has a museum: anvil weddings occurred here until 1940. Lockerbie, 6 miles north-west of Ecclefechan on the A74, is a market town, once notorious for the violent feuds of the local Maxwells and Johnstones. Lochmaben Castle, on a loch off the A709, 4 miles from Lockerbie, is a ruined stronghold which was a favourite residence of James IV, King of the Scots. Three miles south of Lochmaben, off the B7020, is Rammerscales (open July to September), a Georgian manor house with pleasant gardens.

315

CULLODEN BATTLEFIELD
HIGHLAND

On the B9006, 5 miles east of Inverness.
Tourist Information Centres: Castle Wynd, Inverness (01463) 234353 and 62 King Street, Nairn (01667) 52753 (seasonal opening only).

One of the most moving places in Britain to visit is the piece of ground where on 16th April 1746 the army commanded by the 25-year-old Duke of Cumberland, 9,000 strong, defeated the 5,000 men led by Prince Charles Edward. The defeat at Culloden was followed by a brutal massacre of the wounded which earned Cumberland his nickname 'Butcher'. Prominent among the Highlanders who fought heroically and fell in the Stuart cause were Macdonalds, Camerons, Frasers, Mackintoshes, Mackenzies and Stewarts of Appin, but there were Scots on both sides, and members of the same families on both sides – in some cases by deliberate policy.

On the battlefield today, markers indicate the position at the opening of the battle and the sites of mass graves. The memorial cairn erected in 1881 is close to the scene of some of the fiercest fighting. The National Trust for Scotland visitor centre gives a good audio-visual account of the battle.

IN EASY REACH Inverness is the administrative capital of the whole Highland Region. There are Jacobite relics in the museum in Castle Wynd, with good displays on Highland history and the clans, and excellent Highland silver. One of the immediate consequences of the '45 Rising was the building of Fort George, 12 miles to the north-east of Inverness on the Moray Firth, reached by way of the A96 and the B9006. It is an outstanding piece of 18th-century military architecture. The regimental museum of the Seaforth and Cameron Highlanders is here.

Cawdor Castle (not open until May), with its echoes of *Macbeth*, is 8 miles north-east of Culloden Moor. The castle is a pleasant building – a 14th-century keep with substantial additions and notable gardens. Its interior has interesting portraits and tapestries.

Folk Festival

Easter weekend brings the three-day folk festival to Inverness, which has been helping to preserve an important part of the Gaelic folk tradition of the Highlands since 1969. Most of the performers are professionals and there are quality guest acts from this country and abroad, with traditional songs and music from Scotland, England, Wales, Ireland and America. The festival's purpose is to keep interest in folk music alive in the Highlands and there is usually a special concert for children.

Known variously as Bonnie Prince Charlie and the Young Pretender, Charles Edward Stuart (inset) led the Jacobites at Culloden in his bid to gain a kingdom. The main picture below shows the prince's men charging for the last time. The Scots lost 1,200 men in the battle, the English 76.

—————— **316** ——————

CULZEAN CASTLE
STRATHCLYDE

Off the A719, 4 miles west of Maybole. Tourist Information Centres: 39 Sandgate, Ayr (01292) 284196 and Bridge Street, Girvan (01465) 4950.

Culzean Castle Events

The castle and its surrounding country park make a delightful setting for numerous events during the spring and summer. These kick off with the annual Family Fun Run in April, over an arduous up-and-down course of six miles. Although everyone goes at his own pace and it is not a race, every year sees determined competitors bent on winning it.

As the year progresses, there are craft fairs, sheepdog trials and a classic car rally. A particularly attractive event is the Country Pursuits Weekend in August with its demonstrations of crafts, falconry, archery and thatching.

Enthroned on a cliff 150ft above the sea, the great house of Culzean (pronounced 'Cullane') was built for the Kennedys, Earls of Cassilis and subsequently Marquesses of Ailsa, who long dominated this stretch of the coast. The architect Robert Adam designed a splendid blend of romantic, fortified exterior and elegantly civilised interior, which incorporated the older house on the site. The work was completed in 1790. The castle is now in the care of the National Trust for Scotland. Notable features inside include the circular saloon looking out over the sea; an armoury, with weapons intended for use against Napoleon, should he have had the temerity to invade the Kennedy's domain; and a fine collection of paintings, furniture and mirrors. President Eisenhower was presented with an apartment at Culzean and there is a display which traces his link with the house.

Culzean Castle's elegant oval staircase, complete with Corinthian pillars and a delicate balustrade, was added in the final stages of Robert Adam's remodelling, which took place over several years. The castle is recognised as one of his masterpieces

IN EASY REACH The Kennedys were buried in the now ruined Collegiate Church at Maybole, on the A77, the centre of the Carrick district. Two miles south-west of Maybole, on the A77, are the substantial remains of Crossraguel Abbey, which are mainly of the 15th century: a member of the Kennedy family roasted one of its abbots in soap. Two miles from the abbey, along the A77, is Kirkoswald, where you can see Souter Johnnie's Cottage, the home of the village cobbler who was the crony of Tam o'Shanter in Burns's poem. The cottage is now a small museum, with life-sized statues of the characters in the story. Turnberry, on the coast 3 miles further on from Kirkoswald, is noted for its golf course

—————— **317** ——————

DALKEITH PARK
LOTHIAN

On the A68, 7 miles south-east of Edinburgh.
Tourist Information Centres: The Library, White Hart Street 0131 660 6818, Brunton Hall, Musselburgh 0131-665 6597 (seasonal opening only) and 3 Princes Street, Edinburgh 0131-557 1700.

The parkland and woods of Dalkeith Palace, just outside Dalkeith, form a pleasant country park with walks, nature trails and picnic places. The twin North Esk and South Esk rivers run through the grounds and one of the trails leads over the North Esk across Robert Adam's handsome Montagu Bridge of 1792. There are good views of the palace, which belongs to the Scotts of Buccleuch and, although not open to the public, is worth looking at. A stately Palladian pile, it was built to a design by Vanbrugh in 1711 for the Duchess Anne, child-bride and widow of the Duke of Monmouth who was the natural son of Charles II.

IN EASY REACH Three miles to the north-west of Dalkeith Park, on the outskirts of Edinburgh, is the formidable bulk of Craigmillar Castle, one of Mary, Queen of Scots's favourite residences. The double curtain walls surround an L-shaped 14th-century tower house. To the south-west of the castle, off the B7003, Rosslyn Chapel is noted for its intricate 15th-century stone carvings. South-east of Dalkeith, Crichton Castle lies west of the A68. It comprises an elegant 16th-century house designed by an Italian architect built on to an older tower house. North-east of Dalkeith, at Prestonpans, a former colliery is occupied by the Scottish Mining Museum, and has an enormous beam engine as one of its exhibits.

318

DRUMLANRIG CASTLE
DUMFRIES AND GALLOWAY

Off the A76, 3 miles north of Thornhill.
Tourist Information Centre, Whitesands, Dumfries (01387) 53862.

Set in a very fine park, the huge house of Drumlanrig Castle is built round an inner courtyard, with a square tower at each corner and a roofscape bristling with cupolas and chimneys. Standing on the site of a medieval Douglas fortress, it was completed in 1691 for the 1st Duke of Queensberry, who is said to have been so horrified at its cost that he spent only one night in the place. The second duke was virtual ruler of Scotland under Queen Anne (and there is an enormous monument to him in the church at Durrisdeer, off the A702). After a period in the hands of a notoriously profligate duke, 'Old Q', the estate passed by marriage to the Scotts, Dukes of Buccleuch, in 1810. The house contains a wealth of Old Master paintings, plus family portraits by Kneller, Reynolds, Ramsay and Gainsborough, and furniture and silver. There are also relics of the Young Pretender to be seen in the bedrooms he used in 1746.

IN EASY REACH Twelve miles south of Drumlanrig Castle, off the A76, is Ellisland Farm on the west bank of the Nith. Robert Burns lived there from 1788 to 1791 and composed *Tam o'Shanter* in that time. Personal relics of the poet are on display. (Visitors are advised to phone in advance.) Nine miles north-west of Drumlanrig on the A76, is Sanquhar, which boasts the oldest post office in Britain, it having been in operation as far back as 1783. North-east from here, 6 miles along the B797, is Wanlockhead, high up in the Lowther Hills, where lead had been mined from Roman times until quite recently (gold and silver too). Here you can explore an 18th-century lead mine at the Museum of the Scottish Lead Mining Industry.

319

GALLOWAY FOREST PARK
DUMFRIES AND GALLOWAY, STRATHCLYDE

Traversed by the A712 and the A714.
Tourist Information Centres: Dashwood Square, Newton Stewart (01671) 402431
(seasonal opening only) and Whitesands, Dumfries (01387) 53862.

Golden eagles and peregrine falcons, deer and feral goats, red squirrels and wildcats, otters and pine martens inhabit 240 square miles of wild country in inland Galloway, in a landscape of mountains, moors and conifer forests. Most of the range called the Rhinns of Kells is in the park and there are several peaks above 2,000ft, topped by The Merrick at 2,765ft, the highest point in the south of Scotland. The park is best explored on foot, along its numerous trails. For the motorist, the A712, here christened 'the Queen's Way', runs 19 miles through lovely countryside between Newton Stewart and New Galloway.

Along this road, beside man-made Clatteringshaw's Loch, is the Galloway Deer Museum, where there are hides for viewing the red deer and displays on the geology and natural history of the area. Close by, the granite boulder called Bruce's Stone commemorates an early victory over the English here in 1307. The Raider's Road runs 110 miles through the forest to the Black Water of Dee.

The extensive Galloway Forest Park lies in one of the wildest regions of Britain. Remote little lochs containing pike, scattered between the mountains, are one of its features

— 320 —

ISLE OF ARRAN
STRATHCLYDE

Ferries travel to Brodick from Ardrossan, and in summer only, to Lochranza from Claonaig in Kintyre. Tourist Information Centre, The Pier, Brodick (01770) 302140.

Swimming, boating and pony-trekking are among the pleasures of Arran, an island in the Firth of Clyde, about 20 miles long by 10 miles wide. It is noted for its gentle climate, sandy beaches and impressive cliffs and mountains. The Isle of Arran Heritage Museum (not open until Easter) at Brodick has a collection tracing the geology, archaeology and local history of the island.

Arran's showplace is Brodick Castle, which belonged to the Dukes of Hamilton. The castle is medieval in origin, but was enlarged and remodelled in the 1840s by the tenth duke. The house is rich in paintings, silver and porcelain, and especially in sporting pictures and trophies. The twelfth duke's only daughter and heiress married the Duke of Montrose in 1906 and her influence on the castle is considerably apparent today. It was she who created the rhododendron gardens, one of the finest in Britain. On her death in 1957, the estate passed to the National Trust for Scotland, and the grounds are now a country park.

Above the castle rises Goat Fell, at 2,868ft, the island's highest peak. Other points of interest include ruined Lochranza Castle, near the northern tip of Arran, and the prehistoric standing stones and tombs of Tormore, on Machrie Moor, on the western side of the island.

Goat Fell Race

Anyone determined to beat the record time of 1 hour 13 minutes and 13 seconds for running 8 miles to the top of Goat Fell (above) and back down again should pay the entry fee of £1 and join the annual race: though you will not have time to admire the panoramic prospect from the summit when you reach it. The race, first staged in 1953, is held on Arran on a Saturday in mid-May and it takes most of the runners two hours or more to complete the run. The race is held under the rules of the Scottish Amateur Athletics Association.
The prone figure (above) of a winner shows how gruelling the race is.

●

●

— 321 —

NEW LANARK
STRATHCLYDE

Off the A73, 1 mile south of Lanark.
Tourist Information Centre, Horsemarket, Ladyacre Road, Lanark (01555) 661661.

This Industrial Revolution site is a veteran star of many films and television programmes, and in the early 19th century was the scene of the socialist reformer Robert Owen's experiments with ideas far ahead of their time. The cotton mill complex here was built in the 1780s, deep in the Clyde Gorge, in order to use power from the river. Robert Owen ran the mill from 1800 to 1825, among his innovations being schools for children up to 12 years old, at which age they went into the mill. The story of New Lanark is told through the eyes of a 10-year-old mill girl – Annie McLeod. The mills, the workmen's houses and principal buildings have been restored, and there's a good history trail and workshops.

Close by in the wooded gorge are the beautiful Falls of Clyde, in a nature reserve run by the Scottish Wildlife Trust, where you might see red squirrels, kingfishers, otters and badgers. An old dyeworks here is now a visitor centre.

IN EASY REACH Lanark is a market town, known for traditional ceremonies including its peculiar Whuppity Scoorie custom in March. To the south-east, Biggar, on the A702, is home to the enjoyable Gladstone Court Museum, where 19th-century shops, workshops, a schoolroom and a bank can be explored. Other aspects of Biggar's local history can be investigated in Greenhill Covenanters' House. Three miles west of Lanark off the B7018, the National Trust for Scotland owns Blackhill, a prehistoric hill-fort with excellent views over the Clyde Valley. Near Crossford, 5 miles north-west of Lanark, off the A72, Craignethan Castle (limited opening before April) is a Hamilton Stronghold of the 16th century. It was once a refuge of Mary, Queen of Scots and is said to be haunted by the queen, minus her head.

Whuppity Scoorie

In the town of Lanark, on the evening of 1 March, a crowd gathers by the parish church of St Nicholas. The children in the crowd are each armed with a tightly wadded paper ball on the end of a piece of string. At 6 o'clock the church bell sounds, and the children charge around the church three times, hitting each other fiercely with the paper balls on the way. In earlier times the game was played by the young men of the town, not the children. The origin of this peculiar custom which is called 'Whuppity Scoorie' (or 'Stoorie'), is unknown, but it is thought to have something to do with driving winter away.

●

— 322 —

THE NORTH-WEST HIGHLANDS
HIGHLAND

Tourist Information Centres: Ullapool (01854) 612135 (seasonal opening only), Lochinver (015714) 330 (seasonal opening only), Durness (01971) 511259 (seasonal opening only) and The Square, Dornoch (01862) 810400.

Sea-lochs bite deep into a coastline studded with fishing villages, cliffs and coves. Inland, miles of solitary moors, remote lochs and mountain peaks, burns and bogs, with few roads or settlements, constitute one of the wildest regions in the country.

Ullapool, on the A835, was founded as a fishing village in 1788 and is now a holiday base and the port for the ferries to the Outer Hebrides. Boat trips in the summer explore the coast where there are plenty of seals and seabirds to be seen. You can find out about life in the past here in Ullapool, including the Highland clearances, in the Loch Broom Museum at the harbour.

Twelve miles south-east of Ullapool, on the A835, is the spectacular Corriechalloch Gorge, where the River Droma tumbles 150ft down the Falls of Measach. North of Ullapool, there's the empty wilderness of the Inverpolly National Nature Reserve to explore, with an information centre at Knockan Cliff on the A835, 13 miles from Ullapool. Further north beside Loch Assynt on the A837 is ruined Ardvreck Castle, the seat of the MacLeods of Assynt, where Montrose was taken prisoner in 1650. This scenic road goes by Loch Assynt and continues westward to Lochinver, a popular centre for touring the coast.

The northward road from Loch Assynt, the A894, runs to Kylesku and on via the A838 through a mountain wasteland to Durness, a pleasant village on the north coast 37 miles from Kylesku. Durness is close to several interesting places, including the craft village of nearby Balnakeil. The bay at Balnakeil is overlooked by the ruins of the 17th-century Old Church. From Durness you can go by boat and bus to Cape Wrath, the headland on Scotland's north-west corner, which has staggering views to the Hebrides and Orkney Islands.

323

PERTH
TAYSIDE

Tourist Information Centre, 45 High Street
(01738) 638353.

Arts Festival and Flambeaux procession

Since it was first held in 1972, the twelve-day Perth Festival of the Arts, at the end of May each year, has established itself as one of the best and liveliest of its kind in Scotland. Classical music, drama and the visual arts are its mainstays, but you might also find brass bands, jazz, folk music and dance on offer, plus ballet, puppets, poetry-readings and crafts.

Right at the tail-end of the year, on 31 December, the Flambeaux Procession burns the old year out in style at Comrie in Perthshire. At midnight a pipe band leads local men through the town carrying blazing 12ft poles, wrapped in sacking and soaked in paraffin. Other Comrie folk, in fancy dress, follow cheerfully behind.

Spectacular fireworks at the Perth Festival of the Arts held every May

An inland port on the River Tay, Perth has a long and colourful history. North Inch, one of the town's pleasant riverside parks, was in 1396 the scene of a formal battle between two clans, each side represented by 30 men, who fought each other to the death. Near the park today are peaceful Georgian streets, including Rose Terrace, where John Ruskin grew up. Balhousie Castle, in Hay Street, is home to the museum of one of the most famous of Scottish regiments, the Black Watch, named after its dark tartan. The museum and art gallery in George Street has instructive displays and the Lower City Mills has a working waterwheel and oatmeal milling demonstrations.

IN EASY REACH On the eastern edge of Perth, on the A85, Branklyn Garden covers only 2 acres, but it may well be the best 2-acre garden in Britain, noted especially for its alpine plants. Two miles north-east of Perth, on the A93, Scone Palace is located on a site of great historic interest. The palace was rebuilt in 1808 by William Atkinson for the 3rd Earl of Mansfield and today contains a wealth of fine paintings, French furniture, clocks, porcelain and ivory objects.

Huntingtower Castle, 2 miles west of Perth, on the A85, is one of Scotland's most historic castles where the Ruthvens held James VI prisoner. North of Perth, 13 miles along the A9, is Dunkeld, where the ruined cathedral is set romantically beside the rippling Tay. The National Trust for Scotland owns the two rows of 'Little Houses' which date from the late 17th century.

—————————————— 324 ——————————————

ST ANDREWS
FIFE

On the A91.
Tourist Information Centre, 70 Market Street (01334) 72021.

Golf Week

Exactly when golf began, and who invented it, are matters of controversy. What is not in dispute is the exalted position held by the town of St Andrews in the history of the game. As far back as the 1400s, golf was being played here on the open ground beside the sea. In 1754 the Society of St Andrews Golfers was established by 22 enthusiasts, who described the game as an 'ancient and healthful exercise'.

The society became the Royal and Ancient Golf Club in 1834 by courtesy of King William IV and it is now the game's recognised ruling body.

Every year, during the second half of April, Links Golf St Andrews organise the Golf Week, which provides a 'special package', golfing holiday, with accommodation, meals and entertainment, tuition by the local professionals and play on the course, culminating on the last day with a round on the venerated Old Course itself. No special arrangements are made to entertain spouses or children who (perish the thought) might not care for golf, however, there is plenty for them to do and to see in and around St Andrews.

At opposite ends of the sea front of St Andrews are the 'temples' of the town's two 'religions' – Christianity and golf – in the form of the ruined cathedral and the Royal and Ancient Golf Club, whose august clubhouse looks out over the revered Old Course. Golf has taken over, but St Andrews was once a major religious centre and the seat of Scotland's oldest university, founded in the 15th century. Monuments commemorate the Protestant martyrs who were burned here for their convictions during the 16th century.

Part of the cathedral's east end stands impressively sentinel over the remains of what was once an enormous church. Here too are the ruins of the older, 17th-century church of St Rule, who brought here the relics of St Andrew, Scotland's patron saint. There is a fine view from the 108ft tower of the church. Close by are the ruins of the castle, with a grim, bottle-shaped dungeon, 24ft deep, and a mine and counter-mine to explore, left over from a 1540s siege. Guided tours of the university (July to mid-September) start from the porter's lodge of St Salvator's College, North Street.

IN EASY REACH Leuchars, on the A919, 5 miles north-west of St Andrews, is known for its Norman church. Less than a mile to the east of Leuchars is Earlshall Castle, restored by Sir Robert Lorimer in the 1890s and famous for its topiary garden. Six miles south-west of the castle, on the A91, is the old town of Cupar. Two miles south of here, on the A916, is Hill of Tarvit, set in pleasant grounds. It is an elegant country house built by Sir Robert Lorimer in 1906 and in the care of the National Trust for Scotland. There is a notable collection of paintings, porcelain and tapestries. Just a mile from the house you can explore 16th-century, Scotstarvit Tower. At Ceres, 2 miles east of Hill of Tarvit, on the B939, the Fife Folk Museum has examples of the local domestic and agricultural life of the past.

Travelling ten miles south-east of St Andrews on the A918 will take you into the East Neuk (east corner) of Fife, with its string of attractive fishing villages and picturesque harbours stretching from Crail to Elie. The story of the fishing industry and the local people is well told at the Scottish Fisheries Museum in Anstruther, four miles from Crail. From Anstruther there are boat trips to see puffins and other seabirds on the Isle of May in the Firth of Forth. Inland lies Kellie Castle, another rewarding National Trust for Scotland property which is well worth a visit. There is a lovely Victorian garden here.

St Andrews Old Course, with the Royal and Ancient Golf Club clubhouse on the left

---
325

THE BLACK ISLE AND EASTER ROSS
HIGHLAND

Tourist Information Centres, North Kessock (0146373) 505,
The Square, Strathpeffer (01997) 421415 (seasonal opening only)
and The Square, Dornoch (01862) 810400.

The Black Isle is not an island but a promontory 16 miles long, lying between the Moray Firth and the superb natural harbour of the Cromarty Firth, a quiet and pleasant area, with sandy beaches and good birdwatching. (Why 'black' is something of a mystery). Fortrose, on the A832, is a sailing resort, with a ruined medieval cathedral. Ten miles away, Cromarty is an attractive town on the northern tip of the Black Isle. Here is the cottage where Hugh Miller, writer and theologian, a pioneer geologist and student of fossils and fairies, was born in 1802. This early-18th-century cottage is preserved as a shrine to him by the National Trust for Scotland.

Easter Ross is the mainland area of mountains and forests north and west of the Cromarty Firth. There's a museum of local history in the 18th-century Town House at Dingwall on the A862, with information about General Sir Hector MacDonald's distinguished military career in the 19th century. He is also commemorated by a tower on nearby Mitchell Hill. Five miles to the west on the A834 is Strathpeffer, an elegant Victorian spa town where you can still take the waters in the Pump Room. There are crafts and a good doll museum at Strathpeffer Station visitor centre.

Running alongside the Cromarty Firth and later the Dornoch Firth, the A9 comes to Dornoch, a holiday resort which still retains the character of a cathedral town. The cathedral was largely rebuilt in the 19th century and is now a parish church. The showplace of the area is 12 miles further north of Dornoch, on the A9, outside Golspie, where Dunrobin Castle, the great baronial palace of the Earls and Dukes of Sutherland, reposes grandly in beautiful grounds above the sea. The castle was rebuilt in the 1850s by Sir Charles Barry, and the interiors were designed by Sir Robert Lorimer around 1920. There are splendid paintings and tapestries. The lovely gardens are modelled on those of Versailles.

326

BURNS COUNTRY
STRATHCLYDE

Tourist Information Centre,
39 Sandgate, Ayr (01292) 284196.

A thatched whitewashed cottage in the Ayrshire village of Alloway, 2 miles south of Ayr on the B7024, is the principal shrine to the memory of Robert Burns. He was born here on 25 January 1759 and spent the first 7 years of his life here. Next door there are relics, letters and manuscripts in the Burns Museum. Also in the village is the Land o' Burns Centre, which contains information about the poet's life and times, and includes an audio-visual display. Near by is the Burns Monument, in the classical style which was thought appropriate to his muse in 1823. Take a look too at the single-arched bridge over the River Doon and the ruined Auld Kirk, which both appear in *Tam o' Shanter*.

Alloway is on the southern outskirts of Ayr, unsurpassed 'for honest men and bonnie lasses' and also as a base for exploring this part of Scotland. Burns was baptised in the 17th-century Auld Kirk of Ayr, and the two bridges which are the subject of one of his poems are still here. At Irvine, 12 miles north of Ayr on the A78, the old street called Glasgow Vennel has been restored to its appearance in the 1780s. Burns worked there, dressing flax, at this time.

To the east of Irvine is Kilmarnock, on the A71, which has more connections with the life of the poet Burns and an 80ft monument to him in Kay Park. For a change from Burns, there's Dean Castle, where the collection of exhibits includes musical instruments and arms and armour. The museum and art gallery of the Dick Institute in Kilmarnock has items on local archaeology and natural history. Mauchline, 7 miles south-east of Kilmarnock, on the A76, is where Burns married Jean Armour in 1788. Their house in Castle Street, is now a museum, and Poosie Nansie's Tavern, which they knew, is still in business.

At Tarbolton, off the B743, to the west of Mauchline, there is an additional important landmark in Burns' life to be seen at the Bachelor's Club, now owned by the National Trust for Scotland. Here Burns and his friends founded a debating society. Auchinlech, 5 miles south-east of Mauchline on the A76, switches attention to another Scottish literary giant – James Boswell. He was buried in the mausoleum at the old parish church, which has been turned into an interesting museum commemorating his life and work.

A Burns leaflet is available from both the Ayrshire and Dumfries and Galloway Tourist Boards and will guide you to all these places, and also south to Dumfries, where the poet spent the last years of his life and where he and his wife are buried (see Caerlaverock Castle entry).

Marymass Festival

In August of the year 1563 Mary, Queen of Scots paid a visit to the town of Irvine on the Ayrshire coast and was entertained at Seagate Castle. This was two years after her return from France to take up the reins of government in Scotland, when she was in her early twenties. Beautiful, high-spirited and charming, she made such an impression on the town that, ever since, the occasion has been remembered in the annual Marymass Festival in August. There's a procession past the castle (now a roofless ruin) and the Marymass Queen is crowned, dressed as the Queen of Scots and attended by her 'Marys', on the model of the queen's four ladies-in-waiting, who were all called Mary. This is the climax of the Marymass Fair, which is much older and goes right back to the 12th century. Horse-races, in which lumbering Clydesdales take part, are also part of the festivities. The races are said to be even older than the fair itself.

Common Ridings and
Arts Festival

*In medieval Dumfries
there was a court which
did its best to force
quarrelling neighbours
to make up their
differences and be
reconciled. It has left its
name behind it in Guid
Nychburris Week (good
neighbours' week),
around the middle of
June. This follows the
general pattern of the
Border area's common-
riding festivities, with a
riding of the town's
boundaries, the crowning
of the Queen of the
South and general
jollifications. A few
weeks earlier, at the end
of May, also in
Dumfries, the Dumfries
and Galloway Arts
Festival occurs. It has
been bringing
professional talent in
music, dance and drama
to the town since 1979.
The festival concentrates
particularly on classical
music, ballet, traditional
jazz, folk music, plays
and the visual arts.*

327

CAERLAVEROCK CASTLE
DUMFRIES AND GALLOWAY

*On the B725, 8 miles south of Dumfries.
Tourist Information Centre, Whitesands, Dumfries (01387) 53862.*

Moated, rose-red, profoundly romantic-looking, the ruins of 'the fort of the lark' dominate the marshes and flats along the Solway Firth. A carving of the Maxwell coat of arms is proudly displayed over the doorway of the formidable gatehouse, which stands at the apex of a triangle of curtain walls, with drum towers at the other corners. Caerlaverock endured five major sieges between 1300 and 1640. Inside, in contrast to the battlemented exterior, you will find the 1st Earl of Nithsdale's Renaissance-style mansion of 1634, its rooms decorated with heraldic carvings and scenes from classical mythology: all empty now, however, and open to the sky.

The marshes and mudflats of the Caerlaverock Nature Reserve, stretch for 6 miles along the shore of the Nith Estuary and the Solway Firth. The natterjack toad breeds here and in winter the reserve is home a great variety of wildfowl.

IN EASY REACH Just to the east of the Caerlaverock Nature Reserve, off the B725, is the parish church of Ruthwell (pronounced 'Rivvel') which contains a famous and beautiful cross of the 8th century. It is richly carved with reliefs depicting Gospel scenes, including a moustached Jesus, and with lines in the runic alphabet from *The Dream of the Rood*, an Anglo-Saxon poem in which Christ's cross describes the Crucifixion.

Dumfries, on the A75, is a tourist centre with an attractive waterfront along the River Nith. Robert Burns lived here for five years until his death in 1796 and this story is told in the Robert Burns Centre in Mill Road. His house in Burns Street is now a museum. He and his wife are buried in the Burns Mausoleum behind St Michael's Church. Also of interest are the Dumfries Museum and Camera Obscura at the Old Observatory in Church Street and the Old Bridge House Museum in Mill Road.

328

THE CAIRNGORMS
HIGHLAND AND GRAMPIAN

Tourist Information Centre, Grampian Road, Aviemore, Highland (01479) 810363.

Topped by Ben Macdui at 4,300ft, and with five other peaks above 4,000ft, the Cairngorms form Britain's premier mountain mass, a magnet for climbers, walkers and in winter, skiers. The Cairngorms National Nature Reserve, the biggest in the country, is home to the eagle and the wild cat, the stag and the capercaillie – a grouse the size of a turkey. In the Glen More Forest Park you may see reindeer, introduced here from Sweden in the 1950s. The Forestry Commission's information centre is on the 'ski road' which leads eastwards from Aviemore to the highest peaks.

Since the 1960s, Aviemore had developed into a lively all-year-round resort town. The Strathspey Railway runs steam trains along 5 miles of track from their station near the British Rail station at Aviemore to Boat of Garten, where the ospreys nest in the Loch Garten Nature Reserve. You can find out all about the Highlands at the Landmark Visitor Centre, Carrbridge, on the B9153.

Going south from Aviemore, attractions are strung like pearls along the thread of the Spey Valley. In the Highland Wildlife Park south of Kincraig, 8 miles from Aviemore on the B9152, you can see Highland cattle, deer, wolves, eagles, bison and other animals that are, or once were, native to the region. The RSPB has a nature reserve at Loch Insh, near Kincraig, off the B970, which attracts multitudes of birds. For the history of the Highlands and Islands, consult the Highland Folk Museum at Kingussie, 12 miles south-west of Aviemore.

329

CAITHNESS
HIGHLAND

*Tourist Information Centres: Riverside, Thurso (01847) 62371 (seasonal opening only)
and Whitechapel Road, Wick (01955) 2596.*

The old county of Caithness covered the desolate moors and peat bogs of Scotland's north-eastern corner. The northern coast of this area looks across the treacherous tidal races of the Pentland Firth in the Orkneys, with wonderful views from vantage points like Dunnet Head, the most northerly spot on the mainland of Britain. The ferry port for Orkney is Thurso, which in the 19th century flourished on the export of paving-stones from the local quarries. Dounreay, with its nuclear reactor, is 9 miles to the west of Thurso. The visitor centre here has audio-visual displays and models to interpret the nature of atomic power. There is also fine coastal scenery in this area.

Travelling east for 12 miles along the coast from Thurso, on the A836, will bring you to a small road leading to the gardens of the Queen Mother's Castle of Mey. They are sometimes open to the public in summer. John o'Groats, a further 6 miles east, is Britain's northernmost village. Here you can take boat trips to see the seals on the island of Stroma.

Running down the eastern Caithness coast are towering cliffs, with occasional crumbling castles. Wick is an old Viking settlement, once a herring fishing port: the Heritage Centre has the story. Further south, half-way between Ulbster and Lybster, off the A9, is the Hill o'Many Stanes, a mysterious Bronze Age monument consisting of 22 rows of 8 small stones. Back on the A9 at Dunbeath, 21 miles south-west of Wick, the Laidhay Croft Museum preserves memories of a vanished way of life.

--- 330 ---

DALMENY HOUSE
LOTHIAN

Off the A90, 3 miles east of South Queensferry. Tourist Information Centres: 3 Princes Street, Edinburgh 0131-577 1700 and Burgh Halls, The Cross, Linlithgow (01506) 844600.

Dalmeny House was built in 1815 by William Wilkins for the 4th Earl of Rosebery, who demanded and got a grand Tudor mullion-windowed mansion in the English style, peppered with chimney-pots and turrets. His son, the fifth earl, was Prime Minister briefly in the 1890s and owner of a Derby-winning racehorse. He married a Rothschild and the house today contains French furniture from Mentmore, the opulent Rothschild house in Buckinghamshire which the Roseberys inherited. There are also relics of Napoleon, including his St Helena furniture. The house is set in gracious parkland on the shore of the Firth of Forth.

The Ferry Fair and Burry Man

On the second Saturday in August every year, South Queensferry holds its Ferry Fair. The town was for centuries the port for ferries across the Forth and has been staging its fair for the last 300 years. This regular event is preceded by a most unusual custom when, on the day before the fair, a nightmare figure stalks the streets, covered from head to toe with thistle burrs, which give the effect of some atrocious disfigurement. The figure is called the Burry Man (see left). He has a cap of flowers on his head and in his hands he holds two large bunches of flowers on striped poles. He is led about by two attendants, who collect money for charity. It is believed to be lucky to meet him on his rounds. The origins and rationale of this strange custom are unknown, but it is said that the town would suffer serious misfortune if it were ever dropped.

IN EASY REACH From South Queensferry, the Forth is crossed by two spectacular bridges, both of them masterpieces of engineering: the 1890 rail bridge and the 1964 road bridge. Off the A904, 2 miles to the west of South Queensferry, is another exceptionally fine aristocratic mansion. This is Hopetoun House, the Marquess of Linlithgow's stately 18th-century home designed by William Adam and his sons. There are splendid staterooms, paintings, furniture and china, and a museum to be seen indoors, and deer and rare St Kilda sheep in the park. West of Hopetoun is the House of the Binns, off the A904, an elegant 17th-century house with fine plaster ceilings. Four miles to the south-west, on the A706, is Linlithgow, with its ruins of the royal palace where Mary, Queen of Scots was born, and the handsome church of St Michael in which she was baptised.

After crossing the Forth by the road bridge (the A90), you come to Dunfermline. There you will find the ruins of the abbey, and what little is left of the old royal palace. The birthplace of Andrew Carnegie is now a museum to the great industrialist. Seven miles west of Dunfermline is Culross, off the A985, where the National Trust for Scotland has preserved a remarkable example of a pre-Industrial Revolution Scots town.

Right: fireworks
during the Festival :
Below right: the castle
from Princes Street
Gardens, where many
statues of famous
Scotsmen can be seen

331

EDINBURGH
LOTHIAN

*Tourist Information Centres: 3 Princes Street 0131-577 1700 and Edinburgh
Airport 0131-333 2167.*

International Festival

*Edinburgh is packed
out for three weeks at
festival time in August
– usually the last three
weeks of the month.
Street entertainers and
musicians, art
exhibitions and a lively
range of off-beat
'fringe' attractions
supplement the main
musical and theatre
programme. A specially
popular event is the
military searchlight
tattoo, staged in front
of the dramatically
floodlit castle, with
massed pipes, drums,
military bands and a
cast of hundreds.*

*The idea of the
festival was first
discussed during World
War II and it was
launched in 1947, in the
hope of encouraging
peaceful co-operation
among the nations as
well as bringing
visitors and revenue to
the city. A leading
figure in the early years
was Sir Rudolf Bing.
The festival has grown
into the most
important and
successful event of its
kind in Britain.
Edinburgh's Lord
Provost, in the first
year of the festival,
committed the city to
providing a centre
where all that was best
in music, drama and
the arts could be
experienced in ideal
surroundings, and that
promise has been kept.*

'The Athens of the North' is a city of style and distinction, noted among other things for its unrivalled array of statues and monuments, and its prestigious annual festival. It owes its existence to the great precipitous rock on which the castle stands – a defensible site first inhabited far back in prehistoric times. The castle today looks more like a barracks than a fortress, with points of interest ranging from the Honours of Scotland (the royal crown and regalia) to Sir Robert Lorimer's dignified Scottish National War Memorial of 1927, and including the apartments of Mary, Queen of Scots and the room where James VI (later James I of England) was born.

From the castle, the Royal Mile leads down to Holyrood Palace. On the way it passes the Outlook Tower, with a camera obscura providing a panorama of the city, and Gladstone's Land, a tall tenement building where you can catch a glimpse of Edinburgh life as it was in the 17th century. Lady Stair's House near by is a museum to Sir Walter Scott, Robert Burns and Robert Louis Stevenson.

St Giles's Cathedral is known for its crown spire and for the chapel of the Order of the Thistle, designed by Sir Robert Lorimer in 1911. Inside the cathedral there are monuments to the gallant Montrose, hanged in 1650, and to the man principally responsible for the hanging – Archibald Campbell.

Further along the Royal Mile, in High Street, are the Wax Museum with its chamber of horrors, and the excellent Museum of Childhood, 'the noisiest museum in the world'. The city's local history museum is in Huntly House, Canongate.

At the end of the Royal Mile stands the royal palace of Holyrood, rebuilt in the 1670s. It was here that Rizzio was stabbed to death in front of Mary, Queen of Scots; here that Mary married Bothwell; and here that both Cromwell and the Young Pretender held court in their time. In the grounds are the ruins of Holyrood Abbey.

Princes Street, the city's main street, is bordered by pleasant gardens. Here there is the 1840s monument to Sir Walter Scott, Edinburgh's answer to London's Albert Memorial, and close by is the National Gallery of Scotland housed in an 1850s building by William Playfair, with a very distinguished collection of paintings, including works by Scottish artists.

In addition you might include in your visit the two branches of the Royal Museum of Scotland in Chambers Street and Queen Street, the latter for its Scottish exhibits; the Scottish National Portrait Gallery in Queen Street; the tombs and memorials in Greyfriars churchyard; the monuments on Calton Hill; and the Royal Botanic Garden in Inverleith Row, one of the oldest botanic gardens in Britain, noted especially for its rhododendron collection.

--------------------------- 332 ---------------------------

FALKLAND PALACE
FIFE

Falkland is on the A912, 11½ miles south-west of Cupar.
Tourist Information Centre, Market Street, St Andrews (01334) 72021.

Falkland Palace, now looked after by the National Trust for Scotland, was a favourite country retreat of the later Stuart sovereigns. Here they would go hawking and hunt deer and wild boar in the forests of Fife. Formerly the site of an old MacDuff castle, the estate came to the royal house by way of marriage in the 14th century and knew a violent history of murder and torture. James III and James IV were responsible for building the palace, and James V brought in French craftsmen to decorate the south and east ranges with medallions of figures from classical mythology in the Renaissance style. Mary, Queen of Scots spent happy days here, 'playing the country girl'.

The palace occupied three sides of a square. The south range and part of the east range are intact, thanks to restoration work in the 19th century by the Marquess of Bute. Visitors can see the bakehouse, the library, the chapel royal, and the king's bedchamber with its splendid golden four-poster. Outside, the pleasant garden, re-created after World War II, contains the 'real' (or royal) tennis court constructed for James V in 1539; it is still playable.

Beyond the castle, in Falkland town, there are some charming 17th- to 19th-century houses and cobbled streets. This was Scotland's first conservation area.

IN EASY REACH South-west of Falkland across the Lomond Hill, about 11 miles away, is Loch Leven with its romantic-looking castle situated on an island which can be reached by ferry from Kinross. Mary, Queen of Scots was held prisoner in this castle for almost a year. On the south bank of the loch, the RSPB runs the Vane Farm Nature Centre, on the B9097, a haven for wildfowl, where you can also see displays giving information on the wildlife and geology of the area. To the south of Loch Leven, off the B920, the Lochore Meadows Country Park has been created almost as if by magic out of a derelict mining landscape.

--------------------------- 333 ---------------------------

FLOORS CASTLE
BORDERS

Just north of Kelso on the A6089.
Tourist Information Centres: Town House, Kelso (01573) 223464 (seasonal opening only) and Murray's Green, Jedburgh (01835) 863688.

With its host of battlements, towers, turrets, cupolas and chimneys, and beautifully positioned above the River Tweed, Floors Castle made an ideal setting for part of the film *Greystoke*. The huge house was built by William Adam (father of Robert Adam) in the 1720s, but owes its appearance today mainly to William Playfair, who started work here for the 6th Duke of Roxburghe in 1838. The American heiress who married the eighth duke had the interiors remodelled to display her superlative collections of tapestry and furniture. Floors belonged to the formidable Borders dynasty of Ker (pronounced 'Care') until the third duke, cruelly frustrated in love, took a vow of celibacy and the title and estate passed to the Innes clan in 1805.

IN EASY REACH In Kelso there is a fine view of Floors Castle from the bridge John Rennie built over the Tweed in 1803. The town's major attractions are its splendid market square, with the town hall and handsome Georgian buildings, and the ruined abbey which was destroyed by the English in 1545. Seven miles west of Kelso, off the B6404, Smailholm Tower stands in solitary splendour above a loch. From it there are magnificent views.

Six miles north-west of Kelso, off the A6089, is the beautiful Georgian mansion of Mellerstain. William Adam built the wings of the house in 1725 and his son Robert built the central block 40 years or so later. There are sumptuous Robert Adam interiors, with fine 18th-century furniture and paintings, plus impressive terraced gardens leading down to the lake.

North-east from Kelso, 9 miles away on the A698, is Coldstream, where Border armies used to ford the Tweed. The place gave its name to the Coldstream Guards, and the local museum in the market square has a section illustrating the history of the regiment.

Less than a mile to the west of Coldstream, off the A697, the lovely grounds of The Hirsel, the seat of the Douglas-Homes, are open in the summer. Here there is a craft centre and nature trails around the lake and along the Leet valley.

●

Civic Weeks and Ram Sales

The Civic Week in July is Kelso's local festival, with the ride led by the Kelso Laddie, also known as The Whipman, with his Right Hand Man and Left Hand Man at his side. On the Saturday they ride to Yetholm, close to the border itself, where they pick sprigs from a fir tree to wear.

At Coldstream the Civic Week is in August, when the riders led by the Coldstreamer go across the border to Flodden Field, where the Scots went down to a disastrous defeat at the hands of the English in 1513. A wreath is laid on the monument to the brave men of both sides.

Later in the year one of the great events in the Borders today are the ram sales at Kelso, where in one September day up to 6,000 animals may be sold in 15 or more auction rings.

●

---- 334 ----

FYVIE CASTLE
GRAMPIAN

Off the A947, 8 miles south of Turriff.
Tourist Information Centres: Fordoun, Fyvie (01651) 891597 (seasonal opening only)
and Collie Lodge, Banff (01261) 812419.

Acquired by the National Trust for Scotland in 1984, Fyvie Castle with its five great towers has claims to be the most imposing Scots baronial mansion in the country. It is set in a handsomely landscaped park. The castle goes back originally to the 13th century, but the interior bears the opulent stamp of Alexander Forbes-Leith, a Scottish-American steel magnate created Lord Leith of Fyvie in 1905. He had the house restyled and furnished in the utmost of Edwardian luxury and installed in it his collection of Raeburns – the finest anywhere in private hands – along with paintings by Gainsborough, Romney, Opie and others, as well as tapestries and arms and armour. An earlier feature of the castle is the superb 17th-century wheel staircase, rising five floors in the central tower.

IN EASY REACH South-east of Fyvie Castle, via the B9005 and Methlick, the National Trust for Scotland also owns Haddo House, the elegant Georgian home of the Gordons, Marquesses of Aberdeen. The house was designed in 1731 by William Adam. Today it stands in a splendid park. Inside there is a fine collection of portraits to be seen and a chapel by G E Street. At Pitmedden, 5 miles to the south on the B999, the Trust owns the formal 'Great Garden' originally laid out in 1675 and re-created by the Trust in the 1950s. The Museum of Farming Life on the same estate has an interesting historical collection.

Two miles north-west of Pitmedden, off the B999, is Tolquhon Castle, a late-16th-century conversion of a fortified mansion. Although roofless, much of the structure is still of interest in so far as it depicts domestic life in times past.

---- 335 ----

GLAMIS CASTLE
TAYSIDE

On the A94, 5 miles south-west of Forfar.
Tourist Information Centres: 40 East High Street , Forfar (01307) 467876
(seasonal opening only) and Market Place, Arbroath (01241) 872609.

Magnificently turreted and battlemented, this 'storybook' castle of Glamis in the former county of Angus is the setting for *Macbeth* and is reputedly haunted by the ghost of a 16th-century Lady Glamis who was burned at the stake for witchcraft. More prosaically, Glamis (pronounced to rhyme with 'arms') has been the home of the Lyons, Earls of Strathmore, for 1,600 years. It was enlarged and rebuilt in the 17th century, round an older L-shaped tower. The Old Pretender stayed here in 1716 and there are mementoes of him to be seen in the house. The Queen Mother grew up here – her father was the 14th Earl – and visitors can see the rooms provided for her as Duchess of York. In the village of Glamis, the Angus Folk Museum, housed in an attractive row of 19th-century cottages has an excellent collection of items illustrating a wide range of local history. The collection and the cottages are in the care of the National Trust for Scotland.

IN EASY REACH The National Trust for Scotland also owns the house in which J M Barrie, author of *Peter Pan*, was born. The house is to be found in Brechin Road, Kirriemuir, 5 miles north of Glamis on the A928. It has been restored to its former character around the time of Barrie's birth in 1860.

Forfar, 6 miles away on the A926, and famous for the 'Forfar Bridie', has a museum of local history. A mile or so to the east of Forfar, off the B9113, are the ruins of Restenneth Priory where the tower base and archway date back to around AD700.

To the south of Glamis, on the A929, is Dundee, where the *Discovery*, in which Captain Scott sailed to the Antarctic, is open to the public in Victoria Dock. Also of interest here are the observatory on Balgay Hill and the town's museums and art galleries. Seventeen miles away on the coast north-east of Dundee, via the A92, is the fishing town of Arbroath, known for its 'smokies', or smoked haddocks. You can find out about these and many other aspects of Arbroath's history in the museum in the Signal Tower. There is also a fishing industry trail along the coast.

Annual Shinty Games

July brings the Annual Shinty Games to Dundee (see below) with competitions for senior and junior clubs, for women and for beginners. Local groups and hockey and rugby teams enter sides, and there are contests of individual skills as well. Shinty is an ancestor of hockey and a close relative of the Irish game of hurling, which involves hitting a ball with a curved stick called a 'caman' and driving it through the goal, the 'hail'. Two ways in which shinty differs from hurling are that only the goalkeeper is allowed to handle the ball and the Scottish stick has a narrow blade, not a broad one. Shinty is now played twelve-a-side, but in the past in the

Highlands any number could play and a game might last all day. There were sometimes games between rival clans. Shinty was brought to the western Highlands by the original Scots – invaders from Ulster – who settled in Argyll. It was revived in the 1880s after almost dying out earlier in the 19th century.

336

THE GREAT GLEN
HIGHLAND

*Tourist Information Centres: Fort William (01397) 703781, Car Park, Fort Augustus
(01320) 6367 (seasonal opening only) and Castle Wynd, Inverness (01463) 234353.*

The Great Glen is the geological split which slices through the Highlands from Inverness on the Moray Firth to Fort William and Loch Linnhe. The Caledonian Canal, a tremendous feat of 19th-century engineering, was constructed by Thomas Telford to create a direct route between the North Sea and the Atlantic, bypassing Cape Wrath. No longer big enough for most seagoing vessels, it is used by small boats and there are enjoyable cruises from Inverness and Fort Augustus.

The A82 runs the whole 60-mile length of the glen from Fort William up to Inverness, past ruined castles and wooded lochs. North of Spean Bridge, in the area where many commandos trained during World War II, the Commando Memorial honours those who fell. At Fort Augustus, the Great Glen Heritage Exhibition tells the story of the glen from the Picts to the present day. From Invermoriston, the A887 branches off for the Western Isles.

The A82 continues along the west side of Loch Ness, which is 24 miles long, a mile wide and extremely deep. Surely few people come this way without keeping an eye out for the monster – which St Columba saw and admonished as far back as the 6th century. The Cobb Memorial was built in the memory of John Cobb, who was killed here in an attempt to break the waterspeed record in 1952. Ruined Castle Urquhart, on its promontory protruding into the loch was once a stronghold of the Grants. At Drumnadrochit, the Loch Ness Monster Centre provides a good survey of the evidence about the elusive beast.

337

ISLE OF BUTE
STRATHCLYDE

*Reached by ferries from Wemyss Bay or Colintraive.
Tourist Information Centre, 15 Victoria Street, Rothesay (0170050) 2151.*

Rothesay, on the island of Bute, was once a spa and is now a popular Firth of Clyde holiday resort and yachting centre. You can find out all about the island's history and wildlife at the Bute Museum, Stuart Street. Rothesay Castle is one of the best preserved medieval fortresses in Scotland, a royal castle, much scarred by war. Its circular curtain wall is 30ft high and surrounded by a moat. A formidable barbican was added in the 16th century when the King of Scots used the castle as a base against the Lords of the Isles.

Fifteen miles long and 3 miles wide, Bute is separated from the Argyll mainland to the north by the narrow and beautiful channel called the Kyles of Bute. The car ferry across to Colintraive on the mainland takes only a few minutes and brings you into the Cowal Peninsula, where you can explore the 100 square miles of the Argyll Forest Park and its mountains, lochs and forests.

Dunoon, on the A815, is a resort on the Firth of Clyde. There are ferries from here across to Gourock to the east. North from Dunoon, near Ardbeg, are the Kilmun Arboretum, on the A880, with trees from all over the world, and the Younger Botanic Garden, on the A815, famous for its rhododendrons, azaleas and giant redwoods.

●

Festivities on Bute

The month of August brings 10 days of lively events to Rothesay, beginning with the Summer Show of the Bute Agricultural Society. There are classes for cattle and sheep, a horse show, trade stands and agricultural equipment on display. This leads straight into the Highland Festival, distinguished by its sailing regatta, angling contests, raft race in the bay, ceilidhs, old time dancing and art exhibitions. Conducted walks and tours explore the island and there are breezy boat cruises, while pipers, accordion bands and folk groups perform in the town's gardens. On the last day the festival culminates in the Bute Highland Games, with the British pipe band championships, Highland dancing contests, wrestling, athletics and a half marathon.

●

--- 338 ---

ISLE OF MULL
STRATHCLYDE

Reached by ferries from Oban and Lochaline, and from Kilchoan (summer only). Tourist Information Centre, The Pier, Tobermory (01688) 2182.

The island is 24 miles long and 26 miles across, but its western shoreline is deeply indented by sea-lochs and it has altogether 300 miles of coast, with magnificent sea views and impressive cliffs, especially in the south-west. Inland, the moors, covered in wildflowers rise to Ben More, 3,169ft, the highest point in Mull. The only town Tobermory, at the northern end of the Sound of Mull, has an attractive waterfront and yachting harbour, where you may hear enticing stories of sunken treasure from a Spanish Armada galleon which sank here in 1588.

At Craignure, on the east of the island, is the Mull and West Highland Railway which operates both steam and diesel trains on the ten-and-a-quarter inch gauge line, from Craignure just over a mile to Torosay Castle. Much of Torosay Castle is open to the public together with its delightful Italian terraced gardens, designed by Sir Robert Lorimer. The Scottish baronial architecture is complemented by the magnificent setting and inside the house are portraits, a study of the Antarctic, an Edwardian library and archive rooms.

From Dervaig in the north and Fionnphort in the south-west, there are boat trips in summer to see the remarkable basalt stacks of the island of Staffa offshore, and you can admire Fingal's Cave, which inspired Mendelssohn's overture. Fionnphort is also the port for Iona.

--- 339 ---

ISLE OF SKYE
HIGHLAND

Reached by ferry from Kyle of Lochalsh, or from Mallaig or Glenelg. Tourist Information Centre, Portree (01478) 2137.

Black, precipitous and wreathed in mist, the Cuillin Mountains (pronounced 'Coolin') rear up in the south-west of Skye. There are thrilling views of them along the B8083 from Broadford to Elgol, where you can take a boat trip to Loch Coruisk in the heart of the Cuillin Range. This loch is widely regarded as the most spectacular in all Scotland.

There's much else to enjoy in the 600 square miles of this delightful island. The way of life here a century ago in the old, peat-warmed crofts can be explored in the Black House Museums at Colbost on the B884, and Luib on the A850. The Skye Museum of Island Life is at Kilmuir (on the northern peninsula), near which is the grave of Flora Macdonald. It was in what is now the Royal Hotel in Portree that Flora bade a last farewell to Prince Charles Edward.

Dunvegan Castle, off the A850 in the west, has been the home of the MacLeod chiefs since at least the 12th century, and besides an extremely grim dungeon, it contains the famous 'fairy' flag of the Macleods, said to have been given to the fourth chief by his wife, who herself was of the 'wee folk'. The hereditary pipers to the Clan MacLeod were the MacCrimmons, the most famous dynasty of pipers in Scotland. The Piping Centre at Borreraig (north of the folk museum at Colbost) pays tribute to them and tells the tale of the pipes. In the south at Carbost the there are tours round the famous Talisker Distillery. At the Clan Donald Visitor Centre in Armadale, just off the southern end of the A851, there is a castle with a museum and gardens.

Skye Week

Close to the beginning of August, usually the first Wednesday of the month, Portree warms to the colour and romance of the annual Highland Games, which involve piping competitions, Highland dancing, tug-o-war, athletics and field events such as tossing the caber and throwing the hammer (and the wellie). The games, first held in 1878, are nowadays held the week after the Skye Folk Festival which hosts many concerts, ceilidhs and lunchtime sessions of local and national folk musicians. Gala days, craft fairs, festivals of Gaelic music and culture, street fairs, piping and archery competitions, sea angling competitions, sheep dog trials and watersport days are just some of the many annual events taking place throughout the summer months.

The Cuillins of Skye rise up behind Elgol

— 340 —
INVERARY CASTLE
STRATHCLYDE

Inverary is on the A83, near the head of Loch Fyne.
Tourist Information Centres: Inverary (01499) 2063 and Campbeltown
(01586) 552056.

Inverary is the capital of the formidable Clan Campbell, whose chief is MacCailean Mor, otherwise the Duke of Argyll. In the 1740s the third duke decided to rebuild both the town and his ruined ancestral castle in grand baronial style. Designed by the Welsh architect Roger Morris, the house has been called a 'toy fort on a huge scale'. The fifth duke had the interiors redesigned by Robert Mylne later in the 18th century and in the 1870s Anthony Salvin was called on to give the place an even more fairy-tale appearance. Today we can see Mylne's rooms sumptuously decorated in the French manner and impressive arrays of arms, paintings, furniture, porcelain and tapestries. Family portraits include one of Princess Louise, Queen Victoria's daughter, wife of the ninth duke. There is also a museum recalling Inverary's role as a combined operations training centre during World War II.

IN EASY REACH The A83 runs north-east from Inverary over the 860ft mountain pass called 'Rest and be thankful', with access to the northern reaches of the Argyll Forest Park (see separate entry). Two miles south from Inverary, the A83 passes the Argyll Wildlife Park, on the bank of Loch Fyne, which has rare owls, wild cats, wallabies, deer and goats. The Auchindrain Open Air Museum of Country Life, 4 miles further along the A83, is an old Highland township which has been restored to illustrate vividly the way of life of poor Highlanders in the past.

Another 5 miles along the A83 brings you to the exceptionally rewarding Crarae Glen Gardens, with their rare trees and flowering shrubs laid out in a glen close to the loch.

— 341 —
JEDBURGH ABBEY
BORDERS

Jedburgh is on the A68, 11 miles south of Kelso.
Tourist Information Centre, Murray's Green,
Jedburgh (01835) 863435.

On the side of a hill above the Jed Water, the monastery ruins of Jedburgh are dominated by the impressive church, which is roofless but otherwise almost intact. Particularly striking is the beautiful west front, with its 15th-century rose window. The abbey was founded in the 12th century for Augustinian canons from France. Often attacked and looted during Border conflicts, it was finally sacked by the English in the 1540s. The abbey is now in the charge of the Scottish Development Department, which has provided an interesting display in the visitor centre describing the life of the canons. It appears that they wore black habits at all times (even in bed). They lived under monastic discipline, but went out preaching and ministering to the people of the area.

A town trail guides you around Jedburgh, which has the chequered and violent history common to all the Border towns. There is a good museum in the picturesque house in Queen Street where Mary, Queen of Scots stayed for a month in 1566. Another small museum of interest is in the early-19th-century prison, on the site of the castle which was demolished in 1409. The prison had three blocks, each for a different category of prisoner.

IN EASY REACH Two miles south of Jedburgh, off the A68, the old Border stronghold of Ferniehurst Castle has been restored and opened to the public (limited opening in summer). Further west in Teviotdale, 10 miles from Jedburgh on the A698, is Hawick (pronounced 'Hoick'), where the exhibits at the Wilton Lodge Museum cover the history of the Borders and the important local knitwear industry. It is worth the drive 16 miles south from Hawick on the B6399 to see the unforgettably grim keep of Hermitage Castle, bleak stronghold of the Wardens of the Middle March, with a long history of bloodshed and cruelty. Mary, Queen of Scots visited her lover Bothwell here from Jedburgh in 1566.

Highland Games

At the Traditional Highland Games at Inverary in July you can enjoy the spectacle of tossing the caber (seen here) throwing the hammer, and the piping and Highland dancing competitions which are an accepted part of this type of occasion. This is one of more than 70 Highland Gatherings now held in Scotland every year, and so popular that they have spread to the Lowlands. The Highland clans used to meet at gatherings and test their strength and fighting abilities in contests, but today's Highland Games have a 19th-century stamp on them. They generally begin with a parade of massed pipers leading clansmen in kilts and bonnets, and the events are likely to include running and hurdling races, as well as field events. Among the latter is the peculiarly Scottish sport of tossing the caber, a pole anything up to 19ft long. The sport may have begun as a practical way of throwing a tree-trunk across a river or a ravine to serve as a bridge.

342

KIRKCUDBRIGHT
DUMFRIES AND GALLOWAY

Tourist Information Centres: Harbour Square, Kirkcudbright (01557) 330494 (seasonal opening only) and Whitesands, Dumfries (01387) 53862.

The harbour of Kirkcudbright was offered to the Spanish Armada in 1588 (so the story goes) by one of the Maxwells, a Roman Catholic and hereditary steward of this area. Formerly a flourishing port and the county town of its own shire, Kirkcudbright (pronounced 'Kirk-oo-bree') is a pleasant place, with its attractive waterfront and elegant houses, and its artists' colony. The Stewartry Museum, St Mary Street has a lively collection of material on life in Galloway in the past and on such local notables as John Paul Jones. Overlooking the harbour are the ruins of Maclellan's Castle, built in the 16th century by Sir Thomas Maclellan, whose elaborately decorated tomb is in Greyfriars Church. John Paul Jones was once imprisoned in the Tolbooth, in the High Street – now an arts centre. Broughton House, also in the High Street, was the home of the central figure of the Kirkcudbright school of painters, the Australian-born Edward Hornel, who died in 1933: you can see his work here, and his Japanese garden too.

Logan Botanic Garden, where southern hemisphere plants flourish — thanks to the Gulf Stream

IN EASY REACH South-east of Kirkcudbright, 5 miles away off the A711, are the ruins of Dundrennan Abbey, where Mary, Queen of Scots spent her last night on Scottish soil in 1568, before crossing the Solway Firth to England and her long captivity. A mile to the west, off the A75, is the implacable-looking tower of Threave Castle standing on an island in the River Dee. This stronghold of the Black Douglases still has the projection above the doorway, from which the Douglas chiefs were wont to hang a 'tassel' – anyone who had incurred their displeasure. About a mile away, on the south side of the A75, are the more peaceable precincts of Threave Gardens, where the National Trust for Scotland raises superb spring daffodils. Near by is the Threave Wildfowl Refuge on the Dee, to which ducks and geese flock in winter.

343

LOGAN BOTANIC GARDEN
DUMFRIES AND GALLOWAY

Near Port Logan, off the B7065, 10 miles south of Stranraer. Tourist Information Centres: Bridge Street, Stranraer (01776) 702595 (seasonal opening only) and Whitesands, Dumfries (01387) 53862.

The Rhinns peninsula, projecting into the Irish Sea from Stranraer like a hammer head, enjoys the Gulf Stream's blessing of a gentle climate which encourages exotic, southern hemisphere plants to grow in the gardens. The queen of them is Logan Botanic Garden, where palm trees, giant tree ferns and what elsewhere would be greenhouse plants flourish cheerfully in a 14-acre outdoor site. The garden is now an offshoot of the Royal Botanic Garden, Edinburgh. It was created around the turn of the century by the McDouall family, who pioneered the art of peat-gardening here.

A mile further south along the B7065, on the shore of Logan Bay, is a tidal fish-pool, 30ft deep and 50ft round, constructed in 1788 to supply the lairds of Logan with cod. The fish in it are tame enough to be fed.

IN EASY REACH At the southern tip of the Rhinns peninsula are the impressive granite cliffs of the Mull of Galloway. Here there is an RSPB reserve, home to multitudes of seabirds. Just north from Logan Botanic Garden, on the A716, are the gardens of Ardwell House, well known for daffodils, rhododendrons and roses.

Stranraer, on the A75, is a holiday resort and ferry port for Ireland. The Wigtown Museum, George Street, covers the history of what used to be Wigtownshire. To the east, 3 miles away from Stranraer on the A75, are the beautiful gardens of Castle Kennedy, famous for magnolias, rhododendrons and monkey-puzzle trees. The gardens are set between two lochs and close to the ruins of an old castle, the home of the Earls of Stair, which burned down in 1716.

A further 7 miles east, off the A75, the chapter house and cloister walls of Glenluce Abbey stand in the valley of the Water of Luce. It was home to the medieval wizard Michael Scot, whose books are said to be buried here.

344

MANDERSTON
BORDERS

On the A6105, 2 miles east of Duns.
Tourist Information Centres: High Street, Coldstream (01890) 882607
(seasonal opening only) and 3 Princes Street, Edinburgh 0131-557 1700.

The entrance to Manderston's beautiful stable courtyard – not surprisingly an important feature of the estate as it was built for racecourse owner Sir James Miller

Grand Edwardian country houses may be fairly few and far between in this area, but Manderston is one of the grandest, with all the opulent comfort of the days just before World War I. It was built for Sir James Miller, a Derby-winning millionaire racehorse owner. The architect, John Kinross, instructed to spare no expense, designed a mansion in the Georgian style with sumptuous interiors modelled on those of Robert Adam (Lady Miller's family home was Kedleston Hall, the great Robert Adam palace in Derbyshire). Sir James died at Manderston in 1906, soon after the house was finished. Its features include the painted ceilings, the ballroom in Sir James's racing colours of primrose and white, the silver-balustraded staircase and the Blue John Ware collection. The lavish 'below stairs' quarters are of special interest: the housekeeper's room, the servants' hall, the larders, sculleries, and the rest. Outside are an impressive marble dairy, astonishingly luxurious stables and beautiful formal gardens.

IN EASY REACH Duns, 2 miles west of Manderston, is a market town in the farming area called the Merse. The trophies won by Jim Clark, the world-champion racing driver, who was killed in 1968, can be seen in the Memorial Room to him at 44 Newton Street. The A6105 and B6355 lead north-east from Duns to Chirnside, where Jim Clark is buried. The B6355 then continues on to Eyemouth, a picturesque fishing port and seaside resort. Most of the items on display in the Eyemouth Museum, Auld Kirk, are related to the fishing industry and local life. In Coldingham, 3 miles north-west of the A1107, are the ruins of Coldingham Priory, where the B6438 runs on north-east to St Abbs. The titanic cliffs of St Abbs Head are a National Nature Reserve, crowded with seabirds.

345

ROYAL DEESIDE
GRAMPIAN

Balmoral is on the A93, 8 miles west of Ballater.
Tourist Information Centres: Station Square, Ballater (013397) 55306
(seasonal opening only) and Kincardine and Deeside Tourist Board,
Bridge Street, Banchory (01330) 822066.

Braemar Gathering

It was Queen Victoria's enthusiasm for Highland Games which did much to establish their popularity. The games, now held regularly at Braemar (see right), were staged several times at Balmoral in the 19th century, at her invitation. It is said that the Braemar Gathering goes back ultimately to the 10th century and the days of King Kenneth II, and that King Malcolm Canmore gave a prize to the clansman who was first up and down Creag Choinnich, the hill behind Braemar Castle. However this may be, the modern series of gatherings, begun in 1832, was organised by the Braemar Highland Society. The events included tossing the caber and the Creag Choinnich race, but the latter was stopped by Queen Victoria in 1850 because it was taking too heavy a physical toll on the winners. The Braemar Gathering of today (held on the first Saturday in September) with its massed pipe bands and Highland finery is the most prestigious event of its kind and is attended by members of the royal family (see above) and thousands of other spectators.

The grounds of Balmoral, enlivened with statues and memorials, are open from May to July, when the royal family is not in residence. The castle is not open to the public, but there is an exhibition in the ballroom describing royal life here. This was Queen Victoria's beloved Highland home, and the Prince Consort had much to do with the design of the Scots baronial-style house, completed in 1855. The little church at Crathie near by also has many royal associations.

Six miles west along the scenic valley of the Dee, via the A93, is Braemar, where the most prestigious of all Highland Gatherings is held in September every year. It was here in 1715 that the Old Pretender's standard was raised by the Earl of Mar. Here also, in a cottage on the Glenshee road, Robert Louis Stevenson wrote *Treasure Island* in 1881. On the north side of the village is Braemar Castle, the home of the Farquharsons. It was garrisoned by government troops after both the 1715 and the 1745 uprisings. A minor road runs west from Braemar to Linn of Dee, a famous beauty spot 5 miles away.

There are many enjoyable drives and walks in this extremely attractive area of mountains and forests. Ballater, 17 miles east of Braemar, is a good touring centre: it was developed as a health spa by the Farquharsons early in the 19th century. Eighteen miles to the north-east along the B9119 is one of the jewels in the National Trust for Scotland's crown: graceful Craigievar Castle, like a Walt Disney fantasy, but real enough. Inside are elaborate ceilings and a secret stair.

346

STIRLING CASTLE
CENTRAL

Tourist Information Centres, 41 Dumbarton Road, Stirling (01786) 475019 and
Motorway Service Area, M9/M80 junction 9 (01786) 814111 (seasonal opening only).

Crouched high on a great rock, Stirling Castle guards a strategically critical crossing of the Forth, a point on which much of the history of Scotland has turned. It is doubtful if any fortress in the kingdom has seen a more turbulent history: armies on the march, battles, murder and sudden death have been commonplace. Most of the castle we can see today dates from the 15th and 16th centuries when the Scottish kings lived here. Their palace is a Renaissance masterpiece with a multitude of statues, grotesque figures and gargoyles. There is an impressive Great Hall and a chapel royal rebuilt by James VI (I of England), who spent his grim childhood here. Also housed here is the regimental museum of the Argyll and Sutherland Highlanders.

The town of Stirling formed around the castle and spread gradually down the hill. Its history can be fruitfully explored at the Stirling Smith Museum, Dumbarton Road. Just outside the town to the south-east, in a loop of the Forth, are the ruins of Cambuskenneth Abbey. A mile to the north-east of Stirling, off the B998 and high up on a 360ft crag, is the striking 1869 memorial to Sir William Wallace, the Scots patriot who defied Edward I. It contains, among other things, what is believed to be the hero's gigantic sword.

IN EASY REACH The battlefield of Bannockburn, where Robert the Bruce decisively defeated the English in 1314, is 2 miles south of Stirling along the A872: a little disappointing today. Located 5 miles north-west of Stirling on the A84 are the lions, tigers, penguins and elephants of the Blair Drummond Safari and Leisure Park, which also has a chimpanzee island, performing sea-lions and a fun-fair. Three miles further northwards on the A84, Doune has an extremely impressive castle and a good motor museum.

347
TRAQUAIR HOUSE
BORDERS

Traquair is off the B709, 1 mile south of Innerleithen.
Tourist Information Centres: High Street, Peebles (01721) 720138 and Halliwell's
House, Selkirk (01750) 20054 (both seasonal opening only).

In visiting this very romantic, secluded house on the bank of the Tweed, you are following the footsteps of 27 Scottish and English monarchs who have been here before you. The outside of the house still looks as it did at the end of the 17th century. The house incorporates a pele tower which goes all the way back to the 1100s. Tall, grey and austere, with little windows and rounded towers and turrets, Traquair is a home of lost causes – Roman Catholic religion and Jacobite politics. Its famous Bear Gates were shut when Prince Charles Edward passed through them in 1745, never to be re-opened until a Stuart returns to the throne. Inside there is a labyrinth of stone-flagged passages and winding stairs, with a a secret priest's room and an escape stairway, family relics, mementoes of Mary, Queen of Scots, and Jacobite glass. The laird brews a potent old ale in his brewhouse and there are craft workshops to enjoy as well as attractive gardens.

IN EASY REACH The Scottish Museum of Woollen Textiles is at Walkerburn, 2 miles east of Innerleithen on the A72. If you follow the river 9 miles to the south-west along the B712 you can enjoy the rare trees and shrubs of the Dawyck Botanic Garden. West from here at Broughton, reached by way of the B712 and A701, the John Buchan Centre keeps the memory of the author alive. Near by is Broughton Place, a modern Scots baronial-style house designed by Sir Basil Spence in 1938. The drawing-room and main hall are open as an art gallery in summer.

348
THE WHISKY TRAIL
GRAMPIAN

Dufftown is on the A920.
Tourist Information Centres: The Square, Dufftown (01340) 820501 (seasonal opening
only) and 17 High Street, Elgin (01343) 542666.

Malt whisky enthusiasts can spend a happy day following a 70-mile trail which visits eight different distilleries (but are asked to let someone else do the driving). A good point at which to start is Glenfiddich Distillery, a mile north of Dufftown, off the A941. The business was founded in the 1880s by the Grant family, who have owned it ever since. In the reception centre an audio-visual introduction to the history and manufacture of the noble fluid is provided for visitors. The Dufftown Museum in The Square also has information on the whisky business in this area, as well as local history displays.

The other distilleries which may be visited are Strathisla at Keith 11 miles north-east of Dufftown; Tamnavulin on the B9008 three miles east of Tomintoul; Cardhu and Tamdhu, both off the B9102 at Knockando; The Glenlivet, six miles south of Ballindalloch off the B9136; Glenfarclas, off the A95, some 8 miles south-west of Craigellachie; and Glen Grant at Rothes on the A941. Speyside Cooperage is at Craigellachie on the A941.

For a change from whisky there are plenty of other points of interest in this area. On the northern outskirts of Dufftown is Balvenie Castle, a ruined medieval stronghold of the Comyns, turned into a stylish house in the 16th century. Ballindalloch Castle on the A95, south-west of Glenfarclas Distillery, dates from the 16th century and has fine paintings and furniture. At Huntly on the A920 east of Dufftown are the impressive ruins of the principal stronghold of the Gordons, Marquesses of Huntly, for many years the leading family in this area: most of the present remains date back to 1550. Six miles south of Huntly on the B9002, near Kennethmont, the National Trust for Scotland owns Leith Hall, an attractive country house with extensive grounds.

Peebles' Customary and Art Festivals

The Beltane Festival at Peebles in June is one of the Border area's common-riding celebrations. During the festivities the Beltane Queen is crowned. The festival was revived in 1899. Beltane was the great Celtic festival which marked the opening of the second half of the Celtic year. The Peebles riders go out to Neidpath Castle on its rock above the Tweed. Originally a stronghold of the Frasers, in the 17th century it surrendered to Cromwell's cannon after a protracted siege, and afterwards belonged to the Douglases, Dukes of Queensberry. Later in the year, at the turn of August and September, comes the Peebles Art Festival, first held in 1981. It involves almost entirely amateur groups and includes a busking championship.

Labels from three distilleries on the Malt Whisky Trail

---- **349** ----

EAST LOTHIAN
LOTHIAN

Tourist Information Centres: Town House, High Street, Dunbar (01368) 863353 and Quality Street, North Berwick (01620) 2197.

The Coastal plain between the Firth of Forth and the Lammermuir Hills is a country of notable golf courses, headed by Muirfield, and of grim ruined castles. The kingpin of these castles is Tantallon, 3 miles east of North Berwick on the A198. The 14th-century stronghold of the Red Douglases, Earls of Angus, on its great rock above the sea, was virtually impregnable with its 50ft curtain wall on three sides, and a cliff on the fourth. Far less is left of the castle that guarded the harbour 9 miles away at Dunbar, now a popular resort town on the A1. To the west of Dunbar, a cliff-top path leads through the John Muir Country Park along a delightful stretch of coast.

Near East Linton, 6 miles west of Dunbar on the A1, the National Trust for

Grain has been milled on the site of Preston Mill for some 700 years. At one time several such mills were strung out along the lower Tyne, but this is the only survivor

Scotland owns Preston Mill, a 16th-century watermill on the River Tyne restored to working order, and a dovecot at Phantassie a short walk away. A mile or so further west along the Tyne, there is Hailes Castle, a ruined Hepburn stronghold, with barbaric-looking dungeons. A mile south of East Linton, the 700ft hump of Traprain Law looms up on the skyline.

The old town of Haddington, 5 miles west of East Linton along the A1, has a good history trail. A mile to the south of Haddington is Lennoxglove (open until September only), for many years the home of the Maitlands of Lethington, now owned by the Duke of Hamilton. It has fine portraits, furniture and porcelain.

From Haddington the A6137 runs north-west to Aberlady on the Firth of Forth, where birds and seals populate what is now a nature reserve. Near by, the comprehensive collection of ancient vehicles at the Myreton Motor Museum is worth seeing.

At Dirleton, 4 miles north-east of Aberlady on the A198, is an impressive ruined castle, linked with the turbulent and outlawed Ruthven family.

---- **350** ----

GLEN COE
HIGHLAND

Glen Coe Visitor Centre is on the A82, and is 18 miles south of Fort William. Tourist Information Centres: Ballachulish (018552) 296 (seasonal opening only), Fort William (01397) 703781 and Argyll Square, Oban (01631) 63122.

The tragic massacre of Glen Coe was carried out on an icy February night in 1692, when a party of Campbells turned on the local Macdonalds, who had sheltered them. Some 40 Macdonalds, were slaughtered and others, driven from their homes, died of exposure.

The pass of Glen Coe is best approached from the south on the A82, over the desolation of Rannoch Moor, and on the right sort of lowering day, it has a spectacular grimness to match its black past. High peaks and jagged rocks thrust up on either side, hemming in the stream and the road. This is splendid walking and climbing country, with wild cats, red deer, golden eagles and peregrine falcons among its wildlife. The National Trust for Scotland's Visitor Centre at Glencoe village provides an excellent introduction to the area, and in the small Glencoe and North Lorn Folk Museum here you can see a number of interesting local exhibits (open until September only).

IN EASY REACH The A82 runs on westwards from Glencoe to Ballachulish. Here the A828 will take you on for 31 miles south to join the A85 near the impressive ruined MacDougall castle of Dunstaffnage. This castle dates mainly from the 13th century. The A85 continues south to Oban in Strathclyde. Oban is a busy tourist town, a cruising centre and a ferry port for Mull and the Western Isles. Here visitors can watch the art of making paperweights at the Oban Glass Studio on the Heritage Wharf.

If you choose to go north from Ballachulish, the A82 will take you along the

eastern side of Loch Linnhe to Fort William, below Ben Nevis. The West Highland Museum, Cameron Square, provides informative displays on the history and wildlife of the area, including material on the '45 Rising, tartans, local industries, the Caledonian Canal, and Ben Nevis itself. The main tourist path from Glen Nevis to the top of Britain's highest mountain, 4,406ft, will take you 8 hours to go up and come down. Less energetically, a minor road folllowing the river for 10 miles explores the wild scenery of Glen Nevis at the foot of the mountain.

351

INVEREWE GARDEN
HIGHLAND

On the A832 near Poolewe, 7 miles north-east of Gairloch.
Tourist Information Centres: Ullapool (01854) 612135 (seasonal opening only) and Auchtercairn, Gairloch (01445) 2130.

Inverewe Garden lies on the latitude of Labrador and Leningrad, but it has the blessing of the warm air off the Gulf Stream. Thus exotic plants from the Pacific and South America, South Africa and the Himalayas are allowed to create a panoply of colour almost the whole year round in a magnificent setting on the shore of Loch Ewe. When Osgood Mackenzie set to work here in 1862, there was only a heather moor and a single diminutive willow tree, but now giant forget-me-nots, exotic lilies, and bamboos jostle other rare plants among the sheltering firs and pines. Inverewe was given to the National Trust for Scotland in 1952.

IN EASY REACH This coastal stretch of Wester Ross is distinguished by some of Britain's most breathtaking scenery, of mountains, sea-lochs and forests. Gairloch is a popular holiday centre for the area. Its heritage museum (open Easter to September only) illustrates how crofting life was carried on here in the past, illicit whisky still and all. The A832 runs on south-west from Gairloch past the Victoria Falls and Loch Maree, a magnificent 12 miles of water beneath towering peaks, and on to Kinlochewe. Here you can take the A896 south-west to the Beinn Eighe National Nature Reserve's 10,000 acres of mountains and moors, abounding in wildlife, and then move on to the National Trust for Scotland's spectacular estate on Loch Torridon. The Countryside Centre at Torridon has audio-visual displays which tell you all about the wildlife here. In addition, there is a small red-deer museum at Mains.

●

Ben Nevis Hill Race

The Ben Nevis hill race at the beginning of September is a gruelling trek and scramble up and down Britain's highest peak (see above), starting from New Town Park in Fort William. Some 500 competitors attack the mountain, with the fastest of them taking about an hour to reach the summit and half that time or less to descend again, gaining time by 'riding the scree' on the way down. The first of these races on record was in 1895 and was won by a Mr Swan of Fort William (the temperature on top of Ben Nevis, incidentally, averages 7 degrees Centigrade less than down below in Fort William and snow is liable to fall at any time of year, so if you are going up the mountain in the ordinary way, take warm clothes.)

●

352

IONA
STRATHCLYDE

Reached by boat from Fionnphort, Isle of Mull.
Tourist Information Centre, The Pier, Tobermory (01688) 2182.

Barren and windswept, a few minutes by boat from the south-western tip of Mull, the diminutive island of Iona is a profoundly venerated place and has an almost tangible atmosphere of being special and set apart. Most of it is now in the care of the National Trust for Scotland. Visitors are not allowed to bring their cars, but Iona is easily covered on foot.

It was on the southern shore that St Columba and a few companions landed from Ireland in AD563. The saint's Latin name means 'dove', which gives an entirely misleading impression of his very forceful character. He founded a monastery here, from which missionaries went out to convert Scotland and the north of England to Christianity. St Oran's cemetery near by was the burial ground of the early Kings of Scots (including Duncan and Macbeth), or so tradition has it. Certainly, later on the Lords of the Isles and other leading Highland chiefs were laid to rest here. St Oran's chapel is the oldest building still standing on Iona.

Nothing is left of the Celtic monastery. It was repeatedly sacked in Viking raids during which many monks were massacred. Early in the 13th century a Benedictine monastery and nunnery were established here. The pink granite ruins of the nunnery church are very attractive. The abbey church, restored in this century, is now the cathedral. Some of the other monastery buildings have been restored and there are several exceptionally fine Celtic crosses on view.

353

THE ROADS TO THE ISLES
HIGHLAND

Tourist Information Centres: Fort William (01397) 703781. Mallaig (01687) 2170, Shiel Bridge (01599) 81264 and Kyle of Lochalsh (01599) 4276 are seasonal opening only.

Eilean Donan Castle – linked to the shore by a causeway – and the village of Dornie, from Totaig across Loch Duich

The 'Road to the Isles' of the well-known song written during World War I is the A830. It runs 45 miles from Fort William (see separate entry) west to Mallaig, a port for Skye and the Inner Hebrides. This road runs through lovely country beside Loch Eil and on to Glenfinnan, where there is a superb view down the 20-mile length of Loch Shiel. It was here on 19 August 1745 that Prince Charles Edward raised his standard with backing from the local Macdonalds and Cameron of Lochiel. A 65ft monument, with a statue of a Highlander on top, marks the spot. It was erected in 1815 by Alexander Macdonald of Glenaladale. The National Trust for Scotland's visitor centre tells the story. From Glenfinnan the A830 runs on west to Lochailort, where the A861 branches south for the mountains of Moidart and the Ardnamurchan peninsula.

The other route often claimed as the 'Road to the Isles' is the A87, north of the A830. This second route runs from Invergarry 51 miles west to Kyle of Lochalsh. One of the most beautiful roads in Britain, it runs past Loch Cluanie and through Glen Shiel below the towering 3,000ft Five Sisters of Kintail and then to Shiel Bridge. In an exquisite position beside Loch Duich is Eilean Donan Castle, possibly the most photogenic castle in all Britain (open Easter to September), with MacRae and Jacobite relics on view. From Kyle of Lochalsh it's just a short ferry-crossing to Skye.

354

SCOTT COUNTRY
BORDERS

Abbotsford House is on the B6360, 3 miles west of Melrose.
Tourist Information Centres: Abbey House, Melrose (0189682) 2555 and Halliwell's
House, Selkirk (01750) 20054 (both seasonal opening only).

With its mock baronial battlements and turrets, Abbotsford House neatly expresses the character, interests and style of its former owner, the best-selling author who did so much to create the image of 'romantic Scotland'. Sir Walter Scott bought a farm here on the bank of the Tweed in 1812 and later called in the architect William Atkinson to design the house, which he called his 'Delilah'. Inside are personal relics, the famous Raeburn portrait of Scott with one of his dogs, the Chantrey bust of him, an armoury of Scottish weapons and his much-loved collection of historical curios, from Rob Roy's sporran to Montrose's sword and a lock of the Young Pretender's hair. Scott died here in 1832 and the house has remained with his descendants ever since.

IN EASY REACH Rising above the market town of Melrose are the peaks of the Eildon Hills, which have an eerie look and reputation. An Iron Age fort on the northern summit commands a spectacular view. Here the stone for Melrose Abbey was quarried. This Cistercian monastry (within Melrose town) grew rich on its profits from sheep rearing, but was repeatedly sacked by invading English armies. Somewhere in these red, romantic ruins the heart of Robert the Bruce was buried. Also interred here is Michael Scot, the wizard prominently mentioned in Dante's *Inferno*. Part of the abbey has a small museum. Beside the abbey, on the B6360, is the National Trust for Scotland's Priorwood Garden. It has a pleasant orchard walk illustrating 'Apples through the Ages' and a special garden of flowers suitable for drying.

On the B6356 east of Melrose there is a famous prospect from Scott's View, a spot which the author especially loved. This road will take you south to Dryburgh Abbey, where there are substantial remains of the monastery to be seen. Scott lies buried in the abbey church. A statue of him stands in the marketplace at Selkirk, on the A7, south-west of Melrose. Also in the marketplace is Halliwell's House, once an ironmonger's shop and now a good museum of local history.

Border Customary and
Cultural Events

The most stirring relics of the long history of fighting and feuding, raiding and cattle-rustling across the border between England and Scotland are the Border ballads, anonymous poems which tell of heroism and murder, undying love and cruel treachery. In October every other year, the Border Festival aims to increase awareness of the area's heritage in towns and villages throughout the region. Earlier, in June, the Braw Lads Gathering at Galashiels represents the town's common-riding festivity, founded in 1930. It includes a ride to Abbotsford House. June also brings the Selkirk Common Riding, with hundreds of riders following the Standard Bearer on a route through the surrounding countryside. A lament is played for the fallen at Flodden.

355

THE TROSSACHS

CENTRAL

Tourist Information Centre, Main Street, Aberfoyle (018772) 352.

Inset: SS Sir Walter Scott on a trip round Loch Katrine. the loch shows a different face below

Sir Walter Scott made the rippling lochs and rugged mountains of the Trossachs a magnet for tourists with his poem The *Lady of the Lake.* The name 'Trossachs' is generally applied nowadays to the area stretching from the eastern shore of Loch Lomond across to Loch Venachar to the west. This was MacGregor country, and in particular the territory of Rob Roy MacGregor, the outlaw who died in 1734, and whose grave is in Balquhidder churchyard (off the A84). Today much of the region falls within the 40,000 acres of the Queen Elizabeth Forest Park, with its many drives and walks and an abundance of wildlife, including golden eagles in the north.

The park visitor centre is called David Marshall Lodge, and it has an exhibition as well as plenty of information about the forest trails. The lodge is on the B829, a mile north-west of the small town of Aberfoyle, the main tourist base for exploring the Trossachs. The scenic B829 goes on north-west from Aberfoyle to Loch Lomond. A road built specially for tourists back in 1820 runs north for 7 miles from Aberfoyle to Loch Katrine, which is nostalgically plied by a 1900-vintage steamer, *Sir Walter Scott.*

Heading eastwards from Aberfoyle, the A81 runs to Lake of Menteith. On an island in the lake, reached by a ferry, are the ruins of Inchmahome Priory, founded in the 13th century,where Mary, Queen of Scots was hidden as a child.

356

WHITHORN PRIORY

DUMFRIES AND GALLOWAY

Whithorn is on the A746, 18 miles south of Newton Stewart.
Tourist Information Centres: Dashwood Square, Newton Stewart (01671) 402431
(seasonal opening only) and Whitesands, Dumfries (01387) 53862.

During the latter half of the 4th century, at the end of the Roman period in Britain, a little stone church was built at Whithorn by St Ninian. He was, apparently, a local man who had studied in Rome and had returned as bishop of the small group of Christians already established here. This early-Christian centre in the North became a magnet for pilgrims throughout the Middle Ages. The banning of pilgrimages by the Scottish authorities in 1581 struck a heavy blow at the economy of Whithorn.

Remains of St Ninian's church have been found during archaeological digs, and are on view at the Old Town Hall next to the priory which is on the site of St Ninian's church. This priory was built by a 13th-century Lord of Galloway. The 15th-century gatehouse of the priory still stands, as does the nave of the church. There are medieval tombs in the crypt. The museum in Bruce Street has a collection of early crosses and memorial stones, including the oldest Christian tombstone in Scotland, over 1,500 years old.

IN EASY REACH Three miles south-east of Whithorn on the A750 is the small harbour of Isle of Whithorn. Here there are the ruins of another St Ninian's Chapel, built centuries after the saint's death, for pilgrims arriving by sea. Present-day pilgrimages focus on St Ninian's Cave, which he is said to have used as a place of retreat: it is on the coast to the west, off the A747. Further west along the A747, at Monreith, a road leads down to the bay, passing a statue of an otter cast in bronze. This is a memorial to Gavin Maxwell, author of *A Ring of Bright Water,* who grew up in this area.

---- 357 ----

ABERDEEN
GRAMPIAN

Tourist Information Centre, St Nicholas House, Broad Street (01224) 632727.

Despite its nickname, the 'granite city' is a lively holiday resort on the Don and the Dee, noted for its rose gardens and parks, as well as being the supply base for the North Sea oil rigs. It owes its appearance today largely to Archibald Simpson and other local architects who rebuilt much of the city in the local granite during the 19th century. The most remarkable granite building is Marischal College in Broad Street with its intricate Gothic façade. The anthropological museum here is open to the public.

In the 19th century, Aberdeen prospered on shipbuilding and trawling, and it had been a thriving port long before that. Its history is vividly conveyed in the Maritime Museum in Shiprow, in what was once the house of a wealthy merchant, Provost Ross. The harbour and the fish market are well worth exploring and two other merchants' houses are now museums: Provost Skene's House in Guestrow and James Dun's House in Schoolhill. Also in Schoolhill is the Aberdeen Art Gallery, with a special collection of portraits of artists.

The unicorn-topped Mercat Cross in Castle Street is a particularly fine specimen of a civic cross. The late-15th-century chapel of King's College with its lovely crown tower is also recommended for viewing. The oldest part of Aberdeen lies close to St Machar's Cathedral. The cathedral's twin-spired granite austerity disguises the fact that it has a magnificent 16th-century heraldic ceiling inside.

IN EASY REACH To the west of Aberdeen is a remarkable assortment of castles, all now in the care of the National Trust for Scotland. However, only the grounds are open all year. At Drum Castle, 10 miles away off the A93, a bulky 13th-century tower is flanked by a more 'civilised' 17th-century wing. Five miles further west along the A93 is Crathes Castle, a delightful 16th-century tower house with unusual painted ceilings and delightful gardens.

---- 358 ----

COATS OBSERVATORY
STRATHCLYDE

At Paisley, 7 miles west of Glasgow on the A737. Tourist Information Centre, Town Hall, Abbey Close, Paisley 0141-889 0711 (seasonal opening only).

Perched high up above the town of Paisley, in Oakshaw Street, this domed observatory is one of the many benefactions of the Coats family whose thread-making firm dominated Paisley life in the 19th century. The observatory, opened in 1883, is an official weather recording station and inside you can admire items as diverse as the two original telescopes, still in use, an orrery, a receiver for satellite weather pictures and displays on astronomy, meteorology and space, as well as play astronomical computer games.

Paisley is best known for the 'Paisley pattern', copied in fact in the 19th century from Indian shawls. The town museum in High Street, has a marvellous collection of Paisley shawls and is also strong on local history, natural history and ceramics. Close by is the vast pink bulk of the Thomas Coats Memorial Baptist Church built in 1894. There is also a striking war memorial, which depicts World War I soldiers grouped around a formidable mailed knight in armour. You might also take a look at the statues of Coats benefactors outside the elegant town hall, and the early-Stewart tombs in the abbey church.

IN EASY REACH Further west, 4 miles north of Lochwinnoch, there are enjoyable walks and good views in the Murshiel Country Park. At Lochwinnoch itself there is the Community Museum whose exhibits reflect the local agricultural, industrial and social life of the area. The Kelburn Country Centre, 2 miles south-east of Largs off the A78, is noted for its gardens, its ancient yew trees and its magnificent prospects of the Firth of Clyde. From the harbour at Largs there is a ferry service to the island of Cumbrae.

Fireball Ceremony

A dramatic New Year's Eve custom at Stonehaven involves 20 or 30 men parading along the High Street swinging blazing fireballs alarmingly round their heads, 'like demonic hammer throwers' it has been said. The fireballs are made of wire netting stuffed with twigs, kindling, pine cones, old clothes or anything that will burn, and attached to long wires. The idea, according to local tradition, is to drive away evil spirits, but this is just one of many fire ceremonies at this time of the year which may originally have been rites of imitative magic meant to revive the light and heat of the sun at midwinter.

Above the stained-glass window in Coats Observatory features William Herschel - a member of the distinguished German-British family of astronomers

Left: this 10in refractor telescope is one of the Observatory's two original instruments

---
359
DAVID LIVINGSTONE CENTRE
STRATHCLYDE

At Blantyre, off the A74, 8 miles south-east of Glasgow. Tourist Information Centre, Road Chef Services, M74 Northbound, Hamilton (01698) 285590.

The Dr Livingstone involved in that famous encounter with Stanley in Africa was born in Blantyre in 1813 in a tenement housing workers of the Blantyre Cotton Mill on a bank of the Clyde. Here began a career which brought him the admiration of Victorian Britain as a great African explorer and humanitarian, and which led, after his death in Africa in 1873, to a tomb in Westminster Abbey. His birthplace is now part of a museum which describes his life and achievements, and the harsh background from which he came. Here, a 'world fountain' traces his African journeys, and there are paintings and tableaux depicting episodes in his career. In the African pavilion there is an exhibition on life in modern African countries.

IN EASY REACH About a mile east of Blantyre is Bothwell, where the impressive ruins of Bothwell Castle loom up among the woods high above the Clyde. Frequently attacked, taken and retaken, the fortress at one time belonged to the Black Douglases. The oldest part is the 13th-century keep. (The entrance of the castle is at Uddington Cross.)

Immediately to the south of Blantyre, Hamilton (on the A74) is an industrial town whose history is brought to life in the Hamilton District Museum, 129 Muir Street, in the town's oldest building, once a coaching inn. Near by, the Cameronians Museum traces the history of this illustrious regiment since 1689.

South-east of Hamilton on the A74 is Chatelherault Country Park – a fine piece of landscape gardening with a small herd of white cattle.

360
ELGIN
GRAMPIAN

Tourist Information Centre, 17 High Street (01343) 542666.

Burning of the Clavie

The most spectacular event of the year in the town of Burghead is reserved for the darkness of winter. On the night of 11 January, which is the 'old' New Year's Eve, the blazing Clavie is carried through the streets by Clavie King and his men. The Clavie is part of a whisky barrel, which is prepared according to traditional rules and mounted on a long pole. It is filled with bits of wood, which are covered in tar and set alight from a burning peat fetched from a house fire. As the Clavie is carried through the town, followed by hundreds of spectators, bits of charred wood are left by custom at certain houses to bring luck. The Clavie is finally taken to a place where it is set on a stone pillar, specially built for the purpose in 1809, left to burn for a while and eventually smashed to pieces (see right).

There are also plenty of enjoyable events in summer and autumn to entertain visitors to the Elgin area. In July there are the Elgin Highland Games and in September fiddlers and fiddle-orchestras flock to Elgin for the Annual Fiddle Festival, with its competitions for soloists and groups.

This pleasant old town is known for its beautiful ruined cathedral, once centre of the see of Moray and described in the 14th century as 'the glory of the kingdom'. In 1390, however, the bishop made the mistake of excommunicating the formidable Alexander Stewart, known as the 'Wolf of Badenoch', who ruled the North for his father, King Robert II. The Wolf descended on Elgin in a fury with an army of Highlanders and burned the cathedral and most of the town. Even though the cathedral was rebuilt, it was neglected after the Reformation and allowed to fall into ruin. However, the twin western towers survived the Wolf's attentions, and a fine octagonal chapter house also remains to be seen. The Elgin Museum, in High Street, is highly regarded for its fossil collection whilst the Moray Motor Museum has an interesting collection of historic cars and motorcycles; the Cashmere Centre and the Old Mills, a fully restored working 18th-century oatmeal mill, are also of interest.

IN EASY REACH Perhaps the most popular attraction in the Elgin area is Baxters of Speyside Visitor Centre, east of Elgin on the A96, where there are tours of the factory. The new heritage centre, the Buckie Drifter, at Buckie off the A98, offers a hands-on experience of the fishing industry in the Moray Firth.

Above: Glasgow's coat of arms is elegantly interpreted in wrought iron on this lamp-post near the cathedral

Left: the central hall of the City Chambers in George Square – Victorian civic pride at its best

---
361

GLASGOW
STRATHCLYDE

Tourist Information Centre, 35 St Vincent Place 0141-204 4400

'Glasgow's miles better', the slogan announces, tactfully not saying better than 'what'. It is fact a thoroughly enjoyable city, a city of character – furnished with opulent 19th-century architecture, a wealth of museums and galleries, and some intriguing oddities. The most fascinating oddity is the Necropolis (there is a self-guiding leaflet) – a hill crowned with monuments, columns, statues, obelisks and miniature temples, where anyone who was anyone in Victorian Glasgow was buried. This 'city of the dead' is next door to St Mungo's Cathedral, considerably restored in the 19th century. It contains interesting modern stained glass, and the tomb and well of the 6th-century saint Mungo, around whose little wooden church here the city originally grew.

Enjoyable buildings include those designed by Charles Rennie Mackintosh, notably the Glasgow School of Art (1909) in Renfrew Street. Not far away in Sauchiehall Street is his Willow Tea Room. Mackintosh enthusiasts should visit his church at Queen's Cross, which is being restored, and should also go to the Hunterian Art Gallery, Hillhead Street, to see the reconstruction of the interiors of his Glasgow home. There is a major Whistler collection here too.

The city's star attraction is undoubtedly the Burrell Collection, amassed by Sir William Burrell, who died in 1958. The superb Chinese ceramics, jades and bronzes, medieval art, tapestries and stained glass, and French 19th-century pictures, are all most attractively displayed in a purpose-built gallery in Pollok Country Park.

The Glasgow Art Gallery and Museum in Kelvingrove Park, has one of the best municipal art collections in Britain, ranging from Giorgione, Rembrandt and Rubens to Van Gogh, Degas, Cézanne and Dali. You can also feast your eyes on ceramics, glass and silver, clocks, snuff-boxes, pewter, Egyptian antiquities and an exceptional arms and armour collection.

Haggs Castle, in St Andrew's Drive, is a history museum specially for children where a 'hands on' approach is encouraged. The Hunterian Museum, in a building designed by Sir George Gilbert Scott, is particularly informative regarding Scottish geology and archaeology, and has a huge coin collection. For those interested in the history of transport, the Museum of Transport in Kelvin Hall is worth a visit. Finally, something a little different perhaps is the Tenement House in Buccleuch Street, where the National Trust for Scotland has preserved the tiny flat of a Glasgow typist, as it was from 1911 to 1965.

●

Hogmanay

George Square in the heart of Glasgow is packed with revellers on New Year's Eve, come to see the old year out and welcome the new one in with joined hands and the singing of 'Auld Lang Syne'. For reasons which are far from clear, Hogmanay or New Year's Eve was always a more important occasion in Scotland than Christmas. It was and still is a time for feasting, drinking and dancing, and for the custom of first-footing. The first person to cross the threshold of the house after midnight on New Year's Eve will bring good luck or misfortune for the whole of the coming year. It should never be a woman or a red-haired man, but should ideally be a tall man with dark hair. The first-foot brings with him small gifts - bread, money and a piece of coal - and should be kissed by whoever lets him into the house.

●

249

--- 362 ---

LEWIS AND HARRIS
WESTERN ISLES

Reached by ferry from Uig or Ullapool: by air from Glasgow or Inverness. Tourist Information Centres: 26 Cromwell Street, Stornoway (01851) 703088 and Tarbert Street (01859) 502011.

The standing stones at Callanish, on Lewis. Many legends surround their origin and until relatively recently there was a commonly held belief that as the sun rose on Midsummer morning the 'Shining One' walked between the stones, accompanied by the call of a cuckoo. The cuckoo is associated with Tir-nan-Og – the Celtic paradise allegedly drowned beneath the sea

Despite the two names, 'Lewis' and 'Harris', it is all one island, 150 miles long, the largest of the Outer Hebrides. Lewis is the northern part, Harris the southern, and the best-known product of both is Harris tweed. Harris is the hillier of the two parts, but the general impression is one of peaty moorland with no trees, carpets of wildflowers here and there, narrow roads, sheep, beautiful sea views and beaches. The Gaelic language and culture is very much alive here. The Ullapool ferries dock at Stornoway, the main town.

Lewis's most famous attraction is the powerfully impressive complex of standing stones at Callanish, on the A858, which have been standing here in eerie majesty for some 4,000 years. North of Callanish are the folk museum at Shawbost and, 5 miles away, the old Lewis blackhouse at Arnol: a traditional Hebridean dwelling with stone walls and a thatched roof held down against the gales with ropes and heavy stones – no chimney.

Tarbert is the port which receives the ferries from Uig in Skye and the chief shopping centre for Harris. From here a road runs south through Glen Laxdale to Rodel, on the southern tip of the island. Here is a church which was built in the 16th century by the MacLeod chiefs from Skye, who used to bury their standard-bearers here.

Ba' Games

Visitors to Kirkwall on the Orkney islands on Christmas Day, and again on New Year's Day, are likely to see a heaving scrum of men pushing to and fro about the town, shoving and slithering about like an immense jellyfish. The scrum is engaged in the traditional ba' game between the Uppies and the Doonies, from the two halves of the town. The game may go on for hours. the object is to get the ball – a hardy object made of leather stuffed with cork – to one or other of the opposing goals. One of the goals is the harbour, in which the ball must be submerged to score. Sometimes the ball is sneaked out of the mêlée and quietly hurried off to a goal while the scrum plunges and struggles on unwittingly. Legend says the game began with Vikings playing football with the severed head of a captive. Certainly it has been going on for the last 200 years. Visitors are welcome to join in.

--- 363 ---

LOCH LOMOND
STRATHCLYDE

Tourist Information Centre, Balloch Road, Balloch (01389) 53533.

The 'bonnie banks' of Britain's largest natural lake lie in wooded, pastoral country at the southern end of this beautiful 24-mile stretch of water, studded with small islands. The narrow northern end of the loch is hemmed in between towering 3,000ft peaks. The best way of seeing Loch Lomond is the 5-hour steamer trip from Balloch at the southern end. There are boat trips from Balmaha on the eastern shore, too, from where you can explore the nearby island of Inchcailloch. Forest walks start at Balmaha for the western reaches of the Queen Elizabeth Country Park.

There are also pleasant walks and scenery in the Balloch Castle Country Park at the foot of Loch Lomond. From Balloch the A82 runs north along the western shore of the loch, with fine views. Eight miles north is Luss, an attractive village in the ancestral territory of the Colquhouns.

IN EASY REACH South from Balloch, 5 miles down the A82 is Dumbarton, the capital of the ancient Celtic kingdom of Strathclyde in post-Roman times. It is dominated by the castle on its 240ft rock above the River Clyde, a royal stronghold with a colourful past, though most of what remains dates from the 18th and 19th centuries.

North-west of Dumbarton, 8 miles along the A814, is Helensburgh. The great treat here is The Hill House, Upper Colquhoun Street, now in the care of the National Trust for Scotland and designed in the 1900s by Charles Rennie Mackintosh. He supervised every detail of this understated, fascinating house – the furniture, the panelling, the door locks, everything.

364

THE ORKNEY ISLANDS

Reached by ferry from Thurso; or by air from
Aberdeen, Edinburgh, Glasgow, Inverness or Wick.
Tourist Information Centres: Broad Street, Kirkwall (01856) 872856 and
Ferry Terminal building, Pierhead, Stromness (01856) 850716 (seasonal opening only).

The Orkneys consist of 15 sizeable islands and a multitude of little ones, 6 miles from mainland Scotland at the nearest point. Visitors come to enjoy a wealth of prehistoric remains, a blend of quiet farming country with formidable cliff scenery, and memories of two World Wars. From the 9th century to the 15th century the islands were ruled by the Earls of Orkney for the Kings of Norway, though some of the earls were virtually independent. Kirkwall, the island's capital, has several places well worth investigating. Besides the cathedral, there are the ruined palaces of the bishops and the earls, the excellent Tankerness House Museum, which specialises in Orkney history, and the bustling harbour.

To the west of Kirkwall, off the A965 near the Loch of Stenness, is an extraordinary concentration of prehistoric monuments: the enormous burial mound of Maes Howe, the Standing Stones of Stenness and the stone circle called the Ring of Brodgar. On the west coast off the B9056, is the remarkable prehistoric village of Skara Brae, with cramped little stone rooms where people lived 4,000 years ago. North from here, about 7 miles away at Brough of Birsay, are the remains of the 11th-century Earl Thorfinn's hall and church.

The finest cliff scenery is on the island of Hoy, with its 450ft stack, the Old Man of Hoy. The huge harbour of Scapa Flow sheltered the British fleet in both wars, and the German fleet was scuttled here in 1919. Museums based on these war memories are developing rapidly (though not always open all year).

365

THE SHETLAND ISLANDS

Reached by ferry from Aberdeen or Kirkwall; or by air from Orkney.
Tourist Information Centre, Lerwick (01595) 3434.

Lying about 100 miles from the Scottish mainland, and only twice that distance from Norway, the Shetlands group is made up of three principal islands – Mainland, Unst and Yel – and a mass of smaller ones. The landscape is high, open moorland of peat and heather. Trees are scarce. There are spectacular cliffs and stacks along the coasts, which are penetrated by long fiords, called *voes*. Ruled by the Earls of Orkney in the past, the Shetlands share the Norse traditions and sympathies of the Orkneys. You can find out all about their history in the Shetland Museum in the capital of the Shetland's, Lerwick, which has taken on a fresh lease of life as a North Sea oil port since the 1970s. In the Shetland Museum you can also find out about Shetland knitwear and Shetland ponies, and trace the history of the islands.

On the southern outskirts of Lerwick is Clickhimin Broch, an impressive circular fortress with walls 17ft high and 18ft thick. At the southernmost tip of the island, near the airport, 20 miles from Lerwick, is Jarlshof, with remains of settlements from the Stone Age on into modern times.

Other places to visit, but not open during winter, include the agricultural museum at Veensgarth, the modern oil terminal of Sullen Voe, and the formidable bulk or Monsa Broch, a well-preserved Iron Age tower on its island – which can only be visited in summer, by boat.

Up Helly Aa

One of the most spectacular ceremonies in Britain occurs on the last Tuesday night in January at Lerwick in the Shetlands. It is called the Up Helly Aa and was invented about a hundred years ago to replace an earlier blazing tar-barrel custom. The ceremonies begin after dark with a procession through the town of hundreds of guisers in weird and colourful costumes and head-dresses, holding tall, flickering torches. There are groups with duck's heads for instance, or dressed as clowns. A band accompanies them and so does a replica Viking longship, which has a dragon's head at the prow, complete with brawny Viking warriors in horned helmets (see below). The longship is drawn to an open space where the guisers with their burning torches surround it. After a ritual which includes the singing of a Christian Socialist hymn, at a signal the guisers hurl their torches into the air. They fall in a fiery rain on the longship, which catches fire and burns fiercely to the exultant glee of the crowd. The rest of the night is spent in dancing and revelry.

Index

ACKNOWLEDGEMENTS

The Automobile Association wishes to thank the following photographers, organisations and libraries for their assistance in the compilation of this book.

ALLSPORT 185 *Grand National* BATH FESTIVAL SOCIETY 15 *Bath Festival* BEAULIEU MOTOR MUSEUM 84 *Record breakers* I BELCHER 101 *Painting canal ware,* 101 *Narrowboat rudder* A W BESLEY 21 *Helston Floral Dance,* 28 *Royal Cornwall Show* BODLEIAN LIBRARY 178 *Manuscript* BOURNEMOUTH TOURIST BOARD 31 *Clowns Festival* E A BOWNESS 201 *Dove Cottage,* 201 *Cumbrian wrestling,* 203 *Friars Crag* BOWES MUSUEM 181 *Swan* BRITAIN ON VIEW 115 *Flatford Mill* BRITAIN WATERWAYS BOARD 100/1 *Buckby Locks* CHICHESTER THEATRE 59 *Chichester Theatre Co* D CORRANCE 218 *Ballatar,* 219 *Edinburgh Festival,* 221 *Honours of Scotland,* 232 *Edinburgh Castle* CULTURAL RESOURCE CENTRE 213 *Viking Festival* P DAZELEY 229 *St Andrews* DEAN & CHAPTER LIBRARY DURHAM 178 *St Cuthbert* ENGLISH HERITAGE 56 *Richborough Castle, Pevensey Castle,* 178/9 *Mount Grace Priory* EXETER FESTIVAL SOCIETY 19 *Exeter Festival* A GILLESPIE 243 *Ben Nevis hill race* GRANADA TELEVISION 206 *Coronation Street* D HARDLEY 238 *Logan Botanic Gardens* N HORNE 40 *Raft Race* KIT HOUGHTON 123 *Burghley Horse Trials* JARROLDS COLOUR LIBRARY 135 *King's College choir* ROD KERRY 82 *Didcot* LITCHFIELD DISTRICT COUNCIL 128 *Samuel Johnson's birthday* THE MANSELL COLLECTION 56/7 *Old Battery Shoeburyness,* 223 *Bonnie Prince Charlie,* 223 *Culloden Battle* MARY EVANS PICTURE LIBRARY 72 *Boating at Henley,* 221 *Monarch of the Glen,* 221 *Stewart tartan,* 221 *Campbell tartan,* 221 *Heart of Midlothian* G P MATTHEWS 165 *String quartet* S & O MATTHEWS 87 *Tunbridge ware* J MORGAN 144/5 *Royal National Eisteddfod* NATIONAL TRUST 27 *Stourhead,* 31 *Clevedon Court* NATURE PHOTOGRAPHERS 1 *Red Admiral (SCB)* 2, 5 *Red Admiral (RT)* 3 *Red Admiral (EAJ)* 67 *Mallard drake (EAJ),* 85 *New Forest leaves (MKW)* NOTTINGHAM COUNTY LIBRARY 130 *Nottingham Goose Fair* PLYMOUTH NAVY DAYS 35 *Navy day* K REDPATH 13 *Well Cap cover* ROCHESTER CITY COUNCIL 69 *Dickens Festival* DOC ROWE 11 *Punkie Night,* 14 *Abbotsbury,* 24 *Padstow hobby horse,* 34 *Tolpuddle Martyrs Inn,* 43 *Ottery St Mary,* 44 *Hob Nob,* 58 *Biddenden Dole,* 62 *Olney Pancake Race,* 77 *Fenny Poppers,* 83 *Lewes Bonfire Night,* 98 *Castleton garland,* 103 *Castleton garland,* 106 *Hare Pie Scramble,* 136 *St Ives Strawbear,* 182 *Ashbourne Shrovetide Football,* 182 *Midgley Pace Egg Play,* 186 *Bacup Nutters Dance,* 199 *Burning the Bartle,* 204 *Skipping at Scarborough,* 211 *Haxey Hood Game* SCOTTISH TOURIST BOARD 224 *Culzean Castle,* 225 *Galloway Forest Park,* 234 *Shinty,* 237 *Tossing the caber,* 240 *Braemar games,* BRIAN SHUEL 18 *Marblers & Stonecutters, Corfe,* 20 *Hobby horse, Minehead,* 25 *John Knill,* 30 *Rush Sunday, Bristol,* 46 *Glastonbury thorn,* 55 *Lord Mayor's Show,* 63 *May Morning, Oxford,* 89 *Car rally, Brighton,* 114 *Eyam Plague,* 125 *Abbots Bromley Horn Dance,* 137 *Blidworth Cradle Rocking,* 150 *Common Walk,* 158 *Coracle racing,* 171 *Mari Llwyd,* 188 *Egremont Crab Fair,* 188 *Knutsford Sanding,* 193 *St Wilfred Ripon,* 208 *Egremont Crab Fair,* 210 *Allendale Tar-Barrel Parade,* 231 *Burryman,* 248 *Burning the Clavie,* 251 *Up-Helley-Aa* SPECTRUM COLOUR LIBRARY 11 *Surfing,* 54 *Cowes Regatta,* 80 *Canterbury Cathedral,* 93 *Lord Mayor's Show,* 127 *Ironbridge,* 131 *Windmill, Horsey,* 137 *Canal art,* 149 *Kidwelly Castle,* 152 *Portmeiron,* 164 *Talyllyn Railway,* 180 *Beverley Minster,* 189 *Appleby Fair,* 191 *Town criers, Chester,* 196 *Lindisfarne/Holy Island,* 202 *Blackpool Illuminations* THE SHUTTLEWORTH COLLECTION 65 *Comet* P SHINTON 101 *Entering the caverns* SPRINGFIELDS GARDENS 109 *Flower Parade* D W WARNER 226 *Brodie* C P & *castle, Goatfell Race* WARWICK CASTLE 111 *Warwick Castle* R W WEIR 162/3 *Snowdon Mountain Railway,* 227 *Fireworks at Perth,* 232 *Fireworks at Edinburgh* WEALD & DOWNLAND MUSEUM 88 *Steam threshing* WELSH TOURIST BOARD 142 *Royal Welsh Show,* 143 *Snowdon Race,* 155 *3 Peaks Yacht Race,* 157 *Castel Coch,* 160 *International Music Festival* 167 *Victorian week* WEST AIR PHOTOGRAPHY 12 *Cadbury Camp* T WOODCOCK 101 *Foxton Locks* WOOLSACK COMMITTEE 27 *Woolsack Race* WORLDWIDE BUTTERFLIES 45 *Swallowtail butterfly*

The following photographs are from The Automobile Association's Photo Library.
42 Longleat, 57 Pevensey Castle, Porchester Castle, 112 Alton Towers, 122 Black Country Museum, 161 Llangollen Viaduct, 166 Caernarfon Castle, 191 Chester, 210/11 Hadrian's Wall.
M Adelman 162 Pentre Ifan, 192 Durham Cathedral, 236 The Cullins, 250 Callanish Standing Stones *V Bates* 176 IOM TT races, 195 IOM racing *M Birkett* 99 Chatsworth, 117 Newmarket, 135 King's College *P & G Bowater* 213 York Minster, 242 Preston Mill *P Brown* 83 Glyndebourne House *I Burgum* 156 Bute Park *D Corrance* 214/5 Edinburgh Castle, 232 Edinburgh Castle *R Czaja* 194 Holker Hall *R Eames* 146 Beaumaris Castle, South Stack, 147 Bodnant Gardens, 163a Snowdon Mountain Railway, 188 Tatton Park, 207 Tea Party *R Fletcher* 48 Stonehenge, 73 Nelson, 85 Pony sales *S Gibson* Photography 247 Paisley Coates Observatory, 249 Glasgow City chambers, Lamp-post *A Grierley* 79 Bleinham Palace, 146 Lligwy Burial Chamber *D Hardley* 244/5 Eilean Donan Castle *A Lawson* 13 Dozmary Pool, 16 Brixham, 17 Gwennap Pit, 17 Trevithic statue, 19 Maritime museum, 26 Sezincote House, 29 The Hurlers, 32 Clovelly, 40 Combstone Tor, 47 Morwellham *S Lund* 22 Hay tossing *S & O Mathews* 6/7 Durdle Door, 13 Tintagel, 15 Bath Abbey, 38 Avebury, 41 Gloucester Cathedral, 44 Salisbury Cathedral, 49 Wells museum, 57 Bodiam Castle, 61 The Needles, Statue at Brading, 66 Round Table, Winchester 68 Battle Abbey, 86 Church, 90 Greenwich, 91 Kew Gardens, 104 Ickworth House, 116 Fishing boats, 121 Wimpole Hall, 124 Bass Museum, 129 Norwich Cathedral, 135 Wedgwood vase, 172 Swaledale 192 Chillingham cattle, 197 Malham *E Meacher* 23 Bowood House *C Molyneaux* 105 Lincoln Cathedral, 154 Tenby *R Newton* 30 Clifton Suspension Bridge, 49 Wookey Hole, 102 Speedwell Cavern, 127 Coalbrookdale, 138/9 Snowdon Railway, 163b Snowdon Railway, 179 Byland Abbey, Rievaulx Abbey *F Ruffles* 239 Manderston *R Surman* 107 Mow Cop, 118 Hereford Beacon, 183 Jodrell Bank *M Trelawny* 50/51 Brighton, 71 Hampton Court *R Weir* 235 Loch Ness, 246 SS Sir Walter Scott, Loch Katrine *H Williams* 12 Glastonbury Tor, 20 Lorna Doone Farm, 34 Eypes Mouth, 35 Kynance Cove, 75 National Dairy Museum, 120 The Stiperstones, 150 Llanstephan Castle, 159 Rhosilli Bay, 161 Lleyn Peninsula, 168 Statue, 169 Tintern Abbey, 204 Flamborough Head, 220/1 Glen Coe *T Wood* 94/5 Gnosnall, 132 Anne Hathaway's cottage *J Wyand* 37 Westbury